Indian Navy

Tradesman Mate

Latest Edition
Practice Kit

20 Tests
12 Sectional Test
08 Mock Test

Based On Real Exam Pattern

✓ Thoroughly Revised and Updated

✓ Detailed Analysis of all MCQs

<table>
<tr><td>Title</td><td>: Indian Navy Tradesman Mate</td></tr>
<tr><td>Author Name</td><td>: Mr. Rohit Manglik</td></tr>
<tr><td>Published By</td><td>: EduGorilla Community Pvt. Ltd.</td></tr>
<tr><td>Publishers Address</td><td>: 12/651, First Floor Opp. Arvindo Park, Near Jama Masjid,
Indira Nagar, Lucknow, Uttar Pradesh-226016, India</td></tr>
</table>

Copyright EduGorilla

ISBN : 978-93-90893-79-9

Second Edition

No part of this book may be reproduced, distributed, or transmitted in any form by any means, without the prior written permission of the publisher.

All Right Reserved

© **by EduGorilla Community Pvt. Ltd**

Disclaimer EduGorilla

Although the author and publisher have made every effort to ensure the accuracy of information in this book, we do not assume any responsibility to errors and hereby disclaim any liability to any party for any loss, damage, or disruption caused by errors or omissions, whether such errors or omissions result from negligence, accident, or any other cause.

Compiled and created by EduGorilla Community Pvt. Ltd

Printed By EduGorilla Community Pvt. Ltd.

ROHIT MANGLIK
CEO, EduGorilla

Dear Applicants,

People say *"Success comes to those who work hard."* But I've seen people working hard for their exams day in and day out for marginal success. While others succeed in their examinations by putting in just half the work. So are they God Gifted? No! I believe that it's because they work *smart* and not just *hard*. Similarly, for your exams, you should strategize your preparation so as to increase the likelihood of success. Well with EduGorilla get ready to increase your *chances of selection* in your exam by *16x*.

EduGorilla helps you in not only working *hard* but also working in a *smart and strategic* manner. With EduGorilla's preparation package, you get a chance to make your exam preparation easy, and a fun learning path towards selection. Finding the right path to your preparations can be difficult if you don't know in which direction to head. Don't worry, we have you covered! EduGorilla will be your guide to success in your journey. With our Preparation Package, you can prepare strategically and beat the exam in just one attempt.

EduGorilla's Preparation Package includes-

• **Test Series**   • **Books**

Our preparation package is handcrafted as per the latest changes, expert opinions, and students' discretion. Thus, enabling you to get through each stage of the selection process for your exam.

Our Books are designed by the teachers and experts of the respective exam with a combined 150+ years of experience; to provide you with easy, efficient, and effective learning. Our books are smart, in the sense that not only do they give you the answers to the questions but also provide similar questions for practice.

EduGorilla's competent Test Series gives you real-time experience and confidence through which you can clear your offline or online exam in just one attempt. We currently host 83,000+ mock tests for 1,440+ competitive and academic exams.

Thus, EduGorilla misses no chance to assist you in your preparation and covers all stages of the exam, so that you don't have to look anywhere else.

We provide complete preparation packages for defense, banking, teaching, and other National & State-Level exams. Hence, it doesn't matter which exam you aspire to because you will reach your success.

ALL THE BEST !
Let EduGorilla be your Guide to Success.

Rohit Manglik,
Founder and CEO, EduGorilla

INTRODUCTION

EduGorilla focuses on guiding students to succeed in their examinations. With that in mind, our book, titled "Indian Navy : Tradesman Mate", has been drafted through the collective efforts of our distinguished experts with 150+ years of combined experience. This book consists of questions that are created following the latest changes in the syllabus and exam pattern. We compiled the book on the basis of questions that are most likely to appear in the Indian Navy Tradesman Mate. Through EduGorilla's "Indian Navy : Tradesman Mate" your chances of success will increase 16x.

EduGorilla does this through our Complete Preparation Package. This package consists of well-conceptualized and structured content in the form of questions that are tailor-made according to your needs and will help you practice for exams in a smart way by pinpointing all the necessary information. It also provides hints and solutions, along with a smart answer sheet for your self-evaluation. You can assess your shortcomings and work accordingly on areas that may require more of your attention.

EduGorilla promises to help you succeed in your examination and accomplish your dream goals. We believe in our aspirants and see them at the top of the merit list. And the first step towards the top is to start preparing with us. EduGorilla's "Indian Navy : Tradesman Mate" includes the following attributes.

➤ Well-Researched Content

➤ Top-Notch Quality

➤ Detailed Answers and Analysis

➤ Smart Answer Sheet

➤ Exam Relevant Questions

Therefore, EduGorilla fortifies your preparation and makes it durable enough to help you stand tall and beat the examination.

Indian Navy Tradesman Mate
Scan QR code for Eligibility, Exam Pattern, Syllabus and more.

Book ID: 0598

TABLE OF CONTENTS

General Intelligence and Reasoning

Q.1 Keshav walks 15 km towards the south. He takes a right turn and walks 25 km. He takes a right turn and walks 10 km. In which direction is he from his starting point?

A. South-West   B. South
C. South-East   D. West

Q.2 Direction: In the following question below are given two statements followed by two conclusions. Taking the given statements to be true even if they seem to be at variance from commonly known facts, read all the conclusions and then decide which of the given conclusion logically follows the given statements.

Statements:

I. Some Carrot are Red.

II. All Red are Colour.

Conclusions:

I. Some Colour are Carrot.

II. No Carrot is a Colour

A. Only I follows
B. Only II follows
C. Either I or II follows
D. None follows

Q.3 If in a certain language PROSE is coded as PPOQE, how is LIGHT coded in that code?

A. LIGFT   B. LGGHT   C. LGGFT   D. LLGFE

Q.4 If a mirror is placed on the line AB, then which of the answer figures?

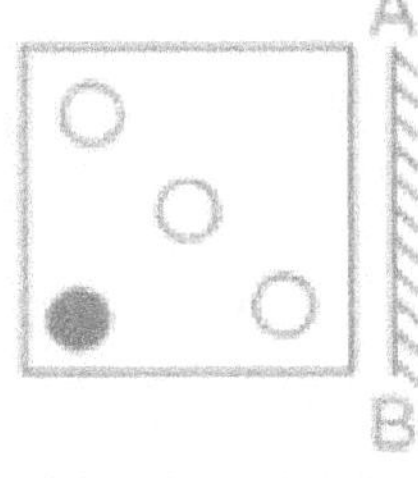

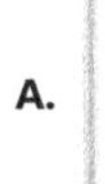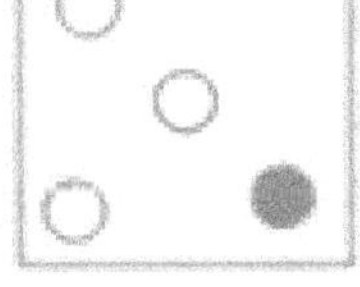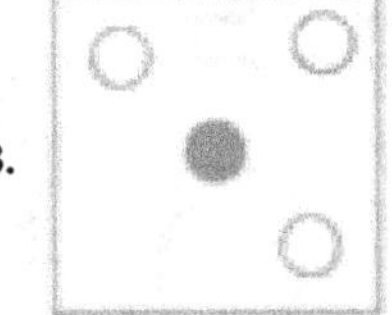

Q.5 Arrange the given words in the order in which they will be arranged in a reverse dictionary and choose the one that comes third.

1. Accouterment

2. Accoutered

3. Accouter

4. Accountancy

5. Accounted

A. Accounted   B. Accoutered
C. Accouter   D. Accountancy

Q.6 In the following question, select the odd letters from the given alternatives.

A. mop   B. prs   C. tvw   D. xyz

Q.7 If the cloud is called air, the air is called water, water is called white, white is called good, good is called green, and green is called a tree, where will the birds fly?

A. Tree   B. Cloud   C. Good   D. Water

Q.8 Select the correct combination of mathematical signs to replace $ signs to balance the given equation.

70 $ 5 $ 2 $ 7

A. ÷, -, =   B. ÷, =, ×   C. ×, =, ×   D. ×, =, ÷

Q.9 Select the related number from the given alternative.

17 : 102 : : 23 : ?

A. 112   B. 138   C. 216   D. 413

Q.10 Deepak remembers his examination is after 23rd December. While his mother remembers his examination is before 25th December. On which date of December is his examination?

A. 24   B. 23   C. 25   D. 26

Q.11 Which of the following jumble words is not a threat to a Computer?

A. RIVUS TANI   B. RIUVS
C. PSAM   D. WARMALE

Q.12 A series is given with one term missing. Select the correct alternative from the given ones that will complete the series.

LM, OP, RS, UV,?

A. WY   B. WX   C. XY   D. XZ

Q.13 In the following question, select the odd word from the given alternatives.

A. School   B. Worker   C. Driver   D. Waiter

Q.14 In the following question, correct the given equation by interchanging two numbers.

28 + 6 × 9 ÷ 3 × 8 ÷ 2 - 5 = 31

A. 6 and 9   **B.** 3 and 6   **C.** 6 and 2   **D.** 6 and 5

Q.15 In a certain code language CAMPHOR is written as 6$3&@52 and SAKE is written as #$98. How is HORSE written in that language?

A. @5#28   **B.** 5@#28   **C.** @528#   **D.** @52#8

Q.16 Which figure represents the relation between Badminton, Tennis, and Racket?

A. 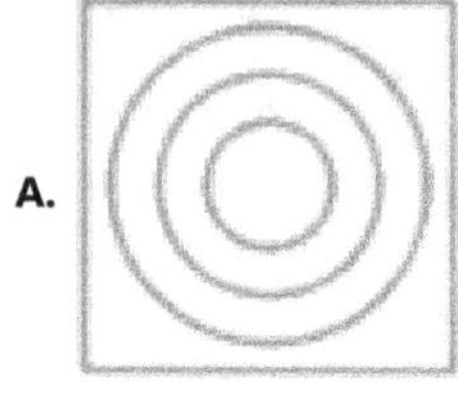   **B.** 

C. 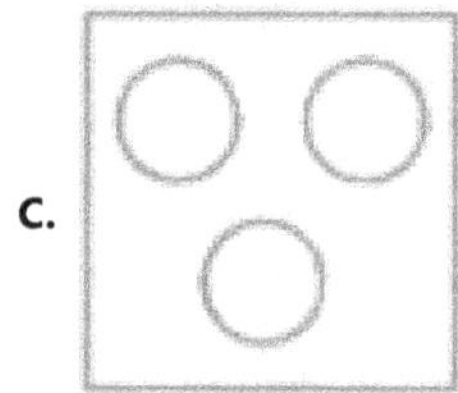   **D.** 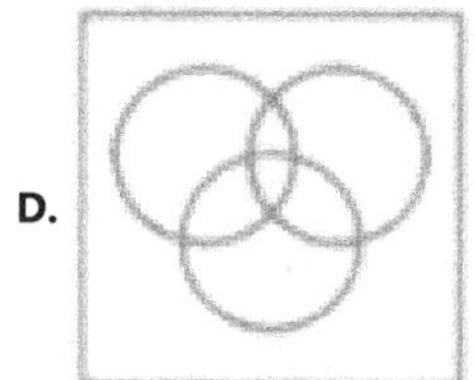

Q.17 A man said to a lady, "Your mother's husband's sister is my mother." How is the man related to the lady?

A. Cousin   **B.** Brother   **C.** Son   **D.** Nephew

Q.18 In the following question, select the related letters from the given alternatives.

NPSA: PRUC: : BLUE:?

A. CMVH   **B.** DNWG   **C.** DNVH   **D.** CMWG

Q.19 From the given answer figure, select the one in which the question figure is hidden/embedded.

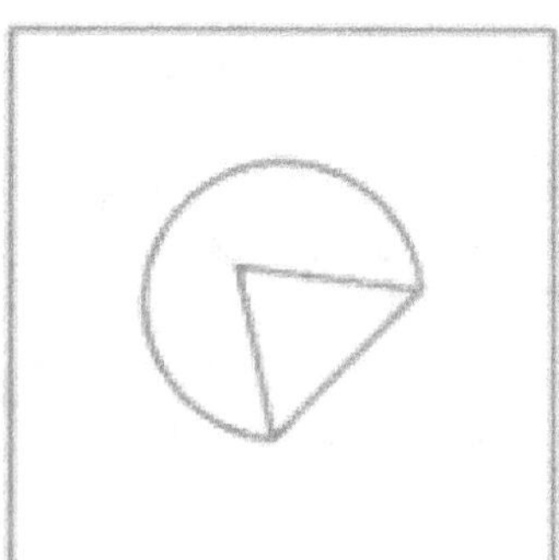

[SSC Stenographer Grade C & D, 2019]

A. 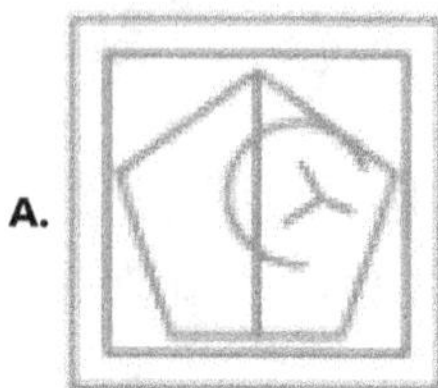   **B.** 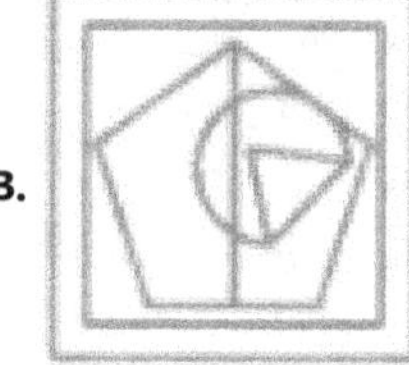

C. 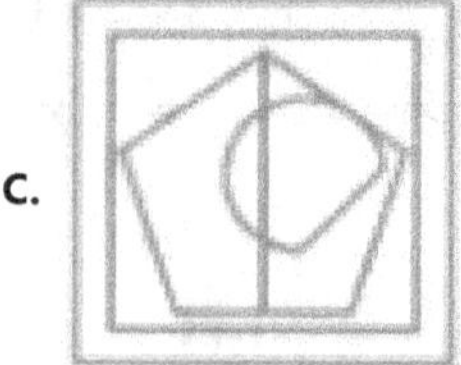   **D.** 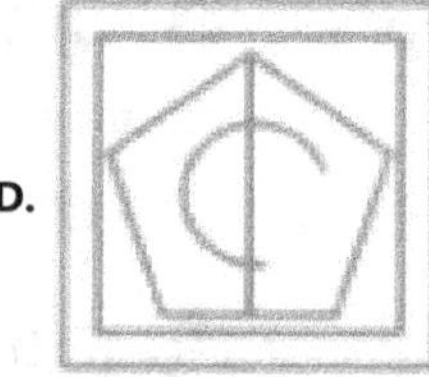

Q.20 Rajat is the brother of Sanjay and Manish is the father of Rajat. Jay is the brother of Shreya who is the daughter of Sanjay. Who is the uncle of Jay?

A.   Rajat
B.   Sanjay
C.   Manish
D.   Cannot be determined

Q.21 Which of the following cube in the answer figure cannot be made based on the unfolded cube in the question figure?

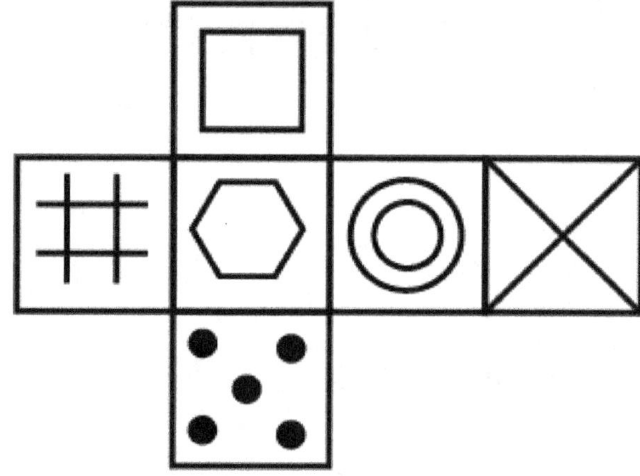

A. 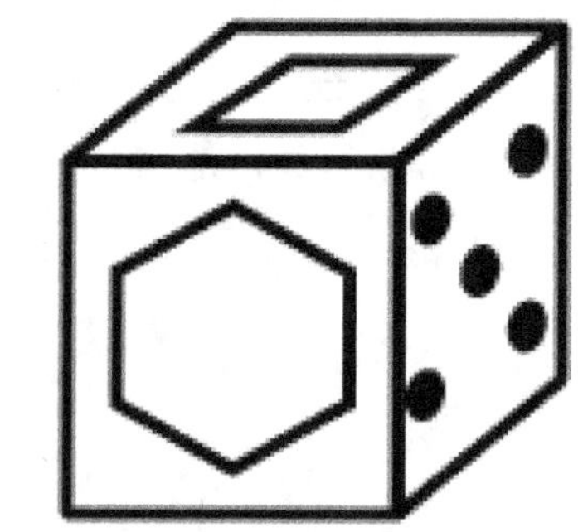

B. 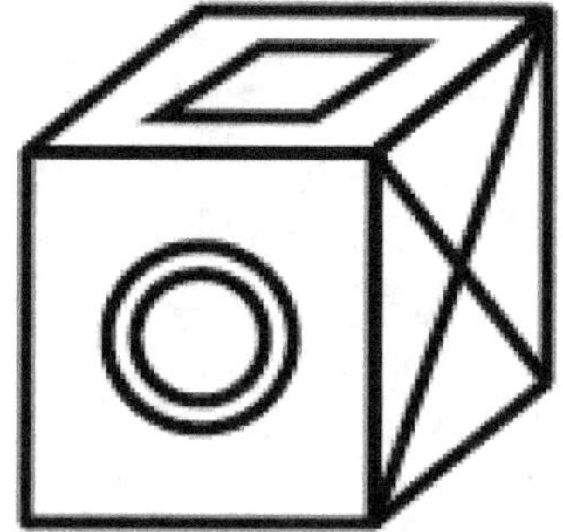

C. 

D. 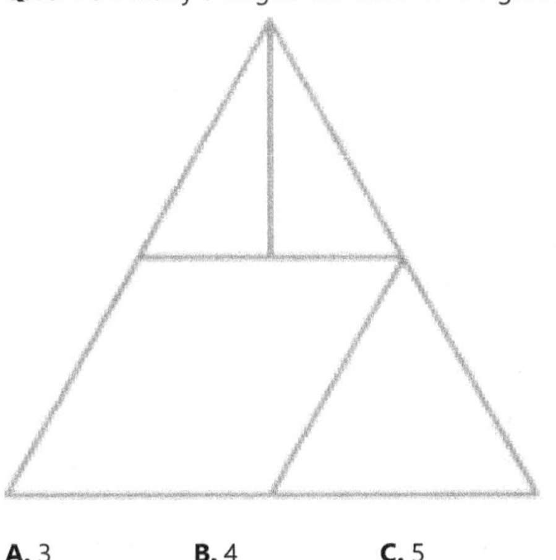

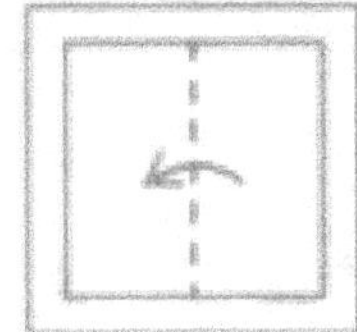 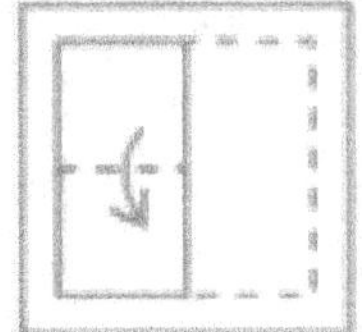 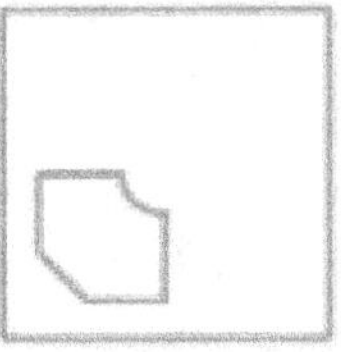

[SSC MTS, 2019], [UP Police Constable, 2019]

A. 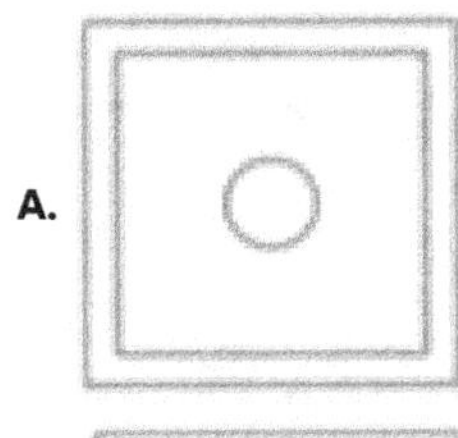 **B.** 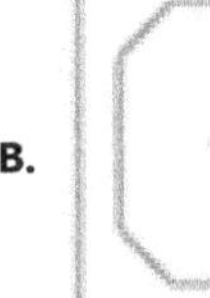

C. 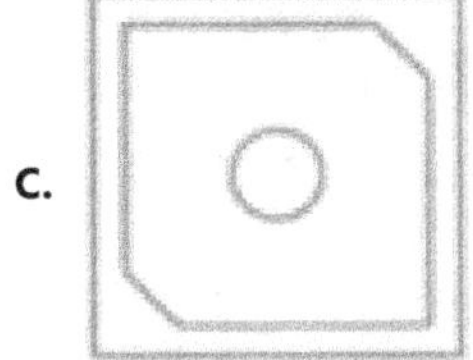 **D.** 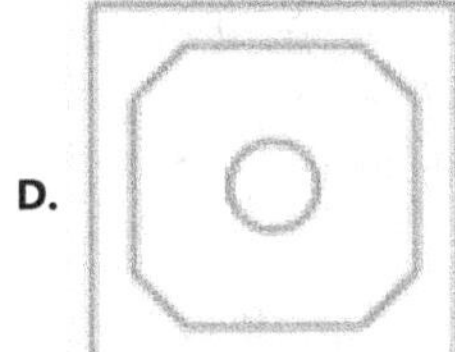

Numerical Aptitude/ Quantitative Ability

Q.22 In the following question, select the missing number from the given series.

1912, 2012, 2133, 2277, 2446, ?

A. 2642 **B.** 2964 **C.** 2738 **D.** 2858

Q.23 How many triangles are there in the given figure?

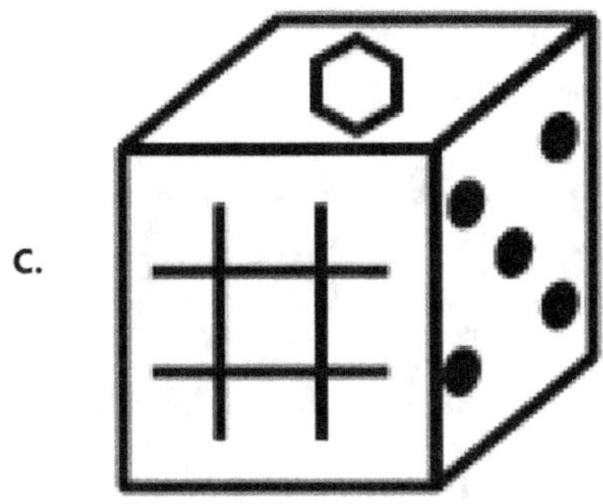

A. 3 **B.** 4 **C.** 5 **D.** 2

Q.24 In the following question, select the number which can be placed at the sign of question mark (?) from the given alternatives.

6	5	22
2	3	10
6	2	?

A. 18 **B.** 16 **C.** 15 **D.** 13

Q.25 A piece of paper is folded and punched as shown below in the question figures. From the given answer figures, indicate how it will appear when opened?

Q.26 When the price of a machine was increased by 20%, the number of machines sold was decreased by 25%. What was the percentage decrease change in the total revenue?

A. 5% **B.** 20% **C.** 15% **D.** 10%

Q.27 Raj got a new chair for 35% discount. Had Raj got no discount, Raj would have had to pay Rs. 224 more. How much did Raj pay for the chair?

A. Rs. 416 **B.** Rs. 640 **C.** Rs. 208 **D.** Rs. 224

Q.28 The price of tea is reduced by 4%. How many kilograms of tea one can buy for the money which was sufficient to buy 48 kg of tea before?

A. 49 kg **B.** 50 kg **C.** 51 kg **D.** 54 kg

Q.29 The average of 10 numbers is X and one of the numbers is 38. If 38 is replaced with 19, then what will be the new average?

A. $X - \frac{1}{2}$ **B.** $X - \frac{1}{19}$ **C.** $X - \frac{19}{10}$ **D.** $X - \frac{19}{9}$

Q.30 Blackberry announced a discount of 25% on their trousers. Vivek went to shop. He wanted to save Rs. 400 in discount. How many trousers should he buy to do so, if each trouser costs Rs. 320?

A. 5 **B.** 4150 **C.** 10320 **D.** 15360

Q.31 If the difference of compound interest and simple interest for 3 years at the rate of 5% per annum is Rs. 11.40, then the principal amount is

A. Rs. 1900 **B.** Rs. 1750 **C.** Rs. 1095 **D.** Rs. 1495

Q.32 The smallest 5-digit number divisible by 41 is _______.
A. 10054 **B.** 10041 **C.** 10004 **D.** 41000

Q.33 A sells a car to B at 10% loss. If B sells it for Rs. 54000 and gains 20%, the cost price of the car for A was
A. Rs. 25000 **B.** Rs. 50000
C. Rs. 37500 **D.** Rs. 60000

Q.34 Paper charge is Rs. 60 per kg. How much expenditure would be there to cover a cube of edge 10 m with a paper, if one kg of paper covers 20 sq.m. area?
A. Rs. 2250 **B.** Rs. 3600
C. Rs. 2700 **D.** Rs. 1800

Q.35 A tree is cut partially and made to fall on ground. The tree however does not fall completely and is still attached to its cut part. The tree top touches the ground at a point 10m from foot of the tree making an angle of $30°$. What is the length of the tree?

A. $10\sqrt{3}$ m **B.** $\frac{10}{\sqrt{3}}$ m **C.** $\frac{\sqrt{2}-1}{10}$ m **D.** $\frac{10}{\sqrt{2}}$ m

Q.36 Summation of 5 consecutive numbers is found out to be 335. If we add the largest and smallest number what will we get?
A. 134 **B.** 150 **C.** 174 **D.** 226

Q.37 An article was sold at 25% loss. Had the article been sold for Rs. 60 more there would have been a profit for 5%. The cost price of the article is
A. Rs. 150 **B.** Rs. 200 **C.** Rs. 250 **D.** Rs. 300

Q.38 The speed of a boat in still water is 9km/hr. It covers a distance of 42 km upstream in 6 hours. What is the speed (in km/hr) of the stream?
A. 1.2 **B.** 1.5 **C.** 1.6 **D.** 2

Q.39 Two trains with their speeds in the ratio of $3:4$ are going in the opposite direction along parallel tracks. If each takes 3 seconds to cross a telegraph post, then the time taken by the trains, to cross each other completely, will be?
A. 3 second **B.** 4 second
C. 7 second **D.** 21 second

Q.40 Three taps $A, B,$ and C can fill a tank in $180, 20,$ and 90 minutes respectively. If all the taps are opened together, then in how many minutes will the tank be filled?
A. 15 **B.** 25 **C.** 30 **D.** 35

Q.41 A can do a work in 12 days. B is 60% more efficient than A, B will complete some work in
A. $7\frac{1}{2}$ days **B.** 8 days **C.** $8\frac{1}{2}$ days **D.** 7 days

Ques (42-45):Direction: The bar chart given below shows the number of mobile phone thefts in 2 cities Delhi and Jaipur from month February 2015 to June 2015.

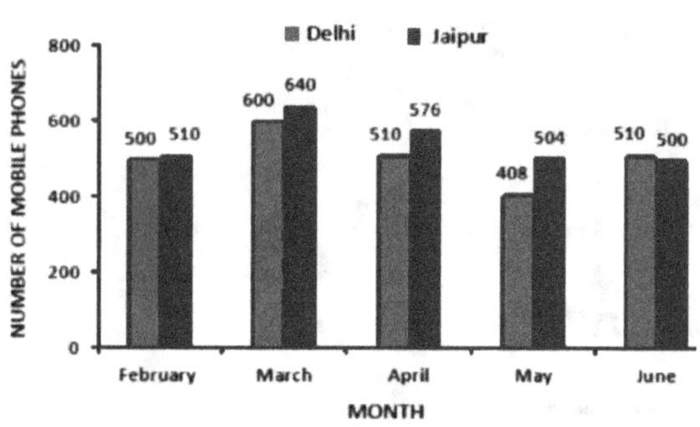

Q.42 For how many months, was the number of mobile phones thefts in Jaipur higher than that in Delhi?
A. 5 **B.** 4 **C.** 0 **D.** 3

Q.43 What is the percentage change in the number of mobile phone thefts in Jaipur from February 2015 to April 2015?
A. 66 **B.** 15.15 **C.** 12.94 **D.** 50

Q.44 In Delhi, what was the percentage change in the number of mobile phone theft from April 2015 to May 2015?
A. 30% **B.** 28% **C.** 20% **D.** 25%

Q.45 What was the average number of mobile phone thefts in Jaipur from February 2015 to June 2015?
A. 550 **B.** 576 **C.** 408 **D.** 546

Q.46 What is the equation of a line having a slope $\frac{-1}{3}$ and y-intercept equal to 6?
A. $x + 3y = 18$ **B.** $x - 3y = 6$
C. $x + 3y = -18$ **D.** $x - 3y = -6$

Q.47 What is the value of $\left(\tan 60° + \frac{1}{3}\right)$?
A. $\frac{(2\sqrt{2}+1)}{2}$ **B.** $\frac{(\sqrt{3}+1)}{\sqrt{3}}$ **C.** $\frac{(3\sqrt{3}+1)}{3}$ **D.** $\frac{(3+\sqrt{2})}{3\sqrt{2}}$

Q.48 In a triangle, one of the angles is three times the smallest and another is two times the smallest angle. Calculate the smallest angle.
A. 60° **B.** 30° **C.** 90° **D.** 45°

Q.49 A metallic hemispherical bowl is made up of steel. The total steel used in making the bowl is 342π cm ^{3}. The bowl can hold 144π cm ^{3} water. What is the thickness (in cm) of the bowl and the curved surface area (in cm ^{2}) of the outer side?
A. $6,162\pi$ **B.** $3,162\pi$ **C.** $6,81\pi$ **D.** $3,81\pi$

Q.50 $\frac{1}{5}^{th}$ of a tank is filled with water. After taking out 8 liters of water, $\frac{1}{6}^{th}$ of the tank remains filled with water. The capacity of the water tank is
A. 240 litre **B.** 280 litre **C.** 320 litre **D.** 520 litre

General English & Comprehension

Ques (51-52):Direction: Find the part with an error in the given sentence.

Q.51 Clues were (A)/ left to guiding the (B)/ team to the next task (C)/. No Error (D)

A. A   **B.** B   **C.** C   **D.** D

Q.52 It being a long day (A)/ she craved for home (B)/ even more than usual (C)/. No Error (D)

A. A   **B.** B   **C.** C   **D.** D

Ques (53-54):Direction: Improve the bracketed part of the sentence.

Q.53 Faded backgrounds in the room had (hint) at abandonment for a long time.

A. Hinting   **B.** Hints

C. Hinted   **D.** No Improvement

Q.54 Rustling leaves made her look up to (finds) that the clear sky was now turning clouded and heavy.

A. Finding   **B.** Find

C. Found   **D.** No Improvement

Ques (55-57):Direction: The sentence given with blanks is to be filled with an appropriate word. Four alternatives are suggested for each question. For each question, choose the correct alternative and click the button corresponding to it.

Q.55 Things continued to burden and she continued to _______ undeterred.

A. Being   **B.** Be   **C.** Have   **D.** Was

Q.56 A good day's work is never felt _______ draining.

A. As   **B.** Of   **C.** Being   **D.** To

Q.57 Sitting _______ the beach, she felt herself becoming the one with the surroundings.

A. On   **B.** Along   **C.** By   **D.** Beside

Ques (58-59):Direction: In the following question, out of the four alternatives, select the word similar in meaning to the word given.

Q.58 Discreet

A. Indiscreet   **B.** Cautious

C. Loud   **D.** Open

Q.59 Essential

A. Optional   **B.** Necessary

C. Unimportant   **D.** Essence

Ques (60-61):Direction: In the following question, out of the four alternatives, select the word opposite in meaning to the word given.

Q.60 Abandon

A. Leave   **B.** Continue   **C.** Desert   **D.** Absolve

Q.61 Negligence

A. Inability   **B.** Irresponsibility

C. Negligent   **D.** Conscientious

Ques (62-64):Direction: In the following question, out of the four alternatives, select the best alternative which best expresses the meaning of the Idiom/Phrase.

Q.62 Let the cat out of the bag.

A. Reveal a secret

B. Free the cat of the bag

C. Let go of something

D. None of the above

Q.63 The ball is in your court.

A. Your chance to hit the ball in that is kept in your court

B. The ball is just lying in your court

C. Your chance to make a decision or a move

D. Your chance to keep the ball in your court

Q.64 Cut corners

A. Cut the corners of something

B. Corners are sharp

C. Cut down on the basic things to save money

D. Cut down the price of something

Ques (65-66):Direction: In the following question, out of the four alternatives, select the alternative which is the best substitute for the phrase.

Q.65 A person who is shy and reserved.

A. Stoic   **B.** Introvert   **C.** Recluse   **D.** Ascetic

Q.66 One who runs away from captivity.

A. Fugitive   **B.** Heretic   **C.** Henpeck   **D.** Lunatic

Ques (67-71):Direction: Read the passage carefully and choose the best answer to each question out of the four alternatives.

This week has seen rounds of tit-for-tat tariffs between the US and China set off by U.S. President Donald Trump levying import duties of 25% and 10% on American steel and aluminum imports, respectively, in early March. Mr. Trump, who has repeatedly used the U.S. trade deficit of over $500 billion as a barometer for the country's lot in the international trade order, has railed against the U.S. being treated "unfairly" by its trading partners, often singling out China. While it is true that China produces approximately half the world's steel and that the European Union, India, and other countries have complained about international steel markets being flooded with Chinese steel, only 3% of U.S. steel is sourced from China. Interestingly, among those exempted from the tariffs are Canada and Mexico, top sources for U.S steel imports. Mr. Trump has linked the threat of tariffs to the North American Free Trade Agreement, a trade deal among the U.S., Canada, and Mexico that Mr. Trump has pried open for renegotiation. Earlier this week China retaliated with tariffs that would impact $3 billion worth of American goods. This was followed by the U.S. proposing tariffs on more than $50 billion of Chinese goods, including in the aerospace, robotics, and communication industries — the outcome of an investigation of several months into whether Chinese policies were placing unreasonable obligations on U.S. companies to transfer technology and hand over the intellectual property while setting up shop in China. Beijing responded with a second round of proposed tariffs impacting a similar value of U.S. imports into China. Mr. Trump has now asked the U.S. Trade Representative to examine if an additional $100 billion worth of goods can be taxed. Since the proposed tariffs have not kicked off, there may be room for negotiation. The economic ties between the countries are deep; China holds some $1.2 trillion in U.S. debt, and it is in everyone's interest to avoid escalating matters. However, the larger cause for concern here is that Mr. Trump continues to undermine the World Trade Organisation and the international world trade order, now that it has served the West well and developing countries are in a significantly stronger position than when the WTO came into existence in 1995. Mr. Trump has pulled out of the Trans-Pacific Partnership, is pushing changes to NAFTA, and has withdrawn from the Paris Agreement to combat climate change. While large-scale protectionism and unilateralism may please some of Mr. Trump's constituents in the short run, undermining existing rules arbitrarily serves no nation, including the U.S., in the long run. In the current climate, it is therefore especially important for India to be a good steward for responsible globalization.

Q.67 Which of the following words is opposite in meaning to the word 'arbitrary'?

A. Erratic

B. Rational

C. Capricious

D. Whimsical

Q.68

Which of the following words is similar in meaning to the word 'escalate'?

A. Deteriorate

B. Intensify

C. Compress

D. Decline

Q.69

Why has the author called it 'tit-for-tat tariffs'?

A. Because in the past a lot of other countries including China have levied duties on imports to support the local industry

B. Because immediately after the US levying import duties China retaliated with tariffs on goods worth 3 billion dollars themselves

C. Because almost all countries have retaliated to US import tariffs by levying heavy charges on US goods themselves

D. None of the above

Q.70 Why according to the author, America levying high import duties on Chinese steel doesn't quite add up?

A. Because the US imports only about 3% of steel requirements from other countries and the rest produced domestically itself

B. Because, the US exports much more steel to China, and the Chinese have already exempted American steel from import duties

C. It is because most of America's steel imports come from Canada and Mexico and both countries are exempted from tariffs

D. None of the above

Q.71 What led US President Donald Trump to levy heavy import duties particularly on the imports from China?

A. Because the US President was very disappointed with the

fact that despite sanctions, China and a few other countries continued to trade with North Korea

B. America's trade deficit with its partners especially China was growing and they felt that the US was being treated unfairly by its trading partners

C. Because the President of America was fearful of the fact that China and a handful of other countries are trying to push America into a debt trap

D. None of the above

Ques (72-73):Direction: In the following question, the first and the last parts of the sentence/passage are numbered (1) and (6). The rest of the sentence/passage is split into four parts and named (P), (Q), (R), (S). These four parts are not given in their proper order. Read the sentence/passage and find out which of the four combinations is correct.

Q.72 1. In the broadest sense, economic development might be viewed as "any growth in real income per capita from whatever source".

(P) And Novack has referred to a very old definition of economic growth, according to which it is a "continuous substantial increase in per capita consumption of goods and services".

(Q) Bach has described it as "growth in the total output of goods and services in the economy".

(R) Substantial production these days depends upon the greater use of technologies.

(S) The substantial consumption of economic goods is possible only when there is substantial production of economic goods.

6. In a narrower sense, therefore, it may be said that economic development refers to "the extensive application of inanimate power and other technologies to the production and distribution of economic goods".

A. PQRS   **B.** QPSR   **C.** SPQR   **D.** RQPS

Q.73 1. We were not born with wings.

(P) Science has given us what God has not.

(Q) Today we can fly to any corner of the world. Rivers and mountains cannot stand in the way.

(R) But we always wished to fly like birds.

(S) How cheap and how easy it is to travel now!

6. Today we can travel even to the moon. Our jets and rockets will carry us there. What a change from the bullock cart to the airplane!

A. PQRS   **B.** QPSR   **C.** RPQS   **D.** RQPS

Q.74 Direction: Select the wrongly spelled word.

A. Horizontal   **B.** Plateau

C. Bureaucrecy   **D.** Fomentation

Q.75 Direction: Select the correctly spelt word.

A. Manageble   **B.** Manageable

C. Managable   **D.** Manegeable

General Awareness

Q.76 With which sport are the following people associated with- Maana Patel, Saloni Dalal, Richa Mishra?

A. Boxing   **B.** Swimming

C. Shooting   **D.** Basketball

Q.77 Who has been voted the BBC Sports Personality of the Year 2020?
A. Sebastian Vettel   **B.** Lewis Hamilton
C. Daniel Ricciardo   **D.** Max Verstappen

Q.78 The privatization of Air India Limited will be completed during the upcoming financial year 2021-22. The government plans to sell how much percent stake in Air India?
A. 100   **B.** 90   **C.** 80   **D.** 70

Q.79 Which of the following movies won the Golden Globe 2020 award for 'Best Motion Picture - Drama'?
A. Joker   **B.** 1917
C. The Irishman   **D.** The Two Popes

Q.80 Currently, how many fundamental rights are recognized by the Indian constitution?
A. Five fundamental rights
B. Six fundamental rights
C. Seven fundamental rights
D. Eight fundamental rights

Q.81 Who is the author of the book 'Law, Justice and Judicial Power – Justice PN Bhagwati's Approach'?
A. Fareed Zakaria
B. Vandana Shiva
C. Mool Chand Sharma
D. Rajiv Malhotra

Q.82 Pathar ki Masjid is a famous tourist place located in which among the following states in India?
A. Bihar   **B.** Telangana
C. Andhra Pradesh   **D.** Madhya Pradesh

Q.83 Who has been named 'Businessperson of the Year' by TIME, in December 2020?
A. Eric Yuan   **B.** Andrew Yang
C. Mark Zuckerberg   **D.** Jack Dorsey

Q.84 Inderkilla National Park is in _______.
A. Himachal Pradesh   **B.** Uttarakhand
C. Chhattisgarh   **D.** Jharkhand

Q.85 'Dhamma' is the _______ word for the Sanskrit term 'Dharma'.
A. Hindi   **B.** Prakrit   **C.** Pali   **D.** Urdu

Q.86 Whom did Babur defeat at the Battle of Khanwa of 1527?
A. Ibrahim Lodi   **B.** Rana Sanga
C. Sher Khan   **D.** Mirza Hakim

Q.87 Capital of Arunachal Pradesh is _______.
A. Aizwal   **B.** Agartala   **C.** Shillong   **D.** Itanagar

Q.88 The title "Governor-General" was changed to Viceroy in which year?
A. 1858 A. D.   **B.** 1885 A. D.
C. 1905 A. D.   **D.** 1917 A. D.

Q.89 What is the unit of Power?

A. Ampere   **B.** Volt
C. Watt   **D.** Kilowatt-hour

Q.90 What is the maximum number of seats fixed for the Rajya Sabha in India?
A. 245 seats   **B.** 252 seats
C. 260 seats   **D.** 250 seats

Q.91 Match the following

	Monument		Country
(1)	Great Pyramid of Giza	(a)	Mexico
(2)	The great wall of China	(b)	Italy
(3)	Colosseum	(c)	Egypt
(4)	Chichen Itza	(d)	China

A. (1)-(b), (2)-(d), (3)-(a), (4)-(c)
B. (1)-(c), (2)-(d), (3)-(b), (4)-(a)
C. (1)-(a), (2)-(d), (3)-(b), (4)-(c)
D. (1)-(b), (2)-(a), (3)-(d), (4)-(c)

Q.92 Which kind of government provides a method to deal with differences and conflicts?
A. Autocratic   **B.** Aristocratic
C. Monarchic   **D.** Democratic

Q.93 Asian Games 2022 will be held in which country?
A. China   **B.** Bahrain
C. Indonesia   **D.** South Korea

Q.94 The type of mirrors used in the headlamp of cars is:
A. Parabolic concave   **B.** Plane
C. Spherical convex   **D.** Cylindrical concave

Q.95 The reason for a swimming pool to appear less deep than the actual depth is
A. Refraction   **B.** Light scattering
C. Reflection   **D.** Interference

Q.96 Bandar Laddu got the Geographical Indication of _______.
A. Andhra Pradesh   **B.** Himachal Pradesh
C. Uttar Pradesh   **D.** Arunachal Pradesh

Q.97 The gas used in the welding and cutting of metals is _______.
A. Ethane   **B.** Methane
C. Acetylene   **D.** Butene

Q.98 The number value 6.022×10^{23} is also called _______.
A. Atomic Number   **B.** Mass Number
C. Avogadro's number   **D.** Dalton's Number

Q.99 What is the full form of MICR?
A. Magnetic Ink Credit Recognition
B. Magnetic Ink Card Recognition
C. Magnetic Ink Character Recognition
D. Magnetic Ink Code Recognition

Q.100 Which Five Year Plan had a motive of 'Faster, More Inclusive and Sustainable growth'?
A. Tenth   **B.** Twelfth   **C.** Seventh   **D.** Eleventh

// Smart Answer Sheet //

Correct — Percentage of students who answered correctly. **Skipped** — Percentage of students who skipped.

Q.	Ans.	Correct	Skipped
1	A	78.31 %	0.0 %
2	A	68.03 %	1.66 %
3	C	40.64 %	1.64 %
4	D	86.71 %	0.0 %
5	C	63.96 %	1.12 %
6	D	59.97 %	1.51 %
7	D	87.36 %	0.0 %
8	B	54.7 %	1.38 %
9	B	60.51 %	1.65 %
10	A	58.41 %	1.88 %
11	A	15.2 %	4.01 %
12	C	41.1 %	1.07 %
13	A	87.14 %	0.0 %
14	C	56.73 %	1.54 %
15	D	61.54 %	1.91 %
16	B	76.1 %	0.0 %
17	A	77.44 %	0.0 %
18	B	66.97 %	1.79 %
19	B	61.06 %	1.61 %
20	A	55.87 %	1.06 %
21	A	48.93 %	1.94 %
22	A	42.38 %	1.13 %
23	C	58.1 %	1.57 %
24	B	40.55 %	1.68 %
25	D	43.37 %	1.32 %
26	D	29.36 %	4.96 %
27	A	63.84 %	1.51 %
28	B	44.35 %	1.82 %
29	C	69.06 %	1.29 %
30	A	59.25 %	1.9 %
31	D	43.81 %	1.67 %
32	C	67.19 %	1.63 %
33	B	46.43 %	1.89 %
34	D	56.48 %	1.82 %
35	A	49.22 %	1.2 %
36	A	45.25 %	1.62 %
37	B	62.77 %	1.94 %
38	D	61.9 %	1.23 %
39	A	68.44 %	1.55 %
40	A	31.63 %	4.1 %
41	A	54.73 %	1.44 %
42	B	77.71 %	0.0 %
43	C	66.13 %	1.89 %
44	C	53.34 %	1.76 %
45	D	23.93 %	3.84 %
46	A	54.7 %	1.27 %
47	C	62.82 %	1.62 %
48	B	45.53 %	1.33 %
49	B	44.03 %	1.33 %
50	A	52.55 %	1.21 %
51	B	79.15 %	0.0 %
52	D	78.17 %	0.0 %
53	C	76.68 %	0.0 %
54	B	85.76 %	0.0 %
55	B	49.57 %	1.23 %
56	A	84.79 %	0.0 %
57	C	67.95 %	1.97 %
58	B	47.11 %	1.29 %
59	B	85.59 %	0.0 %
60	B	48.4 %	1.39 %
61	D	88.59 %	0.0 %
62	A	78.47 %	0.0 %
63	C	89.51 %	0.0 %
64	C	67.58 %	1.34 %
65	B	76.8 %	0.0 %
66	A	63.05 %	1.82 %
67	B	61.52 %	1.13 %
68	B	76.89 %	0.0 %
69	B	57.53 %	1.7 %
70	C	86.61 %	0.0 %
71	B	85.0 %	0.0 %
72	B	18.8 %	4.04 %
73	C	64.35 %	1.45 %
74	C	46.1 %	1.3 %
75	B	83.58 %	0.0 %
76	B	21.06 %	4.16 %
77	B	40.35 %	1.97 %
78	A	40.31 %	2.0 %
79	B	57.99 %	1.55 %
80	B	84.01 %	0.0 %
81	C	59.52 %	1.82 %
82	A	49.0 %	1.89 %
83	A	41.0 %	1.72 %
84	A	56.3 %	1.35 %
85	C	47.85 %	1.09 %
86	B	81.66 %	0.0 %
87	D	89.44 %	0.0 %
88	A	24.81 %	4.58 %
89	C	84.96 %	0.0 %
90	D	65.6 %	1.54 %
91	B	65.19 %	1.88 %
92	D	55.07 %	1.79 %
93	A	79.36 %	0.0 %
94	A	50.05 %	1.88 %
95	A	82.33 %	0.0 %
96	A	47.06 %	1.67 %
97	C	80.53 %	0.0 %
98	C	19.14 %	4.76 %
99	C	40.91 %	1.16 %
100	B	28.59 %	3.21 %

//Hints and Solutions//

1. The movement of Keshav can be traced as follows:

- Keshav walks 15 km towards the south.
- He takes a right turn and walks 25 km.
- He takes a right turn and walks 10 km.

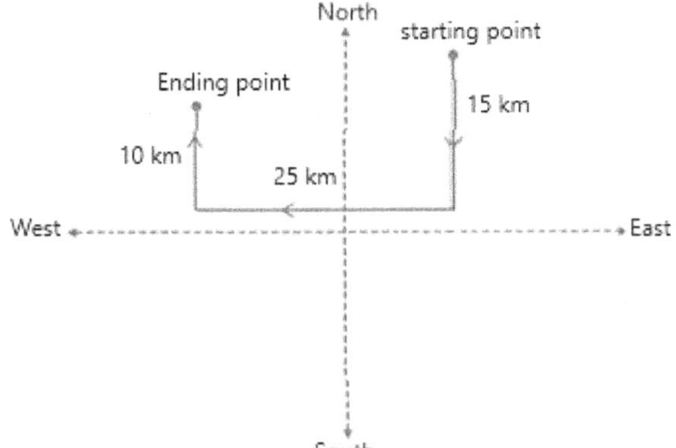

On closely observing the diagram we can say that Keshav is in South West direction from his starting point.

Hence, the correct option is (A).

2. Given:

I. Some Carrot are Red.

II. All Red are Colour.

From these statements the least possible diagram is shown below:

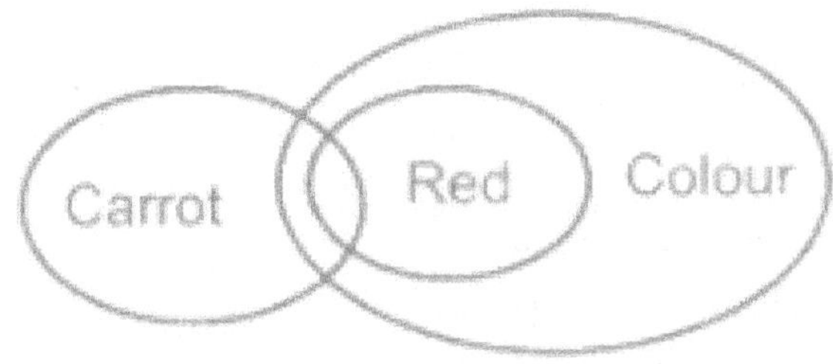

Conclusions:

I. Some Colour are Carrot → follows (It is definitely true).

II. No Carrot is a Colour → not follows (As some carrot will definitely be the colour).

Hence, the correct option is (A).

3. Given:

PROSE is coded as PPOQE

The first, third, and fifth letters are the same but in the place of the second and fourth letters, the previous two letters are used.

So, LIGHT is coded as LGGFT.

Hence, the correct option is (C).

4. The mirror image of the question figure:

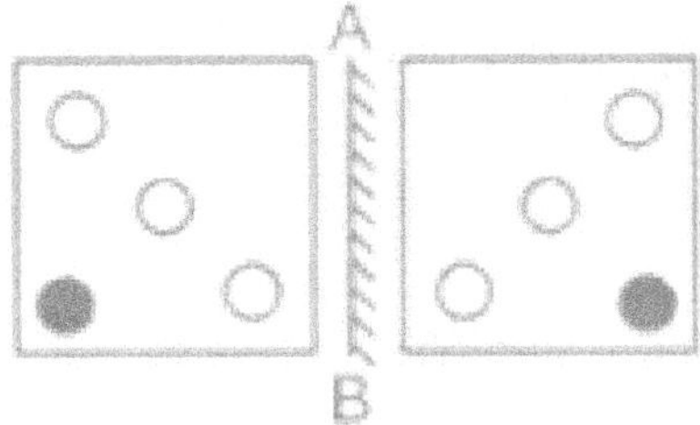

Hence, the correct option is (D).

5. As per the Dictionary order,

1) Accountancy

2) Accounted

3) Accouter

4) Accoutered

5) Accouterment

Reverse dictionary order:

1) Accouterment, 2) Accoutered, 3) Accouter, 4) Accounted, 5) Accountancy

So, 'Accouter' will be the third word in reverse dictionary order.

Hence, the correct option is (C).

6. The pattern followed here is,

1) mop: m + 2 → o + 1 → p

2) prs: p + 2 → r + 1 → s

3) tvw: t + 2 → v + 1 → w

4) xyz: x + 1 → y + 1 → z

So, 'xyz' are the odd letters.

Hence, the correct option is (D).

7. Clearly, the birds fly in the air' and 'air' is called 'water'.

so, the birds fly in the 'water'.

Hence, the correct option is (D).

8. Checking each of the options:

(A) ÷, -, = → 70 ÷ 5 − 2 = 7 → False

(B) ÷, =, × → 70 ÷ 5 = 2 × 7 → True

(C) ×, =, × → 70 × 5 = 2 × 7 → False

(D) ×, =, ÷ → 70 × 5 = 2 ÷ 7 → False

So, the correct combination of mathematical signs is '÷, =, × '.

Hence, the correct option is (B).

9. In 17 : 102

⇒ 17 × 6 = 102

Similarly,

⇒ 23 × 6 = 138

Hence, the correct option is (B).

10. According to Deepak = 23rd Dec < Exam

According to Deepak's mother = Exam < 25th Dec

Clearly, only one date between exist = 24th Dec.

So, Deepak's exam will be on 24th December.

Hence, the correct option is (A).

11. 1) RIVUS TANI = ANTI VIRUS (It is a programme used to remove threats)

2) RIUVS = VIRUS

3) PSAM = SPAM

4) WARMALE = MALWARE

Hence the correct answer is (A).

12. The followed pattern is as follows:

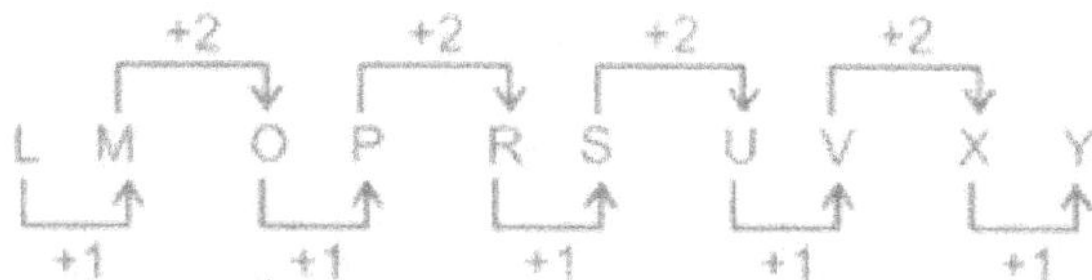

So, 'XY' will complete the given series.

Hence, the correct option is (C).

13. Except for School, all are humans.

Thus, School is the correct answer.

Hence, the correct option is (A).

14. Given equation is 28 + 6 × 9 ÷ 3 × 6 ÷ 2 - 5 = 31

Let's check each of the options,

(A). Interchanging 6 and 9

Equation will become, 28 + 9 × 6 ÷ 3 × 8 ÷ 2 - 5 = 95 ≠ 31

(B). Interchanging 3 and 6

Equation will become, 28 + 3 × 9 ÷ 6 × 8 ÷ 2 - 5 = 41 ≠ 31

(C). Interchanging 6 and 2

Equation will become, 28 + 2 × 9 ÷ 3 × 8 ÷ 6 - 5 = 31

(D). Interchanging 6 and 5

Equation will become, 28 + 5 × 9 ÷ 3 × 8 ÷ 2 - 6 = 82 ≠ 31

So, by interchanging 6 and 2, we get the correct answer.

Hence, the correct option is (C).

15. The codes are as follows,

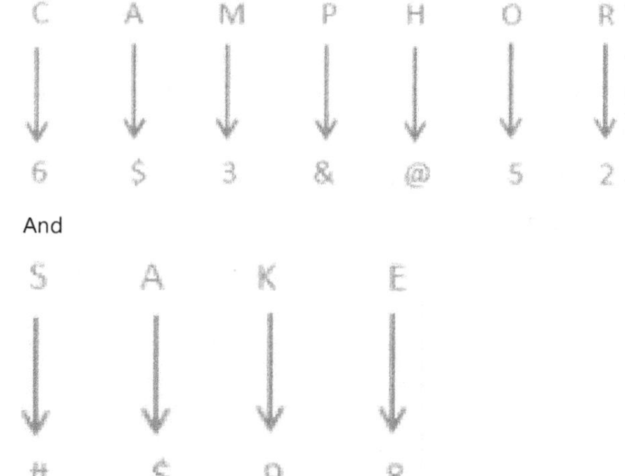

And

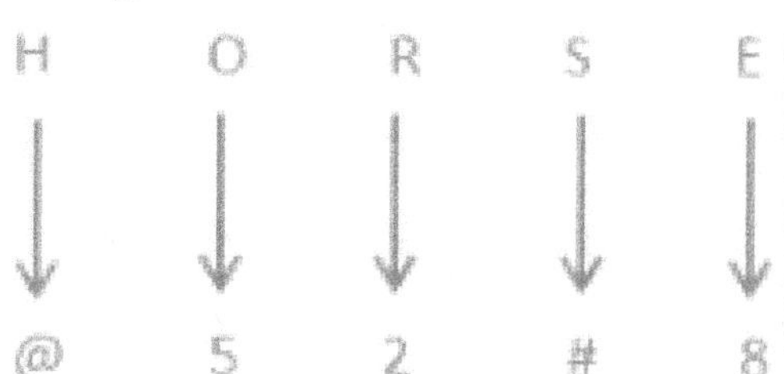

Similarly,

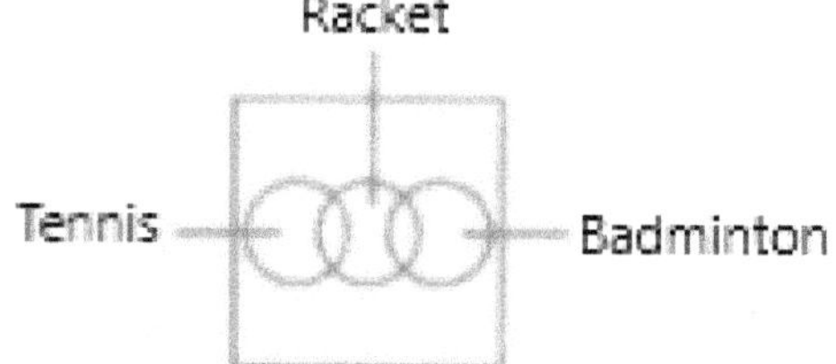

So, HORSE is written as @52#8.

Hence, the correct option is (D).

16. The racket is used in both Badminton and in Tennis. But racket is also used in other games as well.

Hence, the correct option is (B).

17. Your mother's husband: Lady's father

Your father's sister: Lady's aunt

Lady's aunt is Man's mother implies that the man and lady are cousins.

Hence, the correct option is (A).

18. Pattern followed here is,

N + 2 = P, P + 2 = R, S + 2 = U, A + 2 = C.

Similarly,

B + 2 = **D**, L + 2 = **N**, U + 2 = **W**, E + 2 = **G**

Hence, the correct option is (B).

19. The question figure is embedded in the following figure;

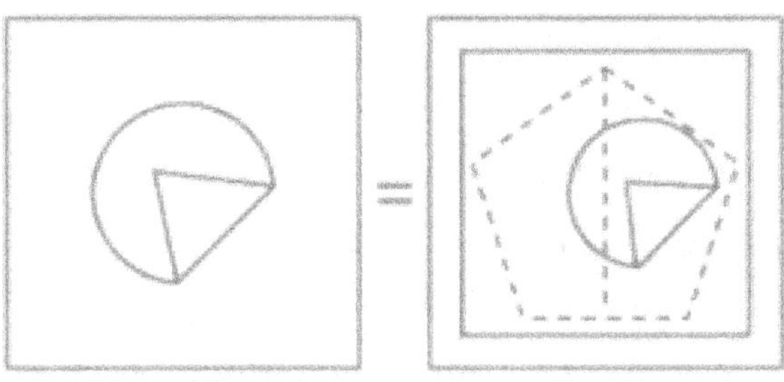

Hence, the correct option is (B).

20.

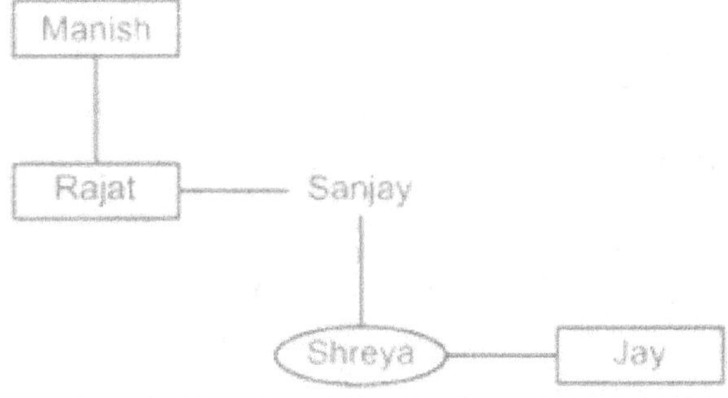

Symbol in Diagram	Meaning
○	Female
□	Male
═	Married Couple
—	Siblings
│	Difference of a generation

So, Rajat is the uncle of Jay.

Hence, the correct option is (A).

21. Face containing five dots and a square should be opposite. So, option (1) cannot be made.

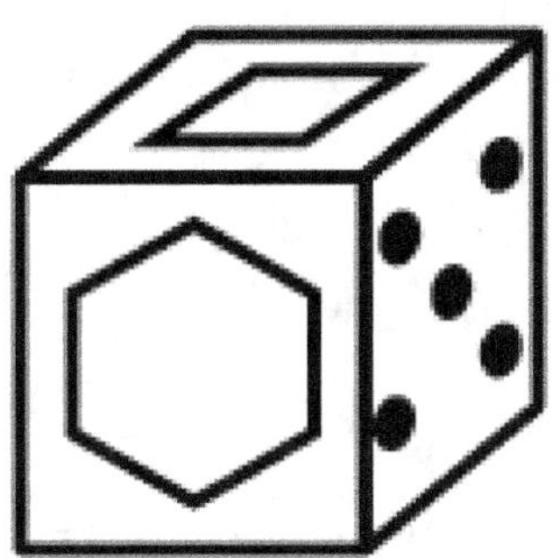

Hence, the correct option is (A).

22. The logic followed here is:

1912 + 100 = 2012

2012 + 121 = 2133

2133 + 144 = 2277

2277 + 169 = 2446

2446 + 196 = **2642**

So, answer is '2642'.

Hence, the correct option is (A).

23.

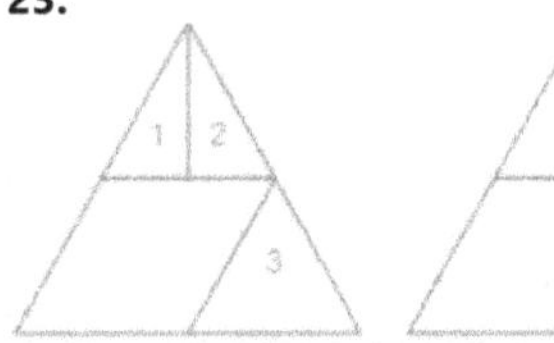 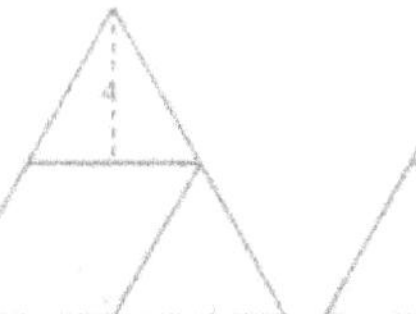 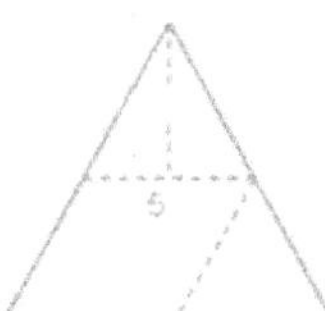

So, there is a total of 5 triangles.

Hence, the correct option is (C).

24. The followed pattern is,

Add the 1st and 2nd columns and multiply the resultant by 2 to get the 3rd column.

In row 1,

6 + 5 = 11, 11 × 2 = 22

In row 2,

2 + 3 = 5, 5 × 2 = 10

Thus, in row 3,

6 + 2 = 8, 8 × 2 = 16

Hence, the correct option is (B).

25.

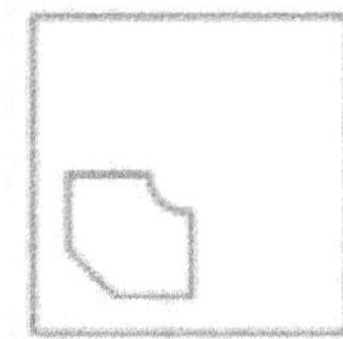 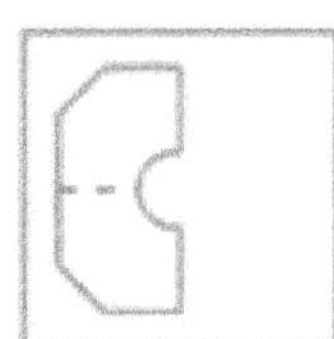 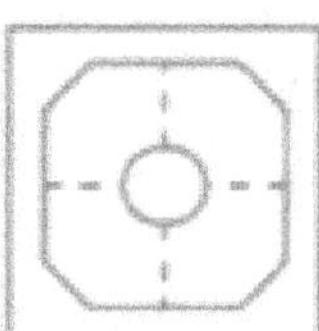

Hence, the correct option is (D).

26. Let the price of a machine be Rs. 100 and let original sales be 100 pieces.

As the price of the machine is increased by 20%.

And the number sold is decreased by 25%.

New price $= 100 + \frac{20}{100} \times 100 = 120$

Number of sales after price rise $= 100 - \frac{25}{100} \times 100 = 75$

Initial revenue $= 100 \times 100 = 10000$

New revenue $= 120 \times 75 = 9000$

Decrease in revenue

$= \left(\frac{(10000-9000)}{10000}\right) \times 100$

$= 10\%$

$\therefore$ Decrease in revenue by 10%.

Hence, the correct option is (D).

27. Given:

Raj got 35% discount

If there was no discount, Raj would pay Rs. 224

This means giving 35% discount $=$ Rs. 224 off

$\therefore 35\%$ of Marked Price $=$ Rs. 224

$\therefore \frac{35}{100} \times$ Marked price $= 224$

$\therefore$ Marked Price $=$ Rs. 640

$\therefore$ Raj paid $= 640 - 224 =$ Rs. 416

Hence, the correct option is (A).

28. Let the original price of 1 kg tea be Rs. 100.

Total money needed to buy 48 kg tea

$= 48 \times 100$

$= 4800$

New price of tea as the price is decreased by 4% per kg,

New price of 1 kg of tea $= 100 - 100 \times \frac{4}{100} = 96$

Quantity of tea bought

$= \frac{4800}{96}$

$= 50$

$\therefore$ As there is reduction in price of 1 kg, one can buy 50 kg of tea in same price.

Hence, the correct option is (B).

29. Average of 10 numbers $= X$

If 38 replaced with 19, then

$\therefore$ The new average will be $= X - \frac{38-19}{10} = X - \frac{19}{10}$

Hence, the correct option is (C).

30. Trouser cost $= Rs.\,320$

Discount is 75% of $320 = Rs.\,80$

For 1 trouser discount is $Rs.\,80$

If Vivek wants to save $Rs.\,400$

So,

He needs to buy $\frac{400}{80} = 5$ trousers

Hence, the correct option is (D).

31. Let $P =$ principal, $R =$ rate of interest and $N =$ time period

Simple interest $= \frac{P \times N \times R}{100}$

Compound interest $= P\left(\frac{1+R}{100}\right)^{n} - P$

Then,

$\Rightarrow 11.40 = P\left(\frac{1+5}{100}\right)^{3} - P - \left(\frac{P \times 5 \times 3}{100}\right)$

$\Rightarrow 228 = 20P\left(\frac{21}{20}\right)^{3} - 20P - 3P$

$\Rightarrow P = \frac{228}{0.1525}$

$\Rightarrow P = 1495$

$\therefore$ Principal is Rs. 1495.

Hence, the correct option is (D).

32. Dividend = Divisor × Quotient + Remainder

When 10,000 is divided by 41, a remainder of 37 is obtained

10000 = 41 × 243 + 37

Now when (41 - 37 = 4) is added to the number, it becomes a multiple of 41 as 41 × 244 = 10004

So, 10004 is the smallest 5-digit number divisible by 41

Hence, the correct option is (C).

33. Given:

B sells for profit of 20%

If gain is $A\%$, then Selling Price $= (100 + A)\%$ of cost price

Selling Price $=$ Rs. $54000 = (100 + 20)\%$ of $CP = \frac{120}{100} \times CP$

$\therefore$ CP for $B = 54000 \times \frac{100}{120} = 54 \times 9 =$ Rs. $45000 = SP$ for A

If loss is $A\%$, then Selling Price $= (100 - A)\%$ of cost price

Selling Price for $A =$ Rs. $45000 = (100 - 10)\%$ of $CP = \frac{90CP}{100}$

$\therefore$ $CP =$ Rs. $\frac{45000 \times 100}{90} =$ Rs. 50000

Hence, the correct option is (B).

34. Total surface area of the cube $= 6a^2$

Where, $a = \dfrac{\text{side}}{\text{edge of the cube}}$

Total surface area of the cube $= 6 \times 10^2 = 600$ sq.m.

1 kg covers 20 sq.m. area, for 600 we need $= \frac{600}{20} = 30$ kg paper.

Expenditure $=$ Rate $\times$ Quantity $=$ Rs. 60×30 kg $=$ Rs. 1800

Hence, the correct option is (D).

35.

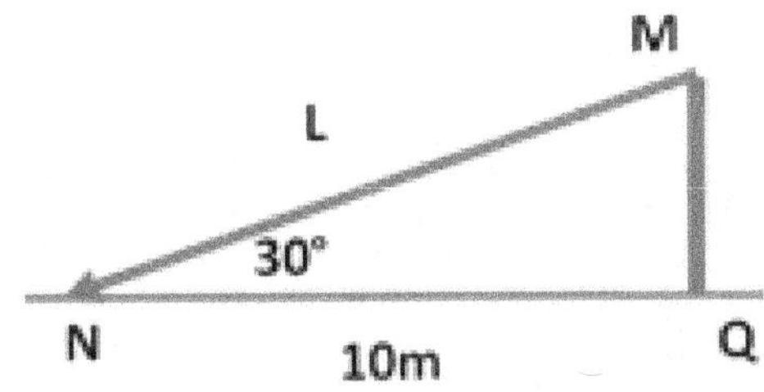

In $\triangle MNQ, Tan30° = \frac{MQ}{NQ}$

$\therefore \frac{1}{\sqrt{3}} = \frac{MQ}{10}$

$\therefore MQ = \frac{10}{\sqrt{3}}$

Also, By Pythagoras theorem, $MN^2 = MQ^2 + NQ^2$

$\therefore L^2 = \frac{100}{3} + 100$

$\therefore L = \frac{20}{\sqrt{3}}$

$\therefore$ Height of tree $= L + MQ$

$= \frac{20}{\sqrt{3}} + \frac{10}{\sqrt{3}} = \frac{30}{\sqrt{3}} = \frac{3 \times 10}{\sqrt{3}} = 10\sqrt{3}$ m

Hence, the correct option is (A).

36. Let 5 consecutive numbers be $N, N + 1, N + 2, N + 3, N + 4$

Sum $= N + (N + 1) + (N + 2) + (N + 3) + (N + 4) = 5N + 10 = 335$

$\therefore N = 65$

Sum of largest and smallest number:

$N + (N + 4) = 65 + 65 + 4$

$= 134$

Hence, the correct option is (A).

37. Let the cost price of an article be Rs. M

Given:

Loss percentage $= 25\%$

Then,

$\Rightarrow 25 = [\frac{(M - S.P)}{M}] \times 100$

$\Rightarrow M = 4M - 4S.P$

$\Rightarrow 3M = 4S.P$

$\Rightarrow S.P = \frac{3M}{4}$

For profit percentage 5%.

$\Rightarrow S \cdot P = \frac{3M}{4} + 60 = \frac{(240 + 3M)}{4}$

$\Rightarrow 5 = [\frac{(\frac{240+3M}{4} - M)}{M}] \times 100$

$\Rightarrow M = 1200 + 15M - 20M$

$\Rightarrow 6M = 1200$

$\Rightarrow M = 200$

$\therefore$ Cost price of an article is Rs. 200

Hence, the correct option is (B).

38. Let, the speed of the stream = x km/hr

Speed of the boat = 9 km/hr

Upstream speed = (9 - x) km/hr

According to the problem,

$\Rightarrow$ 6(9 - x) = 42

$\Rightarrow$ 9 - x = 7

$\Rightarrow$ x = 2

∴ Speed of the stream = 2 km/hr

Hence, the correct option is (D).

39. Let the speed of two trains be $3a$ and $4a$ respectively.

Length of train $= 3a \times 3 = 9a$ meter

Length of other train $= 4a \times 3 = 12a$ meter

Then,

Time taken to cross each other

$$= \frac{(9a + 12a)}{(3a + 4a)}$$

$$= \frac{21}{7}$$

$$= 3 \text{ second}$$

∴ 3 second required to cross each other.

Hence, the correct option is (A).

40. Tap A can fill the tank $= 180$ minutes

Tap A's one-minute work $= \frac{1}{180}$

Tap B can fill the tank $= 20$ minutes

Tap B's one-minute work $= \frac{1}{20}$

Tap C can fill the tank $= 90$ minutes

Tap C's one-minute work $= \frac{1}{90}$

When all the taps are opened together,

$A + B + C = \left(\frac{1}{180} + \frac{1}{20} + \frac{1}{90}\right) = \frac{(1+9+2)}{180} = \frac{12}{180} = \frac{1}{15}$

So, $(A + B + C)$ working together can fill the whole tank in 15 minutes.

Hence, the correct option is (A).

41. Given:

Ratio of time taken by A and $B = 160 : 100$

Then,

$$\Rightarrow \frac{12}{B} = \frac{160}{100}$$

$$\Rightarrow B = \frac{12 \times 5}{8}$$

$$\Rightarrow B = \frac{15}{2}$$

∴ B will complete the work in $7\frac{1}{2}$ days

Hence, the correct option is (A).

42. Number of thefts in Delhi for February, March, April, May, and June is $500, 600, 510, 408,$ and 510 respectively.

Number of thefts in Jaipur for February, March, April, May, and June is $510, 640, 576, 504,$ and 500 respectively.

From the above data:

∴ There are four months where the number of mobile phone thefts in Jaipur higher than that in Delhi.

Hence, the correct option is (B).

43. Number of thefts in Jaipur for February $= 510$

Number of thefts in Jaipur for April $= 576$

Percentage change:

$$= \left[\frac{(576 - 510)}{510}\right] \times 100$$

$$= 12.94\%$$

Hence, the correct option is (C).

44. Number of thefts in Delhi for April $= 510$

Number of thefts in Delhi for May $= 408$

Percentage change

$$= \left[\frac{(510 - 408)}{510}\right] \times 100$$

$$= 20\%$$

Hence, the correct option is (C).

45. Average $= \dfrac{Sum\ of\ elements}{Number\ of\ elements}$

Number of thefts in Jaipur for February, March, April, May, and June is $510, 640, 576, 504,$ and 500 respectively.

Average number of mobile phones thefts in Jaipur from February 2015 to June 2015

$$= \frac{(510 + 640 + 576 + 504 + 500)}{5}$$

$$= \frac{2730}{5}$$

$$= 546$$

∴ Average number of mobile phone thefts in Jaipur from February 2015 to June 2015 is 546.

Hence, the correct option is (D).

46. Let the equation of line be $y = mx + c$

Here, $m = \frac{-1}{3}$ and $c = 6$

$$\Rightarrow y = \left(\frac{-1}{3}\right)x + 6$$

Multiplying above equation by 3

$\Rightarrow 3y = -x + 18$

$\therefore x + 3y = 18$

Hence, the correct option is (A).

47. Given:

$\tan 60° + \dfrac{1}{3}$

$= \sqrt{3} + \dfrac{1}{3}\left[\because \tan 60° = \sqrt{3}\right]$

$= \dfrac{(3\sqrt{3}+1)}{3}$

Hence, the correct option is (C).

48. Let smallest angle (say, ∠A) be a°

According to question:

$\Rightarrow$ ∠B = 3a°

$\Rightarrow$ ∠C = 2a°

Now, by angle sum property of triangle,

$\Rightarrow$ ∠A + ∠B + ∠C = 180°

$\Rightarrow$ a + 3a + 2a = 180°

$\Rightarrow$ 6a = 180°

$\therefore$ a = 30°

Hence, the correct option is (B).

49. Inner volume of the hemispherical bowl $= 144\pi$ cm^3

$\Rightarrow \dfrac{2}{3}\pi r^3 = 144\pi$

$\Rightarrow r = 6$cm

Material used in hemispherical bowl $= 342\pi$ cm^3

$\Rightarrow \dfrac{2}{3}\pi(R^3 - r^3) = 342\pi$

$\Rightarrow (R^3 - r^3) = 513$

Since $r = 6$ cm

$\Rightarrow R^3 = 513 + 216 = 729$

$\Rightarrow R = 9$cm

$\therefore$ Thickness of the bowl $= R - r = 9 - 6 = 3$cm

$\therefore$ Curved surface area of outer side $= 2\pi R^2$

$\Rightarrow 2 \times \pi \times 81 = 162\pi$ cm^2

Hence, the correct option is (B).

50. Given:

Let the capacity of the tank be A liter.

Tank filled with water $= \dfrac{A}{5}$

The amount of water left after draining 8 liters of water from the tank $= \dfrac{A}{6}$

According to the question:

$\Rightarrow \dfrac{A}{5} - 8 = \dfrac{A}{6}$

$\Rightarrow 6A - 240 = 5A$

$\Rightarrow A = 240$

$\therefore$ Capacity of the water tank is 240 liter.

Hence, the correct option is (A).

51. The error lies in the second part of the sentence. The error is in the wrong form of the word, that is, 'guiding' where it should instead be 'guide'.

Correct sentence: Clues were left to guide the team to the next task.

Hence, the correct option is (B).

52. There is no observed error in the given sentence.

All the parts of the sentences are in the correct form and order.

Hence, the correct option is (D).

53. Correct sentence: Faded backgrounds in the room had hinted at abandonment for a long time.

The verb before the bracketed part is had which suggests the sentence to be in the past tense. Thus, hinted here is the right word for improvement.

The formula for the past perfect tense is had + [past participle]. It doesn't matter if the subject is singular or plural; the formula doesn't change.

Hence, the correct option is (C).

54. Finding and found do not hold grammatical sense in the given sentence. This is because the subject must agree with the verb. Here, the subject 'rustling leaves' agrees with the verb 'find'. It maintains the grammar with proper meaning. Thus, made is the right word to be used as an improvement in the given sentence.

Correct sentence: Rustling leaves made her look up to find that the clear sky was now turning clouded and heavy.

Hence, the correct option is (B).

55. 'Be' is the only suitable word from the given options that makes meaningful and grammatical sense in the given sentence.

Correct sentence: Things continued to burden and she continued to be undeterred.

Hence, the correct option is (B).

56. The last three options do not fit in grammatically and are incorrect answers. 'As' makes the right fit because it provides the right meaning.

Correct sentence: A good day's work is never felt as draining.

Hence, the correct option is (A).

57. 'On' the beach refers to the place geographically and not the action of sitting 'by' it. 'Along' does not fit here as it usually defines movement or direction while the action here is sitting still. In comparison with 'by', 'beside' does not fit in very well.

Thus, 'by' is the right word for the given blank.

Correct sentence: Sitting by the beach, she felt herself becoming the one with the surroundings.

Hence, the correct option is (C).

58. Discreet means careful and prudent in one's speech or actions, especially in order to keep something confidential or to avoid embarrassment.

Cautious means are careful to avoid potential problems or dangers.

Hence, the correct option is (B).

59. Essential means absolutely necessary; extremely important.

Necessary means needed to be done, achieved, or present; essential.

Hence, the correct option is (B).

60. Abandon means cease to support or look after (someone); desert.

Continue means persist in an activity or process.

Thus 'continue' is the correct antonym of 'abandon'.

Hence, the correct option is (B).

61. Negligence means failure to take proper care of something.

Conscientious means wishing to do one's work or duty well and thoroughly.

Hence, the correct option is (D).

62. Let the cat out of the bag means to reveal a secret by mistake or by carelessness.

Sentence Usage: He let the cat out of the bag by telling us about his extra ways of income.

Hence, the correct option is (A).

63. The ball is in your court means that one has an opportunity to make a decision or take the next step.

Sentence Usage: It is Hina's decision if she would file a case against her boss for being dishonest as the ball is in her court now.

Hence, the correct option is (C).

64. Cut corners means cutting down on the basic necessities to save money.

Sentence Usage: He cut corners to give his children the basic education.

Hence, the correct option is (C).

65. Introvert- A person who does not freely express himself.

Other options:

Stoic- A person who endures pain without expressing it.

Recluse- A person who lives in solitude.

Ascetic- A person who leads a highly disciplined life.

Hence, the correct option is (B).

66. Fugitive- One who escapes from captivity.

Other options:

Heretic- A person whose actions are against religion.

Henpeck- A person who is controlled by his wife.

Lunatic- A person who is mentally ill.

Hence, the correct option is (A).

67. Arbitrary means based on random choice or personal whim, rather than any reason or system.

Rational means based on or in accordance with reason or logic.

Thus, 'Rational' is the correct opposite of 'Arbitary'

Hence, the correct option is (B).

68. Escalate means increase rapidly.

Intensify means become or make more intense or increase the capacity of something.

Hence, the correct option is (B).

69. Tit-for-tat means 'actions done intentionally to punish other people because they have done something unpleasant to you.' So option (B) explains this between the US and China in which the US's heavy tariff on Chinese goods was met with China levying tariffs on US products.

Hence, the correct option is (B).

70. The author has stated that though America is not the only country to have complained about markets flooding with Chinese steel, its decision to levy heavy tariffs on Chinese Steel is interesting considering the fact that it imports only 3% of steel from the Chinese.

Hence, the correct option is (C).

71. In the first part of the passage, this is very strongly discussed. But the most significant statement is "who has repeatedly used the U.S. trade deficit of over $500 billion as a barometer for the country's lot in the international trade order, has railed against the U.S. being treated "unfairly" by its trading partners."

Hence, the correct option is (B).

72. The passage starts with defining economic development. The next sentence must obviously be Q. it is the only one continuing to describe economic development without referring to any previously un-introduced terms.

And the next sentence must be P because it starts with 'and' and also gives an interpretation of economic development from the point of view of Novack. Novack now introduces consumption into the discussion, which is taken up by sentence S.

And S introduces the concept of substantial production, which is taken up by sentence R.

The term 'technologies', introduced in sentence R, is then utilized to redefine economic development in the concluding statement of the passage.

Thus the correct sequence will be QPSR.

Hence, the correct option is (B).

73. The passage starts with stating that we were not born with wings, and then must naturally point to how we always wished to fly like birds. Thus 1 is followed by R.

The next sentence must now transition us from what we don't have to what we have or how we got it. Thus sentence P is the next sentence ideally. The passage begins to talk about how science has given us what God has not. After this, the passage can talk about what flight is possible today. Thus, the next sentence must be Q.

This can be followed by more information on these flights i.e. S. It ends by saying that today science can even take us to the moon.

Thus the correct sequence will be RPQS.

Hence, the correct option is (C).

74. The wrongly spelled word is Bureaucrecy.

Correct spelling: Bureaucracy

Meaning of Bureaucracy: a system of government in which most of the important decisions are taken by state officials rather than by elected representatives

Hence, the correct option is (C).

75. The correct spelling is manageable.

Meaning of Manageable: Something that can be managed.

Hence, the correct option is (B).

76. Maana Patel, Saloni Dalal, Richa Mishra are all National level swimmers. They have represented India at the Asian Age Group Championships, Indian Championships etc. Maana Patel -- India's third entrant for Tokyo 2020 through universality quota -- holds the national marks in the 50m, 100m and the 200m backstroke races. Delhi's Richa Mishra has as many as five Indian swimming records under her name.

Hence, the correct option is (B).

77. World champion Lewis Hamilton has been voted BBC Sports Personality of the Year 2020.

- One of F1s all-time great drivers, he equaled Michael Schumacher's record of seven world titles with his fourth consecutive championship in 2020.
- It is the second time Hamilton has been crowned Sports Personality of the Year, he first won the award in 2014.

Hence, the correct option is (B).

78.

- The privatization of Air India Limited will be completed during the upcoming financial year 2021-22.
- The government plans to sell its entire 100% stake in Air India, which has not made profits since its merger with Indian Airlines in 2007.
- The winning bidder will also get 100% stake in the national carrier's low-cost arm Air India Express and 50% stake in Air India SATS (AISATS).

Hence, the correct option is (A).

79.

- '1917' won the Golden Globe 2020 award for 'Best Motion Picture - Drama.
- 1917, unfolds in real-time, tracking a pair of British soldiers as they cross the Western Front on a desperate rescue mission.

Hence, the correct option is (B).

80. Under Part-III (Article 12-35) of the constitution, every citizen has provided 6 fundamental rights.

- A total of seven rights were originally provided by the Constitution. 44th amendment (1978 A.D.) removed the right to property and made a legal right 300-A.
- The fundamental rights secure the natural rights of all citizens and it was taken from the constitution of the U.S.A.

Hence, the correct option is (B).

81.

- The President of India, Ram Nath Kovind, received the first copy of the book 'Law, Justice and Judicial Power – Justice PN Bhagwati's Approach' on 8 February 2019.
- The book is written by Mool Chand Sharma.
- Justice Bhagwati has been called the father of Public Interest Litigation in India.

Hence, the correct option is (C).

82.

- Pathar ki Masjid is located in Patna, Bihar.
- It was founded by Parvez Shah, the son of Jahangir, the Mughal Emperor, in 1621.
- It is named so since the structure is built entirely of stones.

Hence, the correct option is (A).

83.

- CEO of Zoom, video conferencing platform, Eric Yuan has been named 'Businessperson of the Year' by TIME for the growth of Zoom in a pandemic.
- He began at WebEx as a coder and soon became integral to the creation of his video-conferencing platform.

- Zoom's software was released in 2013, promoting a free basic service for different-size organizations along with many paid levels.

Hence, the correct option is (A).

84. Inderkilla National Park is in Himachal Pradesh.

Following national parks of Himachal Pradesh are:

National Park	Trick
Simbalbara National Park	Simba
Great Himalayan National Park	Great Himalaya
Pin Valley National Park	Valley
InderKilla National Park	Inder
Khirganga National Park	Khir

Trick: Simba ate kheer with Inder in the valley of the Great Himalayas.

Hence, the correct option is (A).

85. In the Pali language, the Sanskrit word 'Dharma' is termed as 'Dhamma'.

- In Buddhism Dharma means 'Cosmic law and order' or the teaching of Buddha. 'Dharma' is pronounced as 'Dhamma' in Pali.
- Pali is a native language of the Middle Indo-Aryan Indian subcontinent. It is also called 'Magadhan'.

Hence, the correct option is (C).

86.

- The Battle of Khanwa of 1527 was fought between **Rana Sanga of Mewar and Mughal Emperor Babur** after the Battle of Panipat.
- Rana Sanga was defeated in the war. Babur's victory consolidated the new Mughal dynasty in India.

Hence, the correct option is (B).

87. Itanagar is the capital and largest city of the Indian state of Arunachal Pradesh.

- The local food of Itanagar is inspired by Tibetan cuisine.
- Christianity is the largest religion in Arunachal Pradesh, a state of Northeast India bordering China.

Hence, the correct option is (D).

88.

- In 1858, the title 'Governor-General' was converted into viceroy.
- In August 1858, the British Parliament passed an act that abolished the rule of the company.
- The British Governor-General of India was given the viceroy's title which meant the emperor's representative.

Hence, the correct option is (A).

89. The standard metric unit of power is the Watt. As is implied by the equation for power, a unit of power is equivalent to a unit of work divided by a unit of time. Thus, a Watt is equivalent to a Joule/second.

Hence, the correct option is (C).

90. In India, the maximum strength of the Rajya Sabha is fixed at 250.

- Out of which 238 are elected.
- 12 are nominated by the President.

Hence, the correct option is (D).

91.

Great Pyramid of Giza	Oldest and largest of the three pyramids in the Giza pyramid complex	Location – Egypt
Great wall of China	Was built to protect the Chinese states and empires against the raids and invasions of the various nomadic groups of the Eurasian Steppe	Location – China
Colosseum	Is an oval amphitheater in the centre of the city of Rome	Location – Italy
Chichen Itza	A large pre-Columbian city built by the Maya people of the Terminal Classic period	Location – Mexico

Hence, the correct option is (B).

92. Democracy provides a method to deal with differences and conflicts as different people have different opinions and interests. There are free and fair elections in a democracy. Different groups can live with one another in harmony and peace.

Hence, the correct option is (D).

93.

- Chinese city Hangzhou will host the 2022 Asian Games which is a multi-sport event. After Beijing and Guangzhou, Hangzhou will be the third Chinese city to host the Asian Games.
- Asian Games 2018 (18th Asian Games) were held in two Indonesian cities, Palembang and Jakarta from Aug 18 to Sep 2, 2018.

Hence, the correct option is (A).

94. Parabolic concave mirrors converge the light ray coming from focus into long parallel rays.

- Parabolic mirrors are the basis of parabolic antennae and automobile headlights, as well as some megaphones and telescopic mirrors.
- A parabolic reflector is a reflective surface used to collect or project energy such as light, sound, or radio waves.

Hence, the correct option is (A).

95. This happens due to the refraction of light. When light travels from one medium to another it bends, the light rays from the bottom of the pool get bent when they exit the water surface. Our eyes don't take refraction into the account so the swimming pool appears less deep than actual.

Hence, the correct option is (A).

96.

- Bandar Laddu is a sweet, got the Geographical Indication of Andhra Pradesh.
- The staple food of Andhra Pradesh is Rice, which is served with sambar. It is also served with other lentil preparations along with vegetables.

Hence, the correct option is (A).

97. Acetylene is used in welding and cutting metals. Oxygen and acetylene gases (Oxyacetylene) are used and the process is called oxyacetylene welding.

Using Acetylene for welding is an old process. In recent decades this process has become obsolete due to modern arc welding methods which provide better and consistent mechanical properties.

Hence, the correct option is (C).

98. The number value 6.022×10^{23} is called Avogadro's number.

It is the number of elementary particles per mole of a substance.

It is expressed in N_A.

Hence, the correct option is (C).

99. The full form of MICR is Magnetic Ink Character Recognition.

- MICR is used by the banking industry to ease the processing and clearance of cheques and other documents.
- Numbers and characters found on the bottom of checks are printed using the Magnetic Ink.
- When a document that contains this ink needs to be read, it passes through a machine, which magnetizes the ink and then translates the magnetic information into characters.

Hence, the correct option is (C).

100.

- In December 2012, the Planning Commission published the near-final draft 12th Five Year Plan – Faster, More Inclusive and Sustainable Growth.
- The Planning Commission (now Niti Ayog) is an institution in the Government of India, which formulates India's Five-Year Plans, among other functions.

Hence, the correct option is (B).

General Intelligence and Reasoning

Q.1 What will come at the place of the question mark?

2, 3, 6, 15, ?, 123

A. 47   **B.** 42   **C.** 45   **D.** 50

Q.2 Direction: In the following question, select the related word/letters/number from the given alternatives.

GREAT: 12 :: TEXTBOOK:?

A. 23   **B.** 22   **C.** 24   **D.** 21

Q.3 Direction: Select the odd image from the given alternatives.

A.  B. 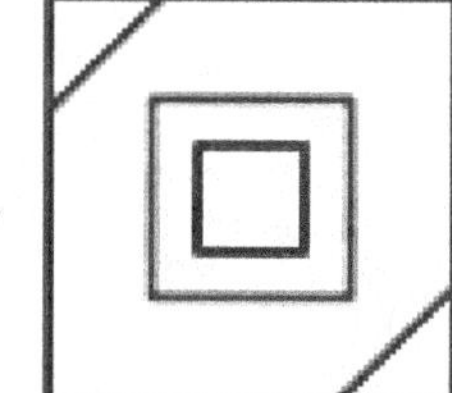

C. 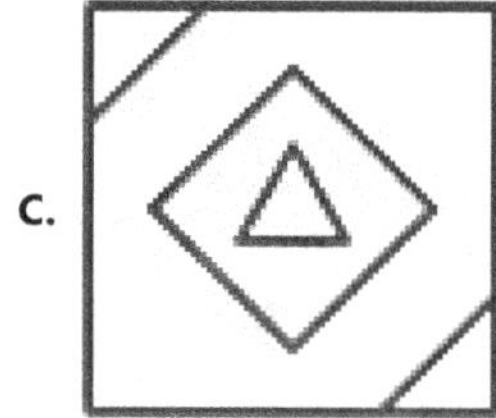 D. 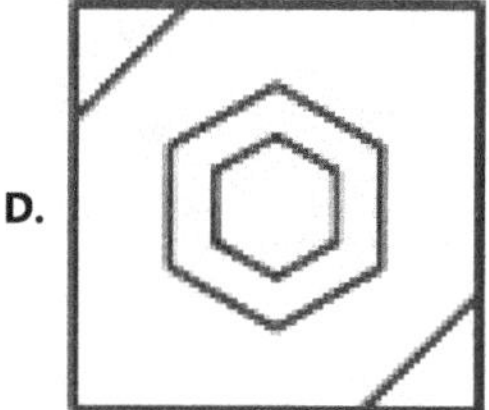

Q.4 Direction: Arrange the given words in the sequence in which they occur in the dictionary

1. Terrible
2. Thaw
3. Thank less
4. Testify
5. Terrain

A. 3, 4, 5, 1, 2   **B.** 2, 1, 5, 4, 3

C. 5, 1, 4, 3, 2   **D.** 2, 1, 3, 4, 5

Q.5 Sunday, Monday, Wednesday, Saturday, Wednesday, Monday, ________________. Which of the following best fits in the blank?

A. Sunday   **B.** Monday

C. Wednesday   **D.** Saturday

Q.6 Direction: Select the missing number from the given responses.

346	96	738
432	18	237
521	?	329

A. 42   **B.** 36   **C.** 44   **D.** 58

Q.7 What will come at the place of the question mark?

8, 6, 9, 23, 87, ?

A. 128   **B.** 226   **C.** 324   **D.** 429

Q.8 In a certain code, THEN is coded as VFGL. How the WORD may be coded?

A. UQPF   **B.** YMTB   **C.** YMVB   **D.** VQFP

Q.9 Which of the following diagrams correctly represents Elephants, Wolves, Animals?

A. 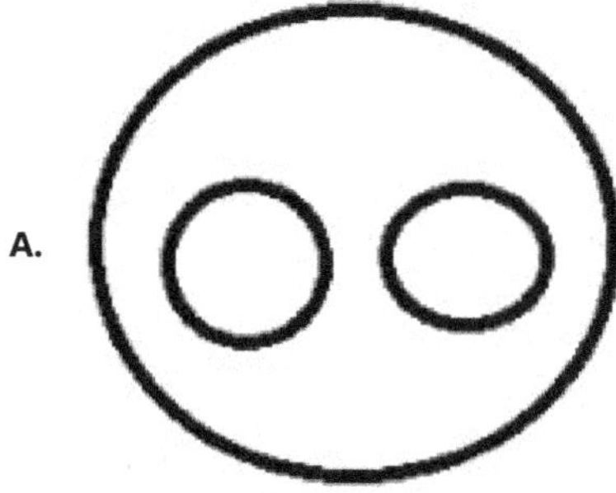

B. 

C. 

D. 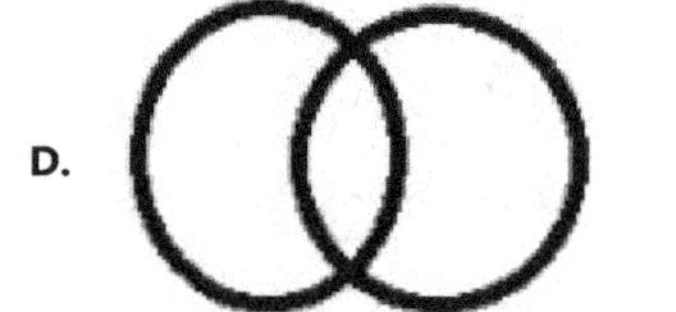

Q.10 If PALAM could be given the code number 43, what code number can be given to PERMIT?

A. 75   **B.** 85   **C.** 81   **D.** 71

Q.11 Direction: In this question, a series is given with one term missing. Select the correct alternative from the given ones that will complete the series.

A, DE, IJK, ?, YZABC

A. LMNO   **B.** PQR   **C.** PQRS   **D.** NOPQ

Q.12 If TOUR is written in a certain code as 1234, CLEAR as 56784, and SPARE as 90847, what will be the 5th digit for SCULPTURE in the same code?

A. 6   **B.** 3   **C.** 0   **D.** 1

Q.13 Find the odd number from the given alternative.

A. 5720   **B.** 6710   **C.** 2640   **D.** 4270

Q.14 Select the odd number from the given alternatives.

A. 169   **B.** 421   **C.** 529   **D.** 289

Q.15 Direction: In the following question, select the word which cannot be formed using the letters of the given word.
CORPORATION

A. PAINT   **B.** ROPE
C. PORTION   **D.** POTION

Q.16 In a certain code, ALTERED is written as ZOGVIVW. How will the word JUSTICE be written in that code?

A. QFHHSWV   **B.** PFGHRXV
C. QFHGRXV   **D.** PFHGSVX

Q.17 Find the odd number from the given alternatives.

A. 626   **B.** 841   **C.** 962   **D.** 1090

Q.18 Arrange the words given below in a meaningful sequence.

1. Rainbow
2. Rain
3. Sun
4. Happy
5. Child

A. 4, 2, 3, 5, 1   **B.** 2, 3, 1, 5, 4
C. 4, 5, 1, 2, 3   **D.** 2, 1, 4, 5, 3

Q.19 Direction: In the following question, select the related word from the given alternatives.

Mathematics : Formulas :: Chemistry : ?

A. Reactions   **B.** Organisms
C. Theorems   **D.** Gravity

Q.20 Select the correct combination of mathematical signs to replace * signs and to balance the given equation:

18 * 6 * 3 * 12 * 24

A. ÷ − = ×   **B.** × ÷ − =   **C.** + ÷ × =   **D.** × = ÷ +

Q.21 Select the correct combination of mathematical signs to replace * signs and to balance the following equation:

8 * 8 * 1 * 7 = 8

A. × ÷ +   **B.** + × ÷   **C.** ÷ × +   **D.** - × ÷

Q.22 Arrange the words given below in a meaningful sequence.

1. Reading
2. Composing
3. Writing
4. Printing

A. 1, 3, 2, 4   **B.** 2, 3, 4, 1   **C.** 3, 1, 2, 4   **D.** 3, 2, 4, 1

Q.23 Direction: In the following figure, the square represents Dietitians, the triangle represents Botanists, the circle represents Psychologists and the rectangle represents Indians. Which set of letters represents Psychologists who are not Botanists?

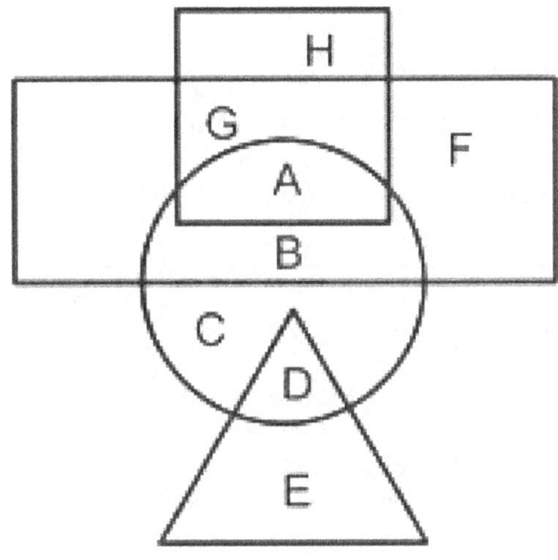

A. D, G, A   **B.** A, B, C   **C.** F, E, C   **D.** H, B, D

Q.24 Direction: In the following question a statement is given, followed by two conclusions.

Statement: Until our country achieves economic equality, political freedom and democracy would be meaningless.

Conclusions:

I. Political freedom and democracy go hand in hand.

II. Economic equality leads to real political freedom and democracy.

A. Only conclusion I follow
B. Only conclusion II follows
C. Either I or II follows
D. Neither I or II follows

Q.25 Direction: In the question, two statements are given, followed by two conclusions, I and II. You have to consider the statements to be true even if it seems to be at variance from commonly known facts. You have to decide which of the given conclusions, if any, follows from the given statements.

Statements:

I: No lighters are fire.

II: All matchboxes are lighters.

Conclusions:

I: No fire are matchboxes.

II: All matchboxes are fire.

A. Only conclusion I follows
B. Only conclusion II follows
C. Both conclusions I and II follow
D. Neither conclusion I nor conclusion II follows

Numerical Aptitude/ Quantitative Ability

Q.26 If $2A = 3B = 8C$, then what is the value of $A : B : C$?

A. $8 : 3 : 2$ **B.** $8 : 4 : 3$
C. $2 : 3 : 8$ **D.** $12 : 8 : 3$

Q.27 An angle is thrice its complementary angle. What is the measure of the angle?
A. 22.5°   **B.** 135°   **C.** 45°   **D.** 67.5°

Q.28 The marked price of an article is 50% more than its cost price. If a discount of 10% is given, then what will be the profit percentage?
A. 35%   **B.** 40%   **C.** 45%   **D.** 30%

Q.29 The average of 9 consecutive numbers is 26. Which is the largest number out of these 9?
A. 42   **B.** 30   **C.** 32   **D.** 31

Q.30 A person bought a certain quantity of sugar at the rate of Rs. 120 per quintal. 10% of the sugar was spoiled. At what price (per quintal) should he sell the remaining sugar to earn 20% profit.
A. Rs. 210 **B.** Rs. 150 **C.** Rs. 220 **D.** Rs. 144

Q.31 The average weight of a class is 52 kg. If a student with weight 118 kg. joins the class, then the new average weight becomes 58 kg. How many total students are there in the class?
A. 19   **B.** 10   **C.** 21   **D.** 18

Q.32 Find the value of $397 \times 397 + 104 \times 104 + 2 \times 397 \times 104$.
A. 250001   **B.** 251001   **C.** 260101   **D.** 261001

Q.33 What is the compound interest (in Rs.) on a sum of Rs. 10000 for 2 years at a rate of 5% per annum compounded annually?
A. Rs. 1000 **B.** Rs. 1025
C. Rs. 1500 **D.** Rs. 1250

Q.34 Find the curved surface area (in cm^2) of a right circular cylinder of diameter 7 cm and height 6 cm.
A. 132 cm^2 **B.** 110 cm^2 **C.** 92 cm^2 **D.** 154 cm^2

Q.35 If $12\cos^2\theta + 8\sin^2\theta = 9$, then what is the value of $\tan\theta$?
A. $\sqrt{7}$ **B.** $\frac{7}{3}$ **C.** 3   **D.** $\sqrt{3}$

Q.36 The LCM and HCF of two numbers are 168 and 6 respectively. If one of the numbers is 24, find the other.
A. 36   **B.** 38   **C.** 40   **D.** 42

Q.37 Two pipes P and Q can fill the tank alone in 120 and 80 hours respectively. If they are opened together, then in how many hours will the tank be filled?
A. 24   **B.** 48   **C.** 100   **D.** 120

Q.38 If P is 25% less than Q, then Q is how much percent more than P?
A. 20%   **B.** 16.66%   **C.** 33.33%   **D.** 12.5%

Q.39 Evaluate $\left(\dfrac{\sin 30°}{\cos 45°}\right) \times \left(\dfrac{\sin 45°}{\cos 30°}\right)$
A. $\frac{\sqrt{2}}{\sqrt{3}}$ **B.** $\frac{2}{\sqrt{3}}$ **C.** $\frac{1}{\sqrt{3}}$ **D.** $\frac{1}{\sqrt{2}}$

Q.40 A sum of Rs. 800 becomes Rs. 1000 in 2 years at simple interest. What is the per annum rate of interest (in percent)?
A. 12.5%   **B.** 25%   **C.** 8.5%   **D.** 17%

Q.41 A, B and C can complete a work in 5, 10 and 30 days respectively. In how many days A, B and C together can complete the same work?
A. 4   **B.** 2   **C.** 3   **D.** 3.5

Q.42 The smallest angle of a triangle is 40° less than the largest angle. If the largest angle is 80°, then find the third angle of the triangle.
A. 40°   **B.** 90°   **C.** 80°   **D.** 60°

Q.43 The speed of a train 150 m long is 45 km/hr. How much time will it take to cross a platform which is 500 m long?
A. 52 sec   **B.** 15 sec   **C.** 9 sec   **D.** 18 sec

Q.44 Four years ago, the ratio of the ages of two sisters was $7 : 9$. If their age ratio after 4 years will be $9 : 11$, find their current ages.
A. 11 year, 13 year   **B.** 18 year, 22 year
C. 25 year, 31 year   **D.** 32 year, 40 year

Q.45 2898 is how much percent of 12600?
A. 19%   **B.** 21%   **C.** 23%   **D.** 27%

Q.46 A gun is fired at a distance of 6.64 km away from Prem. He hears the sound 20 seconds later. Then the speed of sound is:
A. 664 m/s   **B.** 664 km/s
C. 332 m/s   **D.** 332 km/s

Ques (47-50):Direction: Study the chart and answer the question:

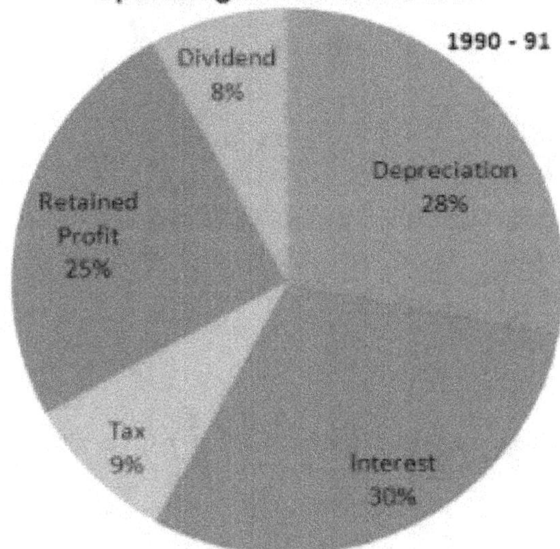

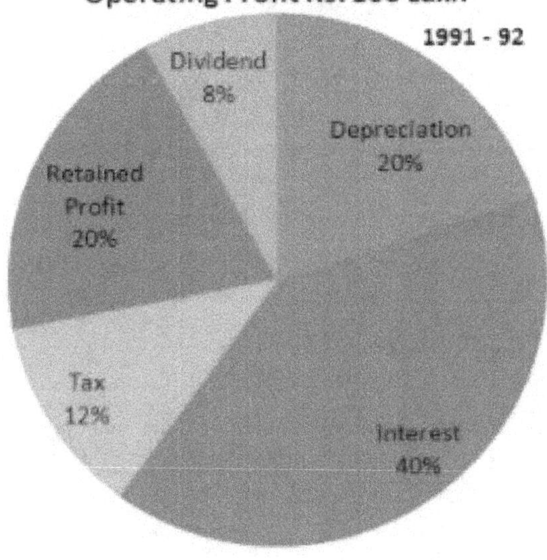

Q.47 The operating profit in $1991 - 92$ increased over in $1990 - 91$ by:

A. 23% **B.** 22% **C.** 25% **D.** 24%

Q.48 The interest burden in $1991 - 92$ was higher than that in $1990 - 91$ by:

A. 50% **B.** Rs. 25 lakh
C. 90% **D.** Rs. 41 lakh

Q.49 If on average, 20% rate of interest was charged on borrowed funds, then the total borrowed funds used by this company is the given 2 year amounted to:

A. Rs. 221 lakh **B.** Rs. 195 lakh
C. Rs. 368 lakh **D.** Rs. 515 lakh

Q.50 The retained profit in $1991 - 92$, as compared to that in $1990 - 91$ was:

A. Higher by 2.5 % **B.** Higher by 1.5%
C. Lower by 2.5 % **D.** Lower by 1.5%

General English & Comprehension

Q.51 Direction: In the following question, some parts of the sentence may have errors. Find out which part of the sentence has an error and select the appropriate option. If a sentence is free from error, select 'No Error'.

The army have been(1)/ called to aid(2)/ in the relief operation.(3)/ No error(4)

A. 1 **B.** 2 **C.** 3 **D.** 4

Q.52 Direction: In the following question, some parts of the sentence may have errors. Find out which part of the sentence has an error and select the appropriate option. If a sentence is free from error, select 'No Error'.

There was no money (1)/ in Rahul's and Roshan's(2)/ joint account. (3)/ No error(4)

A. 1 **B.** 2 **C.** 3 **D.** 4

Q.53 Direction: In the question below, a part of the sentence is underlined. Below are given alternatives to the underlined part which may improve the sentence. Choose the correct alternative. In case no improvement is needed choose 'No improvement.'

Having driving down the lane, I saw a quaint house with green walls and a red roof.

A. Because I was driving down the lane
B. As I was driving down the lane
C. I was driving down the lane
D. No improvement

Q.54 Direction: In the question below, a part of the sentence is underlined. Below are given alternatives to the underlined part which may improve the sentence. Choose the correct alternative. In case no improvement is needed choose 'No improvement.'

Sheena is the most cleverest girl in our class.

A. The cleverest girl
B. The cleverer girl
C. The more clever girl
D. No improvement

Q.55 Direction: In the following question, the sentence is given with a blank to be filled in with an appropriate word. Select the correct alternative out of the four and indicate it by selecting the appropriate option.

I am awful ______ picking vegetables.

A. for **B.** at **C.** of **D.** as

Q.56 Direction: In the following question, the sentence is given with a blank to be filled in with an appropriate word. Select the correct alternative out of the four and indicate it by selecting the appropriate option.

Career ______ the kind of lifestyle one will lead and his/her position in society.

A. determined
B. determines
C. deter

D. has been determined

Q.57 Direction: In the following question, a sentence has been given in direct/indirect speech. Out of the four alternatives suggested, select the one which best expresses the same sentence in indirect/direct speech

He said to her, "What a hot day it is!"

A. He exclaimed sorrowfully that it was a very hot day.

B. He told her that it was a hot day.

C. He exclaimed that it was a very hot day.

D. He said that it was a hot day.

Q.58 Direction: In a sentence has been given in Active/Passive Voice. Out of the four alternatives suggested, select the one which best expresses the same sentence in Passive/Active Voice.

This strategy permits investors to buy shares from unlisted companies.

A. Under this strategy, the investors may be permitted to buy shares from unlisted companies.

B. Under this strategy, the investors have been permitted to buy shares from unlisted companies.

C. Under this strategy, the investors are permitted to buy shares from unlisted companies.

D. Under this strategy, the investors were permitted to buy shares from unlisted companies.

Q.59 Direction: Fill in the blank with the proper form of the verb.

Last month, he ___________ in debt if not for my help.

A. would have been   **B.** had been

C. was   **D.** None of these

Q.60 Direction: Out of the four alternatives, choose the one which best expresses the opposite meaning of the given word.

Foremost

A. Mature   **B.** Premature

C. Unimportant   **D.** Disposed

Q.61 Direction: Out of the four alternatives, choose the one which best expresses the opposite meaning of the given word.

Protects

A. Defends   **B.** Deprives   **C.** Devises   **D.** Deserts

Q.62 Direction: Out of the four alternatives, choose the one which best expresses the meaning of the given word.

Fostering

A. Safeguarding   **B.** Neglecting

C. Ignoring   **D.** Nurturing

Q.63 Direction: Out of the four alternatives, choose the one which best expresses the meaning of the given word.

Transient

A. Permanent   **B.** Brief

C. Momentary   **D.** Both (B) and (C)

Q.64 Direction: Out of the four alternatives, choose the one which best expresses the opposite meaning of the given word.

Recalcitrant

A. Obedient   **B.** Obstinate

C. Stubborn   **D.** Unruly

Q.65 Direction: Out of the four alternatives, choose the one which best expresses the opposite meaning of the given word.

Obliterate

A. Protect   **B.** Destroy

C. Eradicate   **D.** Delete

Q.66 Direction: Out of the four alternatives, choose the one which best expresses the meaning of the given word.

Equitable

A. Partial   **B.** Prejudiced

C. Biased   **D.** Neutral

Q.67 Direction: In the following question, an idiomatic expression or a proverb is highlighted. Select the alternative which best describes its use in the sentence.

After he had atoned for his crimes he **kept his nose clean** and lived a sedate life, till the day he died.

A. To wash his face regularly

B. To maintain personal hygiene

C. To live alone

D. To live a good life and avoid trouble

Q.68 Direction: In the following question, an idiomatic expression or a proverb is highlighted. Select the alternative which best describes its use in the sentence.

She asked him to join their band tour **with no strings attached.**

A. By following their rules

B. By signing a document

C. By tying up the agreement with a string

D. Without any preconditions

Q.69 Direction: In the following question, an idiomatic expression or a proverb is given. Select the alternative which best describes its use in the sentence.

To hit the sack

A. To vent out anger

B. To hit a sack on the floor

C. To go to bed

D. To repress anger

Q.70 Direction: In the following question, an idiomatic expression or a proverb is given. Select the alternative which best describes its use in the sentence.

To hit the nail on the head.

A. To say the correct thing

B. To fool someone

C. To deceive someone

D. Get hurt on your nail

Ques (71-75):Direction: Read the passage given below and then answer the question given below the passage. Some words may be highlighted for your attention. Read carefully.

It's rough when you realize that the true saboteur of your dreams is an insider. If you aren't living up to your highest potential and achieving your goals, blame your brain's own negativity bias. Positive emotions give us access to the control center in the brain that initiates action toward our goals. Yet, the human brain has evolved to prioritize negative emotions, experiences, and memories.

There's a scientific reason why negative inner voices get more air time in your head than positive ones. Our brains are hard-wired to continuously scan for potential threats. Such focus on the possible worst-case scenario contributed to the survival of our early ancestors. Those who were nervous, tense, and attentive to possible danger had a better chance of living to see another day.

As a result, the human brain evolved with a bias towards the negative. Studies show that we recognize and respond more quickly to an angry or sad face, than a happy face. Negative ads and headlines draw more of our attention. Our own shortcomings are far more apparent to us than our achievements. We notice lack more than abundance.

Q.71 Human brains have evolved to focus more on negative emotions. Which of the following is a possible explanation for this?

A. Our conscience finds it easier to believe in negativity

B. Over the years, humans have survived taking in note the worst case scenarios

C. Over the years, we have responded quickly to something joyful as compared to something sad

D. Both (A) and (B)

Q.72 'We notice lack more than abundance'. Which of the following quotes by famous personalities suit this context?

A. Everybody is a genius. But if you judge a fish by its ability to climb a tree, it will live its whole life believing that it is stupid - Albert Einstein

B. If you are born poor, it's not your mistake. But if you die poor, it's your mistake - Bill Gates

C. I cried because I had no shoes, then I met a man who had no feet - Mahatma Gandhi

D. Successful people don't fear failure but understand that it's necessary to learn and grow from – Robert Kiyosaki

Q.73 Which of the following is the closest synonym of the word saboteur as used in the passage?

A. Promoter

B. Facilitator

C. Destroyer

D. Architect

Q.74 According to the passage, what is the effect of having positive emotions?

A. They allow us to deal with depression and anxiety

B. They help us to feel and act confident

C. They warn us of various threats and challenges

D. They help us in initiating action towards our goals

Q.75 Which of the following best describes the tone of the author?

A. Nonchalant

B. Illuminating

C. Vindictive

D. Depressed

General Awareness

Q.76 Which style of Kabaddi is known as "Punjabi Kabaddi"?

A. Standard style of kabaddi

B. Square style of kabaddi

C. Rectangle style of kabaddi

D. Circle style of kabaddi

Q.77 Syed Mushtaq Ali Trophy is associated with which sport?

A. Hockey

B. Cricket

C. Foot Ball

D. Golf

Q.78 Which of the following measures of the money supply is known as 'Broad money'?

A. M_1 **B.** M_2 **C.** M_3 **D.** M_4

Q.79 Which among the following is an example of Indirect tax?

A. Income tax

B. Wealth tax

C. Sales tax

D. Corporate tax

Q.80 When was NABARD established?

A. 1975   **B.** 1980   **C.** 1982   **D.** 1990

Q.81 Which of the following key combinations is used to open Windows Task Manager?

A. Alt + F4

B. Alt + Shift

C. Alt + Enter

D. Ctrl + Shift + Esc

Q.82 What was the theme of the 10-day long Taj Mahotsav which began on 18 February 2020?

A. Sanskriti

B. Parampara

C. Dharma

D. Dharohar

Q.83 Which city bagged the cleanest city award under Swachh Survekshan 2020?

A. Mysore

B. Kochi

C. Indore

D. Bengaluru

Q.84 Which country has formed its first all-woman communication team?

A. New Zealand

B. Myanmar

C. United States

D. Germany

Q.85 What amount of grant has been allotted under "Mission COVID Suraksha", by the Central Government?

A. Rs.100 crore

B. Rs.500 crore

C. Rs.900 crore

D. Rs.1000 crore

Q.86 When is World Hindi Day celebrated?

A. 10 January

B. 11 January

C. 12 January

D. 13 January

Q.87 Which is the world's most polluted city, as per the US Air Quality Index?

A. Delhi

B. New York

C. Beijing

D. Lahore

Q.88 Sonai Rupai Wildlife Sanctuary is a protected area located In the state of.

A. Himachal Pradesh

B. Haryana

C. Jammu and Kashmir

D. Assam

Q.89 Which city is called as the Pittsburgh of India?

A. Jabalpur   **B.** Jamshedpur
C. Jamnagar   **D.** Junagarh

Q.90 Water vapour is:
A. A gas   **B.** A cloud droplet
C. A raindrop   **D.** A snowflake

Q.91 From which state does Dard Aryan Tribe belong?
A. Jammu & Kashmir   **B.** Karnataka
C. Telangana   **D.** Jharkhand

Q.92 Which river is known as the Sorrow of Bihar?
A. Ganga   **B.** Gandak   **C.** Kosi   **D.** Son

Q.93 Chandragupta Maurya died in which among the following places?
A. Kalinga, Odisha
B. Sravanbelgola, Karnataka
C. Pataliputra, Bihar
D. Rajgriha, Bihar

Q.94 At what time of day is the relative humidity normally at a minimum?
A. When the air temperature is highest
B. Just before sunrise
C. About midnight
D. When the air temperature is lowest

Q.95 When was the Quit India movement started for the first time?
A. 1931   **B.** 1942   **C.** 1920   **D.** 1935

Q.96 Who among the following raised Azad Hind Fauj?
A. Jawaharlal Nehru
B. Subhash Chandra Bose
C. Mahatma Gandhi
D. Lala Lajpat Rai

Q.97 Trans-Himalayan rivers are _________.
A. Sutlej, Indus, Ganga
B. Brahmaputra, Indus, Sutlej
C. Brahmaputra, Indus, Ganga
D. Brahmaputra, Sutlej, Ganga

Q.98 What is the SI unit of resistivity?
A. Ohm metre   **B.** Ohm metre^{-1}
C. Ohm^{-1} **D.** Ohm metre^{2}

Q.99 The watermelon model of the atom was given by whom among the following?
A. Niels Bohr   **B.** Rutherford
C. Thomson   **D.** None of the above

Q.100 The Avogadro's Number is _______.
A. 6.023×10^{23} **B.** 6.052×10^{-23}
C. 6.022×10^{20} **D.** 6.032×1023

// Smart Answer Sheet //

Correct — Percentage of students who answered correctly. **Skipped** — Percentage of students who skipped.

Q.	Ans.	Correct	Skipped	Q.	Ans.	Correct	Skipped	Q.	Ans.	Correct	Skipped	Q.	Ans.	Correct	Skipped	Q.	Ans.	Correct	Skipped	Q.	Ans.	Correct	Skipped
1	B	50.93 %	1.32 %	18	B	66.46 %	1.19 %	35	D	48.78 %	1.07 %	52	B	54.88 %	1.37 %	69	C	64.78 %	1.17 %	86	A	82.02 %	0.0 %
2	D	47.67 %	1.45 %	19	A	52.06 %	1.89 %	36	D	43.74 %	1.29 %	53	B	69.92 %	1.76 %	70	A	55.71 %	1.16 %	87	D	64.37 %	1.41 %
3	C	66.41 %	1.21 %	20	B	61.31 %	1.46 %	37	B	48.77 %	1.54 %	54	A	60.9 %	1.47 %	71	B	19.52 %	4.44 %	88	D	64.27 %	1.08 %
4	C	67.63 %	1.42 %	21	C	80.42 %	0.0 %	38	C	81.15 %	0.0 %	55	B	57.79 %	1.43 %	72	C	19.03 %	4.14 %	89	B	61.29 %	1.59 %
5	A	81.04 %	0.0 %	22	D	64.42 %	1.72 %	39	C	32.07 %	4.55 %	56	B	47.2 %	1.83 %	73	C	31.87 %	4.97 %	90	A	56.78 %	1.34 %
6	C	45.5 %	1.42 %	23	B	52.33 %	1.35 %	40	A	43.87 %	1.26 %	57	C	68.88 %	1.04 %	74	D	17.62 %	4.13 %	91	A	45.48 %	1.44 %
7	D	40.55 %	1.33 %	24	B	48.22 %	1.2 %	41	C	65.03 %	1.78 %	58	C	51.85 %	1.72 %	75	B	14.18 %	3.25 %	92	C	63.92 %	1.72 %
8	B	67.11 %	1.85 %	25	A	59.17 %	1.99 %	42	D	53.84 %	1.94 %	59	A	55.72 %	1.76 %	76	D	11.96 %	3.87 %	93	B	55.09 %	1.96 %
9	A	86.08 %	0.0 %	26	D	64.28 %	1.38 %	43	A	53.89 %	1.66 %	60	C	60.96 %	1.52 %	77	B	30.79 %	3.86 %	94	A	63.76 %	1.49 %
10	C	56.54 %	1.08 %	27	D	60.63 %	1.43 %	44	D	42.61 %	1.9 %	61	D	55.43 %	1.93 %	78	C	88.34 %	0.0 %	95	B	57.84 %	1.75 %
11	C	47.46 %	1.6 %	28	A	62.05 %	1.2 %	45	C	85.19 %	0.0 %	62	D	46.25 %	1.7 %	79	C	84.03 %	0.0 %	96	B	68.24 %	1.15 %
12	C	63.23 %	1.94 %	29	B	53.41 %	1.34 %	46	C	40.57 %	1.26 %	63	D	40.66 %	1.07 %	80	C	80.14 %	0.0 %	97	B	52.52 %	1.3 %
13	D	64.0 %	1.96 %	30	D	52.02 %	1.3 %	47	A	65.97 %	1.02 %	64	A	53.21 %	1.38 %	81	D	52.55 %	1.74 %	98	A	63.04 %	1.23 %
14	B	63.6 %	1.11 %	31	B	66.07 %	1.53 %	48	B	63.11 %	1.71 %	65	A	52.44 %	1.03 %	82	A	40.51 %	1.96 %	99	C	15.25 %	3.39 %
15	B	47.37 %	1.95 %	32	B	87.86 %	0.0 %	49	D	68.1 %	1.69 %	66	D	46.14 %	1.27 %	83	C	52.01 %	1.85 %	100	A	45.72 %	1.55 %
16	C	58.68 %	1.86 %	33	B	45.78 %	1.07 %	50	D	51.73 %	1.21 %	67	D	53.55 %	1.34 %	84	C	65.8 %	1.92 %				
17	B	53.47 %	1.86 %	34	A	64.25 %	1.05 %	51	A	56.45 %	1.88 %	68	D	60.28 %	1.78 %	85	C	57.72 %	1.71 %				

//Hints and Solutions//

1. First term → 2

Second term → (2×3-3) = 3

Third term → (3×3-3) = 6

Fourth term → (6×3-3) = 15

Fifth term → (15×3-3) = 42

Sixth term → (42×3-3) = 123

Hence, the correct option is (B).

2. As given in the question,

GREAT → number of letters = 5,

So, 5 × 3 - 3 = 12

Similarly,

TEXTBOOK→ number of letters 8.

So, 8 × 3 - 3 = 21.

Hence, the correct option is (D).

3. Here both the shape, one is smaller in size and the other is larger in size are the same shapes, but in option (C) both shapes are different.

So, option (C) is an odd image.

Hence, the correct option is (C).

4. The dictionary sequence is:

Terrain → **Terrible** → **Testify** → **Thank** less → **Thaw.**

Thus, 5, 1, 4, 3, 2 will be the correct sequence.

Hence, the correct option is (C).

5. Sunday to Monday = no gap

Monday to Wednesday = One day gap.

Wednesday to Saturday = Two days gap.

Saturday to Wednesday = Three days gap.

Wednesday to Monday = Four days gap.

In the next term, there must be five days.

So, Next term would be Sunday.

Hence, the correct option is (A).

6. Logic: Difference between product of digits is middle column.

[Product of digits in third column - Product of digits in first column = Midddle column]

In first row: (7 × 3 × 8) - (3 × 4 × 6) = 168 - 72 = 96

In second row: (2 × 3 × 7) - (4 × 3 × 2) = 42 - 24 = 18

Thus,

In third column: (3 × 2 × 9) - (5 × 2 × 1) = 54 - 10 = 44

Clearly, the missing number is 44.

Hence, the correct option is (C).

7. Given:

8, 6, 9, 23, 87, ?

The pattern is as follow

8 × 1 - 2 = 6

6 × 2 - 3 = 9

9 × 3 - 4 = 23

23 × 4 - 5 = 87

87 × 5 - 6 = 429

Hence, the correct option is (D).

8. Given:

THEN is coded as VFGL.

The pattern is as follows:

T + 2 = V

H - 2 = F

E + 2 = G

N - 2 = L

So,

W + 2 = Y

O - 2 = M

R + 2 = T

D - 2 = B

Hence, the correct option is (B).

9. Elephants and Wolves bear no relationship to each other. But, both of them are animals.

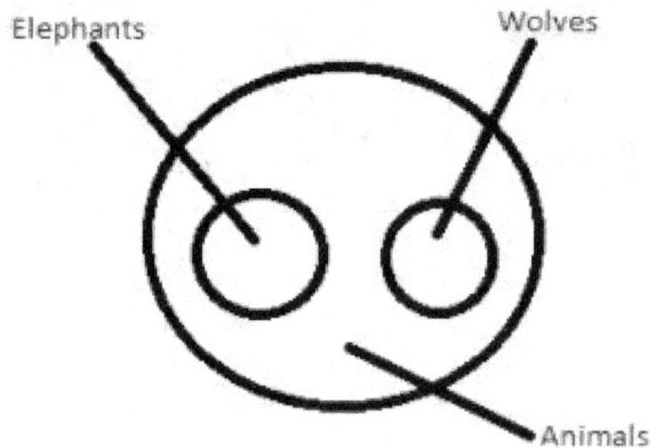

Hence, the correct option is (A).

10.

A	B	C	D	E	F	G	H	I	J	K	L	M
1	2	3	4	5	6	7	8	9	10	11	12	13

N	O	P	Q	R	S	T	U	V	W	X	Y	Z
14	15	16	17	18	19	20	21	22	23	24	25	26

If, PALAM = 16 + 1 + 12 + 1 + 13 = 43.

Similarly, PERMIT = 16 + 5 + 18 + 13 + 9 + 20 = 81.

Hence, the correct option is (C).

11. Firstly, the number of letters in subsequent terms increases by 1, thus there will be 4 terms in place of '?'.

Now the terms follow the following pattern:

A - BC - DE - FGH - IJK - LMNO - PQRS

Thus, the term required will be PQRS.

Hence, the correct option is (C).

12. According to the question,

If TOUR is written in a certain code as 1234, CLEAR as 56784, and SPARE as 90847, then the 5th digit for SCULPTURE in the same code will be-

By, comparing letters and digit, we get-

T = 1

O = 2

U = 3

R = 4

C = 5

L = 6

E = 7

A = 8

S = 9 and

P = 0

So,

S = 9

C = 5

U = 3

L = 6

P = 0

T = 1

U = 3

R = 4

E = 7

As the 5th letter in SCULPTURE is P and '0' is used for P, therefore, 5th digit is the required code which Is '0'.

Hence, the correct option is (C).

13. The pattern is as follow:

(D) 4270 → 4+7+0 = 11 (The sum of all the three digits is not equal to the second digit from left.)

(A) 5720 → 5+2+0 = 7 (The sum of all the three digits is equal to the second digit from left.)

(B) 6710 → 6+1+0 = 7 (The sum of all the three digits is equal to the second digit from left.)

(C) 2640 → 2+4+0 = 6 (The sum of all the three digits is equal to the second digit from left.)

Hence, the correct option is (D).

14. Except 421, all other are square of a number

$13^2 = 169$, $23^2 = 529$ and $17^2 = 289$

Therefore, the odd number is 421.

Hence, the correct option is (B).

15. 2) ROPE: 'E' is not present in CORPORATION, so the word cannot be formed.

1) PAINT: COR**PORA**T**I**ON, so the word can be formed.

3) PORTION: COR**PORA**T**I**ON, so the word can be formed.

4) POTION: COR**PO**RA**TI**ON, so the word can be formed.

Therefore, 'ROPE' cannot be formed from the given word.

Hence, the correct option is (B).

16. Each of the letters of the word ALTERED is replaced by the letter which occupies the same position in the reverse alphabetical order to obtain the code ZOGVIVW. The relation is given as follows:

If,

A	L	T	E	R	E	D
↓	↓	↓	↓	↓	↓	↓
Z	O	G	V	I	V	W

Similarly,

J	U	S	T	I	C	E
↓	↓	↓	↓	↓	↓	↓
Q	F	H	G	R	X	V

Therefore, the correct answer is QFHGRXV.

Hence, the correct option is (C).

17. The pattern here is,

626-1 = 625 = 25^2

962-1 = 961 = 31^2

1090-1 = 1089 = 33^2

Similarly,

841 1 = 840, is not a perfect square

Hence, the correct option is (B).

18. The correct order is:

Rain	2
Sun	3
Rainbow	1

Child	5
Happy	4

Hence, the correct option is (B).

19. In Mathematics we study formulas and in Chemistry, we study Chemical Reactions.

Thus, the answer is Reactions.

Hence, the correct option is (A).

20. Given:

18 * 6 * 3 * 12 * 24

From the second option, we get:

18 × 6 ÷ 3 − 12 = 24

⇒ 18 × 2 − 12 = 24

⇒ 36 − 12 = 24

Hence, the correct option is (B).

21. Given:

8 * 8 * 1 * 7 = 8

From the option (C) we get:

⇒ 8 ÷ 8 × 1 + 7 = 8

⇒ 1 × 1 + 7 = 8

Hence, the correct option is (C).

22. The correct order is:

Writing	3
Composing	2
Printing	4
Reading	1

Hence, the correct option is (D).

23. Square → Dietitians

Triangle → Botanists

Circle → Psychologists

Rectangle → Indians

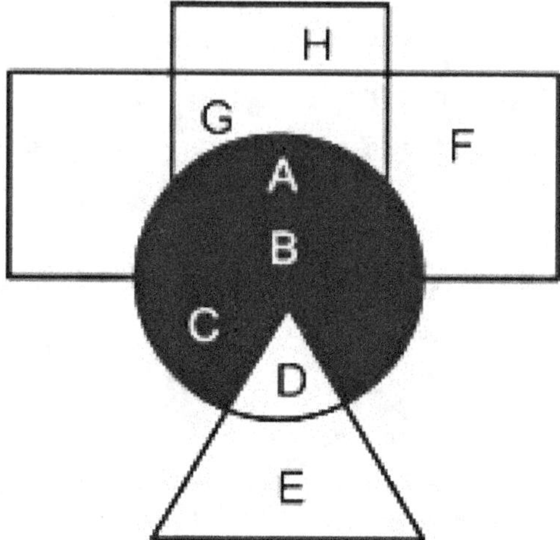

In order to get the letters that represent Psychologists who are not Botanists, the letters should be in a circle but not in a triangle. ABC satisfies the given condition.

Hence, the correct option is (B).

24. There is nothing mentioned about the relation between political freedom and democracy. So, I does not follow. But II directly follows from the given statement.

Hence, the correct option is (B).

25. Consider the following least possible Venn diagram,

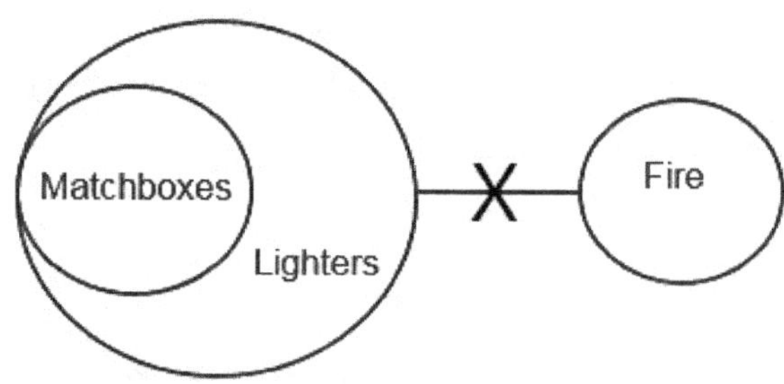

Conclusions:

I. No fire are matchboxes → True (It is definitely true as no fire can be matchboxes).

II. All matchboxes are fire → False (It is definitely false because it is not possible).

So, the only conclusion (I) follows.

Hence, the correct option is (A).

26. Given:

$$2A = 3B = 8C$$

Let, $2A = 3B = 8C = k$

$$\therefore A : B : C = \frac{k}{2} : \frac{k}{3} : \frac{k}{8}$$

$$\Rightarrow A : B : C = 12 : 8 : 3$$

Hence, the correct option is (D).

27. An angle is thrice its complementary angle.

Let the angle be x.

Then, complementary angle = (90° - x)

Given that,

x = 3 (90° - x)

x = 270° - 3x

4x = 270

$\Rightarrow$ x = 67.5°

$\therefore$ The measure of the angle x = 67.5°

Hence, the correct option is (C).

28. Given,

Marked Price $= 50$

Discount $= 10\%$

Formula used:

$Discount\ \% = \dfrac{(MP - SP)}{MP \times 100}$

$SP = MP - \left(\dfrac{Discount\%}{100}\right) \times MP$

Let the cost price be Rs. X

Marked price $= X + \left(\dfrac{50}{100}\right) \times X = 1.35X$

Discount $= 10\%$

$SP = 1.5X - \left(\dfrac{10}{100}\right) \times 1.5X = 1.35X$

Profit $\% = \dfrac{(SP - CP)}{CP} \times 100$

Profit $\% = \dfrac{(1.35X - X)}{X} \times 100 = 35\%$

Hence, the correct option is (A).

29. Let, 9 consecutive numbers,

$\Rightarrow (x - 4), (x - 3), (x - 2), (x - 1), x, (x + 1),$
$(x + 2), (x + 3), (x + 4)$

$\therefore$ Sum of 9 consecutive numbers,

$\Rightarrow (x - 4) + (x - 3) + (x - 2) + (x - 1) + x + (x + 1) + (x + 2) + (x + 3) + (x + 4)$

$\Rightarrow 9x$

$\therefore$ Average of 9 consecutive numbers,

$\Rightarrow \dfrac{9x}{9}$

$\Rightarrow x$

According to problem,

$\Rightarrow x = 26$

$\therefore$ Largest number among these,

$\Rightarrow x + 4 = 26 + 4 = 30$

Hence, the correct option is (B).

30. Let a person bought a quantity of sugar be M quintal.

The price of sugar at 1 quintal $=$ Rs. 120

Total price of M quintal sugar $= 120\,M$

10% of sugar is spoiled.

Good quantity of sugar remain $= 90\%$ of $M = \dfrac{9\,M}{10}$ quintal

Profit percentage $= 20\%$

$\Rightarrow 20 = \left[\dfrac{(S.P. - 120\,M)}{120\,M}\right] \times 100$

$\Rightarrow 120\,M = 5\,S.P. - 600\,M$

$\Rightarrow 720\,M = 5\,S.P.$

$\Rightarrow S.P. =$ Rs. 144

$\therefore$ The selling price of 1 quintal sugar is Rs. 144.

Hence, the correct option is (D).

31. Formula used:

$Average = \dfrac{Sum\ of\ elements}{Number\ of\ elements}$

Given,

The average weight of a class is 52 kg.

Let the total number of students in a class be n.

Total weight of class $= 52n$

According to the question,

A student with a weight 118 kg joins the class then the average weight becomes 58 kg.

Total weight of a class after new student $= 52n + 118$

$\Rightarrow 58 = \dfrac{(52n + 118)}{(n + 1)}$

$\Rightarrow 58(n + 1) = 52n + 118$

$\Rightarrow 58n + 58 = 52n + 118$

$\Rightarrow 6n = 60$

$\Rightarrow n = 10$

$\therefore$ The total number of students in a class is 10.

Hence, the correct option is (B).

32. Given:

$397 \times 397 + 104 \times 104 + 2 \times 397 \times 104$

According to formula,

$(a+b)^2 = a^2+b^2+2ab$

$= (397)^2+(104)^2+2\times397\times104$

$= (397+104)^2$

$= (501)^2$

$= 251001$

Hence, the correct option is (B).

33. Given:

$$P = \text{Rs. } 10000, \ t = 2 \text{ year}, \ r = 5\%$$

Formula used:

$$\text{Amount } = P\left(1+\frac{r}{100}\right)^t$$

$\text{Amount } = \text{Principal } + \text{Compound interest}$

Now,

$$\text{Amount } = 10000\left(\frac{1+5}{100}\right)^2$$

$$\text{Amount } = 11025$$

$\text{Compound interest } = 11025 - 10000 = \text{Rs. } 1025$

Hence, the correct option is (B).

34. For a right circular cylinder with radius "r" and height "h",

$\text{Curved surface area } = 2\pi rh$

Given,

$$\text{Radius of cylinder } = \frac{7}{2} = 3.5 \text{ cm}$$

$\text{Height } = 6 \text{ cm}$

$\therefore$ Curved surface area of given cylinder $= 2 \times \left(\frac{22}{7}\right) \times 3.5 \times 6$

$= 132 \text{ cm}^2$

Hence, the correct option is (A).

35. Given:

$$12\cos^2\theta + 8\sin^2\theta = 9$$

$$\Rightarrow 4\cos^2\theta + 8(\cos^2\theta + \sin^2\theta) = 9$$

$$\Rightarrow 4\cos^2\theta = 1 \qquad (\because \sin^2\theta + \cos^2\theta = 1)$$

$$\Rightarrow \cos^2\theta = \frac{1}{4}$$

$$\Rightarrow \theta = 60°$$

$\therefore \tan\theta = \tan 60° = \sqrt{3}$

Hence, the correct option is (D).

36. We know that,

Product of two numbers = L.C.M. of those numbers × H.C.F. of those numbers

Let the second number be x.

24 × x = 168 × 6

x = 6 × 7

x = 42

Hence, the correct option is (D).

37. Given,

Pipe P can fill the tank $= \dfrac{1}{120}$ hours

Pipe Q can fill the tank $= \dfrac{1}{80}$ hours

If both pipes are opened together, then the tank will be filled in -

$$= \left(\frac{1}{120}\right) + \left(\frac{1}{80}\right)$$

$$= \frac{20}{960}$$

$$= \frac{1}{48}$$

$\therefore$ If both pipes are opened together, then the tank will be filled in 48 days.

Hence, the correct option is (B).

38. Given:

P is 25% less than Q.

Let the value of Q be x

$\text{Value of } P = x - \dfrac{25}{100} \times x = 0.75x$

Formula used:

Percentage value Q has more than $P = \dfrac{(Difference\ in\ value)}{(Value\ of\ P)} \times 100$

Percentage value Q has more than $P = \dfrac{(x-0.75x)}{0.75\times100} = 33.33\%$

Hence, the correct option is (C).

39. Given:

$$\left(\frac{\sin30°}{\cos45°}\right) \times \left(\frac{\sin45°}{\cos30°}\right) \quad .....(i)$$

As we know,

$$\sin45° = \cos 45° = \frac{1}{\sqrt{2}}$$

$$sin30° = \frac{1}{2}$$

$$cos30° = \frac{\sqrt{3}}{2}$$

Putting the above values in equation (i).

$$\frac{\sin 30°}{\cos 45°} \times \frac{\sin 45°}{\cos 30°}$$

$$= \frac{\frac{1}{2}}{\frac{1}{\sqrt{2}}} \times \frac{\frac{1}{\sqrt{2}}}{\frac{\sqrt{3}}{2}}$$

$$= \frac{\frac{1}{2}}{\frac{\sqrt{3}}{2}}$$

$$= \frac{1}{\sqrt{3}}$$

Hence, the correct option is (C).

40. Given:

Principal $=$ Rs. 800; Amount $=$ Rs. 1000; Time $=$ 2 years

Let rate be $r\%$

Formula used:

Simple interest $= \frac{(Principal \times time \times rate)}{100}$

$$= \frac{(800 \times 2 \times r)}{100}$$

$$= 16r$$

Formula used:

Amount $=$ Principal $+$ Simple interest

$\Rightarrow 1000 = 800 + 16r$

$\Rightarrow 16r = 200$

$\therefore r = 12.5\%$

Hence, the correct option is (A).

41. A alone can do a work $= 5$ days

A's one day's work $= \frac{1}{5}$

B alone can do the work $= 10$ days

B's one day's work $= \frac{1}{10}$

C alone can do the work $= 30$ days

C's one day's work $= \frac{1}{30}$

A, B, and C together can do the work in,

$(A + B + C)$'s one-day's work $= \left(\frac{1}{5} + \frac{1}{10} + \frac{1}{30}\right)$

$$= \frac{(6+3+1)}{30}$$

$$= \frac{10}{30} = \frac{1}{3}$$

Therefore, $A + B + C$ can complete the whole work in 3 days.

Hence, the correct option is (C).

42. Given,

Largest angle = 80°

Smallest angle = Largest angle - 40° = 80° - 40° = 40°

We know that,

The sum of angles of a triangle = 180°

Third angle = 180° - (Sum of largest and smallest angle)

= 180° - (80° + 40°)

= 180° - 120° = 60°

∴ Third angle = 60°

Hence, the correct option is (D).

43. Given:

Speed $= 45$ km/h $= 45 \times \frac{5}{18} = 12.5$ m/s

Train length $= 150$ meter

Platform length $= 500$ meter

According to the formula,

Speed $= \frac{Distance}{Time}$

The total length that needs to be crossed $= 500 + 150 = 650$ meter

Now,

$$12.5 = \frac{650}{Time}$$

Time $= \frac{650}{12.5} = 52$ second

Hence, the correct option is (A).

44. Let their current age be 'x' and 'y' years

Four years ago, the ratio of their ages,

$\Rightarrow (x - 4):(y - 4) = 7:9$

$\Rightarrow 9(x - 4) = 7(y - 4)$

$\Rightarrow 9x - 36 = 7y - 28$

$\Rightarrow 9x - 7y = 8 \quad ---- (i)$

After four years, ratio of their ages,

$\Rightarrow (x + 4):(y + 4) = 9:11$

$\Rightarrow 11(x + 4) = 9(y + 4)$

$\Rightarrow 11x + 44 = 9y + 36$

$\Rightarrow 11x - 9y = -8 \quad ---- (ii)$

Multiplying equation (i) by 11 and equation (ii) by 9 and subtracting equation (ii) from equation (i),

$\Rightarrow 99x - 77y - 99x + 81y = 88 + 72$

$\Rightarrow 4y = 160$

$\Rightarrow y = \frac{160}{4} = 40$ years

SPuttuing the value of y in equation (i),

$\Rightarrow x = \frac{(8+7\times40)}{9}$

$= 32$ year

∴ Their current ages are 32 years and 40 years.

Hence, the correct option is (D).

45. Formula used:

Percentage formula $= \left(\dfrac{Value}{Total\ value}\right) \times 100$

According to the question,

$\Rightarrow 12600 \times x\% = 2898$

$\Rightarrow 12600 \times \frac{x}{100} = 2898$

$\Rightarrow x = \frac{2898\times100}{12600} = 23\%$

Hence, the correct option is (C).

46. The distance travelled by the shot of the gun in 20 sec is 6.64 km.

Distance = 6.64 km = 6.64 × 1000 = 6640 m

$Speed = \dfrac{Distance}{Time}$

Speed $= \frac{6640}{20}$

= 332 m/s

Hence, the correct option is (D).

47. According to the given data,

Required $\%$ increase $= \frac{(160-130)}{130} \times 100$

$= 23.07\% \approx 23\%$

Hence, the correct option is (A).

48. According to the given data,

Interest in $1990 - 91$

$= 30\%$ of 130

$= 39$ lakh

Interest in $1991 - 92$

$= 40\%$ of 160

$= 64$ lakh

So, difference $=$ Rs. 25 lakh

Hence, the correct option is (B).

49. According to the given data,

Total interest

$= (39 + 64)$

$=$ Rs. 103 lakh

This interest is calculated on 20% of the borrowed fund.

So, borrowed funds

$= \frac{103\times100}{20}$

$=$ Rs. 515 lakh

Hence, the correct option is (D).

50. According to the given data,

Retained profit in $1990 - 91$,

$= 25\%$ of 130

$=$ Rs. 32.5 lakh

Retained profit in $1991 - 92$,

$= 20\%$ of 160

$=$ Rs. 32 lakh

∴ Decrease $= \frac{32.5-32}{32.5} \times 100$

$= 1.53\% \approx 1.5\%$

Hence, the correct option is (D).

51. The correct sentence is:

The army has been called to aid in the relief operation.

Part 1 is incorrect. Army here is a collective noun and therefore should take the verb 'has' instead of 'have'.

Hence, the correct option is (A).

52. The correct sentence is:

There was no money in Rahul and Roshan's joint account.

Since it is a joint account, so using two possessives is wrong. It should be used only with the latter noun. So, "Rahul and Roshan's". is the correction.

Hence, the correct option is (B).

53. The correct sentence is:

As I was driving down the lane, I saw a quaint house with green walls and a red roof.

The first part of the sentence is a dangling modifier and in order to make complete sense it needs to be corrected, option (B) is the right way of writing it, as 'because' is used for showing reason and 'before' refers to time. Both are inept here, 'as' means 'while', showing us an ongoing action.

Hence, the correct option is (B).

54. The correct sentence:

Sheena is the cleverest girl in our class.

The double superlative adjective cannot be used in one sentence like in the given "most cleverest", in such cases, only the adjective is used and the antecedent is done away with.

Hence, the correct option is (A).

55. I am awful at picking vegetables.

The correct preposition here is 'at' as someone is awful 'at' an action.' Being awful means 'too bad at doing that thing.'

Hence, the correct option is (B).

56. Career determines the kind of lifestyle one will lead and his/her position in society.

The correct form of the verb here is present tense thus 'determines' which means 'decides; controls' fits here correctly. The word 'deter' means 'discourage.'

Hence, the correct option is (B).

57. The sentence is an exclamation but we cannot add the word 'sorrowfully' here as it is not apt. Also, present tense (it is) changes to past tense (it was). Also, the structure of the sentence changes as 'subject (it) + verb (was) + object (a very hot day)'.

Hence, the correct option is (C).

58. The given sentence is in the active voice. It is a simple form of present tense. The structures for active/passive voices are:

Active: Subject + verb ("s" or "es" with singular noun) + object.

Passive: Object + Is/are/am + verb (IIIrd form) + by + subject.

So, based on the above structures, we can convert the given sentence into passive voice: Under this strategy, the investors are permitted to buy shares from unlisted companies.

Hence, the correct option is (C).

59. Last month, he would have been in debt if not for my help.

This statement requires a present perfect continuous tense and so other options do not fit in the context.

Hence, the correct option is (A).

60. Foremost: Most prominent in rank, importance, or position.

Unimportant: Lacking in importance or significance.

Mature: Fully developed physically, full-grown.

Premature: Occurring or done before the usual or proper time, too early.

Disposed: Inclined or willing.

So, the antonym is Unimportant.

Hence, the correct option is (C).

61. Protects: Keep safe from harm.

Deserts: To abandon that is to stop supporting or looking after.

Defends: Protect from harm or danger.

Deprives: Prevent (a person or place) from having or using something.

Devises: Plan or invent (a complex procedure, system, or mechanism) by careful thought.

So, the antonym is Deserts.

Hence, the correct option is (D).

62. Fostering: Encourage the development of (something, especially something desirable).

Nurturing: Care for and protect (someone or something) while they are growing.

Safeguarding: A measure taken to protect someone or something or to prevent something undesirable.

Neglecting: Fail to care for properly.

Ignoring: Refuse to take notice of or acknowledge; disregard intentionally.

So, The synonym of Fostering is Nurturing.

Hence, the correct option is (D).

63. Transient: Lasting only for a short time; impermanent; temporary.

Brief: Of short duration; not lasting for long.

Momentary: Lasting for a very short time; brief.

Permanent: Lasting or intended to last or remain unchanged indefinitely.

So, the option (B) and (C) are the synonyms of "transient".

Hence, the correct option is (D).

64. Recalcitrant: A person who is obstinate, stubborn, and unruly, i.e. a self-centEred person.

Obedient: A person who follows what is said.

Obstinate: Stubbornly refusing to change one's opinion or chosen course of action, despite attempts to persuade one to do so.

Stubborn: Having or showing dogged determination not to change one's attitude or position on something, especially in spite of good arguments or reasons to do so.

Unruly: Disorderly and disruptive and not amenable to discipline or control.

So, option (A) is the one that best expresses the opposite meaning of the given word.

Hence, the correct option is (A).

65. Obliterate: Destroy utterly; wipe out.

Protect: keep safe from harm or injury.

Destroy: End the existence of (something) by damaging or attacking it.

Eradicate: Destroy completely; put an end to.

Delete: Remove or obliterate (written or printed matter), especially by drawing a line through it.

So, option (A) best expresses the opposite meaning of the given word.

Hence, the correct option is (A).

66. Equitable: Fair and just; impartial.

Neutral: Not engaged on either side specifically; not aligned with a political or ideological grouping a neutral nation.

Partial: Existing only in part; incomplete.

Prejudiced: Having or showing a dislike or distrust that is derived from prejudice; bigoted.

Biased: Unfairly prejudiced for or against someone or something.

So, option (D) best expresses the meaning of the given word.

Hence, the correct option is (D).

67. 'Kept his nose clean' means to behave well and not get into trouble of any kind.

Hence, the correct option is (D).

68. 'With no strings attached' means without any rules or demands or restrictions attached.

Hence, the correct option is (D).

69. The idiom "Hit the sack" means to go to bed in order to sleep.

Example: I've got a busy day tomorrow, so I think I'll hit the sack.

Hence, the correct option is (C).

70. The phrase "Hit the Nail on the Head" refers to doing or saying something that is precisely right.

Example: "You've spotted the flaw, Sally. You hit the nail on the head."

Hence, the correct option is (A).

71. According to the passage, the line in the second paragraph "Such focus on the possible worst-case scenario contributed to the survival of our early ancestors" suggests the reason for humans to focus more on negative emotions rather than on positive ones. Among all the options, option (B) is the correct answer.

Note: We can approach this question by using the method of elimination. Clearly, option (A) is not mentioned in the passage. There is no discussion on conscience – the part of us that makes a moral sense of right and wrong. When we eliminate option (A), option (D) also gets eliminated. Now, we have narrowed down

our options to two – option (C) is incorrect as indicated by the line 'Studies show that we recognize and respond more quickly to an angry or sad face, than a happy face'. Thus, we are left with option (B).

Hence, the correct option is (B).

72. The line 'We notice lack more than abundance' means that we don't notice what we have. We tend to focus on what we don't have often by making comparisons with others. In this process, we lose sight of contentment and end up having a negative outlook.

Option (A) is about judging someone on his/her abilities rather than by using some common yardstick available for everyone.

Option (B) is more about taking charge and having the will to come out of our misfortunes.

Option (D) talks about the learning we can get from our failures.

Option (C) seems appropriate for the context of the discussed line. It talks about how we focus on what we don't have (shoes) until we realize what we do have (feet) which is more important than what we don't have (shoes).

Hence, the correct option is (C).

73. From the context of the passage, we can understand that the word saboteur is used in a negative light. The line 'It's rough when you realize the true saboteur of your dreams is an insider' suggests the negative connotation associated with the highlighted word. The meaning of the word saboteur is a person who sabotages – who destroys things (or makes a mess of a situation) on purpose.

So, we can eliminate option (A) as it is opposite to the word. A promoter is a supporter of an aim or cause.

A facilitator helps us to achieve something by making the action easier. So, option (B) is incorrect as it sheds a positive light if used. An architect is someone who designs buildings and advises in their construction. So, option (D) is out of context.

Hence, the correct option is (C).

74. Option (C) is related to the effect of having negative emotions, as indicated in the passage. So, we can eliminate option (C). Options (A) and (B) seem to be possible effects of positive emotions but this is not mentioned anywhere in the passage. We need to stick to the context.

We can infer from the line 'Positive emotions give us access to the control center in the brain that initiates action toward our goals' that option (D) seems to be the correct answer.

Hence, the correct option is (D).

75. Illuminating means providing clarity, insight, or understanding in order to explain the subject being discussed. This seems the best option because the author does explain why humans are hard-wired to focus more on negative emotions. The points and views presented in the passage are an attempt to make us explain our bias towards negativity.

The tone of the author tells us how the author feels towards the subject being discussed. To be precise – it is the attitude of the author. Clearly, the author is not sad or depressed. One cannot infer that he/she is expressing grief towards the topic of discussion. So, we can eliminate option (D).

Vindictive means having a strong desire for revenge. This is not what the attitude of the author reflects. So, we can eliminate option (C) as well.

Nonchalant is used to describe a person who is behaving in a calm and relaxed way often because he/she is not interested. But to say that the author has not expressed interest in the subject would be incorrect. So, option (A) is also eliminated.

Hence, the correct option is (B).

76. Punjabi kabaddi, also called circle style kabaddi, is a contact sport that originated in the Punjab region, in the northern part of the Indian subcontinent. There are a number of traditional Punjabi kabaddi styles traditionally played in the Punjab region.

Hence, the correct option is (D).

77. The correct answer is Cricket. The Syed Mushtaq Ali trophy is an Indian domestic cricket championship organized by the Board of Control for Cricket in India (BCCI). The championship is named after Syed Mushtaq Ali, the famous Indian cricketer.

Hence, the correct option Is (B).

78. M_3 measure of the money supply is known as 'Broad money.

M_3 is a measure of the money supply that includes M_2 as well as large-time deposits, institutional money market funds, short-term repurchase agreements (repo), and larger liquid assets.

The M_3 measurement includes assets that are less liquid than other components of the money supply and are referred to as "near money," which are more closely related to the finances of larger financial institutions and corporations than to those of small businesses and individuals.

Hence, the correct option is (C).

79. An example of Indirect tax is Sales tax.

Indirect Tax is a tax imposed on an individual or entity which is passed on to other individuals.

It is imposed on products or services which are used by the customer.

Hence, the correct option is (C).

80. NABARD is an apex regulatory body for overall regulation and licensing of regional rural banks and apex cooperative banks in India. It was established on 12th July 1982 by an Act of Parliament.

Hence, the correct option is (C).

81.

- Ctrl + Shift + Esc are used to open Windows Task Manager.
- It is a task manager, system monitor, and startup manager which is included with Microsoft Windows systems.

Hence, the correct option is (D).

82. The 10-day long Taj Mahotsav began on 18 February 2020 with the theme "Sanskriti ke Rang, Taj ke Sang", depicting the vibrant and diverse cultures and traditions of India. Every year the carnival has a different theme which forms the basis of the cultural programmes organized at the carnival.

Hence, the correct option is (A).

83. Madhya Pradesh's Indore has been ranked the cleanest city for the fourth consecutive year under the Swachh Survekshan 2020, the centre's annual survey on cleanliness under the Swachh Bharat Mission. Surat in Gujarat and Navi Mumbai in Maharashtra were ranked second and third.

Hence, the correct option is (C).

84. US President-elect Joe Biden has recently appointed the country's first all-female White House communications team.

He also appointed Jen Psaki, who earlier served as the spokesperson in Barack Obama administration, as the White House Press Secretary. Six other women who had held important positions were appointed in the official Press Team.

Hence, the correct option is (C).

85. The Union Government has launched "Mission COVID Suraksha" and has allotted a package of Rs.900 crore for the same. The grant by the central government would be given to the Department of Biotechnology (DBT) for the Research & Development of Indian COVID-19 vaccines.

The mission aims at the development of approximately 5 or 6 COVID 19 vaccine candidates and ensures their faster availability to the public.

Hence, the correct option is (C).

86.

- World Hindi Day is celebrated every year on January 10.
- World Hindi Day commemorates the anniversary of the first World Hindi Conference held in Nagpur on January 10, 1975.
- The conference was inaugurated by the then prime minister Indira Gandhi in Nagpur.
- World Hindi Day was first celebrated in 2006 by former Prime Minister Dr. Manmohan Singh.

Hence, the correct option is (A).

87. US Air Quality Index: Lahore becomes the world's most polluted city According to data released by the US Air Quality Index (AQI) on air pollution, Pakistan's cultural capital Lahore has been topped as the world's most polluted city. Lahore received a 423 rating in Particulate Matter (PM) rating.

Hence, the correct option is (D).

88. Sonai Rupai Wildlife Sanctuary is a protected area located in the state of Assam in India. This wildlife sanctuary covers 175 km². It is located along the foothills of the Great Himalayan Range. The area was declared as a sanctuary in 1998.

Hence, the correct option is (D).

89.

- Jamshedpur is known as the Steel City of India or Pittsburgh of India for being rich in minerals.

- It is home to many industries like Tata Motors, Tata Steels, Usha Martin Industries, Steel & Wire Products, Tata Pigments, Tayo Rolls Limited, and many other assets.

- This city is also known as the Tatanagar.

Hence, the correct option is (B).

90. Water vapour, water vapour or aqueous vapour is the gaseous phase of water. It is one state of water within the hydrosphere. Water vapour can be produced from the evaporation or boiling of liquid water or from the sublimation of ice. Unlike other forms of water, water vapour is invisible. Under typical atmospheric conditions, water vapour is continuously generated by evaporation and removed by condensation.

Hence, the correct option is (A).

91. Dard is a group of people predominantly found in eastern Afghanistan, in the northern areas and northwest frontier province of Pakistan, and in the Indian state of Jammu and Kashmir.

In heavy fur costumes, flower bouquets adorning their heads, members of the Dard Aryan tribe from Jammu & Kashmir's Ladakh region were in the capital as part of a seminar that extensively discussed the need to preserve their legacy.

Hence, the correct option is (A).

92. The Kosi River is known as the "Sorrow of Bihar" as the annual floods affect about 21,000 km^2 (8,100 sq mi) of fertile agricultural lands thereby disturbing the rural economy.

It has caused widespread human suffering in the past due to flooding and very frequent changes in the course when it flows from Nepal to Bihar.

Hence, the correct option is (C).

93.

- Chandragupta Maurya became a Jain and left for Sravanbelgola, Karnataka along with his Jain guru Bhadrabahu.

- He died by slow starvation at Chandragiri Hill, Sravanbelgola.

- He lived as an ascetic for some years and died of voluntary starvation.

- He was the founder of the Maurya Dynasty in India.

Hence, the correct option is (B).

94. The relative humidity is a measure of the water vapour content of the air at a given temperature. The amount of moisture in the air is compared with the maximum amount that the air could contain at the same temperature and expressed as a percentage.

Hence, the correct option is (A).

95.

Name	Quit India Movement
Start date	8 August 1942
By whom	Mahatma Gandhi
Another name of the movement	August Movement
Where was it launched	Bombay session of the All-India Congress Committee
Slogan attached to the movement	Do or Die

Hence, the correct option is (B).

96.

- Azad Hind Fauj was raised by Subhash Chandra Bose.

- Azad Hind Fauj or Indian National Army was formed in 1942.

- Its aim was to secure Indian independence from British rule.

Hence, the correct option is (B).

97. Trans-Himalayan Rivers are those rivers that are rising beyond the great Himalayas. These rivers, after cutting deep gorges in the great Himalayas, flow into Indian parts.

Example: Indus, Satluj, Brahmaputra.

Hence, the correct option is (B).

98. The resistance offered by a wire of unit length and unit area of cross-section is called resistivity or specific resistance (r).

$$p = R\frac{A}{l} = (ohm)\frac{metre^2}{metre} = ohm\ metre$$

Where,

R = resistance of the wire

A = area of cross-section of the wire

l = length of the wire.

Hence, the correct option is (A).

99.

- The watermelon model or the Plum-Pudding Model was given by Thomson.

- According to this model, an atom is treated as a sphere of radius 10^{-8} cm in which positively charged particles are uniformly distributed whereas the electrons are embedded through them.

- Rutherford later proposed the nuclear atomic model of an atom.

Hence, the correct option is (C).

100.

- The number 6.023×10^{23} is known as the Avogadro's Number.

- It is the number of constituent particles contained in a one-mole amount of substance.

- It helps in understanding the relationship between the molar mass of a substance and the mass of a given sample.

Hence, the correct option is (A).

General Intelligence and Reasoning

Q.1 Which one of the given responses would be a meaningful order of the following?

1. Result
2. Learn
3. Exam
4. Revise
5. Study

A. 4, 3, 5, 2, 1   **B.** 2, 5, 3, 1, 4

C. 5, 2, 4, 3, 1   **D.** 1, 4, 2, 3, 5

Q.2 Which answer figure will complete the pattern in the following question figure?

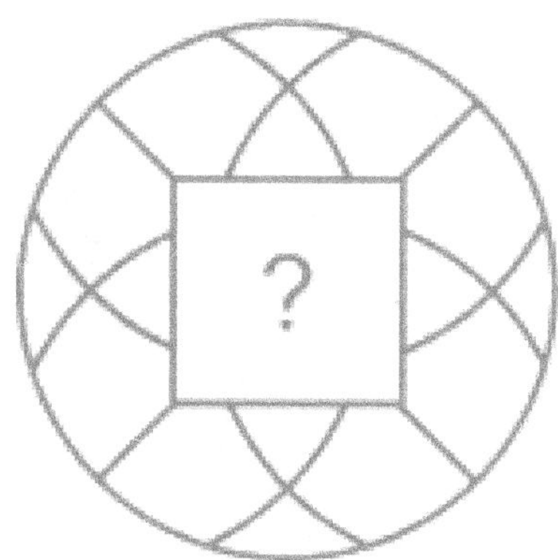

[AFCAT, 2021]

A. 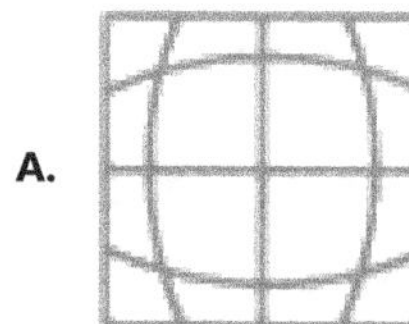   **B.** 

C. 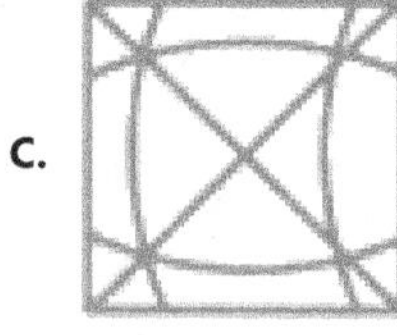   **D.** 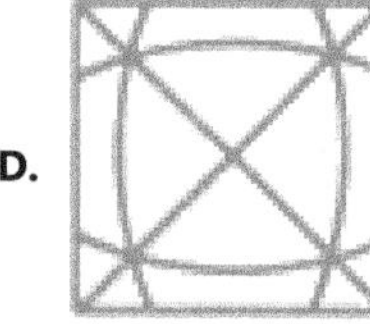

Q.3 If in a certain code language, MACBOOK is written as BCAMKOO, then SIBLING can be written as?

A. LBISGIN   **B.** INGSIBL

C. LBSINGI   **D.** LBSIGIN

Q.4 Directions: In the question given below, two statements are followed by two conclusions. You have to take the given statements to be true even if they seem to be different from the known facts. Read all the conclusions and decide which of the given conclusions logically follows from the given statements.

Statements:

I. Some Carrot are Red.

II. All Red are Colour.

Conclusions:

I. Some Colour are Carrot

II. No Carrot is a Colour

A. Only Conclusion I follows

B. Only Conclusion II follows

C. Either Conclusion I or Conclusion II follows

D. Both Conclusions I and II follow

Q.5 A series is given with one term missing. Select the correct alternative from the given ones that will complete the series.

15, 20, 30, 40, 45, ___, 60, 80, 75, 100, 90

A. 50   **B.** 60   **C.** 55   **D.** 45

Q.6 In the given figure, how many red are pens?

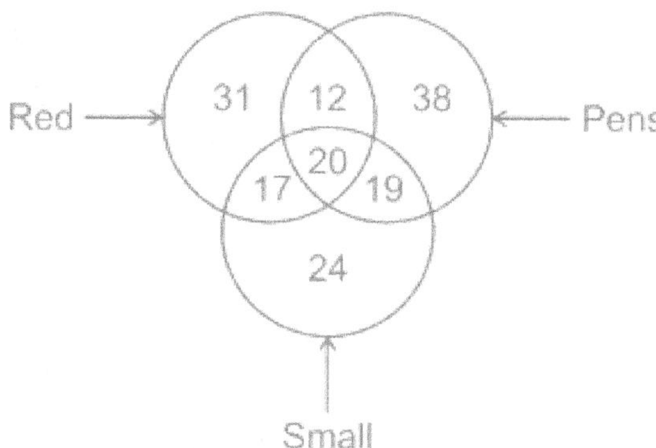

A. 12   **B.** 32   **C.** 20   **D.** 29

Q.7 In the following question, select the odd letter pair from the given alternatives.

A. AP - EQ   **B.** IS - MT   **C.** OC - UB   **D.** EK - IL

Q.8 If 'sit orn tik' stands for 'he is handsome';

'not tik pmr' stands for 'she is beautiful' and

'pmr tnt nit' stands for 'she likes mangoes',

which word would mean 'beautiful'?

A. pmr   **B.** tik

C. not   **D.** can't be determined

Q.9 In the following question, select the number which can be placed at the sign of question mark (?) from the given alternative.

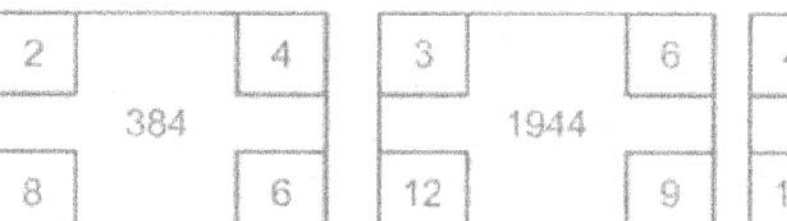

A. 6248   **B.** 7144   **C.** 6144   **D.** 2844

Q.10 A series of figures is given which can be grouped into classes. Select the group into which the figures can be classified from the given responses.

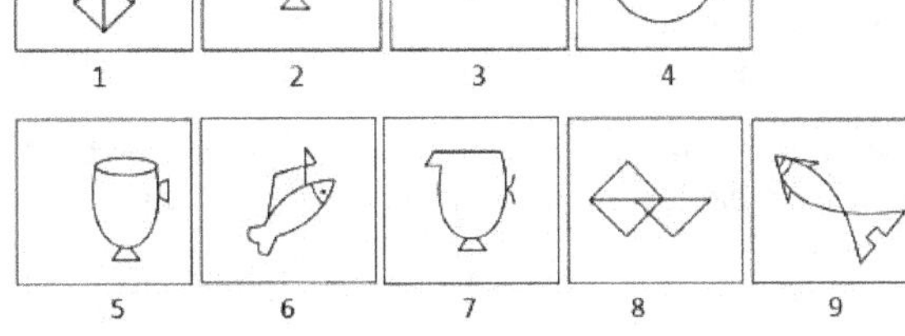

A.   1 3 4, 4 2 5, 6 7 8
B.   1 4 8, 2 5 7, 3 6 9
C.   2 5 6, 3 4 8, 1 7 9
D.   3 4 8, 2 3 5, 1 6 7

Q.11 Introducing Naira with her son, Mansi said, "Her husband is the son-in-law of my mother."

Then, how is Mansi related to Naira's husband?

A. Daughter   **B.** Sister
C. Sister-in-law   **D.** Brother-in-law

Q.12 A piece of paper is folded and punched as shown below in the question figures. From the given answer figures, indicate how it will appear when opened?

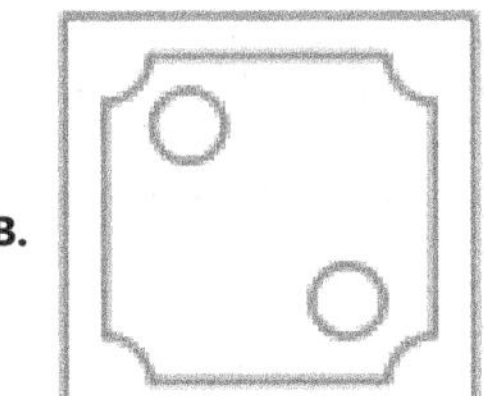

[SSC MTS, 2019], [UP Police Constable, 2019]

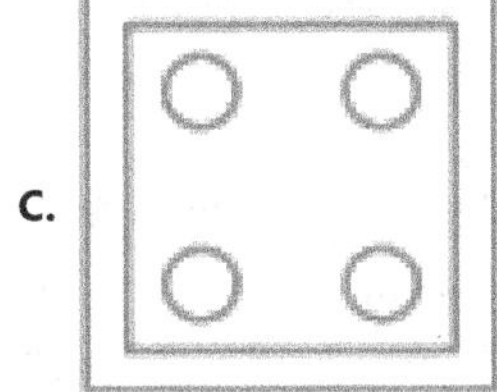
A.

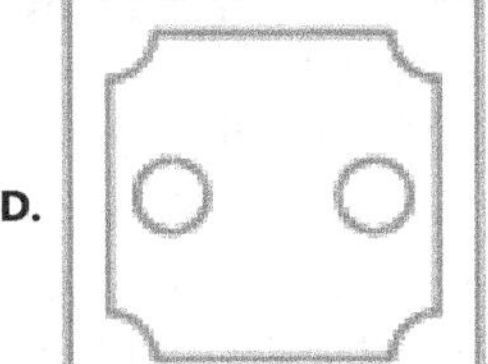
B.

C.

D.

Q.13 Directions: Choose the odd figure from the given alternatives.

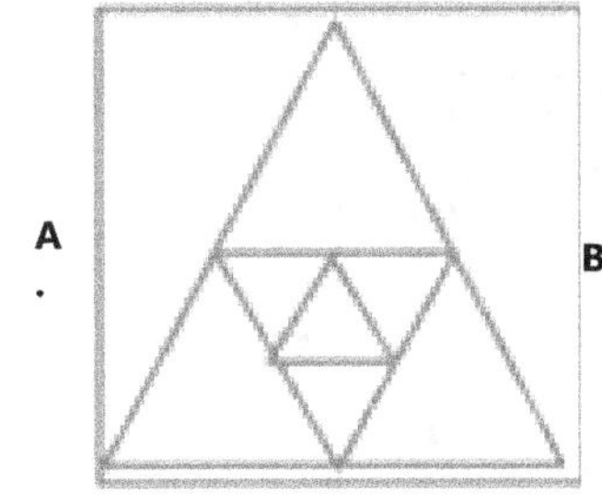
A.

B.

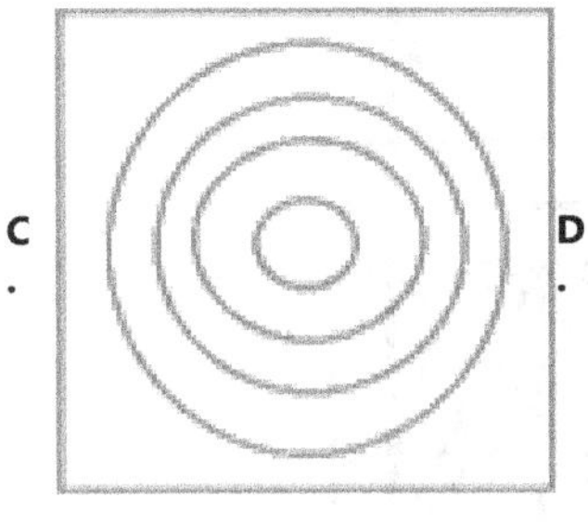
C.

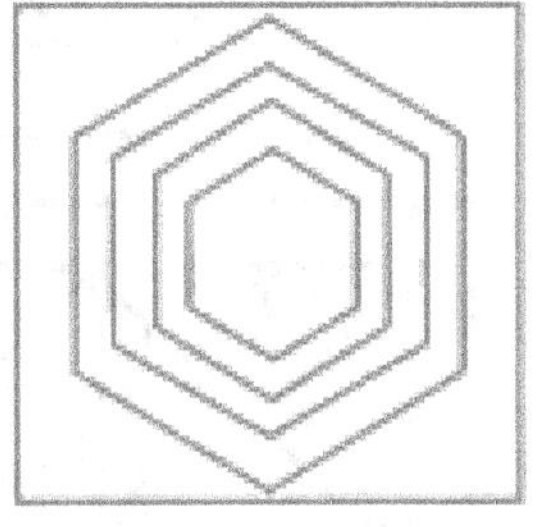
D.

Q.14 In which of the following answer figures, the given question figure is hidden/embedded.

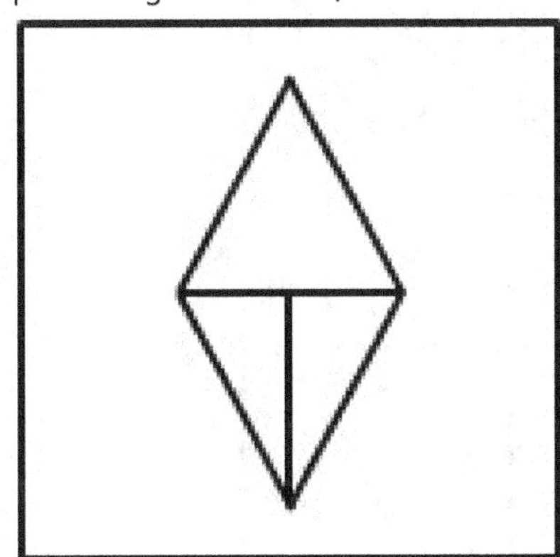

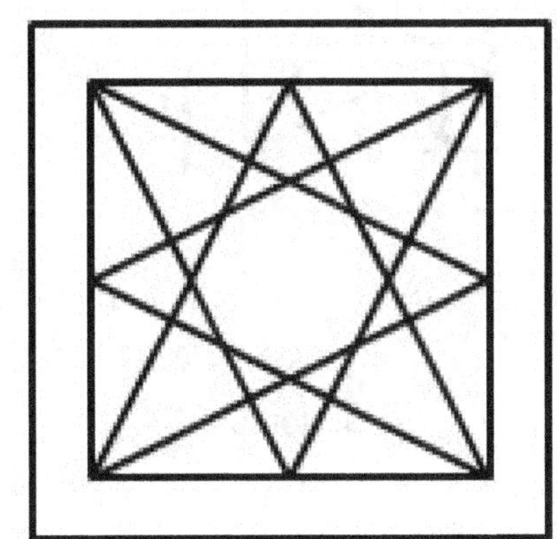
A.

B.

C.

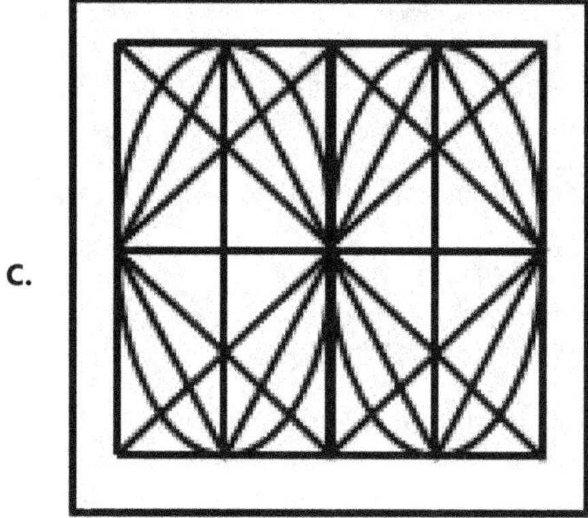

D.

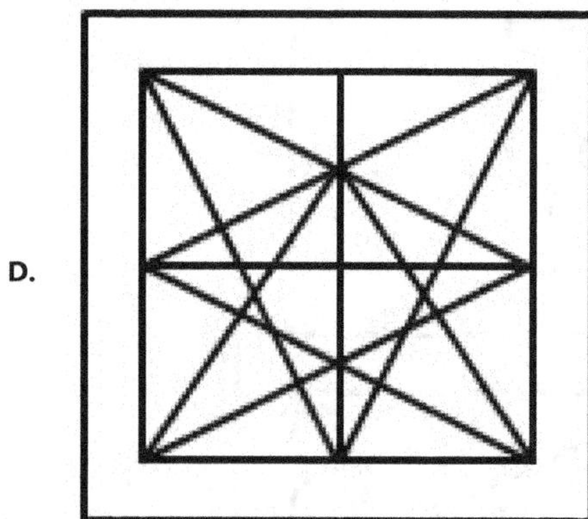

Q.15 Rearrange the jumbled letters to make a meaningful word and then select the one which is different.

A. HHIG   **B.** LATL

C. HHUIHG   **D.** HORTS

Q.16 In a certain code language, '÷' represents ' + ', '-' represents ' × ', ' + ' represents '÷' and ' × ' represents '-'. Find the value of the given expression.

17 - 20 + 5 × 30 ÷ 4 = ?

A. 34   **B.** 42   **C.** 18   **D.** 47

Q.17 In the following question, select the related word from the given alternatives.

Disease : Medicine :: Famine : ?

A. Clouds   **B.** Rainfall   **C.** Lakes   **D.** Ponds

Q.18 A series is given with one term missing. Select the correct alternatives from the given ones that will complete the series.

J, F, ?, D, F

A. C   **B.** M   **C.** G   **D.** H

Q.19 T walks 17 km towards the west. He turns right and walks 15 km. He turns right and walks 17 km. How far (in km) is he from his starting point?

A. 15   **B.** 17   **C.** 32   **D.** 53

Q.20 Each face of the dice is painted with Purple, Red, Yellow, Blue, Gray, and Black as shown in the given figure. What color is painted on the face opposite to the Black color?

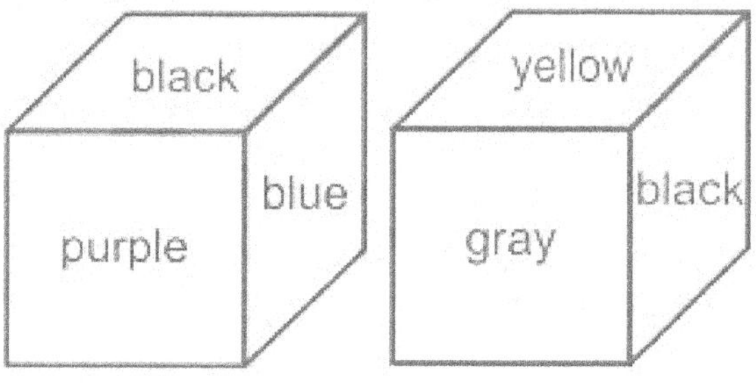

A. Red   **B.** Yellow   **C.** Blue   **D.** Purple

Q.21 In a certain code language, "FIT" is written as "33" and "FAT" is written as "25". How is "KIN" written in that code language?

A. 32   **B.** 36   **C.** 30   **D.** 34

Q.22 How many triangles are there in the given figure?

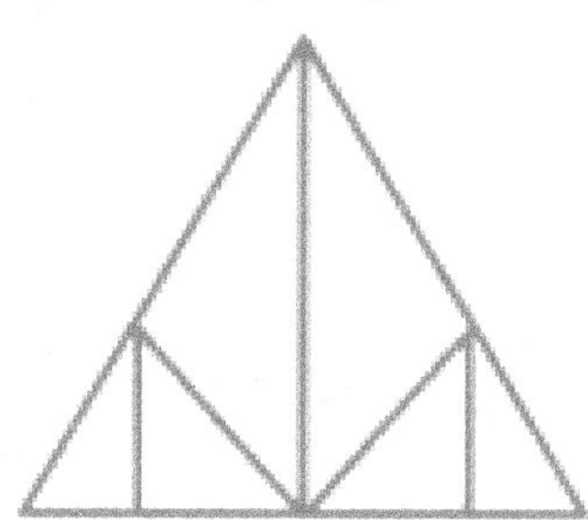

[SSC CGL, 2021]

A. 10   **B.** 11   **C.** 12   **D.** 13

Q.23 Direction: Select the combination of letters that when sequentially placed in the gaps of the given letter series will complete the series.

ac_d_b_cbdd__a_bddb

A. bdcabc   **B.** bdabac   **C.** cbdbcc   **D.** bdbcac

Q.24 Vilas remembers his marriage is after 4th July. While his sister remembers his marriage is before 6th July. On which date of July is his marriage?

A. 4   **B.** 5   **C.** 6   **D.** 7

Q.25 If a mirror is placed on the line MN, then which of the answer figures is the right image of the given figure?

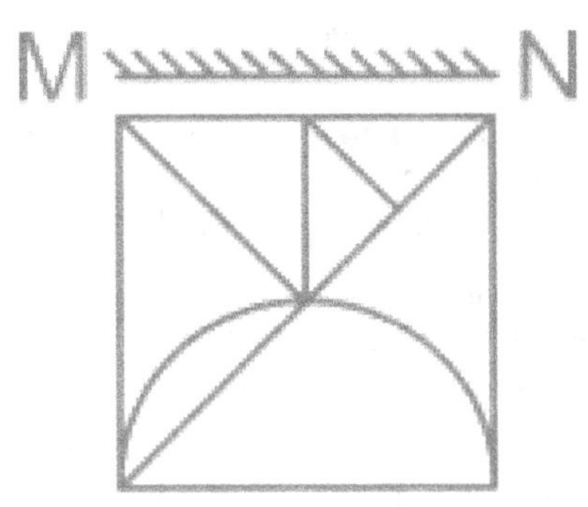

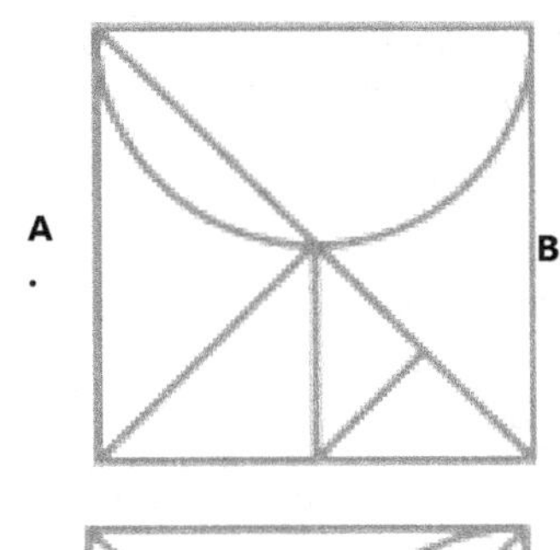
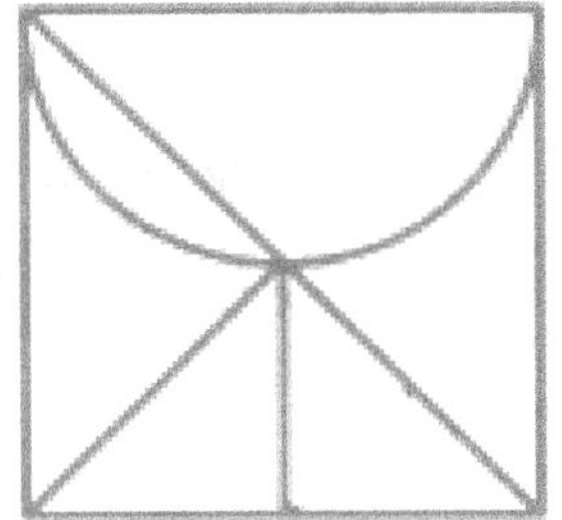

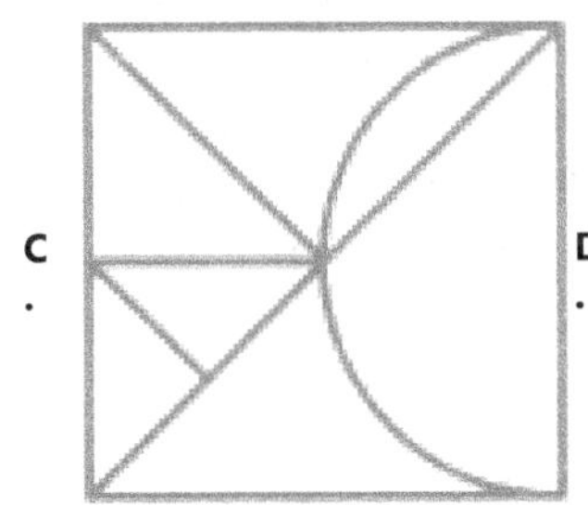
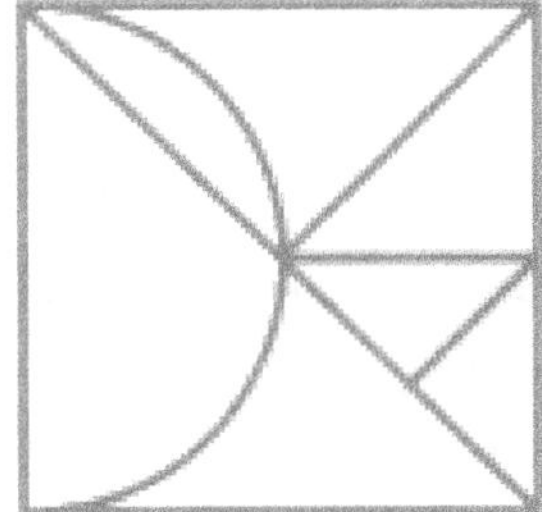

Numerical Aptitude/ Quantitative Ability

Q.26 If $x - y = 6$ and $xy = 40$, then find $x^2 + y^2$

A. 116   B. 80   C. 89   D. 146

Q.27 Mr. Rajesh buys a toy for Rs. 27.50 and sells it for Rs. 28.60. Find the gain percent.

A. 5%   B. 4%   C. 6%   D. 3%

Q.28 A man completes $\frac{5}{8}$ of a job in 10 days. At this rate how many more days will he take to finish the job?

A. 5   B. 6   C. 8   D. 7

Q.29 If A: B=2: 5, B: C=4: 3 and C: D=2: 1, then what is value of A: C: D ?

A. 6: 5: 2   B. 7: 20: 10
C. 8: 30: 15   D. 16: 30: 15

Q.30 The average marks of a student in four subjects is 58. If the student obtains 68 marks in the fifth subject, then the new average is –

A. 60   B. 58   C. 62   D. 64

Q.31 If the two sides of an obtuse-angled triangle are 8 cm and 15 cm and the third side is x then,

A. $7 < x < 23$
B. $7 < x < \sqrt{161}$
C. $17 < x < 21$
D. Cannot be determined

Q.32 A sum becomes Rs. 5832 in 2 years at 8% per annum compound interest. Find the simple interest at 9% per annum for 3 years on the same amount?

A. Rs. 1325   B. Rs. 1375   C. Rs. 1350   D. Rs. 1300

Q.33 A man covers $\frac{3}{5}$ of the total distance by train and the remaining 40 km by bus. What is his total journey (in km)?

A. 50   B. 75   C. 100   D. 150

Q.34 If there is a profit of 20% on the cost price, then the percentage of profit on the sale price is:

A. $16\frac{2}{3}\%$ B. 12%   C. $15\frac{1}{3}\%$ D. 16%

Q.35 The difference between a number and $\frac{2}{7}$th of the number is 100. The number is

A. 130   B. 140   C. 150   D. 160

Q.36 If the price of sugar is raised by 25%, find by how much percent a householder must reduce his consumption of sugar so as not to increase his expenditure?

A. 10   B. 20   C. 18   D. 25

Q.37 The duplicate ratio of $x + 3: x + 7$ is $4: 9$ then find the value of x.

A. 5   B. 3   C. 2   D. 4

Q.38 Age of Pinky and Aditi is 35 and 25 respectively. After how many years the ratio of their ages will be $4: 3$?

A. 5 years   B. 6 years   C. 4 years   D. 7 years

Ques (39-42):Direction: The line graph shows the Sales per employee of a certain company. Study the diagram and answer the following questions.

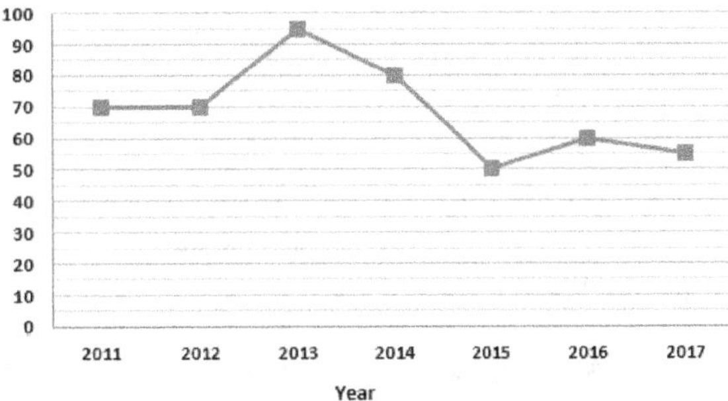

Q.39 If the number of employees of the company was 80 in the year 2015 then what was the sales (in Rs. crore) of the company in the year 2015?

A. 30   B. 40   C. 20   D. 50

Q.40

The Sales per employee in 2012 were greater than that in 2015 by _______.

A. 16.7%   B. 20%   C. 40%   D. 28.5%

Q.41

What was the difference in the Sales per employee (in Rs. lakhs) between the years 2011 and 2015?

A. 15   B. 10   C. 20   D. 5

Q.42

In which year were the Sales per employee greater than that of the previous year?

A. 2014   B. 2015   C. 2017   D. 2016

Q.43 Solve: $40 \div \left[(28 - 13) \div \left\{ (32 - 8) \div \left(5 + \frac{1}{3} \right) \right\} \right] = ?$

A. 10   B. 12   C. 14   D. 16

Q.44 $\triangle PQR$ is right-angled at Q. If $\cos P = \frac{3}{5}$, then what is the value of $\cos R$?

A. $\frac{3}{4}$ B. $\frac{5}{3}$ C. $\frac{4}{5}$ D. $\frac{4}{3}$

Q.45 Rectangle has its length and breadth as 12 cm and 20 cm respectively. If length is increased by 20% and breadth by 10% then what is the percentage change in the area of the rectangle?

A. 30%   B. 31%   C. 32%   D. 33%

Q.46 Solve: $5\frac{1}{5} + 2\frac{2}{15} + 3\frac{2}{3} = ? + 9$

A. 2   B. 4   C. 8   D. 10

Q.47 If a sum becomes thrice at simple interest in 12.5 yr, the rate of interest per annum is

A. $16\frac{2}{3}\%$ B. 16%   C. $16\frac{1}{3}\%$ D. 17%

Q.48 The ratio of the number of boys to the number of girls at a party is 5: 9. If there are 99 girls at the party, the total number of persons at the party are:

A. 99   B. 55   C. 132   D. 154

Q.49 Find the H.C.F. and L.C.M. of 20 and 28.

A. 20, 280   B. 5, 280   C. 10, 140   D. 4, 140

Q.50 Irfan bought a chair for Rs. 517 with a discount of 6% on the marked price. Find the marked price of the chair.

A. Rs. 580   B. Rs. 520   C. Rs. 550   D. Rs. 540

General English & Comprehension

Ques (51-52):Direction: In the following question, a part of the sentence may have an error. Find out which part of the sentence has an error and select the appropriate option. If a sentence is free from error, select 'option (D) i.e No Error'.

Q.51 We are what our thoughts (1)/ have made us; (2)/ so took care about what you think. (3)/ No error (4)

A. 1   B. 2   C. 3   D. 4

Q.52 Stringent penalties have a lower chance (1)/ of being imposed, as compared to fines that (2)/ are proportionate to the offend. (3)/ No error. (4)

A. 1   B. 2   C. 3   D. 4

Ques (53-55):Direction: In the following question, the sentence is given with a blank to be filled in with an appropriate word. Select the correct alternative out of the four and indicate it by selecting the appropriate option.

Q.53 Pilgrims gather here to atone _________ their sins.

A. Of   B. With   C. To   D. For

Q.54 She kept thinking, "How lucky Serena _______!"

A. Can   B. Could be
C. Is   D. Supposedly

Q.55 The four friends are always ready to go to _____ rescue.

A. Each other's   B. One another's
C. Other's   D. None of the above.

Ques (56-58):Direction: In the following question, out of the four given alternatives, select the one which is opposite in meaning to the given word.

Q.56 Opulent

A. Palatial   B. Luxurious
C. Penurious   D. Sedative

Q.57 Palliate

A. Accuse   B. Relieve
C. Condemn   D. Exacerbate

Q.58 Clamorous

A. Noisy   B. Confusion
C. Disturbance   D. Suppression

Ques (59-61):Direction: In the following question, out of the four given alternatives, select the one which best expresses the similar meaning of the given word.

Q.59 Arbitrary

A. Methodical   B. Penetrable
C. Random   D. Artful

Q.60 Penchant

A. Indifference   B. Revulsion
C. Disgust   D. Fondness

Q.61 Hearsay

A. Realise   B. Testimony
C. Buzz   D. Declare

Ques (62-64):Direction: In the following question, out of the four alternatives, select the alternative which best expresses the meaning of the idiom/phrase.

Q.62 Lend me your ear
A. To politely ask for someone's full attention.
B. Begging someone to listen to your grievances.
C. When nobody is willing to hear your side of the story.
D. Call someone for severe scolding.

Q.63 Pedal to the metal
A. Build something big by yourself.
B. Add more protection to an already strong shield.
C. To drive very fast.
D. Push a person to perform to its extreme.

Q.64 Tongue in cheek
A. In an ironic or insincere way.
B. Being practical.
C. Stop yourself from saying something hurtful.
D. Be gutsy and speak the unpleasant truth.

Ques (65-67):Direction: In the following question, out of the four alternatives, select the alternative which is the best substitute of the phrase/sentence.

Q.65 A person or thing that brings bad luck.
A. Felicitous
B. Adventitious
C. Jinx
D. Providential

Q.66 Writing or drawings scribbled, scratched, or sprayed illicitly on a wall or other surface in a public place.
A. Splotch
B. Smudge
C. Graffiti
D. Streak

Q.67 A transcendent state in which there is neither suffering, desire, nor sense of self.
A. Woe
B. Nirvana
C. Depression
D. Despondency

Ques (68-70):Direction: Read the passage carefully and choose the best answer to each question out of the four alternatives.

Will economists prove more helpful today, at a time when the challenges we face are nearly as pressing as those during the Great Depression? Unemployment may not be a severe problem in most advanced countries currently, but large segments of the labor force seem cut off from economic progress. Record levels of inequality and poor earnings prospects for younger, less-educated workers are eroding the foundations of liberal democracies. The rules that underpin globalization are badly in need of reform. And climate change continues to pose an existential threat.

These problems demand bold responses. Yet, for the most part, mainstream economists seem preoccupied with marginal fixes—a tax-code tweak here, a carbon tax there, perhaps a sprinkling of wage subsidies—that leave untouched the structures of power underwriting the rules of the economic game.

Economists can rise to the challenge by adopting a broader vision. Last month, I joined a group of prominent economists to launch an initiative that we have called "Economics for Inclusive Prosperity" (EIP). From labor markets and finance to innovation policies and electoral rules, the goal is to advance ambitious

policy ideas that pay much closer attention to inequality and exclusion—and to the power imbalances that produce them.

Although economists are well-positioned to develop institutional arrangements that go beyond what already exists, their habit of thinking at the margin and sticking close to the evidence at hand encourages an aversion to radical change. But, when presented with new challenges, economists must envision new solutions. Imagination is crucial. Not everything we try will succeed; but if we do not rediscover the value of Roosevelt's credo—"bold, persistent experimentation"—we will certainly fail.

Q.68 The line 'Yet, for the most part, mainstream economists seem preoccupied with marginal fixes' suggests that:

We don't need large-scale solutions from economists.
A. Marginal fixes can solve the problems pertaining to economics in general.
B. Mainstream economists are not interested in solving the problem of unemployment.
C. Though we need to take some bold approaches to solve the problems faced in our economies, mainstream economists are adopting minor fixes.
D. Most part of the solution is derived when the economists choose to apply marginal fixes.

Q.69 What is the meaning of the word aversion used in the passage?
A. A feeling of dislike and hostility.
B. A reasoned judgment.
C. The ability to understand something.
D. Suspicion or fear that something bad will happen.

Q.70 Which of the following statement is correct according to the passage?
A. The economy of advanced countries is severely crippled with unemployment.
B. Climate change poses an existential threat.
C. The full form of EIP is "Economics for Included Prosperity".
D. Both (A) and (C)

Q.71 Select the correctly spelt word.
A. nesessary
B. necessary
C. necessery
D. necassery

Q.72 Select the correctly spelled word.
A. commemorete
B. commemmorate
C. commemorate
D. comemorate

Q.73 Direction: The question below consists of a set of labelled sentences. These sentences, when properly sequenced form a coherent paragraph. Select the most logical order of sentences from among the options.

P: One's language fluency is determined by the quality of reading.

Q: In all cultures and civilizations, much stress is laid on reading but, in modern times, this activity is being ignored.

R: Reading is an essential basic skills-building activity.

S: Besides, vocabulary enrichment, ideas collection, familiarization with different types of writing formats, speaking fluency, etc, all depend upon reading.

A. RSPQ   B. QRPS   C. PQRS   D. RPSQ

Ques (74-75):Direction: Select the most appropriate option to substitute the underlined segment in the given sentence. If there is no need to substitute it, select No improvement.

Q.74 There <u>are too less</u> space for Naveen to park his car in front of the shop.

A. was so few space
B. was too little space
C. were too little space
D. No improvement

Q.75 She is quite capable of looking after herself, <u>aren't she</u>?

A. won't she
B. wasn't she
C. isn't she
D. No improvement

General Awareness

Q.76 Which of the following is one of the hockey stadiums of Madhya Pradesh?

A.   Nehru Stadium, Indore
B.   Aishbagh Stadium, Bhopal
C.   Captain Roop Singh Stadium, Gwalior
D.   Holkar Stadium, Indore

Q.77 To train the tribal sportspersons in traditional Archery, the 'Archery Sports Academy' has been established in Rajasthan at:

A. Udaipur   B. Banswara
C. Jaipur   D. Dungarpur

Q.78 Prithvi Shaw has become the 1st player to breach the mark of how many runs in a single edition of the Vijay Hazare Trophy?

A. 500   B. 600   C. 700   D. 800

Q.79 Which of the following has bagged the best drama series honor at the 48th International Emmy Awards?

A. She   B. Delhi Crime
C. Mirzapur   D. Crime Patrol

Q.80 Where is the Vivekananda Rock Memorial located?

A. Chennai   B. Coimbatore
C. Kanyakumari   D. Madurai

Q.81 Which among the following is the capital of France?

A. Vaduz   B. Baku   C. Paris   D. Libya

Q.82 Who was the son of Chandragupta Maurya?

A. Chandragupta II   B. Ashoka
C. Binbsara   D. Bindusara

Q.83 Special Drawing Rights (SDRs) is related to ________.

A.   World Bank
B.   Reserve Bank of India
C.   World Trade Organization
D.   International Monetary Fund

Q.84 What was the other name of Chanakya?

A. Bhattaswamy   B. Vishnugupta
C. Rajasekhar   D. Visakhadatta

Q.85 Pattachitra is famous for?

A. Dance   B. Painting
C. Puppetry   D. Theatre art

Q.86 Palk strait separates India with which country?

A. Pakistan   B. Bangladesh
C. Indonesia   D. Sri Lanka

Q.87 Air pollution is caused by:

A. Loudspeakers   B. Insecticides
C. Smoke   D. Sewage

Q.88 Who is credited for the construction of the Red Fort in Delhi ?

A. Sikandar Lodi   B. Akbar
C. Jahangir   D. Shah Jahan

Q.89 Who was the chairman of the Constitution Drafting Committee?

A.   Jawaharlal Nehru
B.   Dr. B.R.Ambedkar
C.   Dr. Rajendra Prasad
D.   Sardar Vallabhbhai Patel

Q.90 Between which of the following two planets are the asteroids found?

A. Saturn and Uranus   B. Jupiter and Saturn
C. Mars and Jupiter   D. Earth and Mars

Q.91 The right to vote is in which article of the Indian Constitution?

A. Article 322   B. Article 324
C. Article 326   D. Article 330

Q.92 ________ are defined as the mass movement of rock, debris, or earth down a slope.

A. Earthquake   B. Cyclone
C. Flood   D. Landslide

Q.93 Which among the following is an example of a primary colour?

A. Blue   B. Pink   C. Violet   D. Yellow

Q.94 Who invented Space Pen?

A. Paul C. Fisher   B. Rudolf Diesel
C. Richard Taylor   D. Alexander Fleming

Q.95 Which among the following is NOT a 3rd Generation Computer system?

A. DCM   B. IBM-370
C. IBM-360   D. CDC-1700

Q.96 Which of the following is **NOT** a programming language?

A. C   B. C++   C. Frontline   D. Python

Q.97 What is the capital of Indonesia?

A. Zagreb   B. San Jose   C. Jakarta   D. Nicosia

Q.98 Which of the following process is used to strengthen the glass?

A. Case hardening   B. Normalizing
C. Annealing   D. Tempering

Q.99 In Jan 2021 , Khelo India Ice Hockey Tournament has been organised at_________.

A. Uttar Pradesh   **B.** Kargil

C. Madhya Pradesh   **D.** Haryana

Q.100 Which of these places was named as the World Book Capital 2020 by UNESCO?

A. Delhi   **B.** Kuala Lumpur

C. Singapore   **D.** Bali

// Smart Answer Sheet //

Correct — Percentage of students who answered correctly. **Skipped** — Percentage of students who skipped.

Q.	Ans.	Correct	Skipped	Q.	Ans.	Correct	Skipped	Q.	Ans.	Correct	Skipped	Q.	Ans.	Correct	Skipped	Q.	Ans.	Correct	Skipped	Q.	Ans.	Correct	Skipped
1	C	85.05 %	0.0 %	18	D	49.46 %	1.99 %	35	B	89.91 %	0.0 %	52	C	57.77 %	1.82 %	69	A	61.32 %	1.23 %	86	D	85.0 %	0.0 %
2	D	89.85 %	0.0 %	19	A	45.39 %	1.64 %	36	B	64.42 %	1.3 %	53	D	88.03 %	0.0 %	70	B	76.23 %	0.0 %	87	C	80.35 %	0.0 %
3	A	69.34 %	1.51 %	20	A	84.31 %	0.0 %	37	A	76.14 %	0.0 %	54	C	84.75 %	0.0 %	71	B	84.43 %	0.0 %	88	D	87.44 %	0.0 %
4	A	59.95 %	1.61 %	21	A	77.83 %	0.0 %	38	A	57.57 %	1.81 %	55	B	87.5 %	0.0 %	72	C	55.84 %	1.7 %	89	B	83.63 %	0.0 %
5	B	64.45 %	1.58 %	22	B	58.98 %	1.77 %	39	B	46.42 %	1.04 %	56	C	50.86 %	1.77 %	73	D	53.17 %	1.28 %	90	C	86.54 %	0.0 %
6	B	89.94 %	0.0 %	23	B	88.58 %	0.0 %	40	C	60.87 %	1.32 %	57	B	80.57 %	0.0 %	74	B	78.85 %	0.0 %	91	C	52.39 %	1.15 %
7	C	54.55 %	1.32 %	24	B	54.7 %	1.36 %	41	C	40.65 %	1.45 %	58	D	44.23 %	1.17 %	75	C	81.72 %	0.0 %	92	D	68.09 %	1.23 %
8	C	67.11 %	1.39 %	25	A	87.42 %	0.0 %	42	D	44.33 %	1.3 %	59	C	46.94 %	1.29 %	76	B	65.58 %	1.31 %	93	A	87.83 %	0.0 %
9	C	59.42 %	1.9 %	26	A	80.63 %	0.0 %	43	B	64.01 %	1.76 %	60	D	40.78 %	1.75 %	77	A	42.24 %	1.49 %	94	A	21.8 %	4.63 %
10	B	69.48 %	1.99 %	27	B	87.46 %	0.0 %	44	C	78.07 %	0.0 %	61	C	45.46 %	1.16 %	78	D	43.91 %	1.42 %	95	A	60.83 %	1.02 %
11	C	59.98 %	1.1 %	28	B	83.12 %	0.0 %	45	C	67.58 %	1.18 %	62	A	53.59 %	1.13 %	79	B	64.56 %	1.8 %	96	C	52.39 %	1.58 %
12	A	78.58 %	0.0 %	29	D	85.44 %	0.0 %	46	A	87.27 %	0.0 %	63	D	64.17 %	1.04 %	80	C	48.55 %	1.11 %	97	C	50.17 %	1.63 %
13	B	83.91 %	0.0 %	30	A	83.29 %	0.0 %	47	B	46.64 %	1.08 %	64	A	83.59 %	0.0 %	81	C	89.96 %	0.0 %	98	C	18.78 %	4.21 %
14	C	83.51 %	0.0 %	31	B	62.22 %	1.7 %	48	D	79.15 %	0.0 %	65	C	60.09 %	1.52 %	82	D	76.86 %	0.0 %	99	B	61.49 %	1.52 %
15	C	40.53 %	1.88 %	32	C	64.64 %	1.38 %	49	D	85.68 %	0.0 %	66	C	20.1 %	4.54 %	83	D	27.6 %	3.77 %	100	B	64.27 %	1.37 %
16	B	64.72 %	1.38 %	33	C	52.15 %	1.18 %	50	C	89.84 %	0.0 %	67	B	61.15 %	1.7 %	84	B	77.52 %	0.0 %				
17	B	82.0 %	0.0 %	34	A	77.0 %	0.0 %	51	C	77.89 %	0.0 %	68	C	85.67 %	0.0 %	85	B	67.35 %	1.59 %				

//Hints and Solutions//

1. The correct sequence will be:

Study → Learn → Revise → Exam → Result

Hence, the correct option is (C).

2.

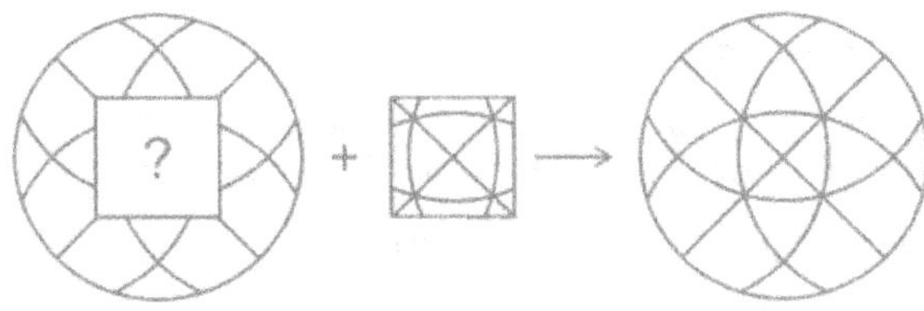

Hence, the correct option is (D).

3. The pattern for the code is as follows,

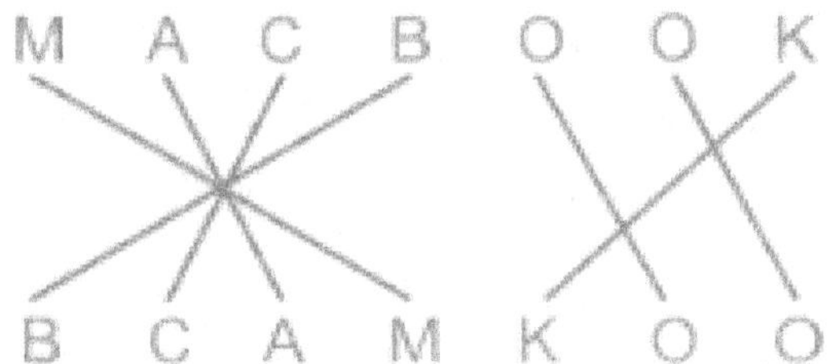

So, SIBLING can be written as LBISGIN.

Hence, the correct option is (A).

4.

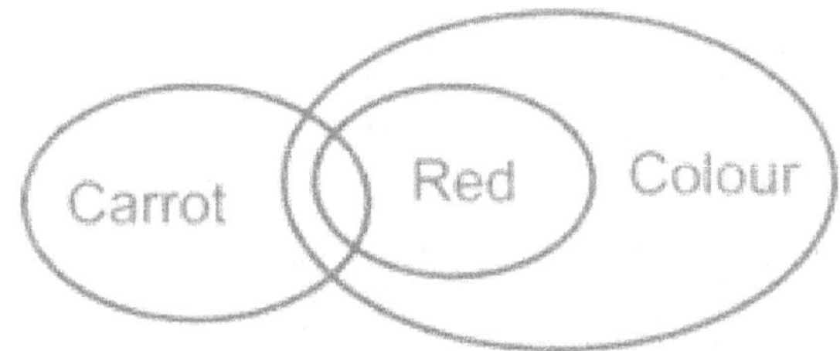

Conclusions:

I. Some Colour are Carrot ⇒ follows (It is definitely true).

II. No Carrot is a Colour ⇒ not follows (As some carrot will definitely be the colour).

Thus, only conclusion I follows.

Hence, the correct option is (A).

5. From the given series, we find that there are two series alternatively.

First is starting with 15 i.e,

15 + 15 = 30

30 + 15 = 45

45 + 15 = 60

Second is starting with 20 i.e,

20 + 20 = 40

40 + 20 = 60

60 + 20 = 80

Hence, the correct option is (B).

6.

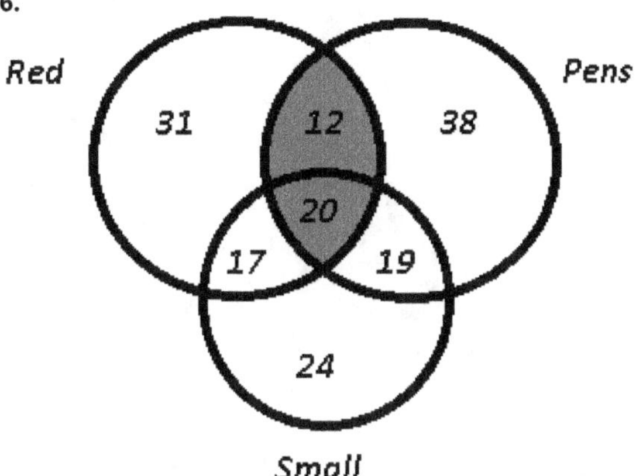

Clearly, the red that are pens are = 12 + 20 = 32. Hence, the correct option is (B).

7. The pattern follow here is

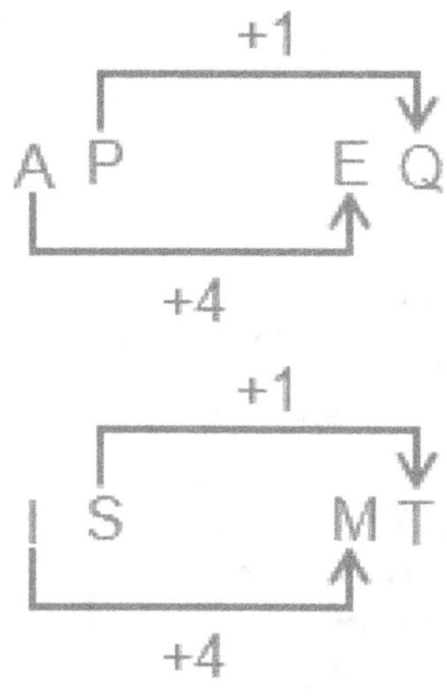

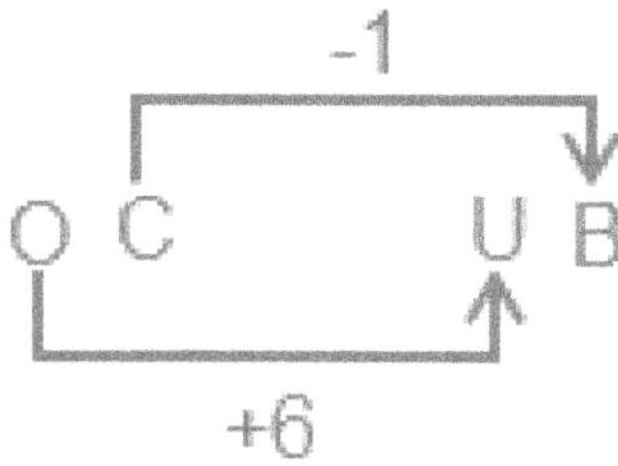

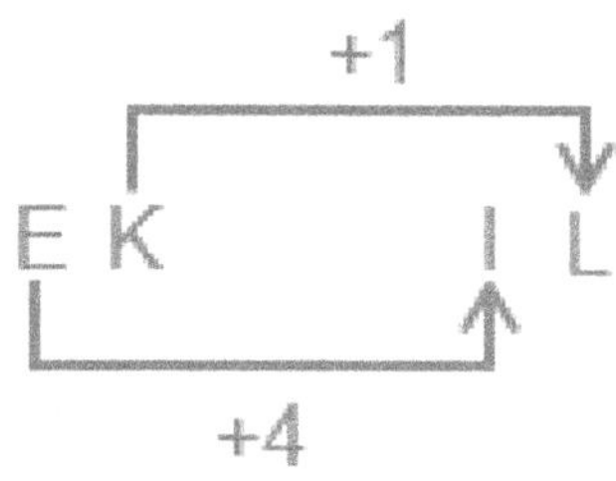

Thus, OC - UB is the odd one.

Hence, the correct option is (C).

8. The words are coded as follows:

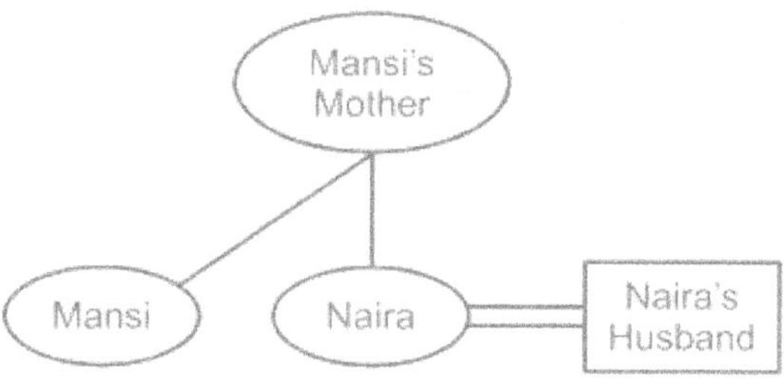

In the first and second statement, the common code word is 'tik' and the common word is 'is'. So, 'tik' stands for 'is'.

In the second and third statement, the common code word is 'pmr' and the common word is 'she'. So, 'pmr' stands for 'she'.

Thus, 'not' stands for 'beautiful'.

Hence, the correct option is (C).

9. The pattern followed here is:

All the numbers on the corners are multiplied to get the number written in the center.

2× 4× 6× 8 = 384

Also, 3× 6× 9× 12 = 1944

Similary,

? = 4 × 8 × 12 × 16 = 6144

Hence, the correct option is (C).

10. In option (B), group 1, group 2, and group 3 have all the shapes similar to each other within their respective groups.

In group 1 the figures are 1, 4 and 8 having triangle.

In group 2, the figures are 2, 5 and 7 which have cylindrical shapes.

In group 3, the figures are 3, 6 and 9 which have a fish-shaped structure.

In all other options, the arrangement is random.

Hence, the correct option is (B).

11. Based on given data, we can draw family tree-

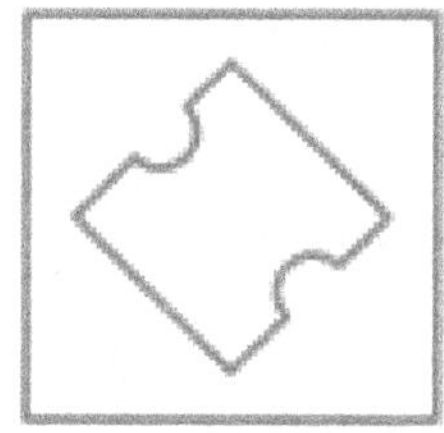
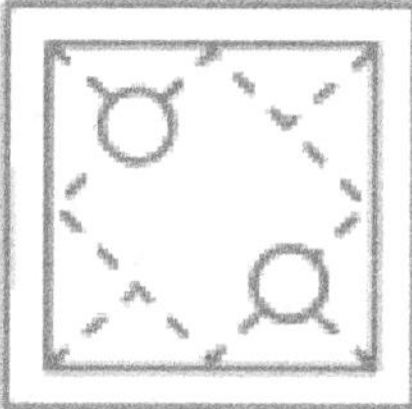

Mansi is the sister-in-law of Naira's husband.

Hence, the correct option is (C).

12. On opening the paper, it will appear like:

Hence, the correct option is (A).

13. In each figure, there are concentric same shapes, like all triangles, all circles, or all hexagons. But in the square figure, we have a line in the center, as shown below.

Thus, the figure given in option (B) is different from other figures.

Hence, the correct option is (B).

14.

Hence, the correct option is (B).

15. Option (C) is the word with the letters HHUIHG that cannot be rearranged to form a meaningful word. But from the remaining options, we can make meaningful words, as follows.

HHIG → HIGH

LATL → TALL

HORTS → SHORT

Hence, the correct option is (C).

16. Given equation: 17 - 20 + 5 × 30 ÷ 4 = ?

Sign	÷	-	+	×
Replacement sign	+	×	÷	-

After replacing the signs:

⇒ 17 × 20 ÷ 5 - 30 + 4

Solving by using the BODMAS rule,

⇒ 17 × 4 - 30 + 4

⇒ 68-30+4

⇒ 42

Hence, the correct option is (B).

17. Medicine prevents the disease.

Similarly, Rainfall prevents Famine.

Hence, the correct option is (B).

18. The pattern followed here is:

⇒ J − 4 = F

⇒ F + 2 = H

⇒ H − 4 = D

⇒ D + 2 = F

Hence, the correct option is (D).

19. The following diagram shows the displacement of T:

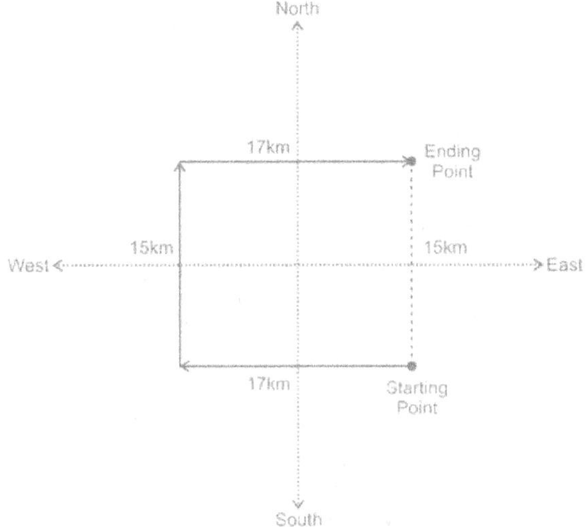

Thus, he is 15 km away from his starting point.
Hence, the correct option is (A).

20. According to the given figures,

Black cannot be opposite to Gray, Purple, Yellow, and Blue, as we can see that all the sides are adjacent to Black.

So, Black is the opposite to Red.

Hence, the correct option is (A).

21. FIT $\rightarrow 6 + 9 + 20 = 35 - 2 = 33$

FAT $\rightarrow 6 + 1 + 20 = 27 - 2 = 25$

Similarly,

KIN $\rightarrow 11 + 9 + 14 = 34 - 2 = 32$

Hence, the correct option is (A).

22.

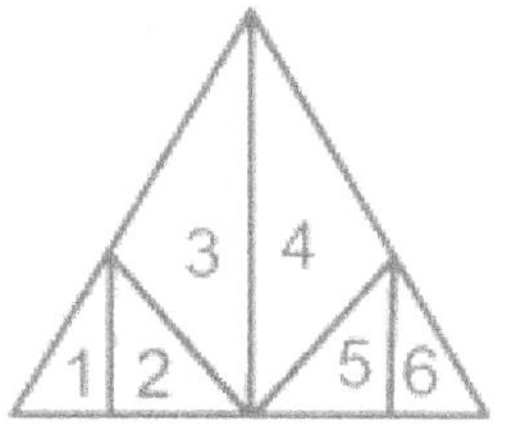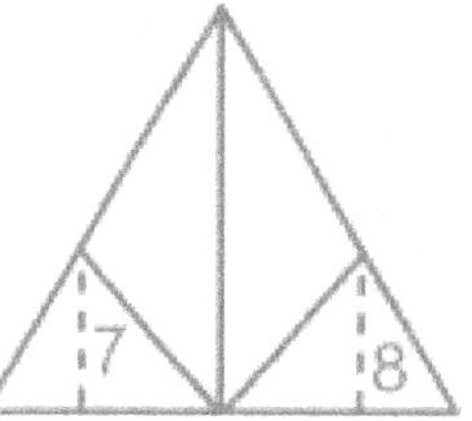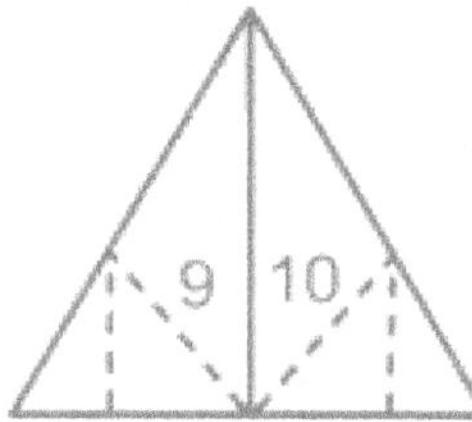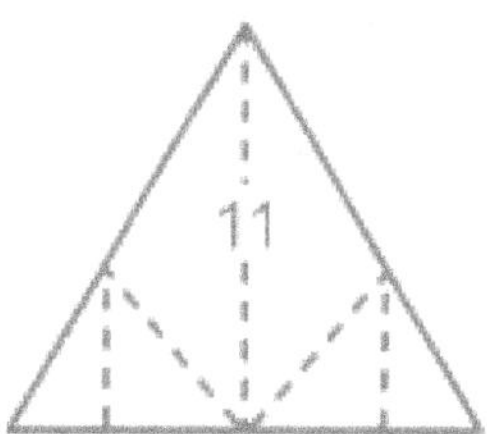

Clearly, 11 triangles are there in the given figure.

Hence, the correct option is (B).

23. The given series follows the following pattern:

acbddb acbddb acbddb

Hence, the correct option is (B).

24. As Vilas remembers his marriage is after 4th July and his sister remembers his marriage is before 6th July, so the date between 4th and 6th July is 5th July which is the marriage date of Vilas.

Hence, the correct option is (B).

25. The mirror image is:

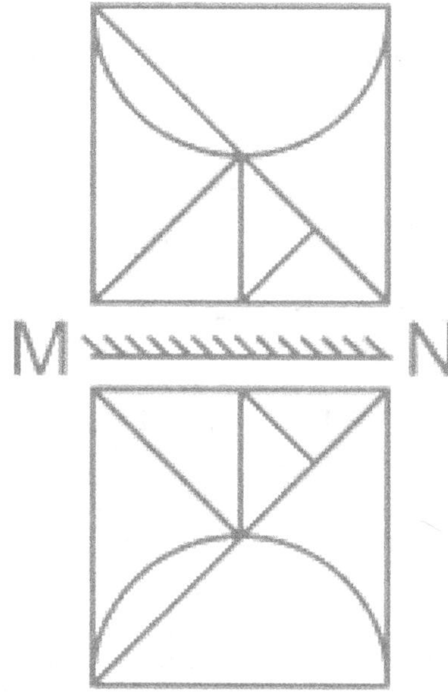

Hence, the correct option is (A).

26. Given,

$x - y = 6$ and $xy = 40$

We know that,

$$x^2 + y^2 = (x - y)^2 + 2xy$$

Substituting the value of $(x - y)$ and xy

$$= (6)^2 + (2 \times 40)$$

$$= 36 + 80$$

$$\therefore x^2 + y^2 = 116$$

Hence, the correct option is (A).

27. We know that,

Gain $=$ Sell Price $-$ Cost Price

So,

$$= \text{Rs. } (28.60 - 27.50)$$

$$= \text{Rs. } 1.10$$

Gain $\% = \dfrac{Gain \times 100}{\text{Cost Price}} = \dfrac{1.10 \times 100}{27.50} = 4\%$

Hence, the correct option is (B).

28. Let the time taken to complete the job be x days,

Therefore,

Time taken to complete $\dfrac{5^{th}}{8}$ of job $= \dfrac{5x}{8}$

So,

$$\Rightarrow \dfrac{5x}{8} = 10 \Rightarrow x = 16 \text{ days}$$

Thus, More time required $= 16 - 10 = 6$ days

Hence, the correct option is (B).

29. A : B = 2 : 5

B : C = 4 : 3

B is the common terms so first of all the value of B should be made equal.

LCM of 4 and 5 is 20.

$A : B = 2 : 5$ (multiply by 4)

$B : C = 4 : 3$ (multiply by 5)

So, A : B : C = 8 : 20 : 15

Now, A: B: C = 8 : 20 : 15

And C : D = 2 : 1

Cis common so its value should be made equal.

LCM of 15 and 2 is 30.

A : B : C = 8 : 20 : 15 (multiply by 2)

C : D = 2 : 1 (multiply by 15)

Now, $A:B:C:D = 16:40:30:15$

Therefore, $A:C:D = 16:30:15$

Hence, the correct option is (D).

30. We know that,

$$\text{Average} = \frac{\text{sum of observations}}{\text{total number of observations}}$$

Given, average marks of a student in four subjects is 58

$\Rightarrow$ sum total in 4 subjects $= 58 \times 4 = 232$

Now, he obtained 68 marks in the 5th subject.

New average $= \frac{(232+68)}{5} = \frac{300}{5} = 60$

Hence, the correct option is (A).

31. The sides a, b and c of an obtuse triangle are related as,

$$\frac{c^2}{2} < a^2 + b^2 < c^2$$

Let $a = x, b = 8$ cm and $c = 15$ cm

$\Rightarrow \frac{15^2}{2} < x^2 + 8^2 < 15^2$

$\Rightarrow 112.5 < x^2 + 64 < 225$

$\Rightarrow 112.5 - 64 < x^2 < 225 - 64$

$\Rightarrow 48.5 < x^2 < 161$

$\Rightarrow \sqrt{48.5} < x < \sqrt{161}$

$\because \sqrt{49} = 7$, we can write

$\therefore 7 < x < \sqrt{161}$

Hence, the correct option is (B).

32. Let Rs. P be the required sum

We know that,

$$\text{Amount} = P\left[\left(1 + \frac{r}{100}\right)^2\right]$$

According to the question,

$\Rightarrow 5832 = P\left[\left(1 + \frac{8}{100}\right)^2\right]$

$\Rightarrow 5832 = P \times 1.1664$

$\Rightarrow P = \frac{5832}{1.1664}$

$\Rightarrow P = $ Rs. 5000

We know that,

$$S.I. = \frac{(P \times R \times T)}{100}$$

Therefore,

$\Rightarrow S.I. = \frac{(5000 \times 9 \times 3)}{100}$

$\therefore S.I = $ Rs. 1350

Hence, the correct option is (C).

33. Let the distance be 'd' km.

If a man covers $\frac{3}{5}$ of the total distance by train, then the remaining distance will be:

Remaining distance $= d - \frac{3d}{5} = \frac{2d}{5}$

According to the question,

$\Rightarrow \frac{2d}{5} = 40$

$\Rightarrow d = 100$ km

Hence, the correct option is (C).

34. Let the CP be x

Profit $= \frac{20}{100} \times x = \frac{x}{5}$

Selling price $= x + \frac{x}{5} = \frac{6x}{5}$

Profit % on selling price $= \frac{\left(\frac{x}{5}\right)}{\left(\frac{6x}{5}\right)} \times 100 = 16\frac{2}{3}\%$

Hence, the correct option is (A).

35. Let the number be X.

$\Rightarrow X - \frac{2X}{7} = 100$

$\Rightarrow \frac{7X - 2X}{7} = 100$

$\Rightarrow X = 140$

Hence, the correct option is (B).

36. Let the price and consumption of sugar be x and y

We know that,

Expenditure $=$ price $\times$ consumption

$\Rightarrow$ Expenditure $= x \times y$

$\Rightarrow$ Price increased by 25% then new cost $= x + 25\%$ of x

$\Rightarrow$ Price increased by 25% then new cost $= 1.25x$

$\Rightarrow$ Reduction in consumption $= \frac{(1.25xy - xy)}{1.25xy}$

$\Rightarrow$ Reduction in consumption $= \left(\frac{0.25xy}{1.25xy}\right) \times 100$

∴ Reduction in $\% = 20\%$

Hence, the correct option is (B).

37. Duplicate ratio $= x + 3 : x + 7$ is $4 : 9$

i.e. $\left(\frac{x+3}{x+7}\right)^2 = \frac{4}{9}$

$\Rightarrow \frac{x+3}{x+7} = \frac{2}{3}$

$\Rightarrow 3x + 9 = 2x + 14$

$\Rightarrow x = 5$

∴ The value of $x = 5$

Hence, the correct option is (A).

38. Let after T years their ages will be in ratio $4 : 3$

According to the question,

$\frac{(\text{Age of pinky} + T)}{(\text{Age of Aditi} + T)} = \frac{4}{3}$

$\Rightarrow \frac{(35 + T)}{(25 + T)} = \frac{4}{3}$

$\Rightarrow 105 + 3T = 100 + 4T$

$\Rightarrow 4T - 3T = 105 - 100$

∴ $T = 5$ years

Hence, the correct option is (A).

39. Sales per employee in 2015 = Rs. 50 lakhs

No. of employees in 2015 = 80

∴ Sales of company in 2015 = 50 × 80 = Rs. 4000 lakhs = Rs. 40 crores

Hence, the correct option is (B).

40. Sales per employee in $2012 =$ Rs. 70 lakhs

Sales per employee in $2015 =$ Rs. 50 lakhs

Difference $= 70 - 50 =$ Rs. 20 lakhs

∴ The Sales per employee in 2012 were greater than that in 2015 by $= \frac{20}{50} \times 100 = 40\%$

Hence, the correct option is (C).

41. Sales per employee in 2011 = Rs. 70 lakhs

Sales per employee in 2015 = Rs. 50 lakhs

∴ Required difference = 70 - 50 = Rs. 20 lakhs

Hence, the correct option is (C).

42. The sales per employee increases in the year 2016 as compared to the previous year

∴ Sales per employee in 2016 is greater than that of the previous year

Hence, the correct option is (D).

43. Given expression,

$40 \div \left[(28 - 13) \div \left\{(32 - 8) \div \left(5 + \frac{1}{3}\right)\right\}\right] = ?$

$\Rightarrow 40 \div \left[15 \div \left\{24 \div \left(\frac{15+1}{3}\right)\right\}\right] = ?$

$\Rightarrow 40 \div \left[15 \div \left\{24 \div \frac{16}{3}\right\}\right] = ?$

$\Rightarrow 40 \div \left[15 \div \left\{3 \times \frac{3}{2}\right\}\right] = ?$

$\Rightarrow 40 \div \left[\frac{15}{\frac{9}{2}}\right] = ?$

$\Rightarrow ? = \frac{40}{\frac{10}{3}}$

$\Rightarrow ? = 12$

Hence, the correct option is (B).

44. In the given $\triangle PQR$

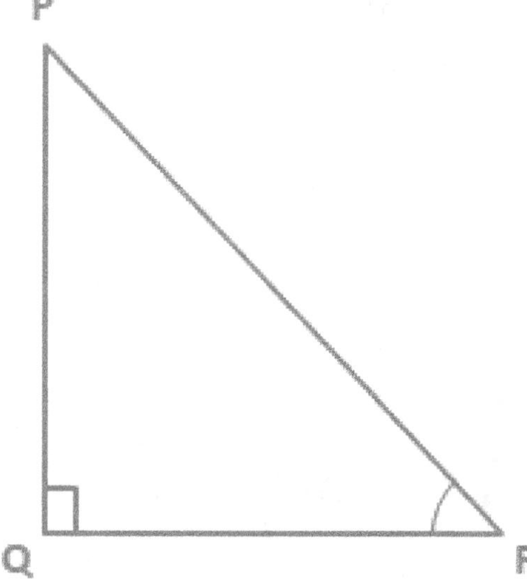

$\Rightarrow \cos P = \frac{base}{hypotenuse} = \frac{PQ}{PR} = \frac{3}{5}$

$\Rightarrow \sin P = \frac{perpendicular}{hypotenuse} = \frac{QR}{PR}$

But, $\sin P = \sqrt{(1 - \cos^2 P)} = \sqrt{1 - \frac{9}{25}} = \sqrt{\frac{16}{25}} = \frac{4}{5}$

$\Rightarrow \frac{QR}{PR} = \frac{4}{5}$

Now, $\cos R = \frac{perpendicular}{hypotenuse} = \frac{QR}{PR}$

$$\therefore \cos R = \frac{4}{5}$$

Hence, the correct option is (C).

45. We know that, Area $=$ Length $\times$ Breadth

According to the given question,

$$= 12 \times 20$$

$$= 240$$

New area $= 12 \times \frac{100+20}{100} \times 20 \times \frac{100+10}{100}$

$$= 316.8$$

Percentage change in the area $= \frac{(316.8-240)}{240} \times 100$

$$= 32\%$$

Hence, the correct option is (C).

46. Given expression,

$$5\frac{1}{5} + 2\frac{2}{15} + 3\frac{2}{3} = ? + 9$$

$$\Rightarrow ? + 9 = \frac{26}{5} + \frac{32}{15} + \frac{11}{3}$$

$$\Rightarrow ? + 9 = \frac{78+32+55}{15} = \frac{165}{15} = 11 - 9 = 2$$

Hence, the correct option is (A).

47. According to the question,

Amount $= 3P$

$$SI = 3P - P = 2P$$

We know that,

$$SI = \frac{(P \times T \times R)}{100}$$

So,

$$\Rightarrow 2P = \frac{(P \times 12.5 \times R)}{100}$$

$$\Rightarrow R = \frac{100}{12.5} = 16\%$$

Hence, the correct option is (B).

48. Let the number of boys be 5x and the number of girls be 9x at the party

Given that there are 99 girls at the party,

So,

$\Rightarrow$ 9x = 99

$\Rightarrow$ x = 11

Total number of Persons at the party = Number of boys + Number of girls

$\Rightarrow$ Total number of Persons at the party = 5x + 9x = 14x

$\Rightarrow$ Total number of Persons at the party = 14 × 11

$\therefore$ Total number of Persons at the party = 154

Hence, the correct option is (D).

49. According to the question,

Factors of 20 = 1, 2, 4, 5, 10, 20

Factors of 28 = 1, 2, 4, 7, 14, 28

$\therefore$ H.C.F. = 4

L.C.M of 20, 28 = 2×2×4×7 = 140

$\therefore$ H.C.F and L.C.M. of 20, 28 are 4 and 140.

Hence, the correct option is (D).

50. Sale price $= S.P =$ Rs. 517

Discount $= 6\%$

Marked price $= M.P$

$$S.P = (1 - 0.06)M.P$$

$$\Rightarrow M \cdot P = \frac{S.P}{0.94} = \frac{517}{0.94} = 550$$

Hence, the correct option is (C).

51. The sentence is talking in a general sense. It is stating a universal truth. So, the present tense should be used. The word 'take' should replace 'took' to make the sentence grammatically correct.

Correct Sentence: We are what our thoughts have made us; so take care about what you think.

Hence, the correct option is (C).

52. The usage of the word 'offend' is incorrect. It should be 'offence' meaning 'a breach of a law or rule; an illegal act' to make the sentence grammatically correct.

Correct sentence: Stringent penalties have a lower chance of being imposed, as compared to fines that are proportionate to the offence.

Hence, the correct option is (C).

53. To 'atone for' one's mistakes/ errors/ failings/ sins is to make up and repent for them.

Correct sentence: Pilgrims gather here to atone for their sins.

Hence, the correct option is (D).

54. The only word that can fit here is 'is' which conveys a proper meaning. It conveys that the person thought that Serena was a very lucky person.

Correct sentence: She kept thinking, "How lucky Serena is!"

Hence, the correct option is (C).

55. 'Each other' is used when referring to two people and 'one another' is used when referring to more than two people.

Correct sentence: The four friends are always ready to go to one another rescue.

Hence, the correct option is (B).

56. Opulent means costly and luxurious or wealthy.

Penurious means extremely poor; poverty-stricken.

Other words:

Palatial means resembling a palace in being spacious and splendid.

Sedative means promoting calm or inducing sleep.

Luxurious means extremely comfortable or elegant, especially when involving great expense.

The meaning of 'penurious' is opposite to that of 'opulent'.

Hence, the correct option is (C).

57. Palliate means to reduce the severity of a disease or its symptoms.

Relieve means to cause to make the disease less severe.

Other options:

Accuse means to say that someone is responsible for a crime.

Condemn means to criticize something or someone strongly.

Exacerbate means making a problem or a negative feeling worse.

Hence, the correct option is (B).

58. Clamorous means making a loud and confused noise.

Suppression means the act of keeping something from happening.

Other options:

Noisy means making or given to making a lot of noise.

Confusion means uncertainty about what is happening, intended or required.

Disturbance means the interruption of a settled and peaceful condition.

Hence, the correct option is (D).

59. Arbitrary means something is based on random choice or chance.

Random means to be done by chance or without any conscious decision.

Other words:

Methodical means to do things in a very ordered and careful way.

Penetrable means allowing things to pass-through.

Artful means clever or skilful.

Hence, the correct option is (C).

60. Penchant means a strong liking for something.

Fondness means a great liking for something or someone.

Other words:

Indifference means lack of interest or concern.

Revulsion means a sense of disgust, feeling that something is unpleasant.

Disgust means a feeling of revulsion or strong disapproval aroused by something unpleasant or offensive.

Hence, the correct option is (D).

61. Hearsay means a piece of information received from someone that might or might not be true (rumour).

Buzz means gossip, rumour, a piece of information heard from others that may not be true.

Other words:

Testimony means a formal written statement that something is true.

Realize means become fully aware of (something) as a fact; understand clearly.

Declare means say something in a solemn and emphatic manner.

Hence, the correct option is (C).

62. The meaning of the idiom 'Lend me your ear' is to ask for someone's full attention.

Sentence usage: My parents are always willing to lend an ear and offer me some helpful advice.

Hence, the correct option is (A).

63. 'Pedal to the metal' means we do something with extremely huge efforts and speed in order to push forward.

Sentence usage: If you put the pedal to the metal, you will finish this work within two days.

Hence, the correct option is (D).

64. 'Tongue in cheek' refers to something that is not serious, not sincere, and is intended to highlight irony in a funny way.

Sentence usage: His work is a tongue-in-cheek perspective on the patriarchal norms of society.

Hence, the correct option is (A).

65. Jinx means someone or something that brings bad luck.

Other words:

Felicitous means used to describe something as suitable / right because it expresses the desired thought.

Adventitious means happening by chance or by accident.

Providential means happening exactly when needed.

Hence, the correct option is (C).

66. Graffiti means words or drawings (especially humorous/funny/rude in nature) made on walls or doors.

Splotch means a large uneven mark or stain.

Smudge means a mark with no particular shape.

Streak means a long thin line or mark which is usually different in color from its surroundings.

Hence, the correct option is (C).

67. Nirvana means a state of freedom in which one is free from suffering and desires.

Other words:

Woe means great sorrow or sadness.

Depression means a mood disorder marked by low mood and feelings of sadness.

Despondency means unhappiness with no hope (similar to depression).

Hence, the correct option is (B).

68. When we consider the premise of the paragraph which uses the given line, we can deduce the meaning being asked. The second paragraph says, 'These problems demand bold responses. Yet, for the most part, mainstream economists seem preoccupied with marginal fixes' which implies that the economists are adopting minor (insignificant/marginal) solutions at a time when bold decisions can have the desirable significance. We need to take major decisions to solve bigger problems and not work towards solving minor fixes.

Hence, the correct option is (C).

69. The meaning of the word aversion is a feeling of dislike often marked with hostility (opposition) which makes the person avoid something.

Hence, the correct option is (A).

70. The word crippled means severely damaged by something or someone. The line 'Unemployment may not be a severe problem in most advanced countries currently' suggests that the economy of advanced countries is not crippled with unemployment. So, option (A) is incorrect.

According to the line used in the first paragraph of the passage, 'And climate change continues to pose an existential threat' option (B) is correct.

The full form of EIP is "Economics for Inclusive Prosperity" and not "Economics for Included Prosperity".

Hence, the correct option is (B).

71. Correct spelling is necessary.

The meaning of the word 'necessary' is 'required, essential'.

Hence, the correct option is (B).

72. The correct spelling is commemorate.

The meaning of the word commemorate means 'to honor the memory of someone or something with a ceremony or object'.

Hence, the correct option is (C).

73.

- Sentence 1- The first sentence should always introduce the subject of the paragraph. Sentence R provides an insight on the subject matter of the paragraph that is reading. The sentence tells us that reading is an essential skill-building activity.

- Sentence 2- The next sentence in this sequence is sentence P. It further explains how someone's language fluency is also determined by the quality of reading.

- Sentence 3- Sentence S is next in sequence as it explains the other things such as vocabulary enrichment, ideas collection, familiarization with different types of writing formats, speaking fluency that is also dependent on reading apart from language fluency. This is evident from the word 'besides', the sentence begins with besides showing how the discussion is continued.

- Sentence 4- The last sentence should always conclude the paragraph. Sentence Q talks about how reading has lost its importance in modern times.

The correct sequence is RPSQ.

Hence, the correct option is (D).

74.

- In the given sentence, the use of 'less' is grammatically incorrect. Here, in the given question, 'little' should be used.

- We know that 'less' is the comparative degree of 'little'. So, we should use less in comparative structures.

- Whereas, the given sentence does not have any kind of comparison. In the given sentence, 'was' should be used instead of 'are' because the given sentence is in the past tense.

Correct Sentence: There was too little space for Naveen to park his car in front of the shop.

Hence, the correct option is (B).

75. The underlined Part "aren't she" is grammatically wrong.

It should have "isn't". We know that singular question tag is followed by a singular negative question tag.

Correct Sentence: She is quite capable of looking after herself, isn't she?

Hence, the correct option is (C).

76. Aishbagh Stadium, Bhopal is one of the hockey stadiums of Madhya Pradesh.

Stadium	Details
Nehru Stadium, Indore	1. It is a cricket stadium with a capacity of about 25,000 spectators in it. 2. It is owned and operated by Indore Municipal Corporation. 3. It is home ground for Holkars in Ranji Trophy.
Aishbagh Stadium, Bhopal	1. It is a field hockey stadium with a capacity of more than 10,000 people in it. 2. It is owned and operated by Madhya Pradesh Government. 3. It is the home ground for Bhopal Badshahs, the World series hockey team.

Captain Roop Singh Stadium, Gwalior	1. It is a cricket stadium with a capacity of about 45,000 people in it. 2. It is owned by Madhya Pradesh Cricket Association (MPCA) and operated by Gwalior Division Cricket Association.
Holkar Stadium, Indore	1. It is formerly known as Maharani Usharaje Trust Cricket Ground which is a cricket stadium. 2. It has a seating capacity of about 30,000 people in it.

Hence, the correct option is (B).

77. To train the tribal sportspersons in traditional Archery, the 'Archery Sports Academy' has been established in Rajasthan at Udaipur.

- Archery Association of India (AAI) came into existence in 1973, with the primary objective to organize, encourage, and promote the game of Archery in the country by providing proper training facilities to Indian Archers.
- Modern FITA/Olympic Archery came to India in 1970 before the game had been chosen as part of the Olympic discipline in Munich, West Germany in 1972.
- Archery Association of India is the national governing body of archery in India.
- Its headquarters are located in New Delhi.
- Its current president is Arjun Munda.
- AAI is a non-profit, government-funded organization affiliated with World Archery Federation (IAF), Asian Archery Federation (AAF), and Indian Olympic Association (IOA) and recognized by the Ministry of Youth Affairs and Sports of India.

Hence, the correct option is (A).

78. Prithvi Shaw has become the 1st player to breach the 800-run mark in a single edition of the Vijay Hazare Trophy.

He achieved the feat during his 73-run knock against UP in the ongoing final of Vijay Hazare Trophy at the Arun Jaitley Stadium in Delhi, in March 2021. A few days back he broke MS Dhoni and Virat's record of the highest individual score by an Indian batsman in a List A chase.

Hence, the correct option is (D).

79.

- Netflix's India Original series "Delhi Crime", helmed by Indian-Canadian director Richie Mehta, has bagged the best drama series honor at the 48th International Emmy Awards.
- The series deconstructs the case of the 23 -year-old physiotherapy intern who was abducted and gang-raped in a moving bus on the night of December 16, 2012.
- The show was released in the year 2019.

Hence, the correct option is (B).

80.

- Vivekananda Rock Memorial is located in Vavathurai, Kanyakumari.
- It was built in 1970 in the honor of Swami Vivekananda.
- It is surrounded by the Laccadive Sea.

Hence, the correct option is (C).

81. Paris is the capital of France.

Country	France
Capital	Paris
President	Emmanuel Macron
Prime Minister	Jean Castex
Currency	Euro, CFP franc

Hence, the correct option is (C).

82.

- Bindusara was the son of the dynasty's founder Chandragupta, and the father of Ashoka.
- He was the second Mauryan emperor of India.
- As per estimates, Bindusara ascended the throne around 297 BCE Bindusara was also known by the name Amritghata.
- To the Greeks, he was known as Amitrochates.

Hence, the correct option is (D).

83. Special Drawing Rights are assets that are maintained by the International Monetary Fund (IMF).

- The unit of SDR is XDR. These rights were created in 1969.
- There are only five currencies in the world which are associated with SDR and those currencies are Chinese Yuan, Japanese Yen, American dollar, Euro, Pound Sterling.

Hence, the correct option is (D).

84.

- Vishnugupta was the other name of Chanakya.
- He was born around 350 BC and is known for his being the chief architect of the Mauryan empire and writing the pioneering work in the Economics and Political Science that is Arthashastra.
- Chanakya was identified with Vishnugupta in a verse in his Arthashastra and also in Panchatantra of Gupta age by Vishnu Sharma.

Hence, the correct option is (B).

85. Pattachitra:

- It is a traditional cloth-based scroll painting from Odisha.
- It became an important art form with the ornamentation of Lord Jagannath in the innermost sanctum.
- The painting depicts the story of Lord Jagannath, his brother Balram and sister Subhadra, Krishna Lila.

Hence, the correct option is (B).

86.

- Palk Strait is a strait that separates India and Sri Lanka.
- It connects the Bay of Bengal with Palk Bay.

Hence, the correct option is (D).

87. Air pollution is caused by smoke.

Air pollution is caused by the release of pollutants in the air that can cause harm to the planet and human life.

Hence, the correct option is (C).

88. Red Fort in Delhi was built by the Mughal Emporer Shah Jahan, his era was considered as the 'Golden Age' for architectures. Some of the popular structures built during his rule are as follows:

- Red Fort or Lal Quila, Delhi
- Taj Mahal, Agra
- Jama Masjid, Delhi
- Jama Masjid, Agra

Hence, the correct option is (D).

89.

- The Drafting Committee of the Constitution was chaired by Dr. B.R Ambedkar.
- B. R. Ambedkar was a wise constitutional expert, he had studied the constitutions of about 60 countries.
- Ambedkar is recognized as the "Father of the Constitution of India".

Hence, the correct option is (B).

90.

- The minor planets of the inner solar system are called Asteroids.
- A large majority of asteroids are found between the planets, Mars and Jupiter.
- Asteroids are composed of minerals and rock.

Hence, the correct option is (C).

91. Article 326 of the Constitution provides that the elections to the House of the People and the Legislative Assembly of every State shall be based on adult suffrage.

For that, a person should not be less than 18 years of age.

Hence, the correct option is (C).

92. A landslide is any geologic process in which gravity causes rock, soil, artificial fill, or a combination of the three to move down a slope.

Causes of Landslide:

- Slow weathering of rocks
- Soil erosion
- Earthquakes
- Volcanic activity

Hence, the correct option is (D).

93.

- Primary colours are those colours which when mixed in specific proportions can form any colour.
- The spectral colours i.e. blue, red and green are the primary colours.
- Secondary colours such as yellow, magenta etc. can be produced by mixing two primary colours in the right proportion.
- Any two colours which when added produce white light are known as complementary colours.

Hence, the correct option is (A).

94. Space pen is a ballpoint pen invented by Paul C. Fisher and made to work in zero gravity, underwater, and at any angle (even upside down). It is also known as Zero Gravity Pen and Fisher Space Pen, and it is sold by Fisher Space Pen Company.

Hence, the correct option is (A).

95.

Generation	Period	Main Computers
I	1940-52	EDVAC, EDSAC, UNIVAC
I	1952-64	IBM-700, 1 BM-1401,1 BM-1620, CDC-1604, CDC-3600
III	1964-71	IBM-360, IBM-370, NCR-395, CDC-1700
IV	1971-Present	APPLE, DCM

Hence, the correct option is (A).

96.

- A programming language is a language that is used to provide instructions to a computer to perform certain specific tasks. Example: C, C++, Java, Python, etc.
- Frontline is a magazine that discusses various topics such as politics, economy, World affairs, etc.

Hence, the correct option is (C).

97.

- The capital of Indonesia is Jakarta.
- The currency of Indonesia is the Indonesian rupiah.
- Indonesia is roughly 4483 kilometers (2786 miles) from India.

Hence, the correct option is (C).

98.

- Annealing is the process that is used to strengthens the glass.
- It is a process in which glass is heated to a specified temperature and then is allowed to cool at a very slow and controlled rate.
- This process is also carried out to relieve residual internal stresses introduced during manufacturing.

- Case-hardening is the process in which the surface of a metal object is hardened, while the deeper layer remains soft.

- Normalizing is a heat treatment process which is used to regulate internal material stress.

- Tempering is a heat treatment process used to increase the toughness of iron-based alloys.

Hence, the correct option is (C).

99. In Jan 2021, Khelo India Ice Hockey Tournament has been organized at Chiktan in Kàrgil, Ladakh.

SDM Shakar Chiktan and the Chief Guest of the event Kacho Asgar Ali khan inaugurated the tournament in the presence of ZPEO Chiktan Ghulam Rasool along with in-charge police post-Chikan.

Hence, the correct option is (B).

100.

- Kuala Lumpur was named as the World Book Capital 2020 by UNESCO in September 2018.

- Malaysia's capital, Kuala Lumpur was selected because of its ongoing development of a knowledge-based society, strong focus on inclusive education and it's population's easy access to reading materials.

- It will undertake a range of initiatives to promote books and reading over the year, beginning World Book and Copyright Day i.e. April 23, 2020.

Hence, the correct option is (B).

General Intelligence and Reasoning

Q.1 In the question given below, two statements are given followed by four conclusions I, II, III, and IV. You have to consider the two statements to be true even if they seem to be at variance from commonly known facts. You have to decide which of the given conclusion, if any, follow from the given statements.

Statements:

All goats are tigers

All tigers are lions

Conclusions:

I. All tigers are goats

II. All lions are tigers

III. No goat is a lion

IV. No lion is a goat

A. Either II or III follows
B. Either II or IV follows
C. Either I or III follows
D. None of the conclusions follow

Q.2 Identify which one of the given alternatives will be another member of the group?

Chandigarh: Puducherry: Lakshadweep:?

A. Gujarat
B. Maharashtra
C. Delhi
D. Sikkim

Ques (3-4):Direction: Find the odd one out.

Q.3 3, 5, 11, 14, 17, 21
A. 21
B. 17
C. 14
D. 3

Q.4 8, 27, 64, 100, 125, 216, 343
A. 27
B. 100
C. 125
D. 343

Q.5 In the following question, select the odd word pair from the given alternatives.
A. Car – Petrol
B. Bulb – Electricity
C. Pen – Ink
D. Pencil – Paper

Q.6 In the given figure, how many are musical toys?

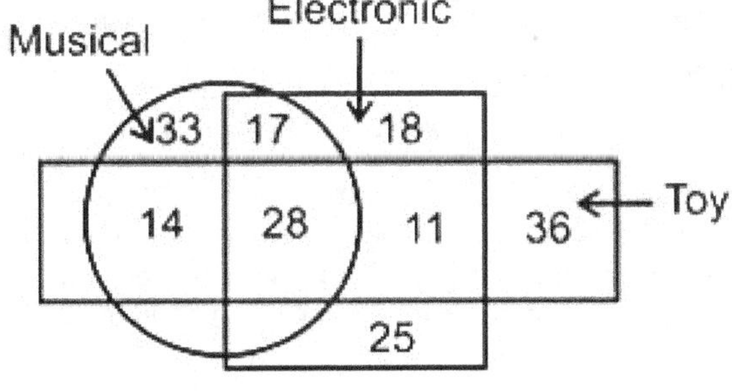

A. 53
B. 61
C. 42
D. 45

Q.7 In a certain code, **FIRE** is coded as **DGPC**. What will be the last letter of the code word for **SHOT**?
A. Q
B. R
C. S
D. P

Q.8 In a certain code the word '**PUSH**' is written as '**NWQJ**', then how will '**CATTLE**' written in the same code?
A. ACRVJG
B. ACRJVG
C. CARVJG
D. CARVGJ

Q.9 In the question given below, two statements are given followed by four conclusions I, II, III, and IV. You have to consider the two statements to be true even if they seem to be at variance from commonly known facts. You have to decide which of the given conclusion, if any, follow from the given statements.

Statements:

All crows are black

Some black things are beautiful

Conclusions:

I. Some black things are beautiful

II. Some beautiful things are black

A. Only conclusion I follows
B. Only conclusion II follows
C. Both conclusions I and II follows
D. Neither conclusion I nor II follows

Q.10 Directions: In the following question, select the one which is different from the other three responses:
A. Shabby – Thriving
B. Solicit – Oppose
C. Slander – Approve
D. Subvert – Demolish

Ques (11-12):Direction: What will come at the place of the question mark?

Q.11 4, 7, 12, 19, 28, ?
A. 49
B. 36
C. 30
D. 39

Q.12 10, 100, 200, 310, ?
A. 430
B. 420
C. 410
D. 400

Q.13 In the following question, select the related word from the given alternatives.

Factory : Production :: Hospital

A. Doctor
B. Nurse
C. Treatment
D. Building

Q.14 Find out which of the figures (A), (B), (C) and (D) can be formed from the pieces given in figure X? (using all pieces only once)

(X)

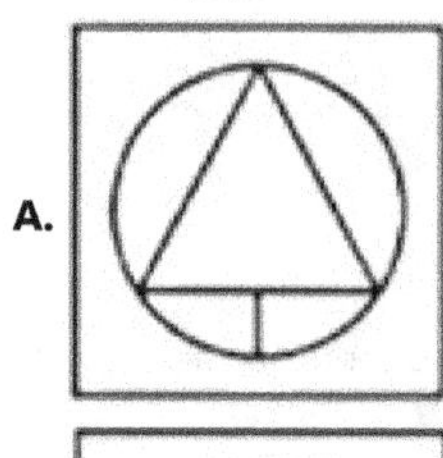

A.

C.

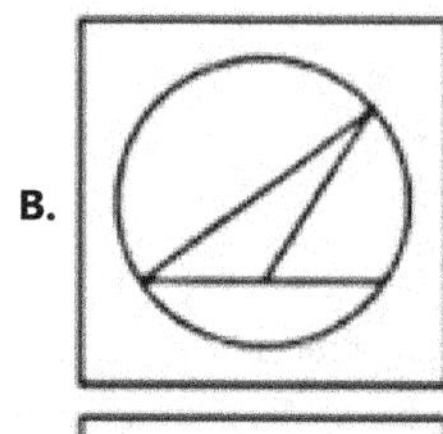

B.

D.

Q.15 Select the related letter from the given alternatives.

YWZX : USVT :: MKNL : ?

A. IGGH　　**B.** IGJH　　**C.** IGJJ　　**D.** IGHH

Q.16 In the following questions, which one set of letters when sequentially placed at the gaps in the given letter series shall complete it?

b _ ac _ cc _ cb _ ab _ ac

A. aabba　　**B.** bbaac　　**C.** cbaba　　**D.** abbbc

Q.17 A series is given, with one term missing. Choose the correct alternative from the given ones that will complete the series.

KlMnO, qRsTu, WxYzA, cDeFg,?

A. iJkLm　　**B.** HiJkL　　**C.** IjKlM　　**D.** hIjKl

Q.18 Find the wrong term in the following series.

1, 8, 28, 64, 125, 216

A. 8　　**B.** 64　　**C.** 28　　**D.** 125

Ques (19-20):Direction: Which interchange of signs will make the following equation correct?

Q.19 $(8 - 8) + 8 \times 32 = 64$

A. ×, +, −　　**B.** −, ÷, +　　**C.** +, ÷, +　　**D.** +, ÷,×

Q.20 $64 - 8 \times 9 \div 8 = 64$

A. + and −　　**B.** ÷ and ×　　**C.** + and ÷　　**D.** − and ÷

Q.21 If + stands for division; × stands for addition; − stands for multiplication; ÷ stands for subtraction, which of the following is correct?

1. $15 \div 5 \times 2 - 6 + 3 = 28$
2. $15 \times 5 + 2 - 6 \div 3 = 56.5$
3. $15 + 5 - 2 \div 6 \times 3 = 3$
4. $15 - 5 + 2 \times 6 \div 3 = 41$

A. 3　　**B.** 1　　**C.** 2　　**D.** 4

Q.22 Identify the diagram that best represents the relationship among the given classes.

Staff, Manager, Worker

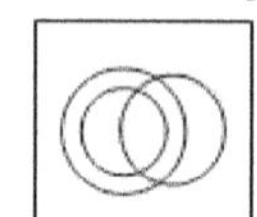 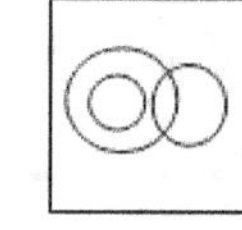 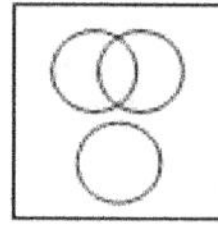

(A)　　　(B)　　　(C)　　　(D)

A. (A)　　**B.** (B)　　**C.** (C)　　**D.** (D)

Q.23 If in a certain code language, SASHWATA is written as RBTGVBUZ then which word would be written as BSPRRCPV?

A. CROOSBOW　　　**B.** CROSSBOW
C. KROSBOOW　　　**D.** CROSSBOX

Q.24 In the given figure, how many cardboard boxes are not white?

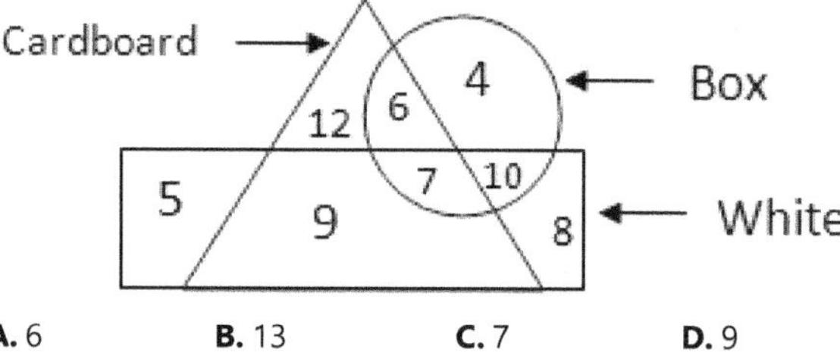

A. 6　　**B.** 13　　**C.** 7　　**D.** 9

Q.25 Direction: Arrange the given words in the order in which they will be arranged in a dictionary and choose the one that comes Third.

i) Dagger
ii) Dangle
iii) Daisy
iv) Damp
v) Dapper

A. Daisy　　**B.** Damp　　**C.** Dagger　　**D.** Dangle

Numerical Aptitude/ Quantitative Ability

Q.26 What is the sum (in Rs.) of money which will become Rs. 26620 at the rate of 10% per annum at compound interest in three years?

A. 20000　　**B.** 22000　　**C.** 25000　　**D.** 26000

Q.27 A circular pond is surrounded by a concrete wall 4 m wide. If the area of the concrete wall surrounding the pond is $\frac{11}{25}$ that of the pond, then the radius (in m) of the pond:

A. 12　　**B.** 20　　**C.** 18　　**D.** 16

Q.28 The lengths of two sides of a right-angled triangle that contain the right angle are a and b, respectively. Three squares are drawn on the three sides of the triangle on the outer side. What is the total area of the triangle and the three squares?

A. $2(a^2 + b^2) + ab$

B. $2(a^2 + b^2) + 2.5ab$

C. $2(a^2 + b^2) + 0.5ab$

D. $2.5(a^2 + b^2)$

Q.29 The average number of days in four consecutive months of year is 30.75. How many such combinations of four consecutive months are possible?

A. 0   **B.** 1   **C.** 2   **D.** 3

Q.30 Annual incomes of Amit and Veer are in the ratio 3 : 2, while the ratio of their expenditure is 5 : 3. If at the end of the year each saves Rs. 1000, then what is the annual income of Amit?

A. Rs. 9000   **B.** Rs. 8000   **C.** Rs. 7000   **D.** Rs. 6000

Q.31 If each edge of cube is increased by 50%, so what will be percentage increase in its surface area?

A. 75%   **B.** 100%   **C.** 125%   **D.** 150%

Q.32 The cost price of an article is Rs. 120. If it is sold for Rs. 102, then what is the loss percentage?

A. 11   **B.** 12   **C.** 15   **D.** 10

Q.33 A profit of 20% is made after giving a discount of 10% on an article. If the marked price of the article is Rs. 3000, then what is its cost price (in Rs.)?

A. 3060   **B.** 2250   **C.** 2500   **D.** 2750

Q.34 What is the value of $(37 + 23)^2 - (37 - 23)^2$?

A. 1908   **B.** 1602   **C.** 1702   **D.** 3404

Q.35 An amount invested at simple interest gives Rs 720 interest at 12% per annum in 3 years. What is the principal amount (in Rs)?

A. 2400   **B.** 1500   **C.** 3000   **D.** 2000

Q.36 An insurance company pays Rs. $3,81,800$ after a new car worth Rs. $4,60,000$ gets completely damaged in an accident. What percent of the car was insured?

A. 83%   **B.** 82%   **C.** 76%   **D.** 78%

Q.37 Solve:

$$38 \div \left[1 - \frac{1}{2} + 2\frac{2}{3}\right] = ?$$

A. 10   **B.** 11   **C.** 12   **D.** 14

Q.38 If $3\cot\theta = 4\cos\theta$, then what is the value of $\cos^2\theta$?

A. $\frac{2}{16}$ **B.** $\frac{-1}{8}$ **C.** $\frac{7}{16}$ **D.** $\frac{9}{16}$

Q.39 What is the simplified value of $\left(\frac{\sec A}{\cot A + \tan A}\right)^2$?

A. $1 - \cos^2 A$ **B.** $2\sin^2 A$

C. $\sec^2 A$ **D.** $\csc^2 A$

Q.40 Solve:

$$\frac{0.796 \times 0.796 - 0.204 \times 0.204}{0.796 - 0.204}$$

A. 0   **B.** 1   **C.** 2   **D.** 3

Q.41 ABDC is a parallelogram in which diagonals AD and BC intersect at O. AE and DF are perpendiculars on BC at E and F, respectively. Which of the following is NOT true?

A. $\triangle ABC \cong \triangle DCB$ **B.** $\triangle AOE \cong \triangle DOF$

C. $\triangle AEB \cong \triangle DFC$ **D.** $\triangle ADC \cong \triangle ABD$

Q.42 If the selling price is Rs. 100 more than the cost price and profit is 20%, then what is the cost price?

A. 600   **B.** 1000   **C.** 800   **D.** 500

Q.43 The ratio of two numbers is $7:10$. If their difference is 96, then what is the smallest number?

A. 210   **B.** 224   **C.** 320   **D.** 276

Q.44 The sides BA and DE of a regular pentagon are produced to meet at F. What is the measure of $\angle EFA$?

A. 60°   **B.** 36°   **C.** 72°   **D.** 54°

Q.45 A and B together can do a piece of work in 10 days and A alone can do it in 30 days. B alone can do the work in how many days?

A. 15   **B.** 12   **C.** 18   **D.** 24

Ques (46-47):Direction: Answer the following questions using the pie chart given.

The total marks scored by them all is 374.

Marks scored in SBI PO Exam

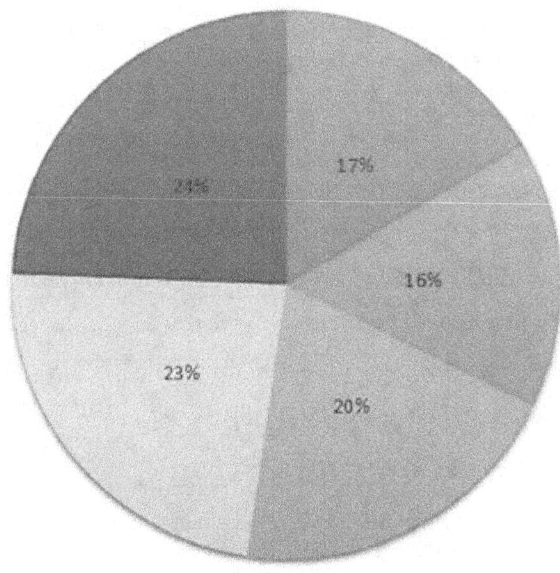

Q.46 What is the approximate difference between the marks scored by the top 2 students and the bottom 2 students?

A. 61   **B.** 45   **C.** 52   **D.** 67

Q.47 What is the approximate central angle subtended by Rakesh in the pie diagram?

A. 72 degrees   **B.** 65 degrees

C. 75 degrees   **D.** 68 degrees

Ques (48-49):Direction: Answer the following questions using the pie chart given.

Total marks scored by them all is 374.

Marks scored in SBI PO Exam

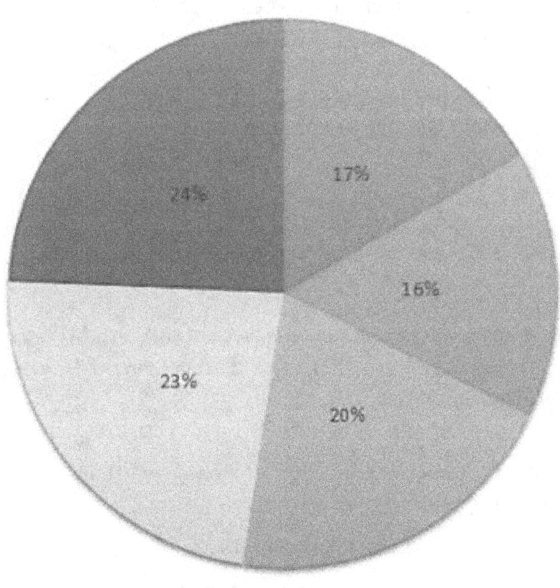

Q.48 What are the average marks scored by the topper and Ramesh in the exam?

A. 92   **B.** 99   **C.** 77   **D.** 88

Q.49 What is the difference between the angle subtended by Ravi and Ram in the pie diagram?

A. 3.5 degree   **B.** 5 degrees

C. 4 degrees   **D.** 3.6 degrees

Q.50 Rs. 6400 are divided among three workers in the ratio $\frac{3}{5} : 2 : \frac{5}{3}$. The share (in Rs) of the second worker is:

A. 3000   **B.** 2000   **C.** 25000   **D.** 2700

General English & Comprehension

Ques (51-52):Direction: Below is given a sentence that is divided in four parts and out of these parts one has an error. Mark that part as your answer if the sentence is correct, mark no error your answer.

Q.51 None (A)/but (B)/am(C)/responsible.(D)/ No Error

A. (A)   **B.** (B)   **C.** (C)   **D.** (D)

Q.52 Don't make stupid excuses. You flunked the exam and I was still furious.

A. Don't make stupid excuses

B. You flunked the exam and

C. I was still furious

D. No error

Ques (53-55):Direction: Fill in the blank with the correct word.

Q.53 We were starving so we really dug _____ when the food finally did arrive.

A. In   **B.** Into   **C.** Up   **D.** Deep

Q.54 If you want to get _____, hone your communication skills.

A. Over   **B.** Upto   **C.** Ahead   **D.** Up

Q.55 The value of education and its _____ can be understood from various aspects of life.

A. Significance   **B.** Significant

C. Signify   **D.** Significantly

Q.56 Doctors are hopeful that he has been cured of the dreaded virus, though they point out it's a little too early to say _______.

A. Rather conclusive   **B.** So conclusively

C. So conclusive   **D.** Most conclusively

Ques (57-58):Direction: In the following question, a sentence has been given in Direct/Indirect speech. Out of the 4 alternatives suggested, select the one which best expresses the same sentence in indirect/Direct speech.

Q.57 "Matthew, the standup comedy circuit is booming right now, maybe you should try your luck there," Chandler said.

A. Chandler suggested to Matthew that the standup circuit was booming right then and that he should try his luck there

B. Chandler suggested to Matthew that the standup circuit was booming right then and that he should try his luck there

C. Chandler urged Matthew to try his luck in the standup circuit as it was booming

D. Chandler requested Matthew to try his luck in the stand-up circuit as it was booming

Q.58 Danneel urged Genevieve to run for student body president.

A. "Genevieve, maybe you should run for student body President." Danneel said

B. "Genevieve you should definitely run for student body President." Danneel said

C. "Genevieve, you could run for student body President." Danneel said

D. "Danneel, you could run for student body President." Genevieve said

Ques (59-60):Direction: A sentence has been given in Active/Passive voice. Out of the four alternatives suggested, select the one which best expresses the same sentence in Passive/Active voice.

Q.59 Kevin ran over the dog while learning how to drive.

A. While learning how to drive, Kevin ran over the dog

B. While driving, the dog was run over by Kevin

C. While learning how to drive, the dog was being run over by Kevin

D. While learning how to drive, the dog was run over by Kevin

Q.60 Raymond was bitten by a snake on his walk in Central Park.

A. Something bit Raymond on his walk to Central Park

B. A snake bit Raymond on his walk in Central Park

C. A snake will bite Raymond on his walk in Central Park

D. A snake has bitten Raymond on his walk in Central Park

Ques (61-64):Direction: Choose the word which is the opposite in meaning to the given word.

Q.61 Scorn

A. Contempt
B. Rapture
C. Ascetic
D. Nimble

Q.62 August

A. Sparse
B. Majestic
C. Illicit
D. Render

Q.63 Throng

A. Teem
B. Strand
C. Abandon
D. Jilt

Q.64 Retort

A. Counter
B. Rebuff
C. Retaliate
D. Plea

Ques (65-67):Direction: In the following question, out of the four alternatives, select the alternative which best expresses the meaning of the idiom/phrase.

Q.65 Get the show on the road

A. Rating something higher on your priority list

B. Putting up a plan or idea into action

C. Getting your things well organized

D. Trying out every possibility to get a result

Q.66 Apple of the eye is something that one

A. Chooses for pleasure

B. Cherishes above everything else

C. Selects minutely

D. Never judges

Q.67 Sit on the fence.

A. To have a greater view while sitting on the fence

B. To be unable or unwilling to commit oneself

C. To be worthless

D. To work lazily

Ques (68-72):Direction: Read the passage carefully and select the best answer to each question out of the given four alternatives.

Culture is defined as a people's way of life. It entails how they dress, how they speak, the type of food they eat, the manner in which they worship, and their art among many other things. Indian culture, therefore, is the Indians' way of life. Because of the population diversity, there is immense variety in Indian culture. The Indian culture is a blend of various cultures belonging to diverse religions, castes; regions follow their own tradition and culture. Indian Culture is one of the oldest cultures in the world. India had an urban civilization even during the Bronze age. The Indus Valley Civilization (HarappanCivilization) dates back to 3300 BC – 1300 BC. Distinct cultures different from each other co-exist together in a single country. Thus, in India, there is unity amidst vast cultural diversity. The way people live in India is reflected in their culture. Unity in Diversity: India is a land of unity in diversity where people of different sects, caste, and religion live together. India is also called the land of unity in diversity as different groups of people co-operate with each other to live in a single society. Unity in diversity has also become the strength of India.

Secularism: The word secularism means equality, impartiality, etc. towards all religions. India is a secular country, which means, equal treatment of all the religions present in India.

Traditions: traditional cultural values Gestures

- Touching feet of elders: Indian tradition has rich cultural values. In India, younger show great respect to their elders. They touch the feet of their elders daily after waking up and especially on festive occasions or before starting an important work.

- Namaste: The gesture of the Namaste greeting is also part of the Indian culture. People greet each other by saying "Namaste" while joining their hands. "Namaste" means "Hello". (Also read, the meaning of Namaste here.)

- Most Indians have a habit of shaking their heads while talking.

Q.68 If I am a cultural, well-behaved Indian, what won't I do?

A. Touch the feet of the elders

B. Join my hands while doing 'Namaste'

C. Wake up early in the morning, especially on the festive occasions

D. Shake my head as a habit while talking

Q.69 Why is India called a unity in diversity?

A. Different groups of people co-operate with each other

B. People of different sects, caste and religion live together

C. It is strength of India

D. All of these

Q.70 Which of the following is not true according to the passage?

A. Culture entails how people dress

B. Culture entails how people speak

C. Culture entails how people worship

D. Culture entails what drawing people draw

Q.71 Based on the above passage, which of the following is NOT true about Indian culture?

A. Indian culture dates back to 3300 BC – 1300 BC

B. Envy religion follows their own tradition and customs

C. Every religion is treated equally in India

D. In India there is unity in diversity

Q.72 What is the reason behind the immense variety in Indian culture?

A. Blend of various cultures

B. Population diversity

C. Cultural diversity

D. Secularism

Q.73 One who is blamed for wrongdoings or mistakes of others.

A. Assailant   **B.** Mugger
C. Scapegoat   **D.** Slasher

Ques (74-75):Directions: Read the following information carefully and answer the question given below-

The questions consist of a set of labelled sentences. Out of the four options given, select the most logical order of the sentences to form a coherent paragraph.

Q.74 A. 15 finalists of more than 12,000 original registrants
B. and theories in the physical or life sciences
C. from around the world who submitted engaging and
D. imaginative videos to demonstrate difficult scientific concepts
E. the three Indian students are among

A. ACDEB   **B.** DAECB   **C.** EABCD   **D.** EACDB

Q.75 A. dozens of UNESCO World Heritage sites
B. in the Mediterranean such as Venice, the Leaning Tower of Pisa
C. and the Medieval City of Rhodes
D. are under severe threat of coastal erosion and
E. flooding due to rising sea levels within the next 100 years

A. BCDEA   **B.** EDBCA   **C.** ABCDE   **D.** ABEDC

General Awareness

Q.76 The number of players in a team of basketball is:
A. 9   **B.** 5   **C.** 6   **D.** 11

Q.77 The first Rajiv Gandhi Khel Ratna Award was given to whom?

[Madhya Pradesh Public Service Commission (MPPSC), 2018]

A. Viswanathan Anand   **B.** Geet Sethi
C. Sachin Tendulkar   **D.** Dhanraj Pillai

Q.78 Atomic number corresponds to the number of _______.
A. Neutrons   **B.** Deutrons
C. Protons   **D.** Electrons

Q.79 Which of the following Union Territories has representation in Rajya Sabha?
A. Andaman and Nicobar Islands
B. Chandigarh
C. Dadra and Nagar Haveli
D. Puducherry

Q.80 Bituminous coal contains _______ of carbon.
A. 81%   **B.** 66%   **C.** 58%   **D.** 91%

Q.81 What are sea waves generated by undersea earthquakes called?
A. Cirque   **B.** Tsunami   **C.** Scale   **D.** Kem

Q.82 Which neighboring country of India lies to the south of the Lakshadweep islands?
A. Sri Lanka   **B.** Bangladesh

C. Myanmar   **D.** Indonesia

Q.83 A boat full of iron nails is floating on water in a lake. When the iron nails are removed, the water level _____.
A. Rises
B. Falls
C. Cannot be determined
D. Remains constant

Q.84 The well-known painting "Bani Thani" belongs to the-
A. Bundi school   **B.** Jaipur school
C. Kangra school   **D.** Kishangarh school

Q.85 Which of the following temple is dedicated to lord sun?
A. Konark   **B.** Modhera
C. Martand   **D.** All of these

Q.86 How is electrical energy (W) related to electrical power?
A. $W = Pt$ **B.** $W = P^2 t$
C. $W = P + t$ **D.** $W = \frac{P}{t}$

Q.87 The 3D-object creation platform named "Poly" is operated by which technology major?
A. Microsoft   **B.** Google
C. Intel   **D.** Amazon

Q.88 First-ever radish crop has been grown in space by which organisation?
A. ISRO
B. NASA
C. European Space Agency
D. Russian Space Agency

Q.89 Which of following forests is known as the "the lungs of the planet earth"?
A. Amazon Rain Forest
B. Mangrove Forest
C. Tundra Forest
D. Taiga Forest

Q.90 National Heritage City Development and Augmentation Yojana (HRIDAY) is implemented in how many cities?
A. 8   **B.** 10   **C.** 11   **D.** 12

Q.91 Which among the following is associated with the provision of appointment of finance commission every 5 years to review the finances of the Panchayats in India?
A. 74th Amendment Act
B. 73rd Amendment Act
C. 77th Amendment Act
D. None of the above

Q.92 Which of the following elements were not found in the form of archaeological remains from Kalibanga?
A. Black bangles   **B.** Firepit
C. Ploughed field   **D.** Couple burial

Q.93 Integrated Child Protection Scheme was launched in the year?
A. 2009-2010   **B.** 2011-2012

C. 2013-2014 **D.** 2015-2016

Q.94 A computer cannot "boot" if it does not have the _____

A. Compiler **B.** Loader
C. Operating system **D.** Assembler

Q.95 Which among the following is INCORRECT pair of 'geographical indicator'?

A. Kangra Tea - Himachal Pradesh
B. Kotpad Handloom fabric - Rajasthan
C. Mysore Silk - Karnataka
D. Pochampally Ikat - Telangana

Q.96 MS-Word is an example of _____

A. An operating system
B. A processing device
C. Application software
D. An input device

Q.97 Who address on the 5th Asia Economic Dialogue (AED) 2021 that was held virtually under the theme "Post Covid-19 Global Trade and Finance Dynamics"?

A. Anurag Thakur **B.** Nirmala Sitharaman
C. Narendra Modi **D.** S. Jaishankar

Q.98 As per the data of the National Statistical Office (NSO), with an estimated GDP of ___% in Q3FY21, India has technically exited from recession.

A. 4 **B.** 1.6 **C.** 0.9 **D.** 0.4

Q.99 Which country's largest bank, has launched the country's first India-dedicated publicly offered investment fund?

A. Nepal **B.** China **C.** Bhutan **D.** Japan

Q.100 Name the 1st Centre of Salt and Soda Ash Production of Tata Chemicals.

A. Mithapur (Gujarat)
B. Haldia (West Bengal)
C. Babrala (UP)
D. Nanded (Maharashtra)

// Smart Answer Sheet //

Correct — Percentage of students who answered correctly.　　**Skipped** — Percentage of students who skipped.

Q.	Ans.	Correct / Skipped	Q.	Ans.	Correct / Skipped	Q.	Ans.	Correct / Skipped	Q.	Ans.	Correct / Skipped	Q.	Ans.	Correct / Skipped	Q.	Ans.	Correct / Skipped
1	D	60.5 % / 1.26 %	18	C	49.58 % / 1.58 %	35	D	29.47 % / 3.98 %	52	C	69.06 % / 1.9 %	69	B	49.17 % / 1.87 %	86	A	46.79 % / 1.18 %
2	C	66.94 % / 1.64 %	19	D	62.71 % / 1.02 %	36	A	56.3 % / 1.45 %	53	A	67.95 % / 1.63 %	70	D	62.72 % / 1.8 %	87	B	44.4 % / 1.7 %
3	C	76.54 % / 0.0 %	20	D	41.43 % / 1.64 %	37	C	87.41 % / 0.0 %	54	C	47.98 % / 1.33 %	71	B	45.9 % / 1.42 %	88	B	41.27 % / 1.13 %
4	B	54.82 % / 1.41 %	21	A	45.03 % / 1.46 %	38	C	64.73 % / 1.96 %	55	A	46.77 % / 1.87 %	72	B	53.06 % / 1.85 %	89	A	46.63 % / 1.8 %
5	D	81.86 % / 0.0 %	22	B	41.26 % / 1.65 %	39	A	49.44 % / 1.63 %	56	B	47.1 % / 1.05 %	73	C	30.81 % / 3.0 %	90	D	55.13 % / 1.37 %
6	C	65.37 % / 1.97 %	23	B	49.44 % / 1.39 %	40	B	66.45 % / 1.98 %	57	B	52.9 % / 1.91 %	74	D	50.35 % / 1.67 %	91	B	61.05 % / 1.91 %
7	B	69.81 % / 1.72 %	24	A	45.99 % / 1.18 %	41	D	51.63 % / 1.72 %	58	B	47.2 % / 1.19 %	75	C	57.87 % / 1.76 %	92	D	69.14 % / 1.05 %
8	A	53.22 % / 1.24 %	25	B	62.09 % / 1.02 %	42	D	52.37 % / 1.13 %	59	D	45.43 % / 1.46 %	76	B	89.87 % / 0.0 %	93	A	68.73 % / 1.54 %
9	B	55.19 % / 1.51 %	26	A	49.62 % / 1.29 %	43	B	78.04 % / 0.0 %	60	B	79.49 % / 0.0 %	77	A	89.07 % / 0.0 %	94	C	86.2 % / 0.0 %
10	D	24.33 % / 4.36 %	27	B	46.74 % / 1.26 %	44	B	40.1 % / 1.17 %	61	A	19.32 % / 3.81 %	78	C	66.89 % / 1.77 %	95	B	15.32 % / 3.78 %
11	D	44.52 % / 1.45 %	28	C	60.24 % / 1.26 %	45	A	40.2 % / 1.38 %	62	B	41.43 % / 1.78 %	79	D	60.36 % / 1.31 %	96	C	80.18 % / 0.0 %
12	A	50.42 % / 1.3 %	29	C	64.6 % / 1.12 %	46	C	53.27 % / 1.32 %	63	A	40.96 % / 1.49 %	80	A	57.03 % / 1.59 %	97	D	42.07 % / 1.59 %
13	C	58.68 % / 1.89 %	30	D	51.39 % / 1.65 %	47	A	54.49 % / 1.39 %	64	D	32.86 % / 3.93 %	81	B	57.46 % / 1.87 %	98	D	63.65 % / 1.26 %
14	A	51.73 % / 1.69 %	31	C	67.31 % / 1.65 %	48	D	66.2 % / 1.71 %	65	B	30.22 % / 4.39 %	82	A	77.2 % / 0.0 %	99	B	49.74 % / 2.0 %
15	B	60.91 % / 1.28 %	32	C	87.72 % / 0.0 %	49	D	62.5 % / 1.46 %	66	B	62.84 % / 1.25 %	83	B	86.26 % / 0.0 %	100	A	63.56 % / 1.81 %
16	A	58.21 % / 1.19 %	33	B	56.77 % / 1.78 %	50	A	17.6 % / 4.12 %	67	B	77.71 % / 0.0 %	84	D	45.57 % / 1.56 %			
17	C	85.88 % / 0.0 %	34	D	82.84 % / 0.0 %	51	C	50.46 % / 1.1 %	68	C	49.35 % / 1.62 %	85	D	57.44 % / 1.38 %			

//Hints and Solutions//

1. According to the statements, the diagram is

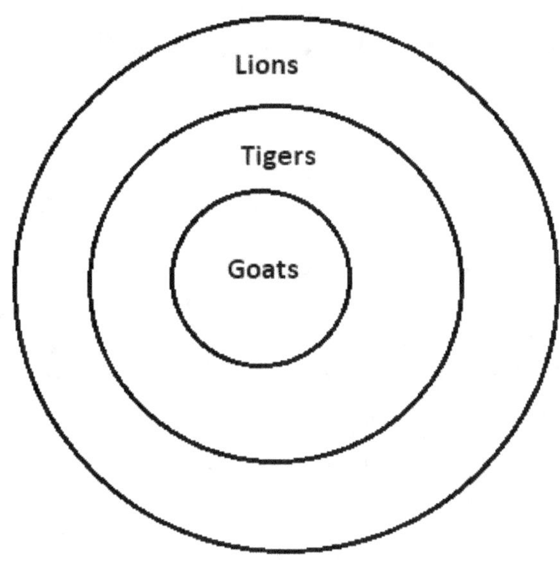

Hence, the correct option is (D).

2. The given series contains the "Union territories of India".

From the given alternatives, Delhi is one of the union territories of India.

Therefore, 'Delhi' is the correct answer.

Hence, the correct option is (C).

3. Each of the numbers except 14 is an odd number.

The number '14' is the only EVEN number.

Hence, the correct option is (C).

4. The pattern is 2^3, 3^3, 4^3, 5^3, 6^3, 7^3.

But, 100 is not a perfect cube.

Hence, the correct option is (B).

5. All except 'Pencil-Paper' are examples of complementary goods.

Hence, the correct option is (D).

6.

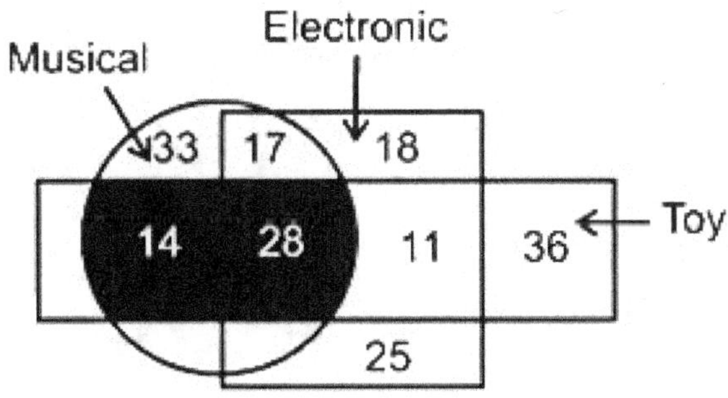

Musical toys: 28 + 14 = 42

Therefore, there are '42' musical toys.

Hence, the correct option is (C).

7. D is used for F.

G is used for I.

P is used for R.

and

C is used for E.

Thus, it is clear that each letter of the word FIRE stands for each corresponding letter of the coded word DGPC two places ahead. By applying the same principle, the letters QFMR will stand for SHOT. So, the last letter of the code word is R.

Hence, the correct option is (B).

8. The given coding language follows a pattern in which the letters at the odd places are obtained by subtracting two from its position and the letters at the even places are obtained by adding two to its position. Therefore, 'CATTLE' can be coded as 'ACRVJG'

Hence, the correct option is (D).

9. According to the statements, the diagram is

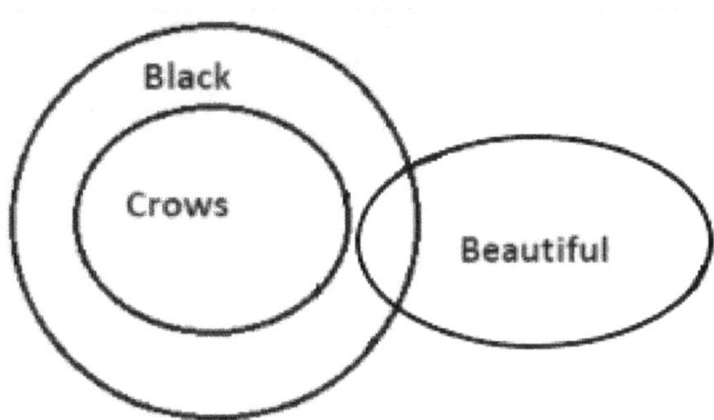

Hence, the correct option is (B).

10. Except Subvert – Demolish, all other pairs of words are antonyms of each other.

Thus, Subvert – Demolish is different from the other three responses as 'Subvert' means 'to undermine the power or authority of someone', and 'Demolish' means 'pulling something down'. This makes both the words synonymous, making Subvert as the correct response.

Hence, the correct option is (D).

11. First term: 4

Second term: 4 + 3 = 7

Third term : 7 + 5 = 12

Fourth term : 12 + 7 = 19

Fifth term : 19 + 9 = 28

Therefore,

Next Terms : 28 + 11 = 39

Hence, the correct option is (D).

12. 1st term : 10

2nd term : 100 = 10 + 90

3rd term : 200 = 100 + 100

4th term : 310 = 200 + 110

5th Term: 430 = 310 + 120

Therefore, the answer is 430.

Hence, the correct option is (A).

13. In Factories, the production of different products is carried out.

Similarly, in Hospitals, the treatment of different diseases and accidents are undertaken.

Thus, the Hospital is related to Treatment.

Hence, the correct option is (C).

14.

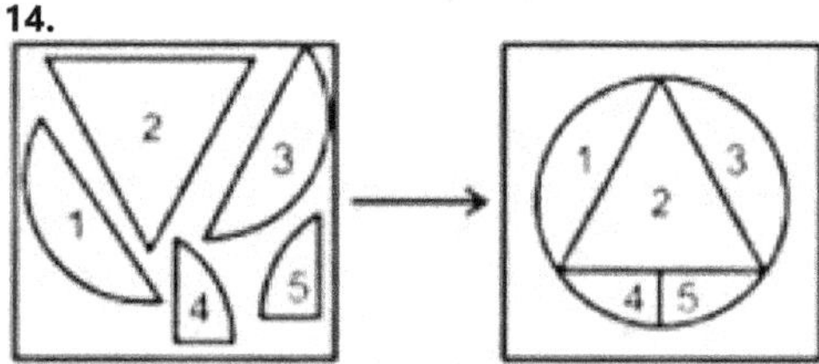

Therefore, the below figure can be formed from the pieces given in the figure (X).

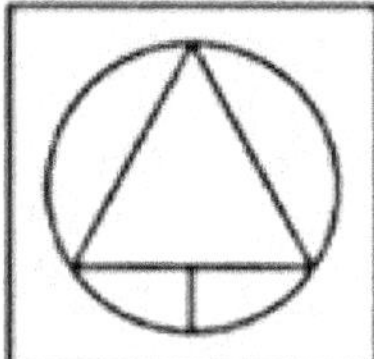

Hence, the correct option is (A).

15. According to the question

YWZX : USVT

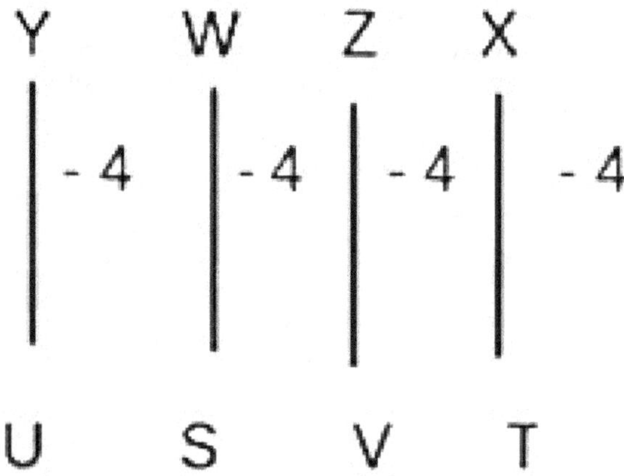

Similarly;

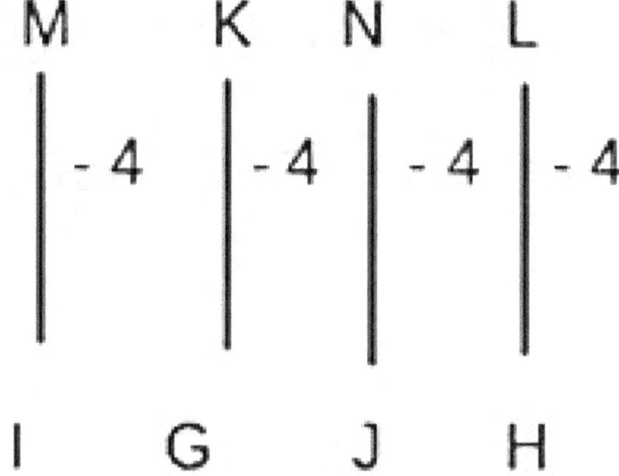

Thus, "IGJH" is the correct answer.

Hence, the correct option is (B).

16. The following pattern of the given series-

b **a** ac/ **a** cc **b** /cb **b** a/b **a** ac

So, a a b b a will be placed in the gap.

Hence, the correct option is (A).

17. The pattern is as follows.

KlMnO (O+2=q) = qRsTu

qRsTu (u+2=W) = WxYzA

WxYzA (A+2=c) = cDeFg

cDeFg (g+2=I) = IjKlM

Hence, the correct option is (C).

18. All are the cubes of some numbers except 28.

$1 = 1^3$

$8 = 2^3$

28 = ... (it should be 27)

$64 = 4^3$

$125 = 5^3$

$216 = 6^3$

Hence, the correct option is (C).

19. Given,

(8 − 8) + 8 × 32 = 64

After interchanging signs from the fourth option, we get:-

⇒ (8 + 8) ÷ 8 × 32 = 64

⇒ 16 ÷ 8 × 32 = 64

⇒ 2 × 32 = 64

Hence, the correct option is (D).

20. Given,

$64 - 8 \times 9 \div 8 = 64$

Putting $(- \ \& \ \div)$ in the equation from the option four,

we get,

$\Rightarrow 64 \div 8 \times 9 - 8 = 64$

$\Rightarrow 8 \times 9 - 8 = 64$

$\Rightarrow 72 - 8 = 64$

$\Rightarrow 64 = 64$

Hence, the correct option is (D).

21. After interchanging the symbol equation 3 will be correct.

Given,

$15 + 5 - 2 \div 6 \times 3 = 3$

After interchanging the symbol

$\Rightarrow 15 \div 5 \times 2 - 6 + 3 = 3$

$\Rightarrow 3 \times 2 - 6 + 3 = 3$

$\Rightarrow 6 - 6 + 3 - 3$

$\Rightarrow 3 = 3$

Hence, the correct option is (A).

22. Some workers may be managers and vice – versa.

All workers and managers are staff.

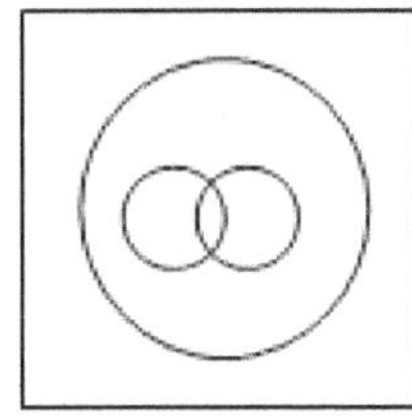

Hence, the correct option is (B).

23. The pattern for this code is as follows

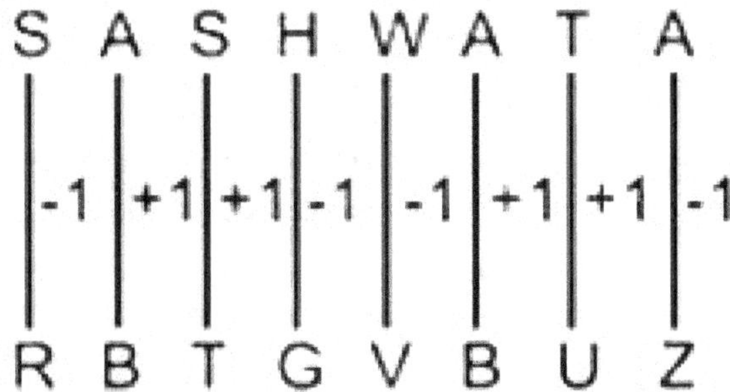

Similarly,

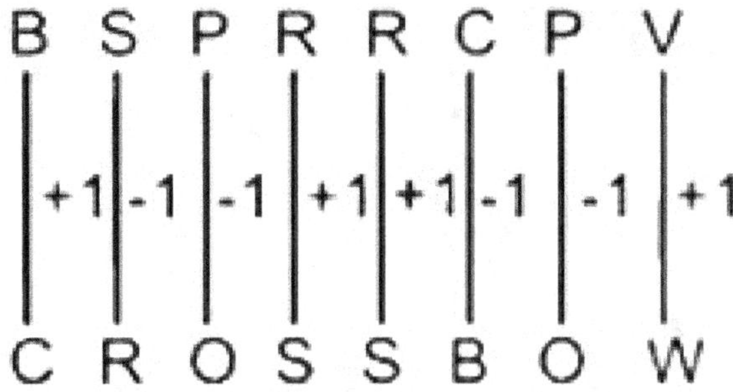

Thus, CROSSBOW is written as BSPRRCPV.

Hence, the correct option is (B).

24. Cardboard boxes that are not white can be represented by the number common to triangle and circle but outside the rectangle. Such a number is '6'.

Hence, the correct option is (A).

25. On arranging given word as per dictionary order,

i) **Dag**ger

ii) **Dai**sy

iii) **Dam**p

iv) **Dan**gle

v) **Dap**per

Thus, "Damp" comes third according to the dictionary.

Hence, the correct option is (B).

26. Let P be the sum of money.

Given,

$t = 3$

$R = 10$

$A = 26620$

$\Rightarrow$ Amount $(A) = P \times \left(1 + \frac{R}{100}\right)^{t}$

$\Rightarrow 26620 = P \times \left(1 + \frac{10}{100}\right)^{3}$

$\Rightarrow 26620 = P \times (1.1)^3 = 1.331P$

$\therefore P = \frac{26620}{1.331} = 20000$

Hence, the correct option is (A).

27. Let the radius of pond $= R$

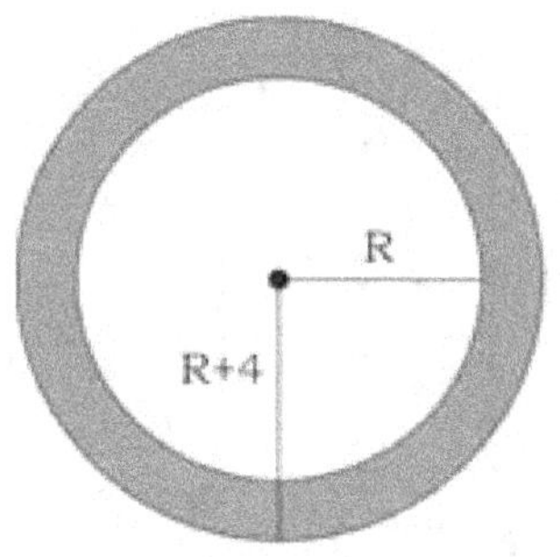

The outer radius of the pond with concrete wall $= (R + 4)$

According to the question,

$$\pi R^2 \times \frac{11}{25} = \pi(R \times 4)^2 - \pi R^2$$

$$R^2 \times \frac{11}{25} = R^2 + 16 + 8R - R^2$$

$$\frac{11}{25} R^2 = 16 + 8R$$

$$11R^2 - 200R - 400 = 0$$

By option (b),

$$R = 20$$

$$11 \times (20)^2 - 200 \times 20 - 400 = 0$$

$$4400 - 4000 - 400 = 0$$

$$0 = 0 \text{ (satisfy)}$$

The radius of pond $R = 20$ cm

Hence, the correct option is (B).

28. $BC = \sqrt{AB^2 + AC^2} = \sqrt{a^2 + b^2}$ (To pythagorean theorem)

$\therefore$ Required total area

$$= a^2 + b^2 + \left(\sqrt{a^2 + b^2}\right)^2 + \frac{1}{2}ab$$

$$= 2(a^2 + b^2) + 0.5ab$$

Hence, the correct option is (C).

29. Average number of days in four consecutive months of year = 30.75

$\Rightarrow$ Sum of number of days in four consecutive months of year = 4 × 30.75 = 123

This is only possible when three of the four months have 31 days and one month has 30 days.

For these combinations, it is possible

May, June, July and August

July, August, September and October.

$\therefore$ Two such combinations are possible.

Hence, the correct option is (C).

30. Amit : Veer

Income 3 : 2

Saving 1000 : 1000

$\therefore$ Income = Expenses + Saving

$$\therefore \frac{3x-1000}{2x-1000} = \frac{5}{3}$$

9x - 3000 = 10x - 5000

x = 2000

$\therefore$ Annual income of Amit is 3x

= 3 × 2000

= Rs. 6000

Hence, the correct option is (D).

31. Surface area of cube $= 6a^2$ where a is the side length

Let the initial length of edge be x

Initial surface area $= 6x^2$

New length $= x + \left(\frac{50}{100}\right) \times x = 1.5x$

New surface area $= 6(1.5x)^2 = 13.5x^2$

Percentage increase in its surface area $= \frac{(13.5x^2 - 6x^2)}{6x^2 \times 100} = 125\%$

Hence, the correct option is (C).

32. Cost price $=$ Rs. 120

Selling price $=$ Rs. 102

$\therefore$ loss percentage

$$= \frac{120-102}{120} \times 100\%$$

$$= \frac{18}{120} \times 100\%$$

$$= 15\%$$

Hence, the correct option is (C).

33. ($M.P =$ Marked price, $C.P =$ Cost price, $S.P =$ Selling price)

Given,

$$M.P = 3000$$

$\because$ Discount $= 10\%$

$\therefore$ Its $S.P =$ Rs. $3000 \times \dfrac{90}{100} =$ Rs. 2700

$$\therefore S.P = C.P + 20 \times \frac{C.P}{100}$$

$$\Rightarrow S.P = C.P \times \left(\frac{120}{100}\right)$$

$$\Rightarrow C.P = S.P \times \left(\frac{100}{120}\right)$$

$$\Rightarrow C.P = 2700 \times \frac{100}{120} = 2250$$

Therefore, the cost price of an article is Rs. 2250.

Hence, the correct option is (B).

34. Given,

$(37 + 23)^2 - (37 - 23)^2$

$\Rightarrow (60)^2 - (14)^2$

$\Rightarrow 3600 - 196$

$\Rightarrow 3404$

Hence, the correct option is (D).

35. $S.I = P \times r \times \dfrac{t}{100}$

$S.I$ = Simple interest

P = Principal

r = Rate

t = time

$S.I = 720$

$$\Rightarrow \frac{(P \times r \times t)}{100} = 720$$

$$\Rightarrow \frac{(P \times 12 \times 3)}{100} = 720$$

$$\Rightarrow P \times 0.36 = 720$$

$$\Rightarrow P = 2000$$

Hence, the correct option is (D).

36. Let, $x\%$ of the car is insured.

According to the problem,

$$\Rightarrow 460000 \times \frac{x}{100} = 381800$$

$$\Rightarrow x = \frac{3818}{46}$$

$$\Rightarrow x = 83\%$$

$\therefore$ 83% of the car is insured.

Hence, the correct option is (A).

37. Given:

$$? = 38 \div \left[1 - \frac{1}{2} + 2\frac{2}{3}\right]$$

$$\Rightarrow ? = 38 \div \left[1 - \frac{1}{2} + \frac{8}{3}\right]$$

$$\Rightarrow ? = 38 \div \left[\frac{1(6) - 1(3) + 8(2)}{6}\right]$$

$$\Rightarrow ? = 38 \div \left[\frac{6 - 3 + 16}{6}\right]$$

$$\Rightarrow ? = 38 \div \left[\frac{19}{6}\right]$$

$$\Rightarrow ? = \frac{(38 \times 6)}{19} = 12$$

Hence, the correct option is (C).

38. Given,

$$3\cot\theta = 4\cos\theta$$

$$\Rightarrow 3\frac{\cos\theta}{\sin\theta} = 4\cos\theta$$

$$\Rightarrow \sin\theta = \frac{3}{4}$$

We know that, $\cos^2\theta = 1 - \sin^2\theta$

$$\Rightarrow \cos^2\theta = 1 - \frac{9}{16}$$

$$\Rightarrow \cos^2\theta = \frac{7}{16}$$

Hence, the correct option is (C).

39. $\left(\dfrac{\sec A}{\cot A + \tan A}\right)^2$

$$= \left(\frac{\frac{1}{\cos A}}{\frac{\cos A}{\sin A} + \frac{\sin A}{\cos A}}\right)^2$$

$$= \left(\frac{\frac{1}{\cos A}}{\frac{\sin^2 A + \cos^2 A}{\sin A - \cos A}}\right)^2 = (\sin A)^2 = \sin^2 A$$

$$= 1 - \cos^2 A$$

Hence, the correct option is (A).

40. Given expression,

$$= \frac{0.796 \times 0.796 - 0.204 \times 0.204}{0.796 - 0.204}$$

$$= \frac{(0.796)^2 - (0.204)^2}{0.796 - 0.204}$$

We know that, $a^2 - b^2 = (a + b)(a - b)$

$$= \frac{(0.796 + 0.204)(0.796 - 0.204)}{0.796 - 0.204}$$

$$= 0.796 + 0.204$$

$$= 1$$

Hence, the correct option is (B).

41.

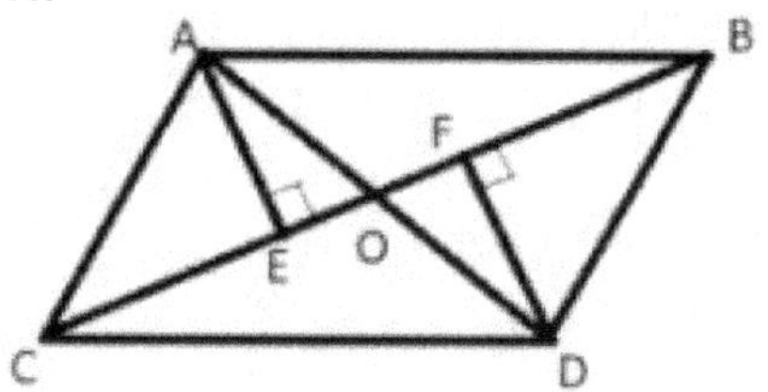

In triangle ABC and triangle DBC,

AC = BD, AB = DC, and BC is the common side so, triangles are congruent.

In triangle AEO and DOF,

Angle AOE = angle DOF (vertically opposite angle)

Angel AEO = angle DFO (both 90°)

And AO = OD (BC bisects AD)

So, the triangles are congruent

In triangle AEB and DFC,

Angle DFC = angle AEB

Angle ABE = angle DCF

CD = AB

Therefore, the triangles are congruent

In triangle ADC and triangle ABD

AC = BD

AD = AD

And CD = BA

Thus, triangle ADC is congruent to triangle DAB. But not congruent to triangle ABD

Hence, the correct option is (D).

42. Gain $\% = \frac{(SP-CP)}{CP} \times 100$

Let the cost price be Rs. x

Selling price $=$ Rs. $(x + 100)$

Profit percentage $= \frac{(x+100-x)}{x} \times 100 = \left(\frac{100}{x}\right) \times 100$

$\left(\frac{100}{x}\right) \times 100 = 20$

$x = 500$

Cost price is Rs. $x =$ Rs. 500

Hence, the correct option is (D).

43. Let the numbers be $7x$ and $10x$

$\Rightarrow 10x - 7x = 96$

$\Rightarrow 3x = 96$

$\Rightarrow x = \frac{96}{3} = 32$

$\therefore$ Smallest number $= 7x = 7 \times 32 = 224$

Hence, the correct option is (B).

44.

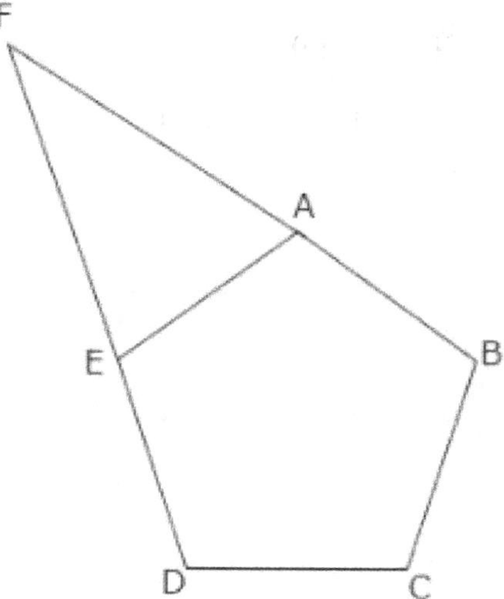

External Angle of a regular pentagon $= \frac{360°}{n} = 72°$

In ΔAEF,

$\angle AEF + \angle EAF + \angle EFA = 180°$

$\Rightarrow \angle EFA = 180° - 72° - 72° = 36°$

Hence, the correct option is (B).

45. A and B together can do a piece of work in one day $= \frac{1}{A} + \frac{1}{B} = \frac{1}{10}$

A alone can do a piece of work in one day $= \frac{1}{30}$

B alone can do a piece of work in one day $= \frac{1}{10} - \frac{1}{30} = \frac{1}{15}$

So, B alone can do a piece of work in 15 days.

Hence, the correct option is (A).

46. From the pie chart, Top 2 students scored 24% + 23% = 47% of total marks

Bottom 2 students scores 17% + 16% = 33% of total marks

Difference = 47 - 33 = 14%

Therefore,

14% of 374 = 52.36 marks = 52 (approx)

Hence, the correct option is (C).

47. From the pie chart, Rakesh scored 20% of total marks.

Therefore, we have 360 degrees $= 100\%$

Then, $20\% = \frac{360}{5}$

$= 72$ degrees

Hence, the correct option is (A).

48. Topper scored 24% of the total marks and Ramesh scored 23% of the total marks.

So, they both scored 47% of total marks between them and so average = 23.5% of 374 = 87.89%

= 88 (approx)

Hence, the correct option is (D).

49. Ravi scored 16% of the total marks and Ram scored 17% and so the difference = 1%

So, we have 100% = 360 degrees

$\Rightarrow 1\% = 3.6$ degrees

Hence, the correct option is (D).

50. Given:

Total amount $= 6400$

Let the first worker's share $= \dfrac{3}{5}x$

Second worker's share $= 2x$

Third worker's share $= \dfrac{5}{3}x$

Then, $\dfrac{3}{5}x + 2x + \dfrac{5}{3}x = 6400$

$\Rightarrow \dfrac{9x + 30x + 25x}{15} = 6400$

$\Rightarrow 64x = 6400 \times 15$

$\Rightarrow x = 1500$

$\therefore$ Second worker's share $1500 \times 2 = 3000$

Hence, the correct option is (A).

51. The final sentence will be " None but me is responsible. Because here but acts as a preposition so it will be followed by an objective form of the pronoun.

Hence, the correct option is (C).

52. Still means at the current moment or present. But *I was* has been used wrongly.

I am still furious.

Hence, the correct option is (C).

53. The correct phrasal verb is 'dug in' which means 'start eating greedily'. Thus option 1 is the correct answer. The other options do not convey the correct meaning.

Hence, the correct option is (A).

54. The correct phrasal verb is 'get ahead' which means 'progress' thus option 3 is the correct word to be placed here. The other options cannot be placed here.

Hence, the correct option is (C).

55. The correct word here is a noun thus 'significance' fits here correctly. Option (A) is the correct answer. Option (B) is an adjective, option (C) is a verb, and option (D) is an adverb.

Hence, the correct option is (A).

56. Option (B) is the correct answer. This is because 'so' means 'to such a great extent' and since the meaning of a verb is to be modified we need an adverb, 'conclusively'.

The sentence implies that though the patient has been cured, doctors find it too early to say this with much great absoluteness.

Option (A) and (C) are incorrect because 'conclusive' is an adjective and we need an adverb.

Option (D) is incorrect because determiner 'most' means 'greatest in amount or degree'. It is not appropriate here.

Hence, the correct option is (B).

57. In converting the sentence to indirect speech, the 'maybe' gets incorporated in the form of the verb 'suggested'. The pronoun 'his' is added instead of 'you' and the pronoun 'your' is replaced by 'his'. The verb 'said' is not needed anymore, the 'now' becomes 'then'.

Thus, the correct sentence is,

Chandler + added verb 'suggested' + to Matthew + that the standup circuit was booming right +'then' + and that + changed pronoun 'he' + should try + changed pronoun 'his ' + luck there.

Hence, the correct option is (B).

58. In converting the sentence to direct speech, the verb 'urged' was incorporated into the new sentence by adding the noun 'definitely'. The verb 'should' is also added. The verb 'said' is added. The 2nd person pronoun 'you' is added.

Thus, the correct sentence is,

"Genevieve, + added pronoun 'you' + added verb 'should' + added noun 'definitely' + run for student body President." Danneel + added verb 'said'.

Hence, the correct option is (B).

59. The original sentence is in active voice, so the answer should be in passive voice. Thus, the pattern will be,

Object (the dog)+ Verb (run over)+ Subject (Kevin)

This automatically eliminates option (A) as it is still in the active voice, the Subject is still acting on the Object, rather than the object being acted on by the Subject. The original sentence is also in the past tense and thus the answer should reflect that, so option (C) is eliminated as it is in the present tense. Option (B) eliminated the verb 'learning' and thus is incomplete and it changes the meaning of the sentence, so this too cannot be the answer.

Hence, the correct option is (D).

60. The original sentence is in passive voice and so the answer has to be in active voice, so the pattern will be –

Subject (the snake) + Verb (bite) + Object (Raymond)

Option (A) is eliminated as it changes the specificity of the Subject to ambiguity – 'snake' to 'something' – and so cannot be the answer. Option (C) is in the future tense while the original sentence is in the past tense which needs to be maintained in the answer and thus option (C) cannot be the answer. Option (D) is again not in the past tense but in the present tense and thus cannot be the answer.

Hence, the correct option is (B).

61. The word 'scorn' means 'a feeling and expression of contempt or disdain for someone or something.' The meanings of the words are:

Contempt means the feeling that a person or a thing is worthless or beneath consideration.

Rapture means a feeling of intense pleasure or joy.

Ascetic means characterized by severe self-discipline and abstention from all forms of indulgence, typically for religious reasons.

Nimble means agile.

Hence, the correct option is (A).

62. The word 'august' means 'having great importance and especially of the highest social class.' The meanings of the words are:

Sparse means thinly dispersed or scattered.

Majestic means having or showing impressive beauty or scale.

Illicit means forbidden by law, rules, or custom.

Render means deliver.

Hence, the correct option is (B).

63. Firstly, let's check the meaning of 'throng' :- To fill in a place or area.

Now, find the meanings of the given options-

Teem- To be full of something.

Strand- To leave from some place.

Abandon- To cease to do something and leave.

Jilt- To reject something or someone suddenly.

Clearly, teem is the most similar in the meaning.

Hence, the correct option is (A).

64. Firstly, let's check the meaning of 'retort' :- It is a quick reply to a question or remark.

Now, find the meanings of the given options-

Plea- To ask for something politely.

Counter- To respond to an action.

Rebuff- To reject in a rude manner.

Retaliate- To attack for being attacked.

Clearly, plea is the most opposite in the meaning.

Hence, the correct option is (D).

65. The idiom 'Get the show on the road ' means putting up a plan or idea into action.

Example - Now that we have completed all the legal formalities, let's get the show on the road.

Hence, the correct option is (B).

66. The phrase apple of my eye refers to something or someone that one cherishes above all others.

Hence, the correct option is (B).

67. To sit on the fence means to not take sides or unable to commit oneself to a particular thing.

E. g. Kim is still sitting on the fence instead of deciding which offer to take.

Hence, the correct option is (B).

68. All the options except (c) are mentioned in the passage. Thus, option (c) has an activity that does not fit in.

Hence, the correct option is (C).

69. It is mentioned in the passage that India has people of different sects, castes and religions live together. It is a strength of India but the reason of calling it so is not this.

Hence, the correct option is (B).

70. All of the options are mentioned in the passage except option (D). It is mentioned 'It entails how they dress, how they speak, the type of food they eat, the manner in which they worship, and their art among many other things.'Thus option (D) is not true according to the passage.

Hence, the correct option is (D).

71. All the options are mentioned in the passage except option (B). It is not written that every religion has its own traditions and customs.

Hence, the correct option is (B).

72. The immense variety in Indian culture is due to the huge population present here. Every region is different from one another. This contributes to the immense variety of culture.

Hence, the correct option is (B).

73. Scapegoat means "a person who is blamed for wrongdoings or mistakes of others."

Assailant: a person who physically attacks another.

Mugger: a person who attacks and robs another in a public place.

Slasher: a sporting competitor who is quick and agile.

Hence, the correct option is (C).

74. The correct order is EACDB.

Since part E is the only independent part and it starts with a definite article 'the', therefore it becomes the first part of the sentence. The word 'among' denotes that there should be a group in the next part. This we get in part A of the sentence.

Since part A talks about 12,000 registrants the next part should give information about them. So part C must follow part A. Now, between part D and part B, D becomes the obvious choice for the fourth part as two 'and' cannot come together. Thus, part D and part B become the fourth and the fifth part respectively.

Thus, the coherent sentence is- 'The three Indian students are among 15 finalists of more than 12,000 original registrants from around the world who submitted engaging and imaginative videos to demonstrate difficult scientific concepts and theories in the physical or life sciences.

Hence, the correct option is (D).

75. The correct order is ABCDE.

When we go through the given parts, we find that they are already arranged in the correct order and form a meaningful sentence.

The sentence speaks about the Heritage sites facing the threats of coastal erosion and floods. The sentence begins with mentioning the UNESCO World Heritage sites and their examples which are under the threat and in later parts sentence talks about the threats they are facing and the time horizon within which these sites may cease to exist.

Thus, the coherent sentence is- 'Dozens of UNESCO World Heritage sites in the Mediterranean such as Venice, the Leaning Tower of Pisa and the Medieval City of Rhodes are under severe threat of coastal erosion and flooding due to rising sea levels within the next 100 years'.

Hence, the correct option is (C).

76. A game of Basketball is played with two teams, with 5 players from each team on the court at one time (that means 10 playing at one time).

Hence, the correct option is (B).

77. Viswanathan Anand was the first recipient of the award.

- He was honored for the performance in the year 1991–92.

Rajiv Gandhi Khel Ratna Award:-

- It is the highest sporting honor of India.
- The recipient(s) is/are honored for their outstanding performance in the field of sports over a period of four years at an international level.
- It was instituted in 1991–92.
- The award comprises a medallion, a certificate, and a cash prize of Rs 25 lakh.
- Abhinav Bindra is the youngest recipient of the award.

Hence, the correct option is (A).

78. The total number of protons in the nucleus of an atom is known as the atomic number.

It is denoted by Z.

Since the number of electrons and protons are the same in an atom, atomic number also corresponds to the number of electrons in an atom but not in the case of ions as in ions, the number of electrons is either more or less than the element.

Hence, the correct option is (C).

79.

Union Territories	Rajya Sabha	Loksabha
1. Andaman and Nicobar Islands	—	1
2. Chandigarh	—	1
3. Dadra and Nagar Haveli	—	1
4. Daman and Diu	—	1
5. Delhi (The National Capital Territory of Delhi)	3	7
6. Lakshadweep	—	1
7. Puducherry	1	1

Hence, the correct option is (D).

80. Bituminous coal contains 81% carbon, 5% hydrogen, 8% oxygen, 1% sulphur, 1.5% nitrogen and 3.5% ash.

It is a dense, black solid which has bright bands. It has a calorific value of about 30 MJ/kg.

It is the most widely used coal because of its high calorific value.

It is dense, compact and normally black in colour.

Hence, the correct option is (A).

81. A tsunami is a series of ocean waves caused by an underwater earthquake, landslide, or volcanic eruption.

Hence, the correct option is (B).

82. Sri Lanka and Maldives are the two island countries that are the Southern neighbours of India.

Maldives island country lies to the south of India

Hence, the correct option is (A).

83. When the iron nails are removed the water tends to fall. It is somewhat related to Archimedes principle. Archimedes' principle states that the upward buoyant force that is exerted on a body immersed in a fluid, whether fully or partially submerged, is equal to the weight of the fluid that the body displaces and acts in the upward direction at the center of mass of the displaced fluid. So when the nail has removed the level of water decreased.

Hence, the correct option is (B).

84. Bani Thani is an India miniature painting painted by Nihâl Chand from the Marwar school of Kishangarh. It portrays a woman who is elegant and graceful.

Hence, the correct option is (D).

85. Konark temple is located in Orissa and is also called black pagoda, Modhera temple is located in Gujarat and Martand Temple is located in J&K and All of these are Dedicated to Lords sun as the entrances east face.

Hence, the correct option is (D).

86. Electric energy (W) is the total work done by an e.m.f. source in maintaining current in the circuit for a given time. Its SI unit is joule (J).

On the other hand, electric power (P) is the rate at which work is done by the e.m.f. source in maintaining current in the circuit. That is,

$$P = \frac{W}{t} \text{ or, } W = Pt$$

Here t is the time for which work is done to maintain the current.

Hence, the correct option is (A).

87. The 3D-object creation platform named "Poly" is operated by the Technology company Google.

Google has proposed to shut down the poly platform from next year, since its service will expire in June 2020. From then on, users will not be able to upload 3D models on the platform.

Hence, the correct option is (B).

88. NASA astronaut Kate Rubins has for the first-time harvested radish crop at the International Space Station.

This is a part of NASA's planet experiment named Plant Habitat-02 (PH-02), which is aimed to understand plant growth in micro gravity conditions. The crops have been harvested in a time of 27 days.

Hence, the correct option is (B).

89. The Amazon Rain Forest is known as "the lungs of the planet earth" since it produces 60% of the oxygen on Earth. It is situated in South America and covers countries like Brazil, Colombia, Peru, Bolivia, Venezuela, etc.

Hence, the correct option is (A).

90. Twelve cities like Ajmer, Amritsar, Amravati, Badami, Dwarka, Gaya, Kanchipuram, Mathura, Puri, Varanasi Velankanni, Warangal were identified for development for the National Heritage City Development and Augmentation Yojana (HRIDAY). The mission period of HRIDAY scheme ended on 31 March 2019.

Hence, the correct option is (D).

91. 73rd Amendment Act 1992 mandates that the state government will appoint a finance commission every five years to review the finances of the Panchayats working in the country. A new Part IX was added in the constitution by this Amendment with the title 'The Panchayats', covering articles from Article 243 to Article 243(O).

Hence, the correct option is (B).

92. Couple burial was found from Lothal and not Kalibanga.

Black bangles, fire pit, ploughed field, a wooden furrow, tiled floors, and bricks have been found at Kalibangan.

Hence, the correct option is (D).

93. Integrated Child Protection Scheme (ICPS) was launched in the year 2009-10 and is dedicated to children. The Scheme is funded by the Central government. This scheme is applicable for children in need of care and protection and children in conflict.

Hence, the correct option is (A).

94. An operating system is the system software that handles the software and hardware resources and provides services for computer programs. SO without an operating system, a computer cannot "boot".

Hence, the correct option is (C).

95.

Geographical Indications	State
Kangra Tea	Himachal Pradesh
Kota Doria	Rajasthan
Kotpad Handloom fabric	Odisha
Mysore Silk	Karnataka
Pochampally Ikat	Telangana

Hence, the correct option is (B).

96. Microsoft Word or MS-Word is an Application software developed by the company Microsoft. It allows users to Type and Save documents.

Hence, the correct option is (C).

97. On February 26-28, 2021, the 5th Asia Economic Dialogue (AED) 2021 was virtually convened by the Ministry of External Affairs (MEA), India and Pune International Centre (PIC) on the theme "Post Covid-19 Global Trade and Finance Dynamics". Its inaugural session was addressed by Union Minister Dr. Subrahmanyam Jaishankar, MEA on "Resilient Global Growth in a Post-Pandemic World". The former Indian Ambassador to China, Pakistan and Bhutan, Mr. Gautam Bambawale is the Convenor of AED 2021.

Hence, the correct option is (D).

98. In accordance with the National Statistical Office (NSO), Ministry of Statistics and Programme Implementation (MoSPI) second advanced estimate, the growth of India's Gross Domestic Product (GDP) is estimated at 0.4% in Q3FY21 (October-December, 2020) stating India's exit from the technical recession. For FY20 also, NSO lowered the economic growth to 4% from 4.2%.

Hence, the correct option is (D).

99. China's largest bank, the Industrial and Commercial Bank of China (ICBC), has launched the country's first India-dedicated publicly offered investment fund. The fund, named the ICBC Credit Suisse India Market Fund, will "invest in exchange-traded funds listed on more than 20 exchanges in Europe and the US that are based on the Indian market

Hence, the correct option is (B).

100. Tata Chemicals established its 1st Centre of Salt and Soda Ash Production 75 years back in Mithapur (Gujrat). On 23 January 2014, it celebrated its Platinum Jubilee (75th year).

Hence, the correct option is (A).

General Intelligence and Reasoning

Q.1 Find out the correct answer for the unsolved equation based on a certain system:

44 + 23 = 201, 61 + 19 = 240, then 89 + 20 = ?

A. 327   **B.** 300   **C.** 256   **D.** 244

Q.2 How many quadrilaterals are there in the given figure?

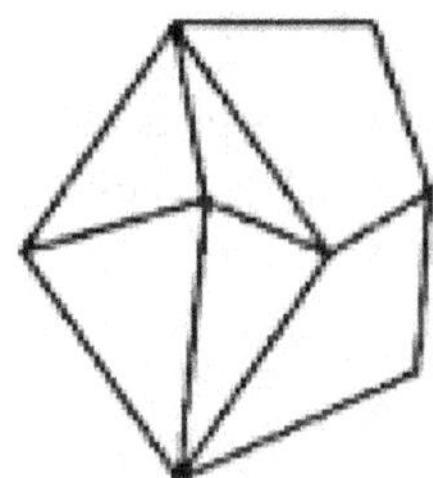

A. 6   **B.** 9   **C.** 7   **D.** 5

Q.3 Arrange the given words in reverse order in which they occur in the dictionary and choose the one that comes second after arranging in reverse order.

Ponder, Polite, Popular, Poodle

A. Polite   **B.** Popular   **C.** Ponder   **D.** Poodle

Q.4 Select the related figure from the given alternatives.

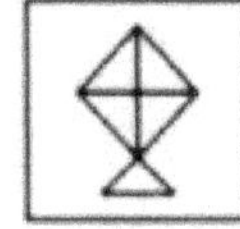 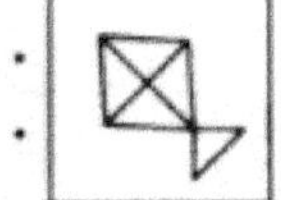 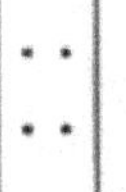  

A. 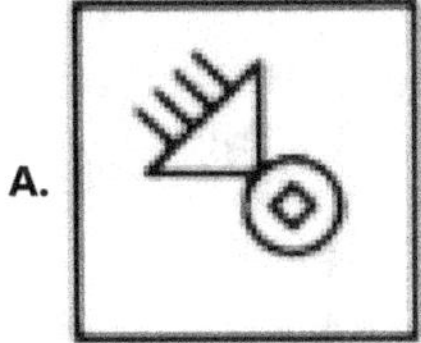   **B.** 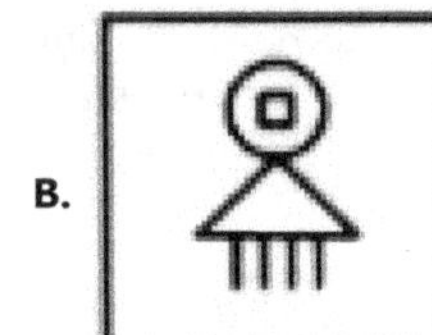

C. 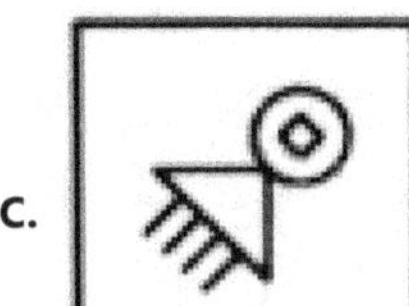   **D.** 

Q.5 Which of the following equation is correct by interchanging the signs × with ÷ and numbers 2 with 3?

A. 12 × 2 + 40 ÷ 2 = 44

B. 23 × 2 + 20 ÷ 2 = 56

C. 13 × 2 + 23 ÷ 4 = 44

D. 23 ÷ 1 + 23 = 64

Q.6 A series is given with one term missing. Select the correct alternative from the given ones that will complete the series.

Ace, King, Queen,?

A. Jack   **B.** Club

C. Heart   **D.** Diamond

Q.7 Chand and Dhyan start from the same point. Chand walks 105 m North, then turns East and walks 55 m, then turns to his right and walks 75 m. At the same time, Dhyan walks 45 m South, then turns to his left and walks 55 m. Where is Chand now with respect to the position of Dhyan?

A. 135 m North   **B.** 75 m North

C. 75 m South   **D.** 135 m South

Q.8 In the following figure, the rectangle represents Fashion designers, the circle represents Equestrians, the triangle represents Campers and the square represents Golfers. Which set of letters represents Equestrians who are not Fashion designers?

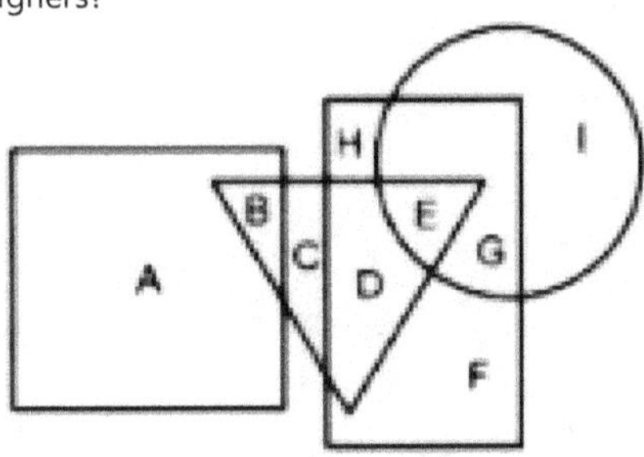

A. EG   **B.** DEG   **C.** I   **D.** E

Q.9 A piece of paper is folded and punched as shown below in the question figures. From the given answer figures, indicate how it will appear when opened?

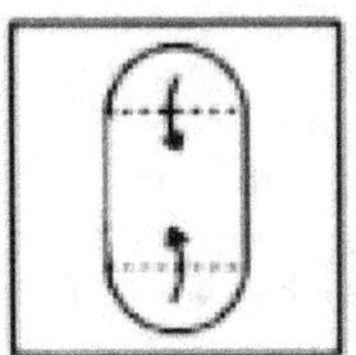  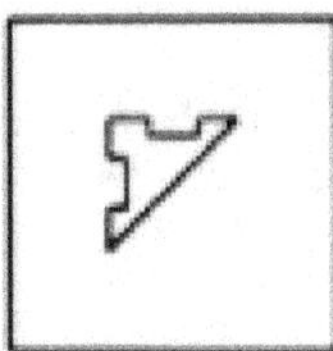

[SSC MTS, 2019], [UP Police Constable, 2019]

A. 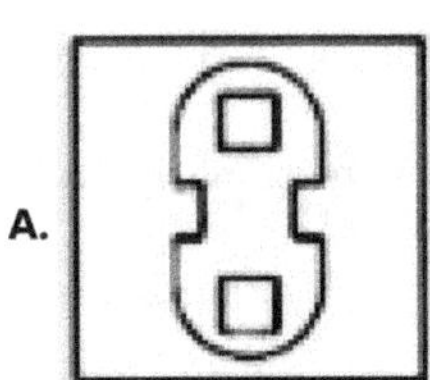   **B.** 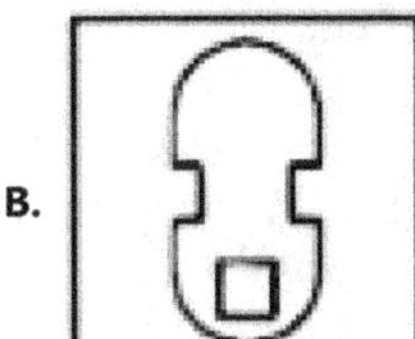

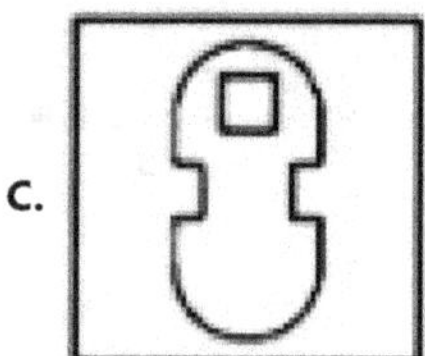 C.

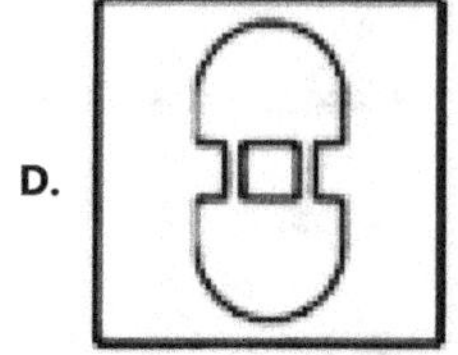 D.

Q.10 In the following question, select the number which can be placed at the sign of question mark (?) from the given alternatives.

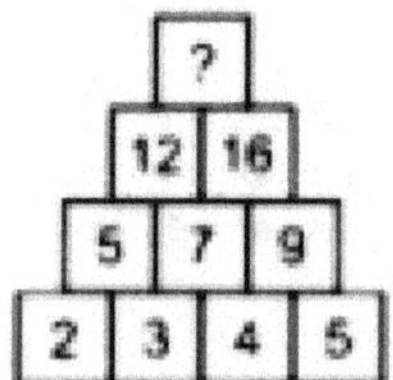

A. 27   **B.** 28   **C.** 26   **D.** 25

Q.11 Direction: Answer the question based on the information given.

Many business offices are located in buildings having 2-8 floors. If a building has more than 3 floors, it has a lift. If the above statements are true, which of the following must be true?

A. 2nd floors do not have lifts
B. 7th floors have lifts
C. Only floors above the 3rd floors have lifts
D. All floors may be reached by lifts

Q.12 In the following question, select the odd letter from the given alternatives.

A. HKN   **B.** RUX   **C.** GJN   **D.** ADG

Q.13 Shiva walks 18 km towards the east. He turns left and walks 37 km. He turns left and walks 24 km. In which direction is he from his starting point?

A. South-East   **B.** North-East
C. North-West   **D.** South-West

Q.14 Six friends P, Q, R, S, T, and U sitting in a straight line facing to the North. P sits on the right end of the line. Q sits second to the right of one who is sitting fifth to the left of P. S sits second to the left of Q. R is not an immediate neighbour of Q. T sits immediate right of Q. how many members are there between P and R?

A. 2   **B.** 3   **C.** 0   **D.** 1

Q.15 Direction: Answer the question based on the information given.

"Some men are definitely intelligent, others are definitely not intelligent, but of intermediate men, we should say, 'intelligent'? Yes, I think, so or no, I shouldn't be inclined to call him intelligent."

Which of the following reflects the intention of the writer well?

A. To call men intelligent who are not strikingly so must be to use the concept with undue imprecision
B. Every empirical concept has a degree of vagueness
C. Calling someone intelligent or not depends upon one's whim
D. There is no need to be as indecisive as the writer of the above

Q.16 How many triangles are there in the given figure?

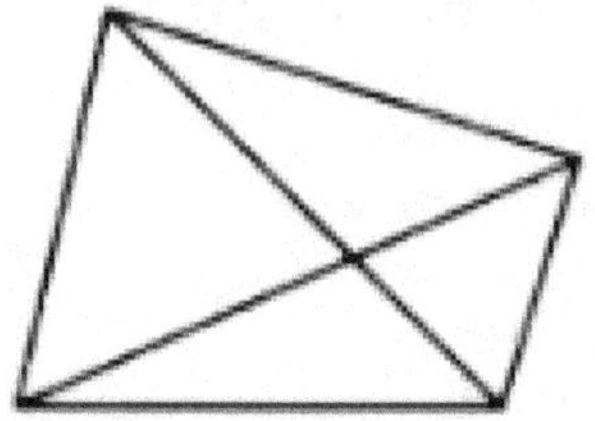

A. 6   **B.** 7   **C.** 8   **D.** 10

Q.17 In the following figure, the rectangle represents Film directors, the circle represents Bikers, the triangle represents Riders and the square represents Asians. Which set of letters represents Film directors who are Riders?

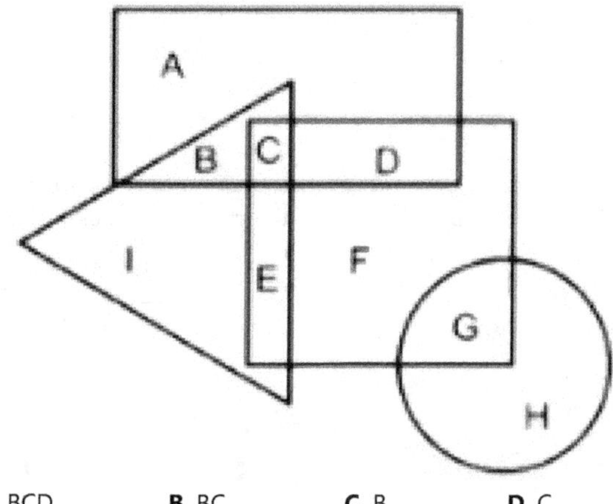

A. BCD   **B.** BC   **C.** B   **D.** C

Q.18 In the following question, four groups of three numbers are given. In each group, numbers are related by a Logic/Rule/Relation. Three are similar on the basis of the same Rule/Relation/Logic. Select the odd one from the given alternatives.

A. 16, 36, 196   **B.** 81, 121, 361
C. 2601, 289, 3969   **D.** 441, 1089, 4761

Q.19 Identify the diagram that best represents the relationship among the classes given below.

Squash, Bowling, Games

A. 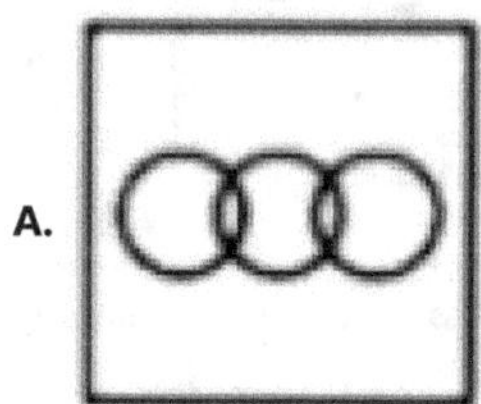   **B.** 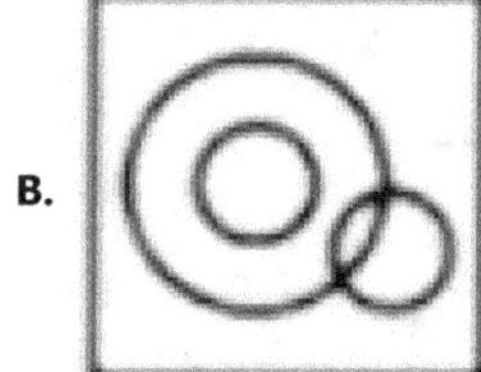

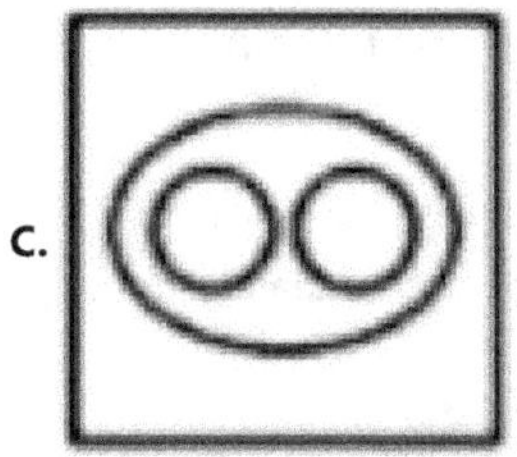

C.

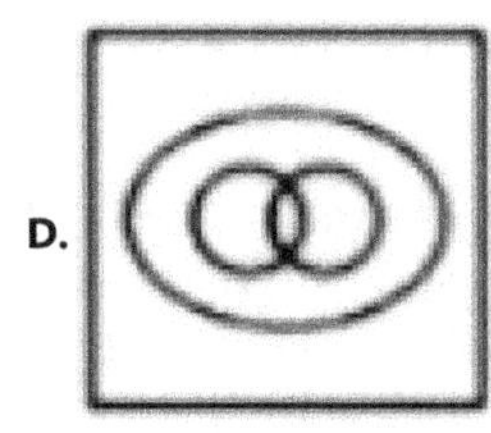

D.

Q.20 Which answer figure will complete the pattern in the following question figure?

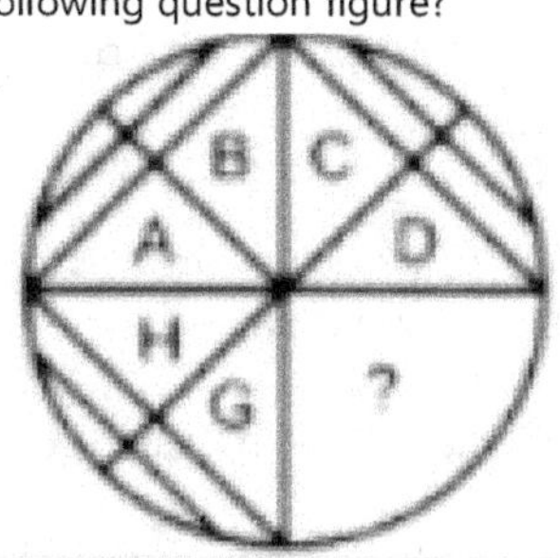

[AFCAT, 2021]

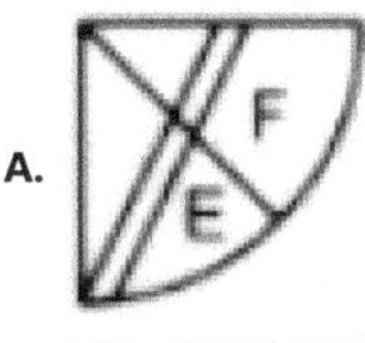

A.

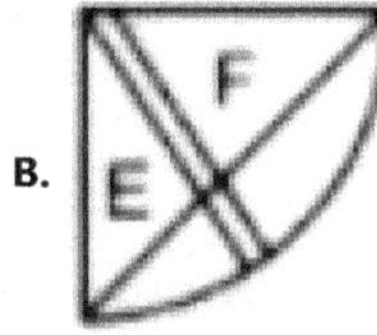

B.

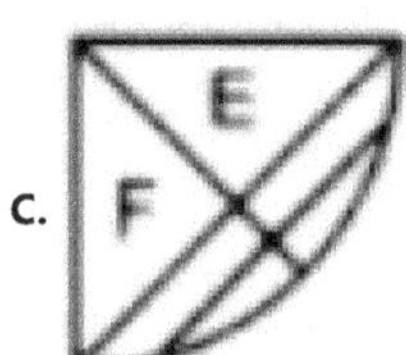

C.

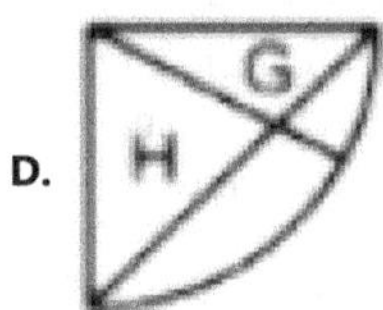

D.

Q.21 If November 2 is Monday, what will be the day after 61 days?

A. Wednesday   **B.** Saturday
C. Tuesday   **D.** Thursday

Q.22 In a certain code language, if COTTON is coded as 325526 and WOOLEN is coded as 122976, then TOWEL will be coded as?

A. 12579   **B.** 21795   **C.** 52179   **D.** 79125

Q.23 In the following question, select the related number from the given alternatives.

41 : 4 : : 37 : ?

A. 34   **B.** 21   **C.** 22   **D.** 16

Q.24 Direction: Find the missing term in the given series.

17, 18, 25, 9,?, 4.5, 37

A. 15   **B.** 32   **C.** 28   **D.** 20

Q.25 Direction: The question is based on a situation. Read the situation and answer the question that follows.

Between 1960 and 1970, ivory poachers in the African nation of Zinbaku killed over 6,500 elephants. During that period, the total elephant population in Zinbaku fell from about 35,000 to just under 30,000. In 1970, new anti-poaching measures were implemented in Zinbaku, and between 1970 and 1980 over 800 poachers were arrested and expelled from the country. Nevertheless, by 1980, the elephant population in Zinbaku had fallen to about 21,000.

Which of the following, if true, would best help to explain the apparent paradox presented above?

A. The poachers arrested in Zinbaku between 1970 and 1980 were rarely sentenced to long prison terms

B. Because of highly publicized campaigns against the slaughter of elephants, demand for ivory fell between 1970 and 1980

C. The elephant population in neighbouring Mombasa rose slightly between 1970 and 1980

D. In Zinbaku, between 1970 and 1980, thousands of acres of forest, the elephant's natural habitat, were cleared for farming

Numerical Aptitude/ Quantitative Ability

Q.26 The average weight of 5 persons decreases by 5 kg when one of them weighing 40 kg is replaced by a new person. The weight (in kg) of the new person is:

A. 14   **B.** 18   **C.** 15   **D.** 17

Q.27 The value of $\sin(45° + \theta) - \cos(45° - \theta)$ is equal to:

A. 1   **B.** 0   **C.** $2\cos\theta$ **D.** $2\sin\theta$

Q.28 The speed of a boat along with the current and against the current is 16 km/hr and 10 km/hr respectively. What is the speed of the boat (in km/hr) in still water?

A. 11   **B.** 13   **C.** 7.5   **D.** 15

Q.29 If the number p is 5 more than q and the sum of the squares of p and q is 55, then the product of p and q is:

A. 10   **B.** -10   **C.** 15   **D.** -15

Q.30 A can do a piece of work in 12 hours, while B can do it in 8 hours. If A and B both work together, so in how many hours the work will be completed?

A. 10 hours   **B.** 4 hours
C. 5 hours 15 minutes   **D.** 4 hours 48 minutes

Q.31 The sum of two interior angles and an exterior angle of a regular polygon is $324°$ then find the number of sides of the polygon?

A. 9   **B.** 8   **C.** 7   **D.** 10

Q.32 What is the unit's place digit in the product (534 × 303 × 441 × 833)?

A. 6   **B.** 4   **C.** 8   **D.** 2

Q.33 Akash purchased an article at a discount of 40% and sold it to Vinay at 10% profit. What is the ratio between the market price and the price for which Vinay purchased the article?

A. 11 : 5   **B.** 50 : 33   **C.** 11 : 7   **D.** 25 : 16

Q.34 A man sold an article at a gain of 10% had he bought it at 10% less and sold it for Rs. 6 more, he would have gained 25%. What did it cost him?

A. 240   **B.** 225   **C.** 200   **D.** 220

Q.35 An amount invested at simple interest gives Rs. 2400 interest at the rate of 12% in 5 years. What is the principal (in Rs.)?

A. 3000   **B.** 4000   **C.** 5000   **D.** 6000

Q.36 The total surface area of a cube is 2166 cm^2. What is the volume of this cube?

A. 6759 cm^3 **B.** 6959 cm^3
C. 6859 cm^3 **D.** 7059 cm^3

Q.37
$$(1 - \sin A)^2 + (1 + \sin A)^2 + (1 - \cos A)^2 + (1 + \cos A)^2$$
is equal to:

A. $\sqrt{2}$ **B.** $\frac{1}{2}$ **C.** 2   **D.** 6

Ques (38-41):Direction: The table below shows the cost of four cars in 5 different towns.

Car	Cost of cars in town (in Rs 1000)				
	T1	T2	T3	T4	T5
C1	914	918	926	998	879
C2	314	325	308	341	317
C3	465	385	442	478	412
C4	238	268	212	199	227

Q.38 What is the difference (in Rs.) between the highest cost of C1 and the lowest cost of C3?

A. 724000   **B.** 575000   **C.** 599000   **D.** 613000

Q.39 What is the average cost (in Rs) of C2?

A. 327000   **B.** 321000   **C.** 336000   **D.** 319000

Q.40 If a person wishes to buy 1 car of each type in T3, then what will be the total cost (in Rs) he has to pay?

A. 1898000   **B.** 2164000   **C.** 1888000   **D.** 1962000

Q.41 What is the ratio of the total cost of 1 unit of all the cars in T2 and the total cost of 1 unit of all the cars in T4?

A. $79 : 99$ **B.** $52 : 59$
C. $79 : 84$ **D.** None of these

Q.42 A can do a piece of work in 14 days and B can do it in 21 days. They begin together but 3 days before the completion of the work, A leaves the work. The total number of days to complete the work is?

A. $10\frac{1}{4}$ **B.** $10\frac{1}{5}$ **C.** $7\frac{1}{5}$ **D.** $7\frac{4}{5}$

Q.43 If 4.5 of $a = 6.5$ of b, then what is $a:b$?

A. $10:13$ **B.** $13:9$ **C.** $13:5$ **D.** $5:9$

Q.44 A number is increased first by 10% and then it is decreased by 20%. What is the percentage change in the number?

A. 12% increase   **B.** 12% decrease
C. 32% increase   **D.** 32% decrease

Q.45 The average weight of 25 bags is 55 kg. the weight of one bag was misread as 65 instead of 56. Find the correct mean value.

A. 55.25   **B.** 54.64   **C.** 55.36   **D.** 55.65

Q.46 What is the compound interest (in Rs) on a sum of Rs. 12000 for 2 years at the rate of 5% per annum compounded annually?

A. 1250   **B.** 1200   **C.** 1230   **D.** 1300

Q.47 If the price of a commodity is decreased by 40% and its consumption is increased by 30%, then what will be the percentage increase or decrease in the expenditure of the commodity?

A. 22% decrease   **B.** 22% increase
C. 12% increase   **D.** 12% decrease

Q.48 A man travelled a certain distance by train at the rate of 25 km/h and walked back at the rate of 4 km/h. If the whole journey took 5 hours 48 minutes, then what was the distance traveled by train?

A. 25 km   **B.** 30 km   **C.** 20 km   **D.** 15 km

Q.49 The sum of three numbers is 98. If the ratio of the first to second is 2 :3 and that of the second to the third is 5 : 8, then the second number is:

A. 20   **B.** 30   **C.** 48   **D.** 58

Q.50 A cloth seller sells 40% of his particular item and recovers the cost price. What will be his profit percentage after selling the complete stock, if he continues to sell the rest of his stock at the same price?

A. 150%   **B.** 250%   **C.** 200%   **D.** 95%

General English & Comprehension

Ques (51-55):Direction: Read the passage and answer the following question.

With how accessible the internet is today, would you believe me if I told you the number of people who go online every day is still increasing?

It is, In fact, "constant" internet usage among adults increased by 5% in just the last three years, according to a few research. And although we say it a lot, the way people shop and buy really has changed along with it -- meaning offline marketing isn't as effective as it used to be. Marketing has always been about connecting with your audience in the right place and at the right time. Today, that means you need to meet them where they are already spending time: on the internet.

Digital marketing is defined by the use of numerous digital tactics and channels to connect with customers where they spend much of their time: online. From the website itself to a business's online branding assets -- digital advertising, email marketing, online brochures, and beyond -- there's a spectrum of tactics that fall under the umbrella of "digital marketing."

The best digital marketers have a clear picture of how each digital marketing campaign supports their overarching goals. And depending on the goals of their marketing strategy, marketers can support a larger campaign through the free and paid channels at their disposal.

Q.51 Why is it surprising that the number of people who go online every day is still increasing?
A. Usage of numerous technologies
B. Even adults are becoming a part of it
C. The accessibility of Internet is huge
D. The strategy of marketing has changed

Q.52 Which does not fall under the umbrella of "digital marketing"?
A. Digital advertising
B. Email marketing
C. Online brochures
D. Better photographs

Q.53 Why is digital marketing gaining so much popularity?
A. It helps businesses to connect with the people at the correct place and time
B. It is easier and faster
C. It is cost-effective and technology-driven
D. It removes the need for human labour

Q.54 What plays the most vital role in digital campaigns?
A. Goals
B. Strategies
C. Digital marketers
D. More campaigns

Q.55 What is the main purpose of digital marketing?
A. To have more campaigns
B. To connect with the customers effectively
C. To increase the brand value
D. To implement more technology in the business.

Ques (56-57):Direction: Choose the word most similar in meaning to the given word.

Q.56 Putrefy
A. Revoke
B. Assimilate
C. Decompose
D. Colloquial

Q.57 Dainty
A. Fester
B. Elegant
C. Fast
D. Noxious

Ques (58-59):Direction: In the following question, out of the four alternatives, select the best alternative which best expresses the meaning of the Idiom/Phrase.

Q.58 Apple Pie Order
A. In random order
B. Related to fruits packing
C. Related to dry fruit packing
D. In perfect order

Q.59 As fit as a fiddle
A. Very weak
B. Recovering from illness
C. Looks fit but not fit actually
D. None of above

Q.60 Direction: Choose the correct alternative which can be substituted for the given sentence.
A person who talks in sleep is called as
A. Philatelist
B. Somnambulist
C. Somniloquist
D. Oneirocritic

Ques (61-62):Direction: Choose the word opposite in meaning to the given word.

Q.61 mollify
A. Appease
B. Irritate
C. Abrogate
D. Acculturate

Q.62 Murky
A. Bright
B. Liturgy
C. Quixotic
D. Pertness

Q.63 Direction: Choose the correct alternative which can be substituted for the given sentence.
Place for ammunition and weapons is called as:
A. Asylum
B. Arsenal
C. Archives
D. Acoustics

Q.64 Find the correct spelling:
A. Accesary
B. Acessarry
C. Acessary
D. Accessary

Q.65 Find the correct spelling:
A. Admittance
B. Admitance
C. Addmitance
D. Admitannce

Ques (66-70):Direction: Fill in the blank with the correct word.

Q.66 Do not push her ____ the problem as she is too young to deal with all this.
A. In
B. Into
C. Up
D. At

Q.67 Small kids carry heavy sacks which ____ their physical development.
A. Is stunting
B. Stunt
C. Was stunt
D. Stunts

Q.68 Education has become ____ commercialized and superficial.
A. Highly
B. High
C. Many
D. Highest

Q.69 Advertisements and promotional campaigns are being ____ by the company.
A. Ran
B. Run
C. Running
D. Runs

Q.70 The most prevalent psychology ____ students today is to fight intense competition
A. With
B. Among
C. Between
D. Beyond

Ques (71-73):Direction: In the following questions, the sentences have been given in Active/ Passive Voice. From the

given alternatives, choose the one which best expresses the given sentence in Passive/ Active Voice.

Q.71 Women like men to flatter them.
A. Men are liked by women to flatter them
B. Women like to be flattered by men
C. Women like that men should flatter them
D. Women are liked to be flattered by men

Q.72 It is your duty to make tea at eleven O'clock.
A. You are asked to make tea at eleven O'clock
B. Your are required to make tea at eleven O'clock
C. You are supposed to make tea at eleven O'clock
D. Tea is to be made by you at eleven O'clock

Q.73 A lion does not eat grass, however hungry he may be.
A. Grass is not eaten by a lion, however hungry he may be
B. Grass is not being eaten by a lion, however hungry he may be
C. Grass is eaten not by a lion, however hungry he may be
D. Grass is being not eaten by a lion, however hungry he may be

Ques (74-75):Direction: In the following questions, a sentence has been given in Direct/ Indirect Speech. Out of the four alternatives suggested, select the one that best expresses the same sentence in Indirect/Direct speech.

Q.74 The speaker said, 'Gentlemen, I am going to discuss the food situation in our country.'
A. Addressing them as gentlemen, the speaker said that he is going to discuss the food situation in their country
B. Addressing them as gentlemen, the speaker said that he was going to discuss the food situation in their country
C. The speaker told the gentlemen that he is going to discuss the food situation in their country
D. The speaker told the gentlemen that I was going to discuss the food situation in our country

Q.75 He said, 'Bravo! You have done well.'
A. He applauded him saying that he had done well
B. He exclaimed him saying that he has done well
C. He exclaimed saying him that he has done well
D. He applauded him saying that I had done well

General Awareness

Q.76 Benson Hedges Cup is related to which of the following sports?
A. Hockey
B. Cricket
C. Football
D. Basket Ball

Q.77 AGMARK is related to:
A. Industry
B. The Indian Railways
C. Agriculture Marketing
D. Agricultural Finance

Q.78 National Education Day is celebrated on _____ every year.
[UP Police Constable, 2018]

A. 27th October
B. 4th March
C. 17th September
D. 11th November

Q.79 'Thang ta', a martial art form is associated with which state of India?
A. Mizoram
B. Nagaland
C. Manipur
D. Tripura

Q.80 Kynrem falls is located in which of following north-east Indian state of India?
A. Assam
B. Sikkim
C. Nagaland
D. Meghalaya

Q.81 Ibn Battuta was a _______ who wrote about his travels to India in the fourteenth century.
A. Persian
B. Egyptian
C. Turk
D. Moroccan

Q.82 Which article has been described as the 'heart and soul' of the Indian Constitution by Dr. B. R. Ambedkar?
A. Article 1
B. Article 21
C. Article 32
D. Article 260

Q.83 In January 2021, the Gujarat government has decided to rename which fruit as 'Kamalam'?
A. Dragon fruit
B. Passion fruit
C. Pomegranate
D. Spirulina

Q.84 The coefficient of static friction is _________.
A. Less than the coefficient of kinetic friction
B. Greater than the coefficient of limiting friction
C. Equal to the coefficient of kinetic friction
D. Equal to the tangent of the angle of friction

Q.85 The sound made by owls is known as _______.
A. Squawk
B. Hoot
C. Warble
D. Cluck

Q.86 The first cloned animal Dolly was a _______.
A. Doy
B. Rabbit
C. Cat
D. Sheep

Q.87 Which of the following option is correct regarding Pradhan Mantri Jeevan Jyoti Beema Yojana?
A. It is a one-year life insurance scheme
B. It is available in the age group of 18 to 50 years
C. It is renewable from year to year
D. All of the above

Q.88 A computer cannot "______" if it does not have the operating system.
A. Compile
B. Load
C. Boot
D. Assemble

Q.89 1 bar is equal to _____ pascal.
A. 10
B. 10000
C. 1000
D. 100000

Q.90 Mass number (A) is given by _______.
A. $A = N - Z$
B. $A = Z + N$
C. $A = Z - N$
D. $A = ZN$

Q.91 Who was the first Chief Election Commissioner of India?
[DSSSB TGT Social Science, 2014]

A. Nagendra Singh
B. Sukumar Sen

C. T N Seshan **D.** T Swaminathan

Q.92 The Indian Standard Meridian in India does not pass through which of the following state?

A. Bihar **B.** Madhya Pradesh
C. Uttar Pradesh **D.** Chhattisgarh

Q.93 USB stands for:

A. Unique Serial Bus
B. Universal Serial Bus
C. Unary Serial Bus
D. Universal Secondary Bus

Q.94 The idea of 'Farr-i Izadi', on which the Mughal kingship was based, was first developed by which one of the following Sufi saints?

A. Shihabuddin Suhrawardi
B. Nizamuddin Auliya
C. Ibn al-Arabi
D. Bayazid Bastami

Q.95 In the modern periodic table while going from top to bottom in a group ______.

A. The size of an atom increases
B. The size of an atom decreases
C. The ionization energy of an atom increases
D. Size and ionization energy of an atom increases

Q.96 Which of the following has entered a partnership with Hyundai Motor India for its highest selling SUV, Creta?

A. Apollo Tyres
B. JK Tyre & Industries Ltd.
C. Bridgestone
D. Goodyear Tire and Rubber Company

Q.97 The first world environment day was celebrated in which of the following years?

A. 1973 **B.** 1974 **C.** 1980 **D.** 1972

Q.98 For the first time in the areca nut sector, 'Sirsi Supari' grown in _______ has received the Geographic Indication (GI) tag.

A. Kodagu **B.** Uttara Kannada
C. Hassan **D.** Bagalkot

Q.99 At which of the following cities had the Prime Minister's Science, Technology and Innovation Advisory Council (PM-STIAC) recommended the setting of the Science and Technology Clusters?

A. Bengaluru
B. NCR-Delhi
C. Pune
D. All (A), (B), and (C)

Q.100 Which of the following has partnered with Niti Aayog to launch the revamped Women Entrepreneurship Platform?

A. Snapdeal **B.** Myntra **C.** Flipkart **D.** Jabong

// Smart Answer Sheet //

Correct Percentage of students who answered correctly. **Skipped** Percentage of students who skipped.

Q.	Ans.	Correct / Skipped	Q.	Ans.	Correct / Skipped	Q.	Ans.	Correct / Skipped	Q.	Ans.	Correct / Skipped	Q.	Ans.	Correct / Skipped	Q.	Ans.	Correct / Skipped
1	A	62.86 % / 1.95 %	18	A	62.47 % / 1.67 %	35	B	48.68 % / 1.79 %	52	D	89.59 % / 0.0 %	69	B	65.32 % / 1.91 %	86	D	68.4 % / 1.77 %
2	C	13.56 % / 4.5 %	19	C	48.59 % / 1.09 %	36	C	47.8 % / 1.65 %	53	A	60.31 % / 1.42 %	70	B	60.94 % / 1.65 %	87	D	43.04 % / 1.84 %
3	D	58.08 % / 1.36 %	20	C	61.93 % / 1.14 %	37	D	48.09 % / 1.6 %	54	A	57.07 % / 1.31 %	71	B	43.66 % / 1.24 %	88	C	60.86 % / 1.15 %
4	D	80.66 % / 0.0 %	21	B	68.71 % / 1.33 %	38	D	46.39 % / 1.78 %	55	B	64.65 % / 1.56 %	72	C	52.9 % / 1.75 %	89	D	67.47 % / 1.64 %
5	D	65.22 % / 1.58 %	22	C	87.29 % / 0.0 %	39	B	42.57 % / 1.31 %	56	C	64.68 % / 1.89 %	73	D	61.34 % / 1.83 %	90	B	55.15 % / 1.8 %
6	A	41.3 % / 1.88 %	23	B	83.3 % / 0.0 %	40	C	85.82 % / 0.0 %	57	B	40.59 % / 1.57 %	74	B	57.19 % / 1.08 %	91	B	40.91 % / 1.38 %
7	B	57.39 % / 1.57 %	24	B	28.46 % / 3.0 %	41	C	47.74 % / 1.35 %	58	D	77.62 % / 0.0 %	75	A	50.94 % / 1.0 %	92	A	65.46 % / 1.53 %
8	C	58.95 % / 1.17 %	25	D	28.7 % / 4.25 %	42	B	43.85 % / 1.7 %	59	D	64.69 % / 1.83 %	76	B	58.57 % / 1.69 %	93	B	79.51 % / 0.0 %
9	A	18.94 % / 3.02 %	26	C	27.03 % / 3.66 %	43	B	81.04 % / 0.0 %	60	C	66.25 % / 1.85 %	77	C	48.45 % / 1.68 %	94	A	22.32 % / 4.02 %
10	B	60.83 % / 1.23 %	27	B	53.87 % / 1.96 %	44	B	67.41 % / 1.98 %	61	B	23.24 % / 4.15 %	78	D	41.58 % / 1.93 %	95	A	65.92 % / 1.06 %
11	B	59.33 % / 1.74 %	28	B	59.97 % / 1.97 %	45	B	52.92 % / 1.42 %	62	A	67.89 % / 1.13 %	79	C	47.1 % / 1.73 %	96	B	43.22 % / 1.66 %
12	C	44.52 % / 1.29 %	29	C	65.35 % / 1.81 %	46	C	51.08 % / 1.46 %	63	B	89.86 % / 0.0 %	80	D	59.64 % / 1.3 %	97	B	40.62 % / 1.54 %
13	C	84.35 % / 0.0 %	30	D	40.59 % / 1.38 %	47	A	63.34 % / 1.48 %	64	D	64.45 % / 1.19 %	81	D	48.42 % / 1.62 %	98	B	45.62 % / 1.63 %
14	C	52.52 % / 1.59 %	31	D	53.01 % / 1.7 %	48	C	45.64 % / 1.8 %	65	A	65.05 % / 1.85 %	82	C	67.52 % / 1.61 %	99	D	42.37 % / 1.05 %
15	A	17.0 % / 3.57 %	32	A	86.42 % / 0.0 %	49	B	48.89 % / 1.14 %	66	B	43.51 % / 1.98 %	83	A	67.72 % / 1.34 %	100	C	61.1 % / 1.37 %
16	C	47.34 % / 1.18 %	33	B	48.81 % / 1.41 %	50	A	58.25 % / 1.85 %	67	D	53.35 % / 1.84 %	84	D	77.64 % / 0.0 %			
17	B	61.95 % / 1.1 %	34	A	55.98 % / 1.86 %	51	C	43.19 % / 1.1 %	68	A	81.44 % / 0.0 %	85	B	67.21 % / 1.16 %			

//Hints and Solutions//

1. The first term is:

44 + 23 = 67

67 × 3 = 201

The second term is:

61 + 19 = 80

80 × 3 = 240

Similarly for 89 + 20

89 + 20 = 109

109 × 3 = 327

Hence, the correct option is (A).

2. The quadrilaterals formed in the given figure are shown below:

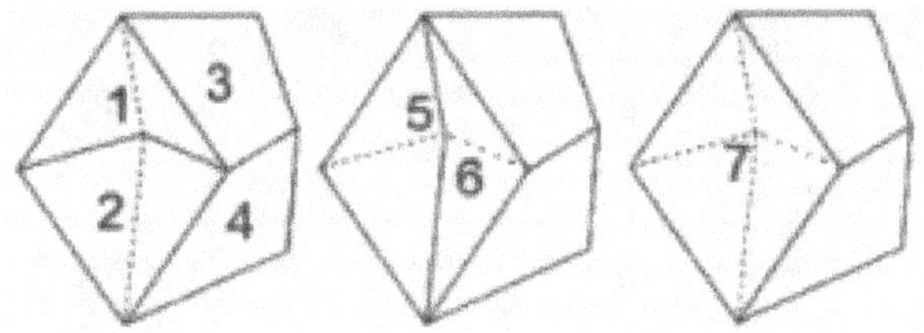

7 quadrilaterals are formed.

Hence, the correct option is (C).

3. On arranging in reverse word as per dictionary order:

i) **Pop**ular

ii) **Poo**dle

iii) **Pon**der

iv) **Pol**ite

So, "Poodle" comes second after arranging in reverse word as per dictionary order.

Hence, the correct option is (D).

4. From the first to the second figure, the image is rotating 45 degrees in the anticlockwise direction.

So, the answer will be option (D) i.e. 45 degrees anticlockwise rotated figure of the first image in the second part.

Hence, the correct option is (D).

5. Interchanging the signs × with ÷ and numbers 2 with 3 in the given equations:

(A). 13 ÷ 3 + 40 × 3 ≠ 44, False.

(B). 32 ÷ 3 + 30 × 3 ≠ 56, False.

(C). 12 ÷ 3 + 32 × 4 ≠ 44, False.

(D). 32 × 1 + 32 = 64, True.

Hence, the correct option is (D).

6. Ace is the highest card in the standard 52 - card deck.

King is the 2nd Highest card in the standard 52 - card deck.

Queen is 3rd Highest card in the standard 52 - card deck.

Jack is the 4th Highest card in the standard 52 - card deck.

Therefore, "Jack" will be next term in the series.

Hence, the correct option is (A).

7. The path taken by Chand and Dhyan is as shown below:

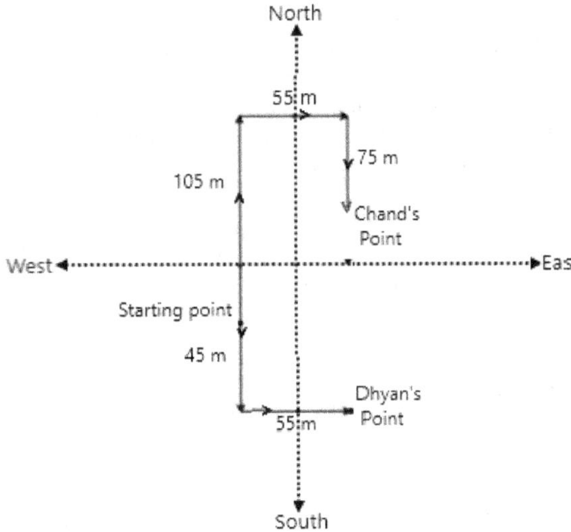

So, Chand is 75 m North with respect to the position of Dhyan.

Hence, the correct option is (C).

8. Given:

- Rectangle represents Fashion designers
- Circle represents Equestrians
- Triangle represents Campers
- Square represents Golfers

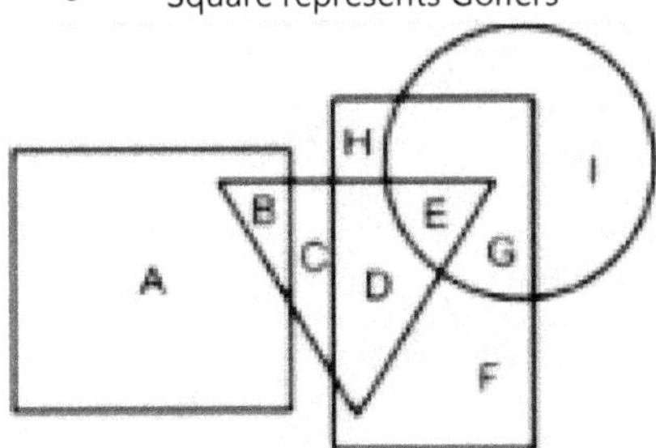

I is the letter which represents Equestrians who are not Fashion designers.

Hence, the correct option is (C).

9. The different orientation on opening the folded and punched paper is as shown below:

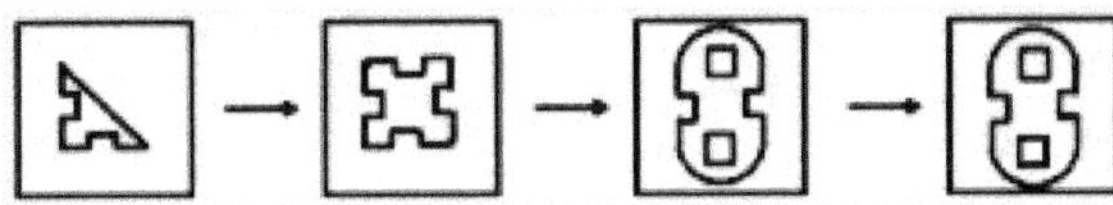

Hence, the correct option is (A).

10. Every number starting from the second row to the top in this tree figure is the sum of the two numbers just below it.

$2 + 3 = 5$; $3 + 4 = 7$; $4 + 5 = 9$ (2nd row)

$5 + 7 = 12$; $7 + 9 = 16$ (3rd row)

$12 + 16 = $ **28** (4th row)

Hence, the correct option is (B).

11. The question states that if the building has more than three floors then it has lifted. Then the buildings, which have to say five floors they have a second floor also, thus the option (A) is wrong. Option (B) is the right answer. Option (C) is wrong, using the same logic as in the case of option (A). Option (D) cannot be definitely true, because had it been the case, then even the building with two floors would have had lifts.

Hence, the correct option is (B).

12. Here, it follows a pattern of + 3 between two consecutive characters as shown below:

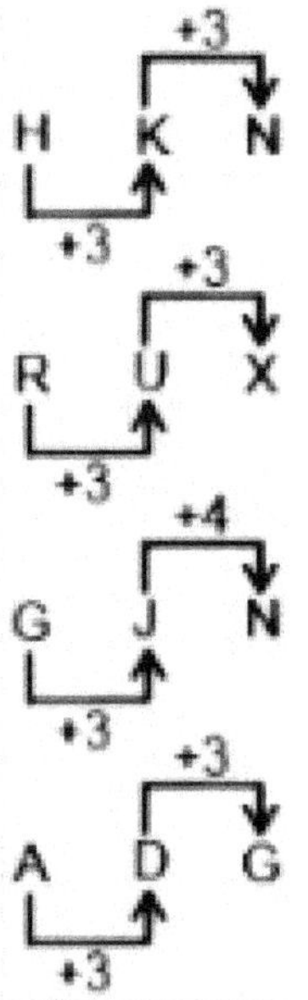

So, GJN is the odd one.

Hence, the correct option is (C).

13. As per the given information:

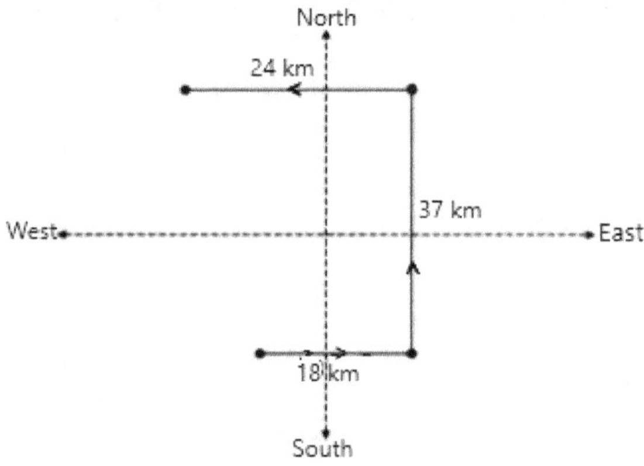

So, Shiva is in the North-west direction from its original position.

Hence, the correct option is (C).

14. From the given information the seating arrangement is shown below:

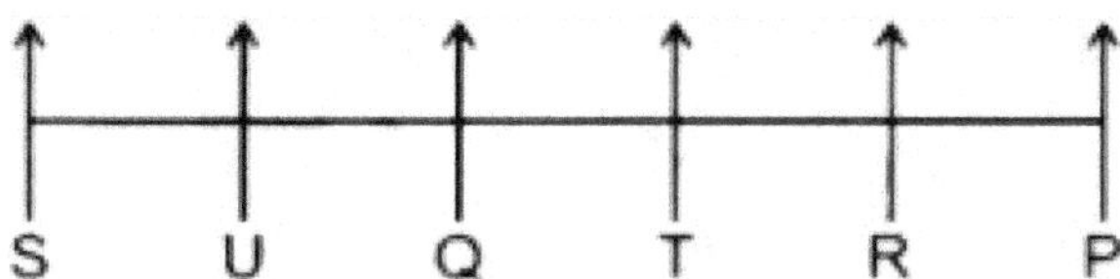

Clearly, there are 0 members between P and R.

Hence, the correct option is (C).

15. The Writer clearly states in the last part of his statement, that he should or should not be inclined to call him intelligent. The only option, which reflects that intention, is the first option and this is the answer.

Option (B) is wrong because we cannot generalize all empirical concepts to be vague on basis of this and it is irrelevant also. Options (C) and (D) are also vague.

Hence, the correct option is (A).

16. The different triangles are shown below:

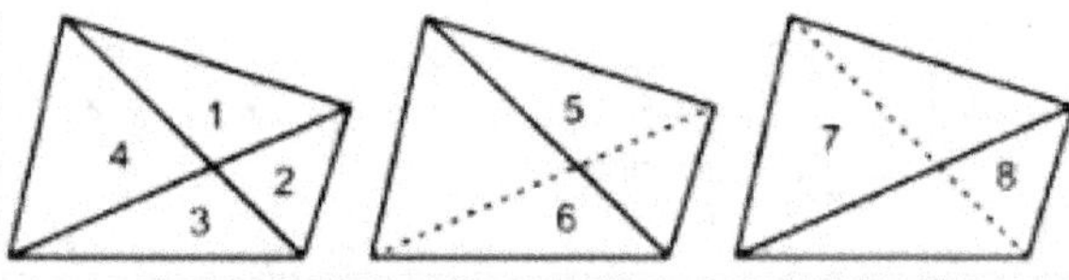

The total number of triangles in the given figure is 8.

Hence, the correct option is (C).

17. Given:

- The rectangle represents Film directors.
- The circle represents Bikers.
- The triangle represents Riders.
- The square represents Asians.

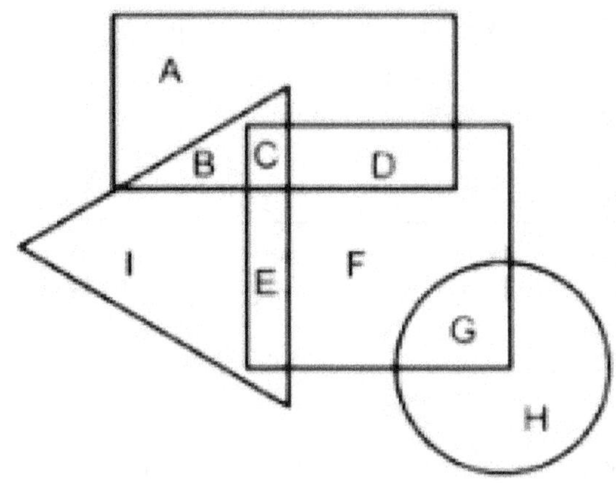

Clearly, Film directors who are Riders are represented by the intersection of rectangle and triangle i.e. BC.

Hence, the correct option is (B).

18. The pattern followed here is:

(A). 4^2, 6^2, $14^2 \rightarrow$ 16, 36, 196

(B). 9^2, 11^2, $19^2 \rightarrow$ 81, 121, 361

(C). 51^2, 17^2, $63^2 \rightarrow$ 2601, 289, 3969

(D). 21^2, 33^2, $69^2 \rightarrow$ 441, 1089, 4761

All groups except "16, 36, 196" are odd number's squares, So, "16, 36, 196" is the odd group from the given alternatives.

Hence, the correct option is (A).

19. Squash and bowling are not related to each other but they both are games.

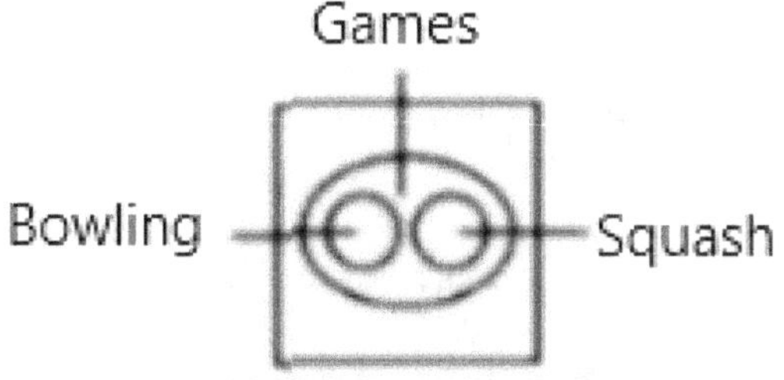

Hence, the correct option is (C).

20.

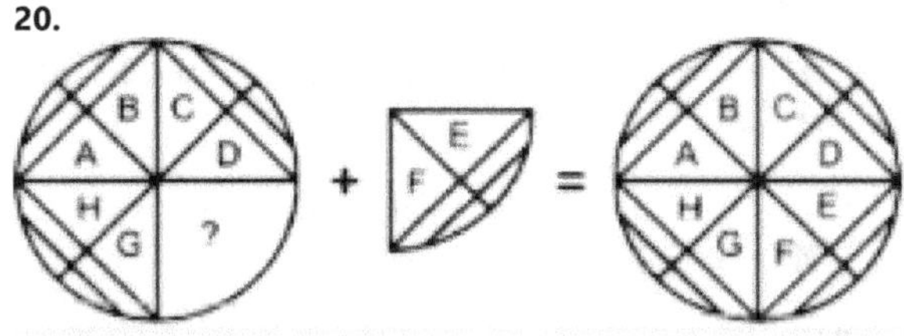

Hence, the correct option is (C).

21. November 2 → Monday

November 3 → Tuesday

November 4 → Wednesday

November 5 → Thursday

November 6 → Friday

November 7 → Saturday

November 8 → Sunday

November 9 → Monday

Thus, each day of the week is repeated after 7 days.

We have to find out for after 61 days, let us consider the multiple of 7 near the value 61,

So, after 63 days, it will be Monday.

Thus after 62 days, it will be Sunday.

Therefore after 61 days, it will be Saturday.

Hence, the correct option is (B).

22. Given:

COTTON is coded as 325526 and WOOLEN is coded as 122976.

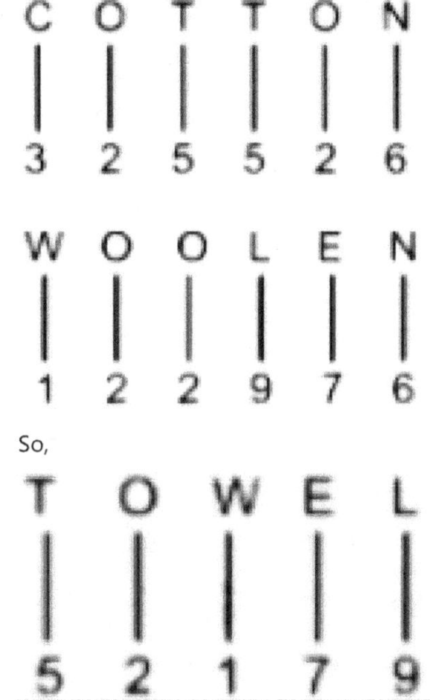

So, TOWEL is coded as 52179.

Hence, the correct option is (C).

23. Given:

41 : 4

The pattern followed here is:

41 = 4 × 1 = 4;

Similarly, from 37:

37 = 3 × 7 = 21

Hence, the correct option is (B).

24. There are two series that merge together.

One is: 17, 25, ?, 37

Here to get the next number, add the sum of the previous number to the previous number.

17 + (1 + 7) = 25

25 + (2 + 5) = 32

32 + (3 + 2) = 37

Other one is: 18, 9, 4.5

Divide the number by 2 to get the next one.

So, the missing term is 32.

Hence, the correct option is (B).

25. The paradox can be explained if an option offers an alternate reason for the decrease in population. Option (D) does that.

Hence, the correct option is (D).

26. The average weight of 5 persons is x.

Let the weight of the new person be y.

Then the total weight of 5 persons initially $= 5x$

New average $= x - 5$

Total weight after one person is replaced $= 5x - 40 + y$

Then,

$$\frac{(5x - 40 + y)}{5} = x - 5$$

$$y - 40 = -25$$

$$y = 15$$

Hence, the correct option is (C).

27. By the trigonometry formula:

$$\sin(A + B) = \sin A \times \cos B + \cos A \times \sin B$$

$$\cos(A - B) = \cos A \times \cos B + \sin A \times \sin B$$

$$\therefore \sin\left(45° + \theta\right) = \sin 45° \times \cos \theta + \cos 45° \times \sin \theta = \frac{1}{\sqrt{2}} \times \cos \theta + \frac{1}{\sqrt{2}} \times \sin \theta$$

$$\therefore \cos\left(45° - \theta\right) = \cos 45° \times \cos \theta + \sin 45° \times \sin \theta = \frac{1}{\sqrt{2}} \times \cos \theta + \frac{1}{\sqrt{2}} \times \sin \theta$$

Given:

$$\sin(45° + \theta) - \cos(45° - \theta)$$

$$= \frac{1}{\sqrt{2}} \times \cos \theta + \frac{1}{\sqrt{2}} \times \sin \theta - \frac{1}{\sqrt{2}} \times \cos \theta - \frac{1}{\sqrt{2}} \times \sin \theta$$

$$= 0$$

Hence, the correct option is (B).

28. Given:

Speed of boat along with the current (Downstream) $= 16$ km/hr

Speed of boat against the current (Upstream) $= 10$ km/hr

Speed of a boat in still water $=$
$$\frac{(Downstream\ Speed + Upstream\ Speed)}{2}$$

$$\therefore \text{Speed of the boat } = \frac{(16 + 10)}{2} = 13 \text{ km/hr}$$

Hence, the correct option is (B).

29. Given:

The number p is 5 more than q and the sum of the squares of p and q is 55.

p = q + 5

p − q = 5   ......(i)

Squaring both sides we get:

$p^2 + q^2 - 2pq = 25$ ......(ii)

$p^2 + q^2 = 55$ ......(iii)

Putting (iii) in (ii)

$\Rightarrow 2pq = 55 - 25$

$\Rightarrow pq = 15$

Hence, the correct option is (C).

30. Given:

A can complete the work in 12 hours

A's one - hour work $= \dfrac{1}{12}$

B can complete the work in 8 hours

B's one - hour work $= \dfrac{1}{8}$

Let the total time taken by A and B to complete the work be x hours

A and B's one - hour work $= \dfrac{1}{12} + \dfrac{1}{8}$

$$\frac{1}{12} + \frac{1}{8} = \frac{1}{x}$$

$\Rightarrow x = 4.8 \text{ hr} = 4 \text{ hr and } (0.8 \times 60) \text{ min} = 4 \text{ hours } 48 \text{ minutes}$

The total time is taken by A and B to complete the work is 4 hours and 48 minutes

Hence, the correct option is (D).

31. Each interior angle in a regular polygon is $(2n - 4) \times \dfrac{90}{n}$

Each exterior angle is $\dfrac{360°}{n}$

The sum is given as $324°$

So,

$$\Rightarrow 2(2n-4) \times \frac{90}{n} + \frac{360°}{n} = 324°$$

$$\Rightarrow 360°n - 720 + 360° = 324°n$$

$$\Rightarrow 36n = 360°$$

$$\Rightarrow n = 10 \text{ sides}$$

Hence, the correct option is (D).

32. Given:

$(534 \times 303 \times 441 \times 833)$

$\Rightarrow$ Unit digit of $(534 \times 303 \times 441 \times 833)$

$\Rightarrow$ Unit digit of $(4 \times 3 \times 1 \times 3)$

$\Rightarrow$ Unit digit of 36

$\Rightarrow 6$

Hence, the correct option is (A).

33. Let the marked price of an article be Rs. x.

$\because$ Discount $= 40\%$

$\therefore$ Akash purchased an article $= C.P$ for Akash $=$ Rs. $0.6x$

$\therefore \quad S.P$ of an article $= C.P + \frac{10 C.P}{100}$

$\Rightarrow S.P = C.P \times \left(\frac{110}{100}\right)$

$\Rightarrow S.P = 0.6x \times \left(\frac{110}{100}\right)$

$\Rightarrow S.P = 0.66x$

$\Rightarrow S.P$ for Akash $= C.P$ for Vinay $= 0.66x$

Required ratio $= \dfrac{M.P}{(C.P \ for \ vinay)} = \dfrac{x}{0.66x} = \dfrac{100}{66} = \dfrac{50}{33}$

Hence, the correct option is (B).

34. Let the C.P. be Rs. 100.

Given:

First S.P. $=$ Rs. 110

Second C.P. $=$ Rs. 90

Gain $= 25\%$

Second S.P. $= 125\%$ of Rs. $90 =$ Rs. 112.50

The difference of two S.P.'s $=$ Rs. $112.50 -$ Rs. $100.00 =$ Rs. 2.50

Actual difference $=$ Rs. 6

Cost price $= \dfrac{6 \times 100}{2.50} = 240$

Hence, the correct option is (A).

35. Given:

Simple Interest (S.I) =Rs 2400

Rate(r)=12%

Time (t)= 5 years

Principle (P)= ?

Simple interest $= \dfrac{(P \times r \times t)}{100}$

$2400 = \dfrac{(P \times 12 \times 5)}{100}$

$P = \dfrac{240000}{60} =$ Rs. 4000

Hence, the correct option is (B).

36. The total surface area of a cube $= 6a^2$

Where, $a =$ side of cube

Given:

Total surface area of a cube $= 2166$ cm^2

$\Rightarrow 2166 = 6a^2$

$\Rightarrow a^2 = \dfrac{2166}{6}$

$\Rightarrow a^2 = 361$

$\Rightarrow a = \sqrt{361}$

$\Rightarrow a = 19$

The volume of a cube $= a^3$

The volume of a cube $= 19^3 = 6859$

$\therefore$ The volume of a cube is 6859 cm^3.

Hence, the correct option is (C).

37. Given:

$(1 - \sin A)^2 + (1 + \sin A)^2 + (1 - \cos A)^2 + (1 + \cos A)^2$

$\Rightarrow (1 + \sin^2 A - 2\sin A) + (1 + \sin^2 A + 2\sin A) + (1 + \cos^2 A - 2\cos A) + (1 + \cos^2 A + 2\cos A)$

$(\because (a \pm b)^2 = a^2 \pm 2ab + b^2)$

$\Rightarrow 4 + 2\sin^2 A + 2\cos^2 A$

$\Rightarrow 4 + 2(\sin^2 A + \cos^2 A)$

$\Rightarrow 4 + 2 = 6 (\because \sin^2 A + \cos^2 A = 1)$

Hence, the correct option is (D).

38. Highest cost of C1 = Rs. 998000

Lowest cost of C3 = Rs. 385000

∴ Difference (in Rs.) between the highest cost of C1 and the lowest cost of C3:

⇒ 998000 - 385000

⇒ Rs. 613000

Hence, the correct option is (D).

39. From the given table:

Cost of C2 in T1 = 314000

Cost of C2 in T2 = 325000

Cost of C2 in T3 = 308000

Cost of C2 in T4 = 341000

Cost of C2 in T5 = 317000

∴ Total cost of C2:

⇒ 314000 + 325000 + 308000 + 341000 + 317000

⇒ 1605000

∴ Average cost of C2:

⇒ $\dfrac{1605000}{5}$

⇒ 321000

Hence, the correct option is (B).

40. From the given table:

Cost of C1 in T3 = 926000

Cost of C2 in T3 = 308000

Cost of C3 in T3 = 442000

Cost of C4 in T3 = 212000

∴ Total cost he has to pay:

⇒ 926000 + 308000 + 442000 + 212000

⇒ 1888000

Hence, the correct option is (C).

41. Total cost of 1 unit all the cars in T2:

⇒ 918000 + 325000 + 385000 + 268000

⇒ 1896000

Total cost of 1 unit all the cars in T4:

⇒ 998000 + 341000 + 478000 + 199000

⇒ 2016000

∴ Required Ratio:

⇒ 1896000 : 2016000

⇒ 237 : 252

⇒ 79 : 84

Hence, the correct option is (C).

42. Given:

A can do a piece of work in 14 days.

B can do it in 21 days.

$A's$ one day work $= \dfrac{1}{14}$

$B's$ one day work $= \dfrac{1}{21}$

$(A + B)'s$ one day work $= \dfrac{1}{14} + \dfrac{1}{21} = \dfrac{5}{42}$

According to the question:

$B's$ 3 day work $= \dfrac{3}{21} = \dfrac{1}{7}$

Remaining work $1 - \dfrac{1}{7} = \dfrac{6}{7}$ (which is completed by A and B together)

So, time taken by A and B to do $\dfrac{6}{7}$ of the work $=$ $\dfrac{6}{7} \times \dfrac{42}{5} = 7\dfrac{1}{5}$ days

∴ Total number of days taken $= 3 + 7\dfrac{1}{5} = 10\dfrac{1}{5}$ day

Hence, the correct option is (B).

43. Given:

4.5 of $a = 6.5$ of b

$\Rightarrow \dfrac{a}{b} = \dfrac{6.5}{4.5} = \dfrac{13}{9}$

Hence, the correct option is (B).

44. Let the number be x.

If the number is increased by 10%, then

The new number will be $= x + 10\%$ of $x = x + 0.1x = 1.1x$

Again, the number is decreased by 20%, then

The new number will be $= 1.1x - 20\%$ of $1.1x = 0.88x$

Percentage change $= (x - 0.88x) \times \dfrac{100}{x} = 12\%$ decrease

Hence, the correct option is (B).

45. The average weight of 25 bags $= 55$

Sum of the weight of 25 bags $= 55 \times 25 = 1375$

The correct sum of 25 bags $= 1375 - 65 + 56 = 1366$

The correct average of 25 bags $= \dfrac{1366}{25} = 54.64$

Hence, the correct option is (B).

46. Let $P =$ Principal, $R =$ Rate % per annum, Time $= n$ years.

When interest is compound annually:

Amount $= P\left(1 + \dfrac{R}{100}\right)^n$

Given:

$P = Rs.\,12000$ and $n = 2$ years and $R = 5\%$

Amount $= 12000\left[1 + \dfrac{5}{100}\right]^2$

$= 12000[1 + 0.05]^2$

$= 12000 \times 1.05 \times 1.05$

$= 13230$

Compound interest $=$ Amount $- P$

Compound interest $= 13230 - 12000 = 1230$

$\therefore$ Compound Interest is Rs. 1230.

Hence, the correct option is (C).

47. Let the price of 1 unit of the commodity $= Rs.\,x$

If the Price is decreased by 40%

Price of 1 unit of the commodity becomes $=$ $Rs.\,(1 - 0.40)x = Rs.\,0.60x$

If consumption is increased by 30%:

1.30 numbers of units consumed in place of 1 unit

Price of 1.30 unit of the commodity becomes $=$ $Rs.\,(1.30 \times 0.60x) = Rs.\,0.78x$

$\therefore$ Percentage decrease in expenditure $= \left[\dfrac{(x - 0.78x)}{x}\right] \times 100 = 0.22 \times 100\% = 22\%$

Hence, the correct option is (A).

48. Let the distance be d km.

We know that:

$Time = \dfrac{Distance}{Speed}$

$\Rightarrow \dfrac{d}{25} + \dfrac{d}{4} = 5$ hours 48 minutes

$\Rightarrow \dfrac{4d + 25d}{100} = \dfrac{29}{5}$

$\Rightarrow \dfrac{29d}{100} = \dfrac{29}{5}$

$\Rightarrow d = 20$ km

Hence, the correct option is (C).

49. Given:

The sum of the three numbers is 98.

The ratio of the first to second is 2 : 3 and that of the second to the third is 5 : 8.

Let the three parts be A, B, C.

According to the question:

A : B = 2 : 3 and B : C = 5 : 8 $= \left(5 \times \dfrac{3}{5}\right) : \left(8 \times \dfrac{3}{5}\right) = 3 : \dfrac{24}{5}$

$\Rightarrow A : B : C = 2 : 3 : \dfrac{24}{5} = 10 : 15 : 24$

$\Rightarrow B = \left(98 \times \dfrac{15}{49}\right) = 30$

Hence, the correct option is (B).

50. Let, total item $= X$

Let, cost price of each item $=$ Rs. a

And selling price of each item $=$ Rs. b

According to the problem:

$\Rightarrow X \times \left(\dfrac{40}{100}\right) \times b = X \times a$

$\Rightarrow b = 2.5a$

$\therefore$ Profit percentage

$\Rightarrow \left(\dfrac{(2.5a - a)}{a}\right) \times 100\%$

$\Rightarrow 150\%$

Hence, the correct option is (A).

51. It is mentioned in the passage 'With how accessible the internet is today, would you believe me if I told you the number of people who go online every day is still increasing?'

Hence, the correct option is (C).

52. It is mentioned in the passage 'From the website itself to a business's online branding assets -- digital advertising, email marketing, online brochures, and beyond -- there's a spectrum of tactics that fall under the umbrella of "digital marketing."

Hence, the correct option is (D).

53. It is mentioned in the passage 'And although we say it a lot, the way people shop and buy really has changed along with it -- meaning offline marketing isn't as effective as it used to be. Marketing has always been about connecting with your audience in the right place and at the right time. Today, that means you need to meet them where they are already spending time: on the internet.'

Hence, the correct option is (A).

54. It is mentioned in the passage 'And depending on the goals of their marketing strategy, marketers can support a larger campaign through the free and paid channels at their disposal.'

Hence, the correct option is (A).

55. It is mentioned in the passage 'Digital marketing is defined by the use of numerous digital tactics and channels to connect with customers where they spend much of their time: online.'

Hence, the correct option is (B).

56.

- The word 'Putrefy' means 'decompose, decay.'
- The word 'Assimilate' means 'to become part of a group.'
- 'Revoke' means 'Cancel' and
- 'Colloquial' means 'Informal.'

Hence, the correct option is (C).

57. The word 'Dainty' means 'Elegant, Delicate.'

The meanings of the other words are:

- Fester ⇒ (of a wound or sore) Becomes septic; suppurate.
- Noxious ⇒ Harmful.

Hence, the correct option is (B).

58. On the eve of inspection, everything was kept in apple-pie order.

Hence, the correct option is (D).

59. As fit as a fiddle means Strong and healthy

Example: He has recovered from illness and now he is as fit as a fiddle.

Hence, the correct option is (D).

60. A person who talks in sleep is called a Somniloquist.

Suffix 'ist' is used to denote a person who is skilled or expert in something.

The word 'Somniloquist' is a Latin word. 'Somni' means sleep and 'loqui' means to talk.

Hence, the correct option is (C).

61. The word 'mollify' means 'appease. Thus 'irritate' is the word having the opposite meaning.

- Abrogate ⇒ Repudiate
- Acculturate ⇒ Assimilate to a different culture, typically the dominant one

Hence, the correct option is (B).

62. The word 'murky' means 'dusky.' Thus 'bright' is the word having the opposite meaning.

- Liturgy ⇒ A forms or formulary according to which public religious worship, especially Christian worship, is conducted.
- Quixotic ⇒ Idealistic
- Pertness ⇒ Impudence

Hence, the correct option is (A).

63. The place for ammunition and weapons is called Arsenal.

The meanings of other words are:

- Asylum – Hospital for mad people
- Archives – Place of collecting public/government/historical records.
- Acoustics – Science of sound

Hence, the correct option is (B).

64. The correct spelling is Accessary.

Please note that do not get confused between Accesssary and Accessory.

Hence, the correct option is (D).

65. The correct spelling is Admittance.

Hence, the correct option is (A).

66. The correct preposition here is 'into' as someone pushes a person 'into' a problem. 'Push someone into a problem' means 'get someone involved in a problem.'

Hence, the correct option is (B).

67. The correct form of the verb is simple present tense and it must be singular as the subject is small kids carrying heavy sacks, which is singular.

Hence, the correct option is (D).

68. The correct word here would be an adverb as it is acting on the adjective 'commercialized' thus 'highly' fits here correctly. Options (B) and (D) are adjectives that are incorrect here. The word 'many' is used with countable nouns and is used to denote numbers thus cannot be used here.

Hence, the correct option is (A).

69. The verb 'run' is correct here as the tense is present progressive thus the other options cannot be placed here.

Hence, the correct option is (B).

70. The correct preposition here is 'among' as something is common 'among' people. The other prepositions do not fit here.

Hence, the correct option is (B).

71. The above given sentence is given in Passive Voice:- Use structure "auxiliary + past participle"

Women like to be flattered by men.

Hence, the correct option is (B).

72. The above given sentence is given in Passive Voice :-

You are supposed to make tea at eleven O'clock.

Hence, the correct option is (C).

73. As per the given above sentence is given in Passive Voice.

Use structure "auxiliary + past participle"

Grass is not eaten by a lion, however hungry he may be.

Hence, the correct option is (D).

74. Addressing them as gentlemen, the speaker said that he was going to discuss the food situation in their country. (Indirect)

said ⇒ addressing

our ⇒ their

that ⇒ conj.

I am ⇒ he was

Hence, the correct option is (B).

75. He applauded him saying that he had done well. (Indirect)

Bravo ⇒ applauded

you ⇒ he

have done (Pr.Per.) ⇒ had done (Past Per.)

Hence, the correct option is (A).

76. The Benson & Hedges Cup was a one-day cricket competition for first-class counties in England and Wales that was held from 1972 to 2002, one of cricket's longest sponsorship deals

Hence, the correct option is (B).

77. Agricultural Marketing is known as AGMARK.

AGMARK acts as a third-party guarantee for agricultural products consumed in India.

AGMARK is a quality certificate that labels a product pure and of necessary quality as per guidelines specified by a governing body.

The quality of an agricultural commodity is based on its intrinsic merit, and these standards are devised keeping in mind International laws and specifications so that we comply with the WTO requirements.

AGMARK is approved by the Directorate of Marketing and Inspection which falls under the Department of Agriculture.

AGMARK comes under the Agriculture Produce (Grading and Marketing) Act of India, 1937.

AGMARK on the products of Pulses, Whole spices, Vegetable oils, Wheat Products, Milk products, Honey, Rice, Tapioca Sago, Seedless tamarind, Besan (Gram flour).

Hence, the correct option is (C).

78.

- National Education Day is celebrated in India on 11th November.
- The day is celebrated as a mark of respect to Maulana Abul Kalam Azad.
- He was a freedom fighter and independent India's first Education Minister (served from 1947 to 1958).
- He was an eminent scholar of Urdu, Persian, and Arabic.
- He was awarded the Bharat Ratna in 1992.

Hence, the correct option is (D).

79.

- 'Thang ta', a martial art form is associated with the Manipur state of India.
- Manipur's popular indigenous martial arts game 'Thang-Ta' will be part of the Khelo India Youth Games 2021 to be held at Panchkula in Haryana.
- Gatka from Punjab, Kalaripayattu of Kerala, and Mallakhamba, a well-known sport played in Madhya Pradesh and Maharashtra will also be part of the Games.

Hence, the correct option is (C).

80.

- Kynrem falls is located 12km from the Chirapunji district in the Khasi Hills of Meghalaya.
- Its height is 305 meter.

Hence, the correct option is (D).

81.

- Muhammad Ibn Battuta was a Moroccan scholar who widely traveled the medieval world and wrote his travel accounts.
- He visited India during the rule of Mohammad bin Tughlaq.

Hence, the correct option is (D).

82.

- Article 32 (Right to Constitutional Remedies) of the Indian Constitution has been described as the 'heart and soul' of the Indian Constitution by Dr. B. R. Ambedkar.
- It gives a citizen the right to approach the Supreme Court or High Court to get resorted any of the fundamental rights in case of their violation.

Hence, the correct option is (C).

83.

- The Gujarat government has decided to rename dragon fruit as 'Kamalam'.
- The state government has applied for a patent to change the nomenclature of dragon fruit, which is largely grown in Kutch, Navsari, and different parts of Saurashtra.
- It looks like a lotus, hence the name 'Kamalam'.
- The fruit is known for its nutritional value and also helps in increasing hemoglobin.

Hence, the correct option is (A).

84. The coefficient of friction between any two surfaces in contact is defined as the ratio of the force of limiting friction and normal reaction between them.

$$\mu = \frac{F}{R}$$

Angle with the resultant of force of limiting friction F and normal reaction R makes with the direction of normal reaction R is angle of reaction.

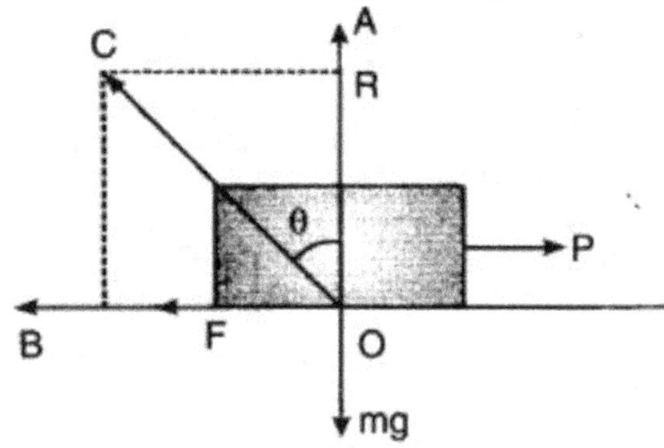

Relation :

In $\triangle AOC$ $\tan\theta = \dfrac{AC}{OA} = \dfrac{OB}{OA} = \dfrac{F}{R} = \mu$

So, $\mu = \tan\theta$

Hence, the correct option is (D).

85.

- The sound made by owls is known as Hoot.
- Squawk is the sound made by Parrots.
- Warble is the sound made by Nightingales.
- Cluck is the sound made by hens.

Hence, the correct option is (B).

86.

- The first mammal cloned from an adult somatic cell, using the process of nuclear transfer was a female domestic sheep name, Dolly from 5 July 1996 – 14 February 2003.
- Keith Campbell, Ian Wilmut with his colleagues at the Roslin Institute, part of the University of Edinburgh, Scotland, and the biotechnology company PPL Therapeutics, based near Edinburgh cloned Dolly.
- The cell used as the donor for the cloning of Dolly was taken from a mammary gland, and the production of a healthy clone, therefore, proved that a cell taken from a specific part of the body could recreate a whole individual.

Hence, the correct option is (D).

87. Pradhan Mantri Jeevan Jyoti Beema Yojana (PMJJBY):

- It is a one-year life insurance scheme.
- It is available in the age group of 18 to 50 years.
- It is renewable from year to year.

Hence, the correct option is (D).

88. An operating system is the system software that handles the software and hardware resources and provides services for the computer programs. So without an operating system, a computer cannot "boot".

Hence, the correct option is (C).

89.

- 1 bar = 1,00,000 pascal.
- The force exerted per unit area is called Pressure.
- Pressure $= \dfrac{Force}{Area}$
- The S.I unit of Pressure is Pascal, denoted by Pa.

Hence, the correct option is (D).

90.

- A mass number of an atom is the integer closest to the nuclear mass. It is denoted by A and expressed as

  A = Z + N

  where Z is the atomic number and N is the number of neutrons in the nucleus of the atom.

- The atomic number is the total number of protons in the nucleus of an atom.
- In $_AX^Z$ where X is the chemical symbol, A represents the mass number and Z represents the atomic number.

Hence, the correct option is (B).

91.

- Sukumar Sen was the first Chief Election Commissioner of India who served from 1950 to 1958.
- The Chief Election Commissioner heads the Election Commission of India and has a tenure of 6 years or up to 65 years of age, whichever is earlier.

Hence, the correct option is (B).

92.

- Indian Standard Time is calculated on the basis of $82.5°$E longitude, in Mirzapur Uttar Pradesh.
- This $82.5°$E is termed as Indian Standard Meridian.
- This line pass through 5 Indian States namely: Uttar Pradesh, Madhya Pradesh, Chhattisgarh, Odisha, Andhra Pradesh.

Hence, the correct option is (A).

93.

- USB stands for Universal Serial Bus.
- A Universal Serial Bus (USB) is a common interface that enables the communication between devices and a host controller such as a personal computer (PC) or smartphone.
- It connects peripheral devices such as digital cameras, keyboards, printers, scanners, media devices, external hard drives, and flash drives.

Hence, the correct option is (B).

94.

- 'Farr-i Izadi' was developed by Sufi saint Shihabuddin Suhrawardi.
- According to Farr-i Izadi, the Mughal ruler receive power from God, there was a hierarchy according to

which the Divine Light was transmitted to the king who becomes the source of spiritual guidance.

Hence, the correct option is (A).

95.

- In the modern periodic table while going from top to bottom in a group the size of an atom increases.

- From left to right in a periodic table, the atomic volume first decreases due to the increase of nuclear charge.

- The number of electrons in the valence shell keeps increasing, results in a decrease of effective nuclear charge due to the shielding effect. Due to this atomic radius increases and thus atomic volume increases.

Hence, the correct option is (A).

96.

- JK Tyre & Industries Ltd. has entered a partnership with Hyundai Motor India for its highest selling SUV, Creta.

- JK Tyre will be offering its UX Royale 215/60 R17 radial tyre with the top end variants of the Hyundai Creta.

- The tyre comes with a 5-rib asymmetric design, variable draft groove technology, stable shoulder tread blocks, waffle groove, and aero wing design.

Hence, the correct option is (B).

97.

- The first World Environment Day was celebrated in 1974.

- World Environment Day is being celebrated every year on 5 June as an annual event to increase the importance of a healthy and green environment in human life.

- This day is celebrated every year to solve environmental issues by implementing some positive environmental actions by the government and organizations.

Hence, the correct option is (B).

98.

- For the first time in the areca nut sector, 'Sirsi Supari' grown in Uttara Kannada has received the Geographic Indication (GI) tag.

- It is cultivated in Yellapura, Siddapura and Sirsi taluks.

- The areca nut has unique features like a round and flattened coin shape, particular texture, taste.

Hence, the correct option is (B).

99.

- Science and Technology Hyderabad Cluster, one of the four such geographic clusters the Centre has proposed to boost science, research and innovation through a collaborative environment, was launched on 8 January 2021.

- The Prime Minister's Science, Technology and Innovation Advisory Council (PM-STIAC) had recommended the setting of the clusters, in Hyderabad, Bengaluru, NCR-Delhi, and Pune.

- The Central government initiative is aimed at encouraging scientific enterprise and pushing individual institutional excellence towards collective performance.

Hence, the correct option is (D).

100.

- Walmart-owned Flipkart has partnered with Niti Aayog to launch the revamped Women Entrepreneurship Platform.

- The Women Entrepreneurship Platform (WEP) is a first-of-its-kind, unified access portal that brings together women from different parts of India to realize their entrepreneurial aspirations.

- The revamped version will also include an additional feature to offer mentorship.

Hence, the correct option is (C).

General Intelligence and Reasoning

Q.1 In the following question, select the number which can be placed at the sign of question mark (?) from the given alternatives.

7	4	2	14
3	5	6	15
6	1	4	?

A. 10 **B.** 11 **C.** 12 **D.** 14

Q.2 If Neha says, "Anusha's father Ramu is the only son of my father-in-law Manish", then how is Bindhu, who is the sister of Anusha, related to Manish?

A. Niece **B.** Daughter

C. Granddaughter **D.** Daughter-in-law

Q.3 In the following question, select the related number from the given alternatives.

5 : 26 : : 1 : ?

A. 21 **B.** 10 **C.** 3 **D.** 2

Q.4 In the following question below are given some statements followed by some conclusions. Taking the given statements to be true even if they seem to be at variance from commonly known facts, read all the conclusions, and then decide which of the given conclusion logically follows the given statements.

Statements:

1. Some cups are tables.

2. Some tables are chairs.

Conclusions:

I. Some chairs are not cups.

II. Some chairs are tables.

A. Only conclusion (I) follows

B. Only conclusion (II) follows

C. Both conclusions follow

D. Neither conclusion (I) nor conclusion (II) follows

Q.5 Identify the diagram that best represents the relationship among the classes given.

Water, liquids, elements

A. 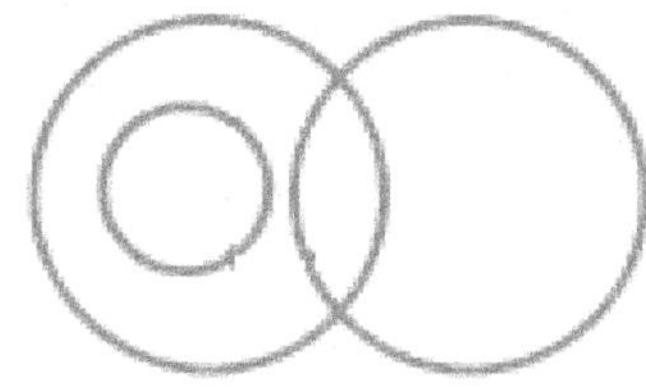

B. 

C. 

D. 

Q.6 There are seven persons Amit, Roshan, Ravi, Priya, Amrita, Arpita, and Mitul. They participated in a competition where they got different positions. Amit scored the first position while Mitul scored the last position. Priya scored the fourth position from the last. Ravi scored one position higher than Priya while Amrita scored one position lower than Priya. Roshan scored higher position than five of them.

Who scored the second-lowest position?

A. Arpita **B.** Amrita **C.** Ravi **D.** Roshan

Q.7 In the following question, select the related letters from the given alternatives.

AB : ZY : : MN : ?

A. ML **B.** OP **C.** NM **D.** XW

Q.8 If a mirror is placed on line AB, then which of the answer figures is the right image of the given figure?

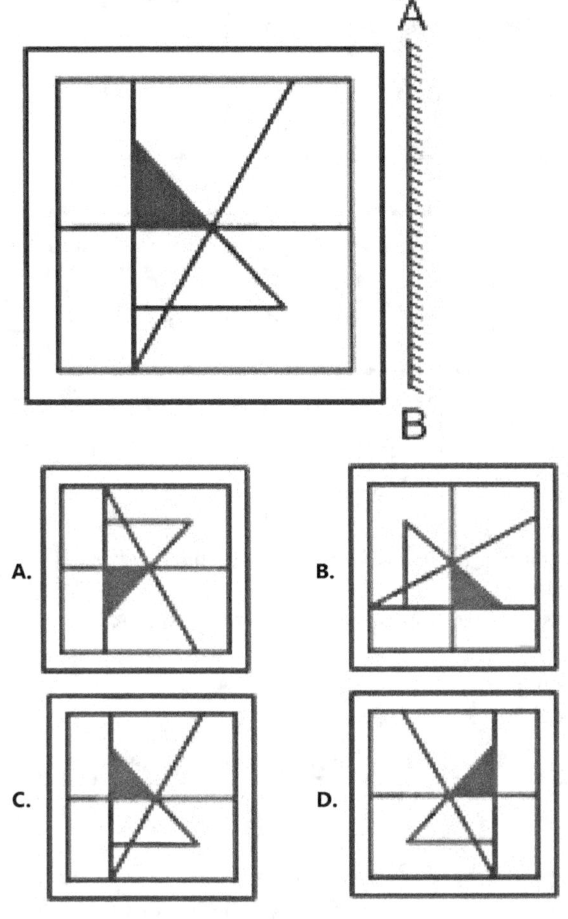

A. 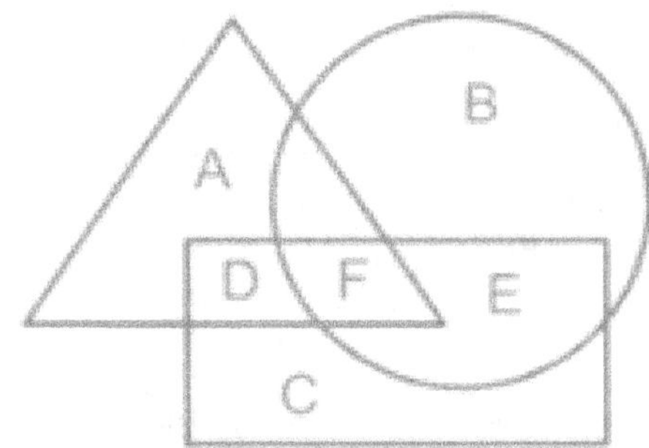

A. f5a   **B.** s6m   **C.** p8k   **D.** n7g

Q.12 Six people A, B, C, D, E, and F are sitting around a circular table facing inwards. A and B are sitting exactly opposite to each other. E is sitting immediately to the right of B. E and F are also exactly opposite to each other. Then which of the following cannot be the position of D.

A.   D is exactly opposite to C
B.   D is exactly between E and A
C.   D is immediate to the right of F
D.   D is immediate to the right of A

Q.13 Direction: Select the correct combination of mathematical signs to replace (*) signs and to balance the given equation.

16 * 6 * 4 * 24

A. ÷, =, ×   **B.** ×, =, ÷   **C.** =, ÷, ÷   **D.** ×, ÷, =

Q.14 Find out which of the figures can be formed by using all the pieces given in the figure.

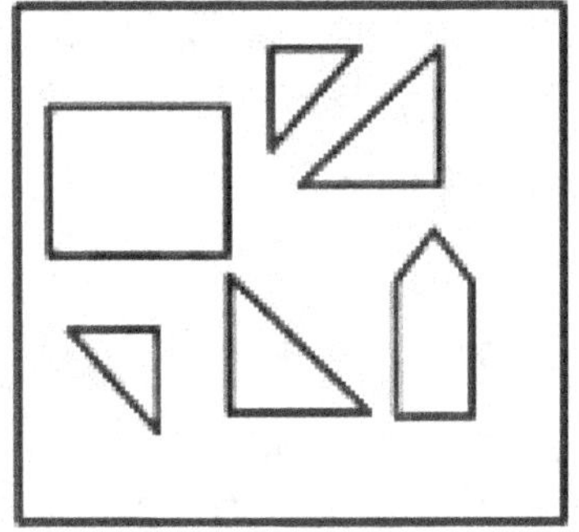

A. 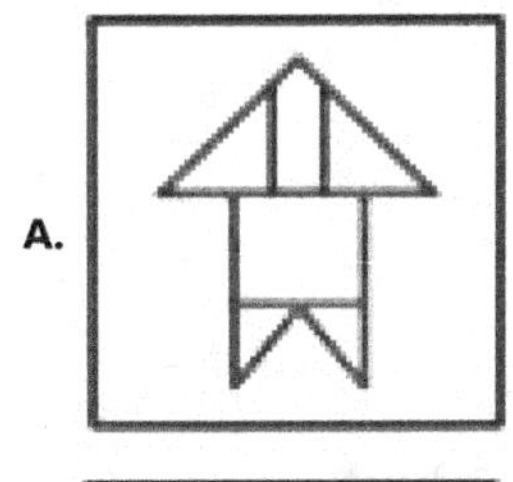   B. 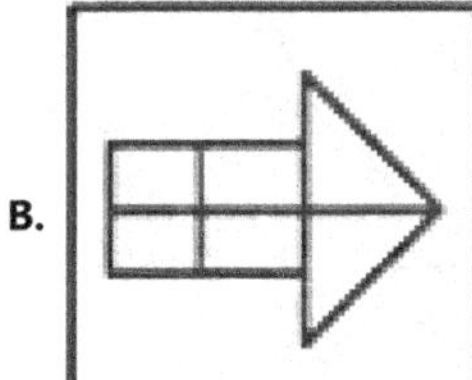

C. 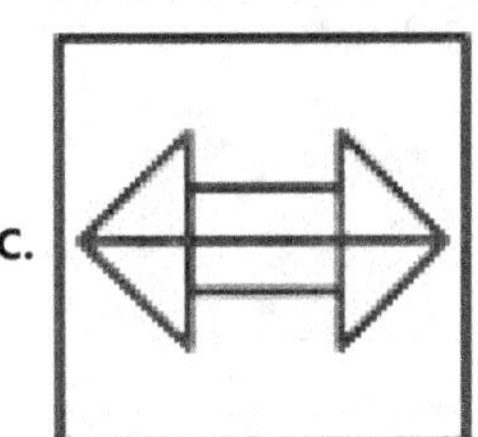   D. 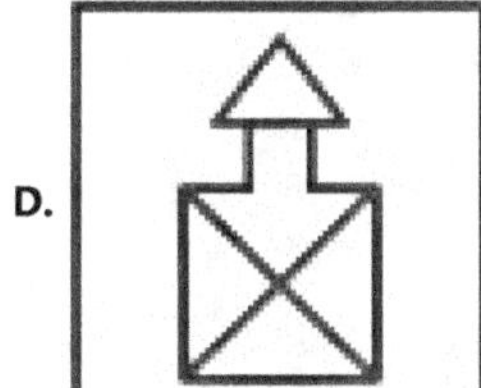

Q.9 In the following figure, the triangle represents Doctors, the circle represents Lawyers and rectangle represents Teachers. Which set of letters represents Teachers who are not Lawyers?

A. DC   **B.** DF   **C.** EC   **D.** DFC

Q.10 In the following question, by using which mathematical operators will the expression becomes correct?

15_9_12_2 = 121

A. -, +, ×   **B.** ×, +, -   **C.** +, ×, -   **D.** ×, -, +

Q.11 In the following question, four groups of numbers and letters are given. Three are similar on basis of some rule/relation/logic. Select the odd one from the given alternatives.

Q.15 A series is given with one missing term. Select the correct alternative from the given ones that will complete the series.

18, 21, 16, 23, 12, 25, ?

A. 9   **B.** 8   **C.** 10   **D.** 12

Q.16 How many triangles are there in the given figure?

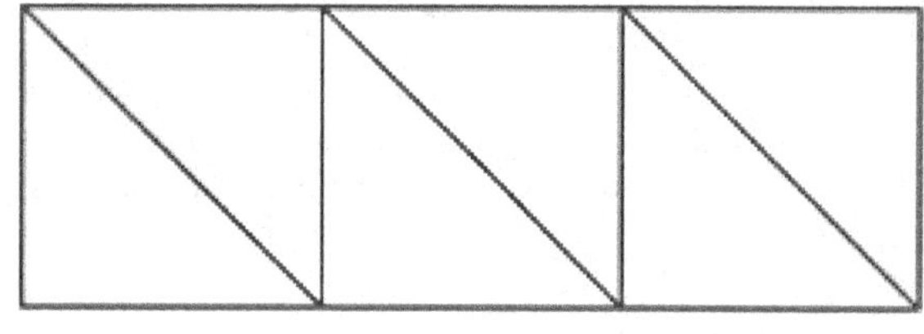

A. 4 **B.** 6 **C.** 5 **D.** 7

Q.17 One evening Rupesh was going toward his house from his office and met his friend Shivam at a crossing. Shivam's shadow was exactly to the left of Rupesh. If they were face to face, which direction was Shivam facing?

A. North **B.** South **C.** East **D.** West

Q.18 In the following question, select the odd word from the given alternatives.

A. Lungs **B.** Nose **C.** Air pipe **D.** Liver

Q.19 Direction: A statement is given followed by two inferences I and II. You have to consider the statement to be true even if it seems to be at variance from commonly known facts. You have to decide which of the given inferences, if any, follow from the given statement.

Statement: After the riots, a curfew was imposed in the whole city.

Inferences:

I. People were asked not to get out of their houses during the curfew.

II. If people go out on the streets during the curfew, the danger of the occurrence of serious violence can increase.

A. Only inference I follow
B. Only inference II follows
C. Both the inferences follow
D. None of the inferences follow

Q.20 Arrange the following options in logical order.

1. Click Print
2. Choose the printer from the pop-menu
3. Change any of the printing options shown if needed
4. Open the item you want to print
5. Choose Print from File menu or Press ctrl+P

A. 45231 **B.** 54321 **C.** 32145 **D.** 12453

Q.21 If the motor is called metro, the metro is called airplane, the plane is called tractor, the tractor is called the ship, the ship is called cart, the cart is called bullet, which is used to plough a field?

A. Motor **B.** Metro **C.** Bullet **D.** Ship

Q.22 In a certain language, BOLLYWOOD is written as CNMKZVPNE, what would be the similar code for the word HOLLYWOOD?

A. CNKMVZNPE **B.** DOOWYLLOB
C. INMKZVPNE **D.** INKMXYZRE

Q.23 Select a suitable figure from the answer figures that would replace the question mark (?).

Question Figure:

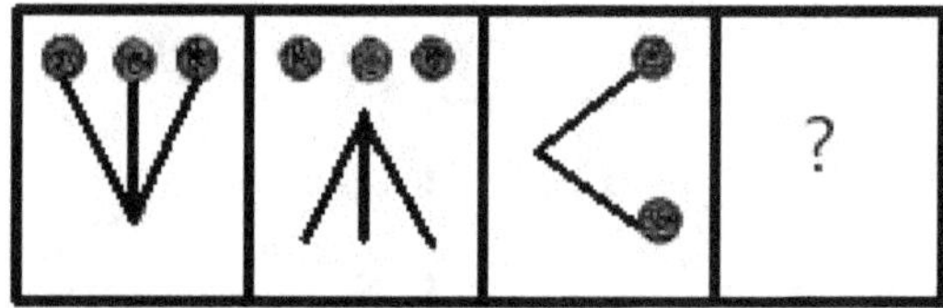

Answer Figure:

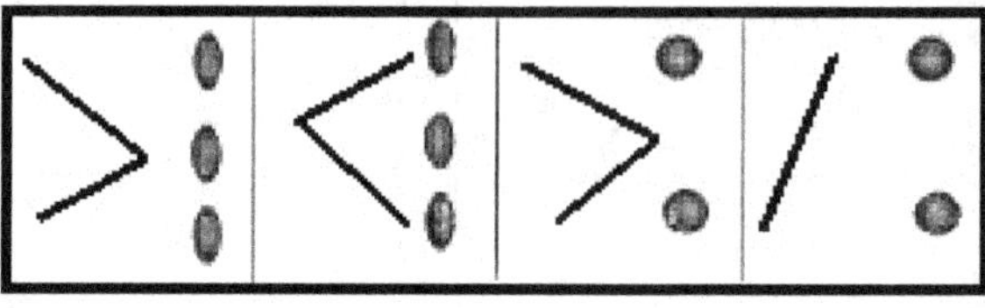

A. 1 **B.** 2 **C.** 3 **D.** 4

Q.24 If 'L' is coded as '24', 'LATE' is coded as '76', then how will 'BIG' is coded in the same way?

A. 33 **B.** 36 **C.** 35 **D.** 39

Q.25 Which of the following terms follows the trend of the given list?

abaBABAB, AbabABAB, ABabaBAB, ABAbabAB, ABABabaB, _______.

A. aBABABab **B.** ABABAbab
C. abaBABAB **D.** AbabABAB

Numerical Aptitude/ Quantitative Ability

Q.26 A and B together complete work in 20 days. B alone can complete the same work in 60 days. They took Rs. 36000 to complete the work. What will be the share of A (in Rs.)?

A. Rs. 18000 **B.** Rs. 24000
C. Rs. 26000 **D.** Rs. 22000

Q.27 The reciprocal of $x + \dfrac{1}{x}$ is

A. $\dfrac{x}{x^2+1}$ **B.** $\dfrac{x}{x+1}$ **C.** $x - \dfrac{1}{x}$ **D.** $\dfrac{1}{x} + x$

Q.28 What is the simplified value of $(1 - \sin A \cos A)(\sin A + \cos A)$?

A. $\sin^2 A - \cos^2 A$ **B.** $\sin^3 A + \cos^3 A$
C. 0 **D.** $\cos^2 A - \sin^2 A$

Q.29 A boat running downstream covers a distance of 28 km in 5 hours. While coming back stream the boat takes 7 hours to cover the same distance. What is the speed of the boat in still water?

A. 4 km/h **B.** 3.6 km/h **C.** 5.6 km/h **D.** 4.8 km/h

Q.30 1000 is first increased by 10% and then it is decreased by 30%. What is the final value?

A. 850 **B.** 770 **C.** 820 **D.** 760

Q.31 P is 60% less than Q. Q is 50% more than R. R is 20% more than S. If S is 1500, then what is the value of P?

A. 1240   **B.** 1080   **C.** 1140   **D.** 960

Q.32 What is the value of 2^{2^3} ?

A. 256   **B.** 1024   **C.** 128   **D.** 64

Q.33 If the compliment of an angle is one-fourth of its supplementary angle, then the angle is

A. 120°   **B.** 60°   **C.** 90°   **D.** 30°

Q.34 A train covers a distance in 50 minutes if it runs at a uniform speed of 48 km/hr. what will be the speed at which the train must run to reduce the time of journey to 40 minutes?

A. 50 km/hr   **B.** 55 km/hr   **C.** 60 km/hr   **D.** 70 km/hr

Q.35 What is the value of $21 + 24 + 27 + \cdots \ldots + 51$?

A. 324   **B.** 396   **C.** 416   **D.** 288

Q.36 The length of a rectangle is four times of its breadth, If the area of the rectangle is 1764 cm ^{2}, then what is the length of the rectangle?

A. 21 cm   **B.** 84 cm   **C.** 44 cm   **D.** 56 cm

Q.37 What is the value of $(3.2 + 2.5)^2 - (3.2 - 2.5)^2$?

A. 32.98   **B.** 33   **C.** 34.11   **D.** 32

Ques (38-40):Direction: The given bar graph shows the number of people who are players of different games. Read the graph carefully and answer the following question.

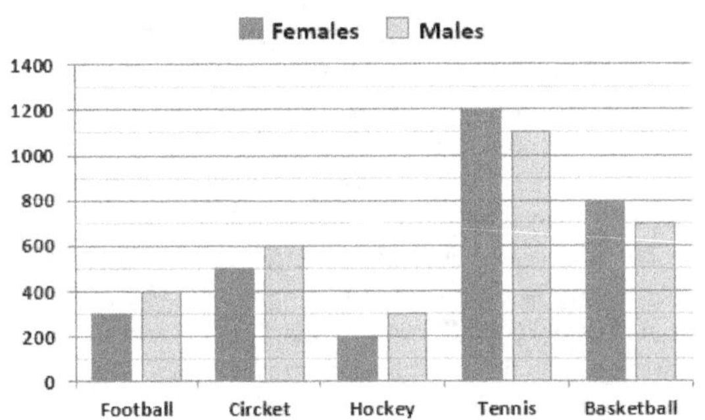

Q.38 What is the ratio of all male players to all female players of all five sports?

A. 29 : 30   **B.** 31 : 30   **C.** 34 : 32   **D.** 27 : 29

Q.39 If the data about the number of female players represented by a pie chart. What is the central angle of the sector representing the number of players of sport cricket?

A. 60°   **B.** 65°   **C.** 75°   **D.** 45°

Q.40 The number of football players is what percent more than the number of Hockey players?

A. 30%   **B.** 40%   **C.** 50%   **D.** 25%

Q.41 If the measure of the interior angle of a regular polygon is $100°$ greater than the measure of its exterior angle then how many sides does it have?

A. 10   **B.** 12   **C.** 9   **D.** 15

Q.42 A profit of 25% is made after giving a discount of 5% on an article. If the marked price of the article is Rs. 2625, then what is its cost price (in Rs)?

A. 2075   **B.** 2135   **C.** 2025   **D.** 1995

Q.43 An amount invested at simple interest gives Rs. 2550 interest at the rate of 17% per annum in 3 years. What is the principal amount (in Rs.)?

A. 4000   **B.** 5000   **C.** 6000   **D.** 4500

Q.44 The area of a circle is 616 cm ^{2}. What is its circumference (in cm).

A. 176   **B.** 88   **C.** 70   **D.** 140

Q.45 Prem buys a table for Rs. 450 and spends Rs. 30 on its transportation. It he sells the table for Rs. 600 what will be his gain percent?

A. 30%   **B.** 25%   **C.** 28%   **D.** 24%

Q.46 On selling an article for Rs. 265 a man loses 4%. In order to gain 12%, for how much he must sell the article?

A. Rs. 283.85   **B.** Rs. 308
C. Rs. 285   **D.** Rs. 298.50

Q.47 The average of 12 numbers is 14. If each number is doubled, then what will be the new average?

A. 28   **B.** 18   **C.** 20   **D.** 24

Q.48 The difference between the simple interest and compound interest on a certain sum of money at the rate of 5% per annum for 2 years is Rs. 34, then what is the principal amount?

A. Rs. 12,600   **B.** Rs. 14,800
C. Rs. 13,600   **D.** None of these

Q.49 The average of $104, 102, 109, A$ and 112 is 109. What is the value of A?

A. 114   **B.** 116   **C.** 118   **D.** 120

Q.50 Three numbers are in the ratio $2 : 3 : 5$. If the sum of their squares is 950, then what are the numbers?

A. 10,15,20   **B.** 10,15,25
C. 20,10,25   **D.** 30,15,25

General English & Comprehension

Ques (51-52):Direction: In the following question, a part of the sentence may have errors. Find out which part of the sentence has an error and select the appropriate option. If a sentence is free from error, select 'No Error'.

Q.51 The committee (1)/ was divided in their opinion (2)/ so no decision was taken. (3)/ No error (4)

A. (1)   **B.** (2)   **C.** (3)   **D.** (4)

Q.52 In spite the mutual (1)/ disagreements, the jury (2)/ has passed a collective statement. (3)/ No error (4)

A. (1) **B.** (2) **C.** (3) **D.** (4)

Ques (53-55):Direction: Fill in the blank with the correct word.

Q.53 Her birthday is _____ the month of November so we have only two weeks in hand to prepare for the party.

A. In **B.** On **C.** For **D.** By

Q.54 I like ______ this book again and again as it strengthens my mind in tough times.

A. To reading **B.** Reading
C. Read **D.** Reads

Q.55 I ______ the essay by tomorrow afternoon by this time.

A. Finished **B.** Would finished
C. Finishes **D.** Will have finished

Ques (56-58):Direction: Choose the word most similar in meaning to the given word.

Q.56 Soothe

A. Allay **B.** Control **C.** Submit **D.** Trepid

Q.57 Admonish

A. Question **B.** Struggle **C.** Applaud **D.** Rebuke

Q.58 Adversity

A. Taunt **B.** Misfortune
C. Illegal **D.** Damage

Ques (59-61):Direction: Choose the word most opposite in meaning to the given word.

Q.59 Praise

A. Bully **B.** Fresco **C.** Scream **D.** Disdain

Q.60 Fanatical

A. Opulent **B.** Funny
C. Tolerant **D.** Aggressive

Q.61 Defray

A. Compose **B.** Repudiate
C. Pour **D.** Burden

Ques (62-64):Direction: In the following question, out of the four alternatives, select the alternative which best expresses the meaning of the idiom/phrase.

Q.62 Sniff test

A. A difficult test
B. To see if something is suitable
C. A test put up for show
D. A test whose results are already known

Q.63 A sorry sight

A. A scene of poverty.
B. A social problem that is talked about a lot.
C. A show put up to gain sympathy.
D. Something sadly neglected.

Q.64 Once bitten twice shy

A. Injured gravely in an accident.
B. Being very sharing of one's belongings.
C. Being cautious of something due to an unpleasant experience in the past.
D. Being very skeptical of fairytales.

Ques (65-67):Direction: In the following question, out of the four given alternatives, select the alternative which is the best substitute of the phrase.

Q.65 A person who believes in the total abolition of war.

A. Groan **B.** Honorary
C. Jitter **D.** Pacifist

Q.66 Carry out a task clumsily or incompetently

A. Bungle **B.** Adept **C.** Apt **D.** Adroit

Q.67 A person who moves stealthily about or loiters near a place with a view to committing a crime.

A. Scrupulous **B.** Prowler
C. Veracious **D.** Unfeigned

Ques (68-72):Direction: Read the passage carefully and choose the best answer to each question out of the four alternatives.

The role of Organic Farming in the Indian Rural Economy can be leveraged to mitigate the ever-increasing problem of food security in India. With the rapid industrialization of rural states of India, there has been a crunch for farmland. Further, with the exponential population growth of India, the need for food sufficiency has become the need of the hour. Furthermore, the overuse of plant growth inhibitors, pesticides, and fertilizers for faster growth of agricultural produce is detrimental to human health and the environment as a whole. The proposition of Organic Farming in the Indian Rural Economy holds good, as an alternative to arrest this problem. The introduction of the process of Organic Farming in the Indian Rural Economy is a very new concept. The huge furor over the overuse of harmful pesticides and fertilizers to increase agricultural output has in fact catalyzed the entry of Organic Farming in the Indian Rural Economy. The process of organic farming involves using naturally occurring and decomposable matter for the growth and disease resistance of different crops. The concept of organic farming in India dates back to 10,000 years and it finds its reference in many Indian historical books.

Q.68 Which factor accelerated the concept of organic farming in India?

A. Shortage of food
B. Overpopulation
C. Overuse of harmful pesticides and fertilizers
D. Lack of funds

Q.69 What is the passage based on?

A. Overpopulation and its impact on farming
B. Deteriorating human health because of rural farming
C. New concepts in Indian farming
D. Factors catalyzing organic farming

Q.70 How would organic farming not be detrimental to human health?

A. It uses advanced chemicals to grow crops.
B. It is not modernized at all.
C. It produces crops in very small amounts.

D. It uses naturally occurring and decomposable matter

Q.71 Which of the following is the tone of the author?

A. Didactic   **B.** Positive
C. Censuring   **D.** Threatening

Q.72 Which of the following can be inferred from the passage?

A. Organic farming has been talked about many years ago in India.
B. Organic farming cannot be a permanent solution.
C. Organic farming is natural but not reliable.
D. It is important to blend organic farming with modernized ways of farming.

Ques (73-74):Directions: Select the most appropriate option to substitute the underlined segment in the given sentence. If there is no need to substitute it, select No improvement.

Q.73 <u>As much as</u> a hundred children gathered to celebrate Independence Day.

A. As long as   **B.** No improvement
C. As high as   **D.** As many as

Q.74 She <u>was looking troubled</u> when the teacher asked her to submit the homework.

A. is look trouble   **B.** was troubling
C. had been trouble   **D.** No improvement

Q.75 Direction: A sentence has been given in Active/Passive Voice. Out of the four alternatives suggested, select the one which best expresses the same sentence in Passive/Active Voice.
Rumi will be competing against Monty in the race.
A. Monty will compete against Rumi in the race.
B. Monty will be compete against Rumi in the race.
C. No passive voice possible
D. Monty will being competed against Rumi in the race.

General Awareness

Q.76 Who among the following cricket player has won the ICC men's ODI player of the decade award, one of the ICC Awards of the Decade?

A. Virat Kohli   **B.** Brett Lee
C. Chris Gayle   **D.** Stuart Broad

Q.77 Which Indian Pace bowler achieved the milestone of 200 Test wickets recently?

A. Mohammed Shami
B. Ravichandran Ashwin
C. Ravindra Jadeja
D. Jasprit Bumrah

Q.78 What is "Augusta National Club" famous for?

A. As a golf club
B. As a tennis club
C. As a badminton club
D. As a football club

Q.79 The force applied perpendicular to the surface of an object per unit area is called____.

A. Gravitational force   **B.** Magnetic force
C. Friction   **D.** Pressure

Q.80 What is the color of the light emitted by the Sun?

A. Red   **B.** Orange   **C.** Yellow   **D.** White

Q.81 Which of the following acids is present in ant bites?

A. Formic acid   **B.** Malic acid
C. Nitric acid   **D.** Perchloric acid

Q.82 Who presides over the Lok Sabha?

A. Speaker
B. President of India
C. Prime Minister of India
D. None of these

Q.83 What was the revenue system during Mughal emperor Akbar's reign called?

A. Jagir   **B.** Iqta   **C.** Mansab   **D.** Zabt

Q.84 Who among the following Mughal Emperors wrote his autobiography in Persian?

A. Babar   **B.** Akbar
C. Jahangir   **D.** Aurangzeb

Q.85 Who among the following was the first Viceroy of India?

A. Warren Hastings   **B.** Lord Hastings
C. Lord Dalhousie   **D.** Lord Canning

Q.86 Who among the following was popularly known as the "secretary of Mahatma Gandhi"?

A. Gopal Krishna Gokhale
B. Sushila Nayyar
C. Mahadev Desai
D. Madeleine Slade

Q.87 Which of the following Pass joins Himachal Pradesh with Leh Ladakh?

A. Aghil Pass   **B.** Niti Pass
C. Bara Lacha   **D.** Lanak La

Q.88 Which of the following is the only river integrated into the Indian Thar Desert?

A. Satluj   **B.** Luni   **C.** Narmada   **D.** Tapi

Q.89 Sunita Lakra announced her international retirement in January 2020, With which sport is Sunita Lakra associated?

A. Tennis   **B.** Cricket
C. Badminton   **D.** Hockey

Q.90 Which of the following is a form of folk music, mainly belonging to the state of West Bengal?

A. Mando   **B.** Kajri   **C.** Baul   **D.** Lavani

Q.91 With which of the following instrument is Pandit Shiv Kumar Sharma associated?

A. Veena   **B.** Sarod   **C.** Sitar   **D.** Santoor

Q.92 _________ is the shortcut key combination to print the data.

A. Ctrl + P   **B.** Ctrl + D

C. Alt + P **D.** Alt − Ctrl + P

Q.93 Memory that temporarily stores data and that can be erased or changed is known as
A. Cache Memory
B. Read Only Memory
C. Flash Memory
D. Random Access Memory

Q.94 Why lichens are used as the best indicator of environmental pollution?
A. Rapidly growing in the polluted atmosphere
B. Highly sensitive to the polluted atmosphere
C. Effectively purify the atmosphere
D. None of the above

Q.95 Which of the following is the most stable ecosystem?
A. Ocean **B.** Mountain
C. Forest **D.** Desert

Q.96 Which of the following will represent Canada in the race for best international feature film at the 2021 Oscars?
A. The Way Back **B.** Bloodshot
C. The Old Guard **D.** Funny Boy

Q.97 What is the pH value of vinegar?
A. 2.5 **B.** 6 **C.** 7 **D.** 5.5

Q.98 Who among the following topped the Forbes India Billionaires List 2020?
A. Mukesh Ambani
B. P.V. Sindhu
C. Rakesh Jhunjhunwala
D. Dr. Ranjan Pai

Q.99 Which of the following countries will host the Commonwealth Shooting and Archery Championships in January 2022?
A. Singapore **B.** Indonesia
C. China **D.** India

Q.100 Which is the form of market where there is lack of competition?
A. Monopoly **B.** Oligopoly
C. Perfect competition **D.** Marketization

// Smart Answer Sheet //

Correct — Percentage of students who answered correctly. **Skipped** — Percentage of students who skipped.

Q.	Ans.	Correct / Skipped	Q.	Ans.	Correct / Skipped	Q.	Ans.	Correct / Skipped	Q.	Ans.	Correct / Skipped	Q.	Ans.	Correct / Skipped	Q.	Ans.	Correct / Skipped
1	C	89.93 % / 0.0 %	18	D	89.88 % / 0.0 %	35	B	42.18 % / 1.67 %	52	A	78.58 % / 0.0 %	69	D	82.66 % / 0.0 %	86	C	45.97 % / 1.43 %
2	C	68.07 % / 1.51 %	19	C	62.35 % / 1.67 %	36	B	77.35 % / 0.0 %	53	A	78.92 % / 0.0 %	70	D	85.47 % / 0.0 %	87	C	44.26 % / 1.83 %
3	D	86.91 % / 0.0 %	20	A	64.31 % / 1.54 %	37	D	49.26 % / 1.96 %	54	B	89.76 % / 0.0 %	71	B	63.17 % / 1.81 %	88	B	44.95 % / 1.01 %
4	B	51.25 % / 1.85 %	21	D	54.08 % / 1.74 %	38	B	83.54 % / 0.0 %	55	D	59.24 % / 1.6 %	72	A	62.3 % / 1.59 %	89	D	51.99 % / 1.02 %
5	A	81.92 % / 0.0 %	22	C	46.07 % / 1.96 %	39	A	68.98 % / 1.11 %	56	A	81.63 % / 0.0 %	73	D	78.82 % / 0.0 %	90	C	25.83 % / 3.84 %
6	A	47.23 % / 1.61 %	23	C	68.81 % / 1.22 %	40	B	87.04 % / 0.0 %	57	D	52.5 % / 1.65 %	74	D	51.02 % / 1.98 %	91	D	51.9 % / 1.18 %
7	C	85.45 % / 0.0 %	24	B	50.6 % / 1.96 %	41	C	67.77 % / 1.21 %	58	B	77.26 % / 0.0 %	75	C	52.04 % / 1.12 %	92	A	89.45 % / 0.0 %
8	D	87.99 % / 0.0 %	25	B	46.79 % / 1.98 %	42	D	63.77 % / 1.14 %	59	D	82.2 % / 0.0 %	76	A	87.11 % / 0.0 %	93	D	79.86 % / 0.0 %
9	A	80.14 % / 0.0 %	26	B	52.47 % / 1.18 %	43	B	85.47 % / 0.0 %	60	C	58.07 % / 1.19 %	77	A	81.15 % / 0.0 %	94	B	68.11 % / 1.9 %
10	C	76.96 % / 0.0 %	27	A	46.97 % / 1.07 %	44	B	85.89 % / 0.0 %	61	B	27.85 % / 3.26 %	78	A	15.43 % / 3.42 %	95	A	88.03 % / 0.0 %
11	C	83.31 % / 0.0 %	28	B	12.97 % / 4.48 %	45	B	89.55 % / 0.0 %	62	B	52.3 % / 1.56 %	79	D	45.53 % / 1.57 %	96	D	63.92 % / 1.57 %
12	D	52.39 % / 1.6 %	29	D	49.74 % / 1.1 %	46	B	82.56 % / 0.0 %	63	D	69.03 % / 1.65 %	80	D	78.2 % / 0.0 %	97	A	43.57 % / 1.37 %
13	D	66.66 % / 1.51 %	30	B	86.2 % / 0.0 %	47	A	77.07 % / 0.0 %	64	C	46.31 % / 1.75 %	81	A	79.34 % / 0.0 %	98	A	86.17 % / 0.0 %
14	A	56.75 % / 1.23 %	31	B	66.54 % / 1.91 %	48	C	67.58 % / 1.99 %	65	D	83.54 % / 0.0 %	82	A	43.81 % / 1.5 %	99	D	79.99 % / 0.0 %
15	B	57.66 % / 1.5 %	32	A	84.27 % / 0.0 %	49	C	88.64 % / 0.0 %	66	A	20.3 % / 3.52 %	83	D	68.69 % / 1.19 %	100	A	55.34 % / 1.01 %
16	B	83.06 % / 0.0 %	33	B	80.53 % / 0.0 %	50	B	47.1 % / 1.35 %	67	B	21.08 % / 4.57 %	84	C	83.34 % / 0.0 %			
17	A	43.74 % / 1.87 %	34	C	76.12 % / 0.0 %	51	B	40.97 % / 1.64 %	68	C	82.7 % / 0.0 %	85	D	77.3 % / 0.0 %			

//Hints and Solutions//

1. The pattern followed here is:

In row 1 → (7 + 4 + 2) + 1 = 13 + 1 = 14

In row 2 → (3 + 5 + 6) + 1 = 14 + 1 = 15

So, the same pattern will be followed:

In row 3 → (6 + 1 + 4) + 1 = 11 + 1 = 12

Hence, the correct option is (C).

2.

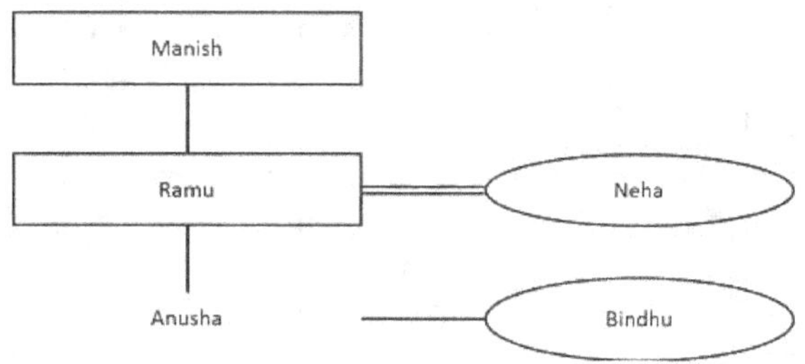

The only son of Neha's father-in-law Manish → Neha's husband

So, Ramu is Neha's husband and Anusha and Bindhu are his children.

Thus, Bindhu is the granddaughter of Manish.

Hence, the correct option is (C).

3. The pattern followed here is,

5 : 26 → (5 × 5) + 1 = 26;

Similarly,

(1 × 1) + 1 = 2

Hence, the correct option is (D).

4. The least possible Venn diagram for the given statements is as follows,

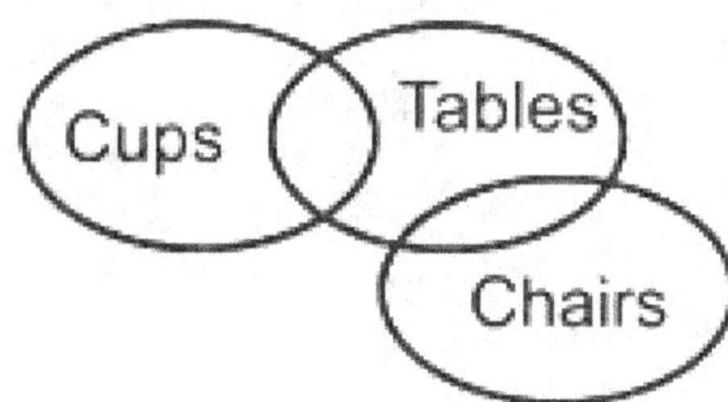

Conclusions:

I. Some chairs are not cups → not follows.

II. Some chairs are tables → follow.

So, only conclusion II follows.

Hence, the correct option is (B).

5. Liquids, water, and elements are represented by the circles. Since water is a liquid, the water circle lies inside the liquid circle.

Some of the elements (but not all the elements) are liquids So, the circles liquid and element intersect. Water is not intersect with each other

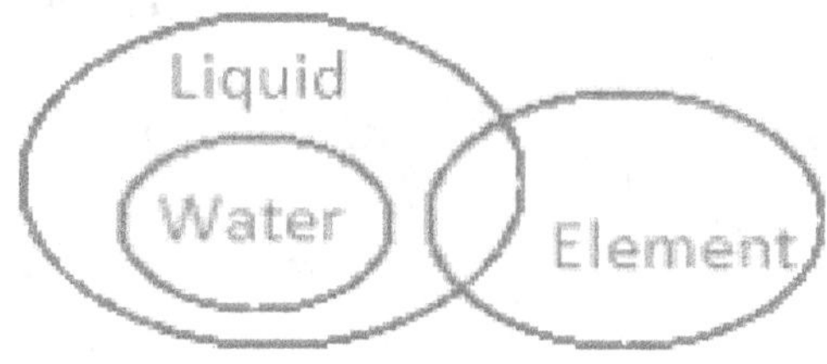

Hence, the correct option is (A).

6. 1) Amit scored the first position while Mitul scored the last position.

Amit > .... > ..... > ...... > ..... > ..... > Mitul

2) Priya scored the fourth position from the last.

Amit > .... > ..... > Priya > ..... > ..... > Mitul

3) Ravi scored one position higher than Priya while Amrita scored one position lower than Priya.

Amit > .... > Ravi > Priya > Amrita > ..... > Mitul

4) Roshan scored higher position than five of them.

(Therefore, Roshan scored second position and Arpita scored second last position)

Amit > Roshan > Ravi > Priya > Amrita > Arpita > Mitul

So, Arpita secured the second-lowest position.

Hence, the correct option is (A).

7. The pattern here is as follows is replacing the letter by its opposite or reverse letter in alphabetical order i.e. A is replaced by Z, B by Y, C by X D by W, and so on as shown in the figure below:

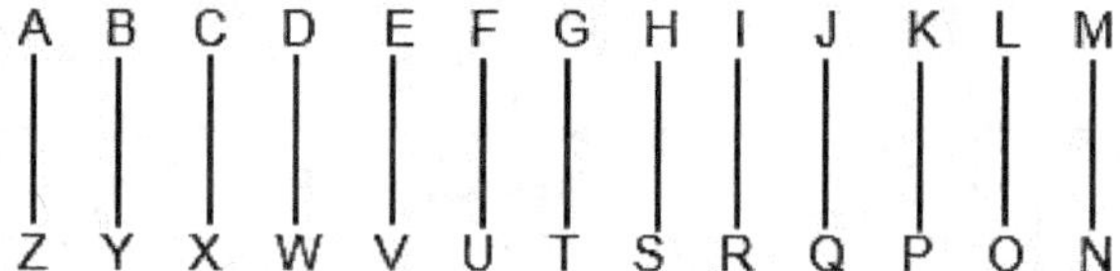

i.e.

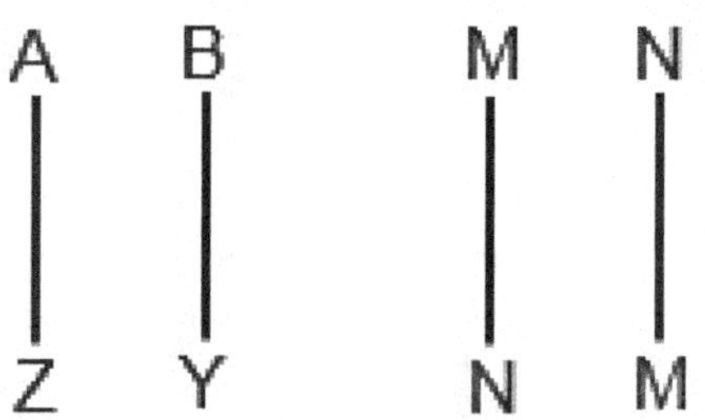

So, NM is the correct alternative.

Hence, the correct option is (C).

8.

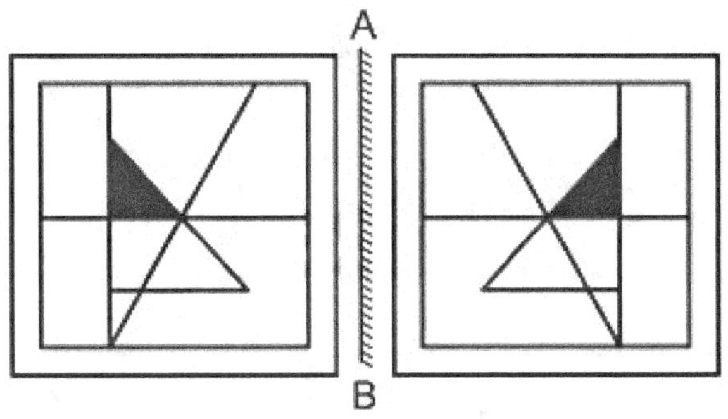

So, option (D) will complete the given question figure.

Hence, the correct option is (D).

9. D $\rightarrow$ Teachers who are doctors but not lawyers.

C $\rightarrow$ Teachers who are neither doctors nor lawyers.

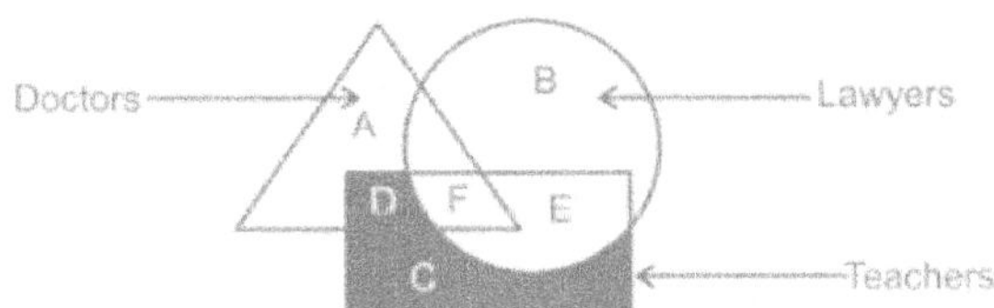

Hence, the correct option is (A).

10. Given: 15_9_12_2 = 121

Following the BODMAS rule,

C) +, ×, - ⇒ 15 + 9 × 12 - 2 = 121

A) -, +, × ⇒ 15 - 9 + 12 × 2 = 30

B) ×, +, - ⇒ 15 × 9 + 12 - 2 = 145

D) ×, -, + ⇒ 15 × 9 - 12 + 2 = 125

So, the correct set of symbols is '+, ×, -'.

Hence, the correct option is (C).

11. According to the alphabetical positions of the letters:

C) p - k = 16 - 11 = 5 ≠ 8

A) f - a = 6 - 1 = 5

B) s - m = 19 - 13 = 6

D) n - g = 14 - 7 = 7

So, 'p8k' is the odd one.

Hence, the correct option is (C).

12. If we arrange the given people around the circular table then we will have the following arrangement

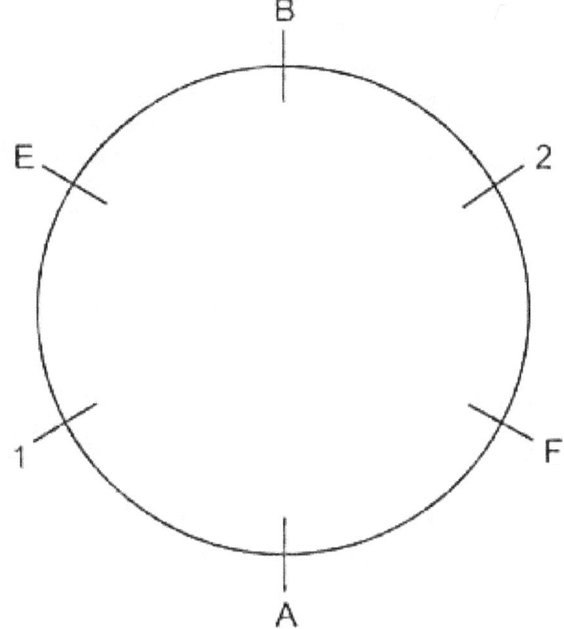

Out of six positions, we are able to fill the 4 positions. Position numbers 1 and 2 will be occupied by C and D in any order, so we will have the following two cases.

Case - 1

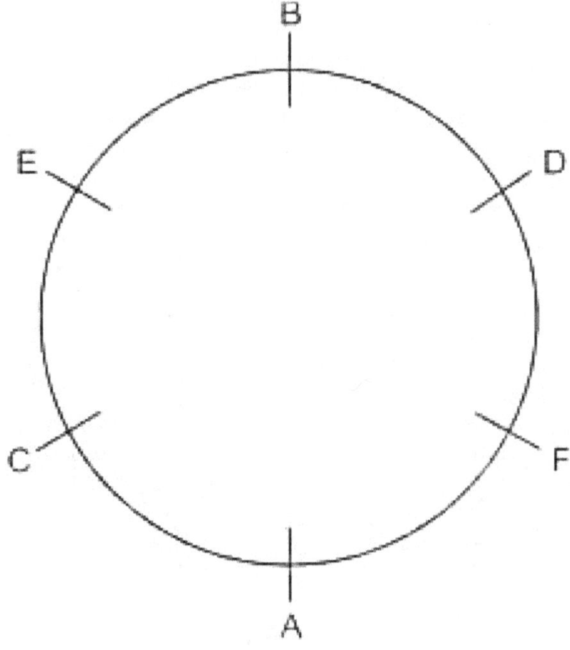

Case - 2

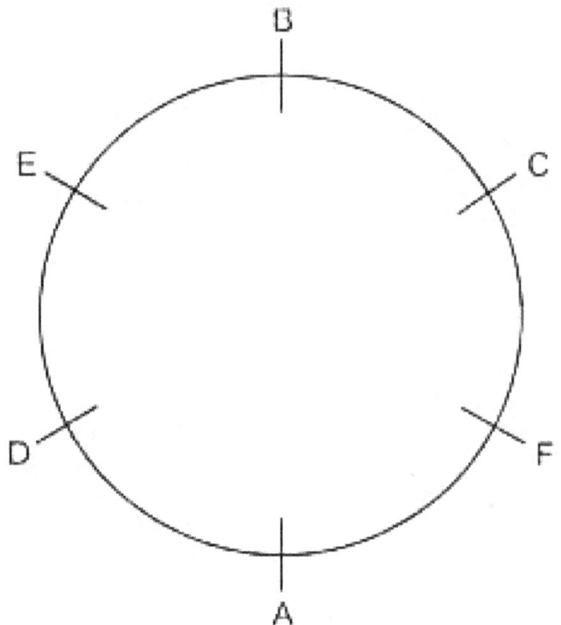

Therefore, if we see all the options, D can never be to the immediate right of A.

Hence, the correct option is (D).

13. Using signs given in option (D) i.e. (×, ÷, =)

16 * 6 * 4 * 24

After putting the signs in place of (*)

Using BODMAS and solving,

$$16 \times 6 \div 4 = 24$$

Hence, the correct option is (D).

14. On arranging the given pieces, we will get the following figure:

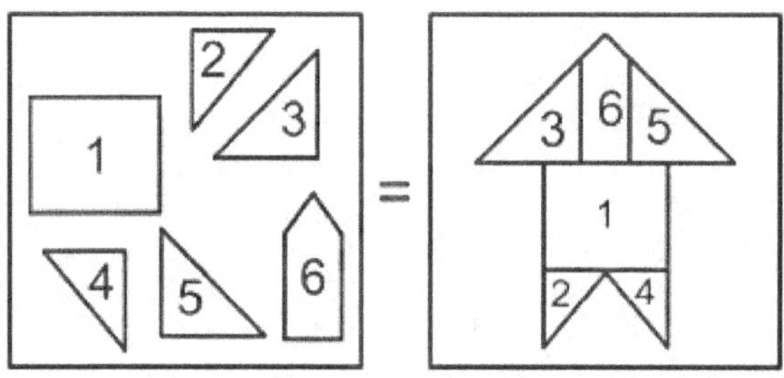

Hence, the correct option is (A).

15. The pattern followed is:

18 + 3 = 21

21 - 5 = 16

16 + 7 = 23

23 - 11 = 12

12 + 13 = 25

Similarly,

A Prime number is added or subtracted to each number, so

25 - 17 = 8

Therefore, "8" is a term which will complete the series.

Hence, the correct option is (B).

16. Let's count the number of triangles on the given figure we get,

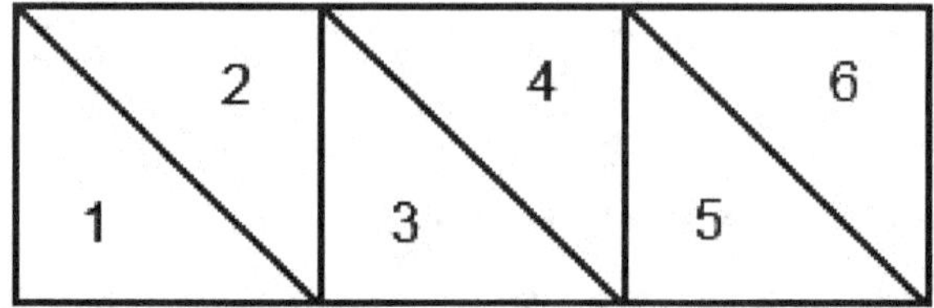

So, there are 6 triangles in the given figure.

Hence, the correct option is (B).

17. In the evening sunsets in the west.

So, the shadow will fall in the east.

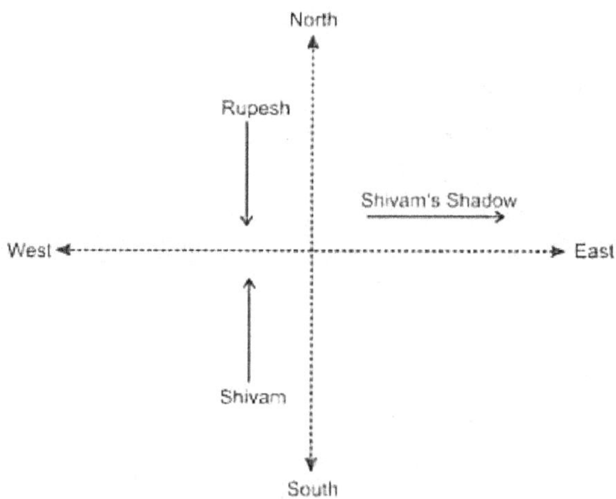

Since the shadow is on the left of Rupesh which is East. Therefore, Shivam is facing North.

Hence, the correct option is (A).

18. Except Liver all other organs, Lungs, Air pipe, and Nose are the parts of the Respiratory system.

Therefore, the Liver is an odd one among the given alternatives.

Hence, the correct option is (D).

19. The fact that a curfew was imposed clearly implies that people were asked to stay indoors for their safety and to avoid undesirable chaos and violence. So, both the inferences follow.

Hence, the correct option is (C).

20. The given options show how to take a printout.

4. Open the item you want to print.

5. Choose Print from the File menu or press ctrl+P.

2. Choose the printer from the pop-menu.

3. Change any of the printing options shown if needed.

1. Click Print.

So, 45231 is the correct order.

Hence, the correct option is (A).

21. A tractor is used to plough a field. But a tractor is called a ship.

Thus ship is used to plough a field.

Hence, the correct option is (D).

22. The pattern followed here is as follows,

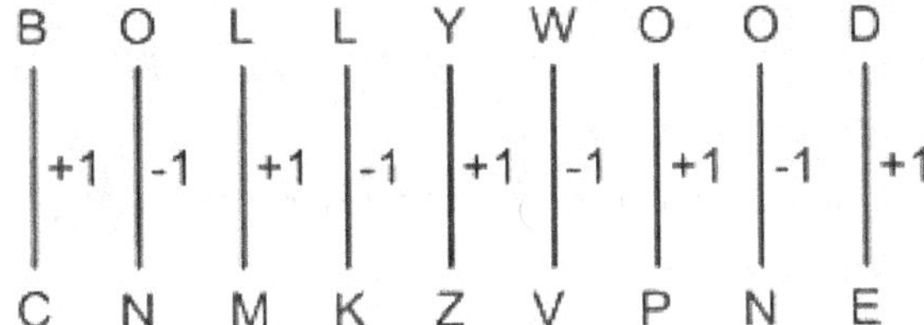

The pattern followed here is starting from the first word we increase one alphabet and then for the next, decrease one alphabet and so on.

Similarly,

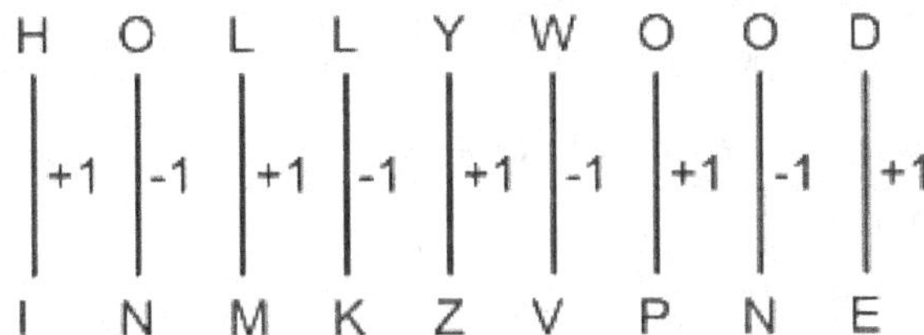

So, the correct answer is INMKZVPNE.

Hence, the correct option is (C).

23. Except for the dots, the remaining part of the figure rotates through 180° and shifts to the opposite side of the square boundary.

Hence, the correct option is (C).

24. According to the coding language:

A	B	C	D	E	F	G	H	I	J	K	L	M
1	2	3	4	5	6	7	8	9	10	11	12	13

Z	Y	X	W	V	U	T	S	R	Q	P	O	N
26	25	24	23	22	21	20	19	18	17	16	15	14

Now, L → 12 → 12 × 2 = 24

LATE → 12 + 1 + 20 + 5 = 38 → 38 × 2 = 76

BIG → 2 + 9 + 7 = 18 → 18 × 2 = 36

So, BIG is coded as '36'.

Hence, the correct option is (B).

25. Here, the position of 'aba' and 'bab' is moving one position forward (i.e. towards right) as shown below,

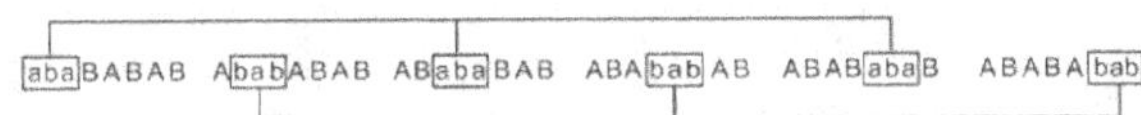

So, the next term in the series is 'ABABAbab'.

Hence, the correct option is (B).

26. B's one-day work $= \dfrac{1}{60}$

Let A can complete the work in x days

Let A's one-day work $= \dfrac{1}{x}$

Total time taken by A and B to complete the work $= 20$

A and B's one-day work $= \dfrac{1}{20}$

$$\dfrac{1}{60} + \dfrac{1}{x} = \dfrac{1}{20} \Rightarrow x = 30$$

A can complete the work in 30 days.

A's one-day work $= \dfrac{1}{30}$

Total work done by A in 20 days $= 20 \times \dfrac{1}{30} = \dfrac{2}{3}$

Total work done by B in 20 days $= 20 \times \dfrac{1}{60} = \dfrac{1}{3}$

Money earned by person $=$ Total money $\times$ Work done by the person

Share of A $= 36000 \times \dfrac{2}{3} = $ Rs. 24000

Hence, the correct option is (B).

27. Reciprocal of $a = \dfrac{1}{a}$

So, Reciprocal of $x + \dfrac{1}{x} = \dfrac{1}{x + \frac{1}{x}}$

$$\Rightarrow \dfrac{1}{\frac{x^2+1}{x}} = \dfrac{x}{x^2+1}$$

Hence, the correct option is (A).

28. Given:

$$(1 - sinA cosA)(sinA + cosA)$$

$$\Rightarrow sinA + cosA - sin^2 A cosA - sinA cos^2 A$$

$$\Rightarrow cosA - sin^2 A cosA - sinA cos^2 A + sinA$$

$$\Rightarrow cosA(1 - sin^2 A) + sinA(1 - cos^2 A)$$

$$\Rightarrow cosA(cos^2 A) + sinA(sin^2 A)$$

$$\Rightarrow sin^3 A + cos^3 A$$

Hence, the correct option is (B).

29. Speed $= \dfrac{distance}{time}$

Speed upstream $=$ Speed of boat $-$ speed of stream

Speed downstream $=$ Speed of boat $+$ speed of stream

Given, boat running downstream covers a distance of 28 km in 5 hours.

$\therefore$ Speed of boat $+$ speed of stream $= \dfrac{28}{5} = 5.6$ km /hr

The boat takes 7 hours to cover the same distance upstream

$\Rightarrow$ Speed of boat $-$ speed of stream $= \dfrac{28}{7} = 4$ km/hr

Adding the two equations, we get

$2 \times$ speed of boat $= 9.6$

$\Rightarrow$ Speed of boat $= 4.8$ km/hr

Hence, the correct option is (D).

30. Initial value = 1000

$\Rightarrow$ After increase of 10% = 1000 + 0.1 × 1000 = 1100

After decrease of 30%:

$\Rightarrow$ 1100 - 0.3 × 1100 = 1100 - 330 = 770

$\therefore$ Final value = 770

Hence, the correct option is (B).

31. Given,

$S = 1500$

$\Rightarrow R = 1500 + 1500 \times \left(\dfrac{20}{100}\right)$

$R = 1500 + 300 = 1800$

$\Rightarrow Q = 1800 + 1800 \times \left(\dfrac{50}{100}\right)$

$Q = 1800 + 900 = 2700$

$\Rightarrow P = 2700 - 2700 \times \left(\dfrac{60}{100}\right)$

$\Rightarrow P = 2700 - 1620$

$\therefore P = 1080$

Hence, the correct option is (B).

32. $\Rightarrow 2^{2^3}$

$\Rightarrow 2^8$

$\Rightarrow 256$

Hence, the correct option is (A).

33. Let the angle be A.

Given,

$90 - A = \dfrac{(180-A)}{4}$

$\Rightarrow 360 - 4A = 180 - A$

$\Rightarrow 180 = 3A$

$\Rightarrow A = 60$

Hence, the correct option is (B).

34. Speed $= \dfrac{Distance}{Time}$

A train covers some distance in 50 minutes if it runs at a uniform speed of 48 km/hr

Distance covered by train $= 48 \times \left(\dfrac{50}{60}\right) = 40$ km

Total time taken to cover this distance is 40 minutes i.e $\left(\dfrac{40}{60}\right)$ hr

New speed of the train $= \dfrac{40}{\frac{40}{60}} = 60$ km/hr

Hence, the correct option is (C).

35. The numbers are $21, 24, 27, \ldots 51$

Using the formula of AP, number of terms in an AP with difference ' d ' and first term ' a ' is given by

N^{th} term $= a + (n - 1)d$

Here N is 51 and $d = 3$

$\Rightarrow 51 = 21 + (n - 1) \times 3$

$\Rightarrow n = 11$

Sum of n terms of an AP $= \dfrac{n}{2}(2a + (n - 1)d)$

Here n is 11, sum $= \left(\dfrac{11}{2}\right) \times (2 \times 21 + (10) \times 3) = 396$

Hence, the correct option is (B).

36. Given:

The area of the rectangle $= 1764$ cm ^{2}

Formula used:

Area of rectangle = length $\times$ breadth

Let the breadth of the rectangle be x then its length is $4x$

Area = length $\times$ breadth

$\Rightarrow 4x \times x = 1764$

$\Rightarrow x^2 = 441$

$\Rightarrow x = 21$

Length of the rectangle $= 4 \times 21 = 84$ cm

- The length of the rectangle is 84 cm

Hence, the correct option is (B).

37. We know that,

$(a^2 - b^2) = (a + b)(a - b)$

$(3.2 + 2.5)^2 - (3.2 - 2.5)^2 = 5.7^2 - 0.7^2$ ...(1)

$\Rightarrow (5.7^2 - 0.7^2) = (5.7 + 0.7)(5.7 - 0.7)$

$\Rightarrow (5.7^2 - 0.7^2) = 6.4 \times 5 = 32$
Hence, the correct option is (D).

38. Total females = 300 + 500 + 200 + 1200 + 800 = 3000

Total males = 400 + 600 + 300 + 1100 + 700 = 3100

$\therefore$ Required ratio = 3100 : 3000 = 31 : 30

Hence, the correct option is (B).

39. $\Rightarrow$ Total numbers $= 3000$

$\Rightarrow$ Number of females in cricket $= 500$

$\Rightarrow 3000$ represents $= 360°$

$\Rightarrow 500$ represents $= \left(\frac{360}{3000}\right) \times 500 = 60°$

Hence, the correct option is (A).

40. $\Rightarrow$ Total number of football players $= 300 + 400 = 700$

$\Rightarrow$ Total number of Hockey players $= 200 + 300 = 500$

$\therefore$ Required percentage $= \frac{(700 - 500)}{500} \times 100 = 40\%$

Hence, the correct option is (B).

41. Formula for Interior angle of a Regular Polygon $= (n - 2) \times \left(\frac{180}{n}\right)$ [Where 'n' is the number of sides of polygon]

Formula for Exterior angle of a Regular Polygon = $\left(\frac{360}{n}\right)$
[Where 'n' is the number of sides of polygon]

$\Rightarrow$ Given $(n - 2) \times \left(\frac{180}{n}\right) = 100 + \left(\frac{360}{n}\right)$

$\Rightarrow (n - 2) \times 180 = 100n + 360$

$\Rightarrow 180n - 360 = 100n + 360$

$\Rightarrow 180n - 100n = 360 + 360$

$\Rightarrow 80n = 720$

$\Rightarrow n = \frac{720}{80} = 9$

$\therefore$ Number of sides $= 9$

Hence, the correct option is (C).

42. Given,

MP of an article $= 2625$

Discount $\% = 5\%$

Then, $SP = MP$ - Discount

$SP = 2625 - 2625 \times 0.05 = 2493.75$

$SP = CP +$ Profit

$SP = CP + CP \times 25\%$

$CP = SP \times \frac{100}{125} = 2493.75 \times \frac{100}{125} = 1995$

Hence, the correct option is (D).

43. Let $P =$ principal amount, $N =$ time and $R =$ rate percent per annum

Then,

Simple interest $= \frac{(P \times N \times R)}{100}$

Given,

Simple interest $=$ Rs. $2550, R = 17\%$ and $N = 3$

$\Rightarrow 2550 = \frac{(P \times 17 \times 3)}{100}$

$\Rightarrow 2550 \times 100 = 51 \times P$

$\Rightarrow P = \frac{(2550 \times 100)}{51}$

$\Rightarrow P = 5000$

$\therefore$ The principal amount is Rs. 5000.

Hence, the correct option is (B).

44. Area of circle with radius ' r ' $= \pi r^2$

$\Rightarrow \frac{22}{7} \times r^2 = 616$

$\Rightarrow r^2 = 196$

$\Rightarrow r = \sqrt{196} = 14$ cm

$\therefore$ Circumference of circle $= 2\pi r = 2 \times 22/7 \times 14 = 88$ cm

Hence, the correct option is (B).

45. Given,

Purchased price of a table $=$ Rs. 450

Transportation charges $=$ Rs. 30

Total cost price of a table

$= 450 + 30$

$= 480$

Cost price of a table $=$ Rs. 480

Selling price of a table $=$ Rs. 600

Profit percentage

$= [\frac{(S.P - C.P)}{C.P}] \times 100$

$= [\frac{(600 - 480)}{480}] \times 100$

$= [\frac{120}{480}] \times 100$

$= 25$

$\therefore$ Profit percentage is 25%

Hence, the correct option is (B).

46. Gain $\% = \frac{(SP - CP)}{CP} \times 100$

Loss $\% = \frac{(CP - SP)}{CP} \times 100$

Let the Cost price of article be x

LoSS $= 4\%$

Selling price of article $= x - \left(\frac{4}{100}\right) \times x = 0.96x$

$0.96x = 265 \Rightarrow x =$ Rs. 276

Now the article is sold at gain

Gain $= 12\%$

Selling price of article $= 276 + \left(\frac{12}{100}\right) \times 276 =$ Rs. 308

Hence, the correct option is (B).

47. Average $= \frac{\text{sum of numbers}}{\text{total numbers}}$

$\Rightarrow 14 = \frac{\text{sum of 12 numbers}}{12}$

$\Rightarrow$ sum of 12 numbers $= 14 \times 12 = 168$

Let the numbers be $a_1, a_2, a_3 \ldots \ldots a_{12}$

$\Rightarrow a_1 + a_2 + a_3 + \cdots \ldots + a_{12} = 168$

If each number is doubled,

Numbers will be, $2a_1, 2a_2, 2a_3 \ldots \ldots 2a_{12}$

$\Rightarrow 2a_1 + 2a_2 + 2a_3 + \cdots . + 2a_{12}$

$\Rightarrow 2(a_1 + a_2 + a_3 + \cdots + a_{12})$

$\Rightarrow 2 \times 168 = 336$

New average $= \frac{\text{sum of numbers}}{\text{total numbers}} = \frac{336}{12} = 28$

Hence, the correct option is (A).

48. Difference between the simple interest and compound interest for 2 years $= \frac{PR^2}{100^2}$

According to Question-

$34 = \frac{P \times 5^2}{100^2}$

P = 34 × 20 × 20 = Rs. 13,600

Hence, the correct option is (C).

49. Average $= \frac{\text{Sum of the terms}}{\text{Number of terms}}$

$\Rightarrow 109 = \frac{(104 + 102 + 109 + A + 112)}{5}$

$\Rightarrow 109 \times 5 = 427 + A$

$\Rightarrow A = 545 - 427 = 118$

Hence, the correct option is (C).

50. Let the three numbers be $2x, 3x$ and $5x$.

The sum of their squares $= 950$

$\Rightarrow (2x)^2 + (3x)^2 + (5x)^2 = 950$

$\Rightarrow 4x^2 + 9x^2 + 25x^2 = 950$

$\Rightarrow 38x^2 = 950$

$\Rightarrow x^2 = \frac{950}{38} = 25$

$\Rightarrow x = 5$

The three numbers are $2x = 10, 3x = 15$ and $5x = 25$

Hence, the three numbers are $10, 15$ and 25.

Hence, the correct option is (B).

51. Collective nouns are used both as singular and plural depending on the meaning. When they mean a single unit, the verb is singular, otherwise, the verb is plural. Also, the pronoun must be singular if the collective noun conveys the idea of one whole and the pronoun must be plural if the collective noun conveys the idea of separate individuals comprising the whole. The error lies in part (2) of the sentence as 'was' is incorrect here and must be replaced with 'were' as the sentence.

Correct sentence:

The committee were divided in their opinion so no decision was taken.

Hence, the correct option is (B).

52. The error lies in part (1) of the sentence as the preposition 'of' is missing after the words 'in spite.' 'In spite of' means 'without being affected by the particular factor mentioned.'

Correct sentence: In spite of the mutual disagreements, the jury has passed a collective statement.

Hence, the correct option is (A).

53. The correct preposition here is 'in' as 'in' is used for expressing a period of time during which an event happens or a situation remains the case.

Correct sentence: Her birthday is in the month of November so we have only two weeks in hand to prepare for the party.

Hence, the correct option is (A).

54. The correct word here is the participle 'reading' as the sentence has been structured.

Correct sentence: I like reading this book again and again as it strengthens my mind in tough times.

Hence, the correct option is (B).

55. The future perfect tense is used to express an action that, the speaker assumes, will have completed or occurred in the future. The other options are incorrect.

Correct sentence: I will have finished the essay by tomorrow afternoon by this time.

Hence, the correct option is (D).

56. Soothe means gently calm (a person or their feelings).

Allay means diminish or put at rest (fear, suspicion, or worry).

Other options:

Control means the power to influence or direct people's behaviour or the course of events.

Submit means accept or yield to a superior force or to the authority or will of another person.

Trepid means timid by nature.

Hence, the correct option is (A).

57. Admonish means to warn or reprimand someone firmly.

Rebuke means express sharp disapproval or criticism of (someone) because of their behaviour or actions.

Other options:

Question means a sentence worded or expressed so as to elicit information.

Struggle means make forceful or violent efforts to get free of restraint or constriction.

Applaud means show approval or praise by clapping.

Hence, the correct option is (D).

58. Adversity means a difficult or unpleasant situation.

Misfortune means bad luck or an unfortunate condition or event.

Other options:

Taunt means a remark made in order to anger, wound, or provoke someone.

Illegal means contrary to or forbidden by law, especially criminal law.

Damage means physical harm that impairs the value, usefulness, or normal function of something.

Hence, the correct option is (B).

59. Praise means express warm approval or admiration.

Disdain means the feeling that someone or something is unworthy of one's consideration or respect.

Other words:

Bully means a person who habitually seeks to harm or intimidate those whom they perceive as vulnerable.

Fresco means a painting done rapidly in watercolour on wet plaster on a wall or ceiling so that the colours penetrate the plaster and become fixed as it dries.

Scream means give a long, loud, piercing cry or cries expressing extreme emotion or pain.

Hence, the correct option is (D).

60. Fanatical means filled with excessive and single-minded zeal.

Tolerant means showing a willingness to allow the existence of opinions or behavior that one does not necessarily agree with.

Other options:

Opulent means ostentatiously costly and luxurious.

Funny means causing laughter or amusement; humorous.

Aggressive means ready or likely to attack or confront; characterized by or resulting from aggression.

Hence, the correct option is (C).

61. Defray means provide money to pay (a cost or expense).

Repudiate means refuse to accept; reject.

Other words:

Compose means write or create (a work of art, especially music or poetry).

Pour means flow rapidly in a steady stream.

Burden means a load, typically a heavy one.

Hence, the correct option is (B).

62. The idiom 'a sniff test' means 'to see if something is suitable'. It is basically an informal reality check of an idea or proposal, using one's common sense or sense of propriety.

Sentence usage: You can't wear that shirt again without washing it—it definitely doesn't pass the sniff test!

Hence, the correct option is (B).

63. The idiom 'a sorry sight' means 'something very untidy or something which is horribly neglected.'

Sentence usage: She confesses that she was a sorry sight back then.

Hence, the correct option is (D).

64. Once bitten twice shy means an unpleasant experience induces caution.

For example, I would never have believed the pictures had I not seen them, and once bitten, twice shy.

Hence, the correct option is (C).

65. Pacifist means a person who believes that war and violence are unjustifiable.

Other options:

Groan means make a deep inarticulate sound conveying pain, despair, pleasure, etc.

Honorary means conferred as an honour, without the usual requirements or functions.

Jitter means feelings of extreme nervousness.

Hence, the correct option is (D).

66. Bungle means to carry out a task clumsily or incompetently; mismanage; mishandle.

Other options:

Adept means very skilled or proficient at something.

Apt means appropriate or suitable in the circumstances.

Adroit means clever or skillful.

Hence, the correct option is (A).

67. Prowler means a person who moves stealthily about or loiters near a place with a view to committing a crime.

Other words:

Scrupulous means a person or process which is careful, thorough, and extremely attentive to details.

Veracious means speaking or representing the truth.

Unfeigned means genuine; sincere.

Hence, the correct option is (B).

68. It is mentioned in the passage ' The huge furor over the overuse of harmful pesticides and fertilizers to increase agricultural output has in fact catalyzed the entry of Organic Farming in India Rural Economy.'

Hence, the correct option is (C).

69. The passage states the factors which catalyze organic farming in India. It talks about food security, inadequate practices in normal farming, etc, and the popularity of organic farming in India.

Hence, the correct option is (D).

70. It is mentioned in the passage 'The process of organic farming involves using of naturally occurring and decomposable matter for growth and disease resistance of different crops.'

Hence, the correct option is (D).

71. The author has a positive tone as the scope of organic farming is being discussed.

Hence, the correct option is (B).

72. Only option (A) can be inferred from the passage as the following line is mentioned: 'The concept of organic farming in India dates back to 10,000 years and it finds its reference in many Indian historical books. '

Hence, the correct option is (A).

73.

- In the given sentence, hundred "children" are countable noun.
- We use "as much as" for uncountable nouns.
- We use "as many as" for countable nouns.
- Therefore, "as much as" should be replaced by "as many as".

Correct Sentence: As many as a hundred children gathered to celebrate Independence Day.

Hence, the correct option is (D).

74.

- The given sentence is in the past continuous tense form of the active voice.
- The rule of making past continuous tense (active voice): Subject + was/were + verb (lst form) + ing + object +(.).
- The adjective 'troubled' is acting as the object.
- Therefore, there is no need for any improvement in the underlined segment.

Hence, the correct option is (D).

75. The given sentence is in future continuous tense, the structure of which is given below:

Subject + will/shall + be + present participle (V1+ing) + Object.

Its passive voice is not possible as the auxiliary verb 'be' can't be used together twice.

Example:

- I shall be writing a novel. (active)
- A novel will be being written by me. (passive)

Hence, the correct option is (C).

76. Virat Kohli has been awarded the ICC men's ODI player of the decade Award.

He also won Sir Garfield Sobers award for the best male cricketer of the past decade.

Other ICC awards of the decade:

Mahendra Singh Dhoni won the ICC Spirit of Cricket Award of the decade.

Ellyse Perry a female all-rounder cricketer from Australia won the following awards:

- ICC female cricketer of the decade.
- ICC women ODI cricketer of the decade.

- Women's T20 Cricketer of the decade.

Hence, the correct option is (A).

77. Mohammed Shami recently achieved the milestone of 200 Test wickets, during the first Test against South Africa.

The 31 -year-old bowler is third-fastest among Indian pacers to reach the landmark, as he achieved this feat in his 55 th Test match. He is only behind Kapil Dev (434), Ishant Sharma (311), Zaheer Khan (311), and Javagal Srinath (236), at present.

Hence, the correct option is (A).

78. Augusta National Golf Club sometimes referred to as Augusta or the National, is a golf club in Augusta. Unlike most private clubs which operate as non-profits, Augusta National is a for-profit corporation, and it does not disclose its income, holdings, membership list, or ticket sales

Hence, the correct option is (A).

79.

- The amount of force exerted (thrust) on a surface per unit area is defined as 'Pressure'.

- It can also be defined as the ratio of the force to the area (over which the force is acting).

- Formula of Pressure: $(P) = \dfrac{Thrust}{Area}$

- Unit of pressure: The SI unit is 'pascals (Pa)'.

Hence, the correct option is (D).

80.

- The color of the light emitted by the Sun is white.

- The white colour is the composition of all the visible light frequencies.

- The highest wavelength of light is Red and the lowest wavelength of light is violet.

Hence, the correct option is (D).

81.

- Formic acid is present in ant bites.

- The sting of an ant contains simple carboxylic acid, which is also known as formic acid.

- The same acid is present in the sting of wasps, bees, etc.

- The chemical formula of formic acid is H-COOH.

Hence, the correct option is (A).

82.

- The Speaker of the Lok Sabha is the person in charge of the Lok Sabha and is elected by general elections.

- Lok Sabha is the lower house of the Parliament of India.

- The Speaker serves for a term of five years.

Hence, the correct option is (A).

83.

- The revenue system during Akbar's reign was called Zabt System.

- In this system, each province was divided into revenue circles with their own rates of revenue for each crop.

Hence, the correct option is (D).

84.

- The fourth Mughal Emperor Jahangir wrote his autobiography 'Tuzuk-e-Jahangiri' in Persian.

- He followed the tradition of Babur, his great-grandfather, had written Baburnama.

- Jahangir went a step ahead and apart from writing the history of his reign, he also included information about his family, politics, and arts.

Hence, the correct option is (C).

85.

- Lord Canning was the first Viceroy of India. His tenure lasted for 6 years from 1856-62.

- After 1858, the post of the Governor-General came to be known as the Viceroy.

Hence, the correct option is (D).

86. Mahadev Desai was popularly known as the "secretary of Mahatma Gandhi". Other names given to him were "a Plato to Gandhi's Socrates", Gandhi's Boswell, and an Ananda to Gandhi's Buddha.

Hence, the correct option is (C).

87.

- Bara Lacha is a high mountain pass that connects Manali and Leh Ladakh.

- It is situated in Jammu and Kashmir at an altitude of 4843 meters above sea level.

Hence, the correct option is (C).

88.

- Luni is the only river integrated into the Indian Thar Desert.

- It originates in the Pushkar valley of the Aravalli Range, near Ajmer, and ends in the marshy lands of Rann of Kutch in Gujarat.

- It was first known as Sagarmati, then after passing Govindgarh, it meets its tributary Saraswati, which originates from PushkarLake, and from then on it gets its name Luni.

Hence, the correct option is (B).

89.

- Sunita Lakra is an Indian field hockey player.

- Lakra has represented her country by being capped in the India women's national field hockey team.

- Lakra announced her retirement from hockey through Hockey India on 2 January 2020.

- Lakra is a part of the 18 member squad which is playing in the 14th edition of the Women's Hockey World Cup.

- Lakra climbed the ladder of ranks in Indian hockey with significant performances at the 17th Asian Games and the 2016 Rio Olympics.

- Lakra completed her 100th international match with a match also against New Zealand in 2017, in the third match of the five-match series.

Hence, the correct option is (D).

90.

- Baul is a form of folk music, mainly belonging to the state of West Bengal.

- The Bauls are a heterogeneous group, with many sects, but mostly Vaishnava-Sahaijyas and Sufi Muslims belong to them.

Hence, the correct option is (C).

91.

- Pandit Shiv Kumar Sharma is an Indian music composer and Santoor player from the state of Jammu and Kashmir.

- He also composed music for many Hindi films in collaboration with Hariprasad Chaurasia (Famous Falutist).

- He was awarded the Sangeet Natak Akademi Award in the year 1985.

- He received the 'Padma Shri Award' in 1991. He also received the Padma Vibhusan in 2001.

Hence, the correct option is (D).

92. In a computer the data can be print on a paper using an output device printer. The shortcut for printing data is Ctrl + P.

Hence, the correct option is (A).

93.

- Random Access Memory (RAM) is a temporary memory that stores input data, or intermediate results, or programs, or instructions, or output.

- It assists in storing data necessary for the processor to do computing.

- It is a volatile memory that is lost when power is off.

Hence, the correct option is (D).

94.

- Lichens are plants that grow in exposed places such as rocks or tree bark.

- Lichens are widely used as environmental indicators or bio-indicators.

- They are highly sensitive to atmospheric pollution and they can be used as air pollution indicators, especially of the concentration of sulfur dioxide in the atmosphere.

- They need to be very good at absorbing water and nutrients to grow there.

Hence, the correct option is (B).

95.

- Structure of an ecosystem refers to its biotic and abiotic factors and the function of an ecosystem includes energy flow and nutrient cycles.

- An ecosystem whose structure and function remains unaltered over a long period of time is considered to be a stable ecosystem.

- Oceans are the most stable ecosystem as they are large, deep, and continuous because of which any change in the structure and function is difficult or can be easily resisted.

Hence, the correct option is (A).

96.

- Deepa Mehta's "Funny Boy" will represent Canada in the race for best international feature film at the 2021 Oscars.

- Based on the best-selling novel by Shyam Selvadurai, the film follows a young boy's sexual awakening in Sri Lanka during the turbulent Tamil-Sinhalese conflict leading up to the civil war.

- The film will premiere on Netflix outside of Canada on December 10.

Hence, the correct option is (D).

97.

- The pH of vinegar is around 2.5.

- Vinegar is acidic.

- Substances with pH levels under 7 are acidic in nature.

Hence, the correct option is (A).

98. Mukesh Ambani:

- Reliance Industries Chairperson Mukesh Ambani topped the Forbes India Billionaires List 2020.

- He received the NDTV Business leader of the year 2010.

- He was also honoured with the Ernst and Young Entrepreneur of the Year India 2000 Award.

- Jeff Bezos topped the World Forbes Billionaires List 2020.

Hence, the correct option is (A).

99.

- India will host the Commonwealth Shooting and Archery Championships in January 2022.

- The medals from the two events were counted for the ranking of competing nations at the Birmingham Games.

- The event was held in Chandigarh in January 2022.

- The Birmingham Commonwealth Games is scheduled to take place from the 27th of July to the 7th of August 2022.

Hence, the correct option is (D).

100.

- A monopoly occurs when one firm that produces a product or service controls the market with no close substitute.

- Once a monopoly is established, a lack of competition can lead the seller to charge consumers high prices.

- A monopoly also reduces the available choices for consumers. The monopoly becomes pure when there is absolutely no other substitute available in the market.

Hence, the correct option is (A).

General Intelligence and Reasoning

Q.1 Directions: In the following question a number series is given. Find the missing number that follows the series.
159, 135, ?, 93

A. 121   **B.** 100   **C.** 113   **D.** 115

Q.2 Direction: In the following question, some statements are given followed by some conclusions. You have to take the given statements to be true even if they seem to be at variance with commonly known facts. Read all the conclusions and then decide which of the given conclusions logically follow the given statements, disregarding commonly known facts.

Statements:

Some dogs are bats.

Some bats are cats.

Conclusions:

I. Some dogs are cats.

II. Some cats are dogs.

A. Only conclusion I follows

B. Only II conclusion

C. Either Conclusion I or II follows

D. Neither Conclusion I nor II follows

Q.3 Direction: Arrange the given words in the order in which they will be arranged in a dictionary and choose the one that comes fourth.

Toothless, Topper, Tomorrow, Tonight, Tower

A. Tonight   **B.** Topper

C. Tower   **D.** Toothless

Q.4 In the following equation, correct the given equation by interchanging the two numbers.

$36 \times 2 + 3 - 10 \div 4 = 18$

A. × and ÷   **B.** × and +   **C.** + and -   **D.** ÷ and +

Q.5 In Question identify the diagram that best represents the relationship among classes given below:

Ornaments, Gold, Silver.

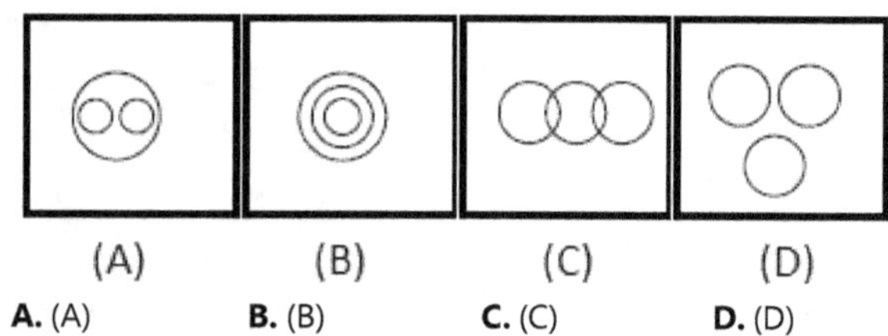

    (A)   (B)   (C)   (D)

A. (A)   **B.** (B)   **C.** (C)   **D.** (D)

Q.6 From the give, alternatives find the alternative that will complete the given series.

Y _ YXZX _ ZY _ ZXYZ _ XZ _ Y

A. ZYXYX   **B.** ZXYZY   **C.** YZXYX   **D.** XYZZY

Q.7 If $18\ (9)\ 3$ and $36\ (30)\ 5$, then what is the value of A in $19\ (A)\ 18$?

A. 33   **B.** 57   **C.** 75   **D.** 96

Q.8 In a certain code, '256' means 'red colour chalk'; '589' means 'green colour flower' and '245' means 'White colour chalk'. Which digit in that code means 'green?

A. 2

B. 4

C. 5

D. Cannot be determined

Q.9 In the following question, select the related word pair from the given alternatives.

Gold : Jewellery : : ? : ?

A. Pulp: Prism   **B.** Furniture: Jute

C. Brick: Wall   **D.** Seed: Book

Q.10 A piece of paper is folded and punched as shown below in the question figure. From the given answer figure, indicate how it will appear when opened?

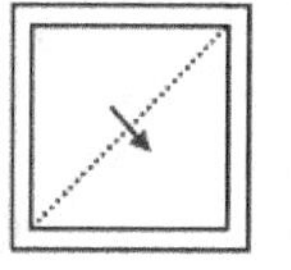 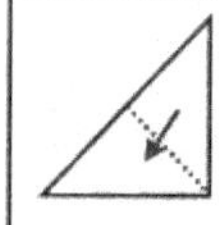 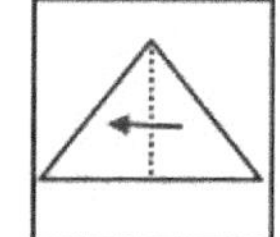 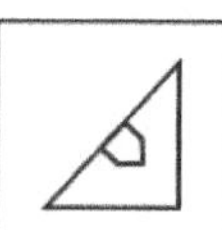

A. 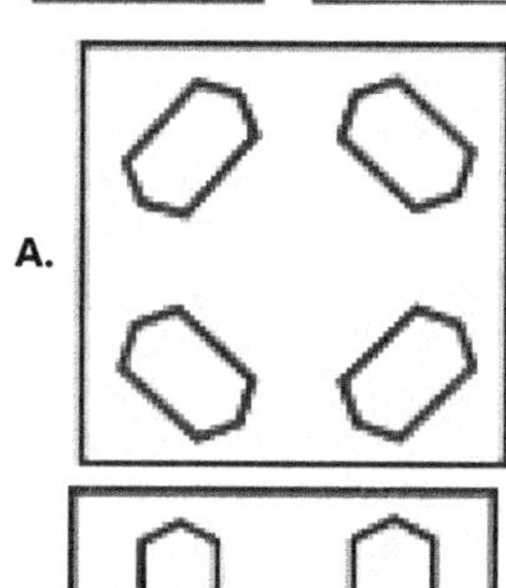   **B.** 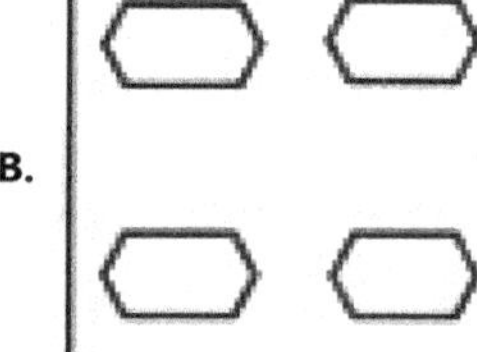

C. 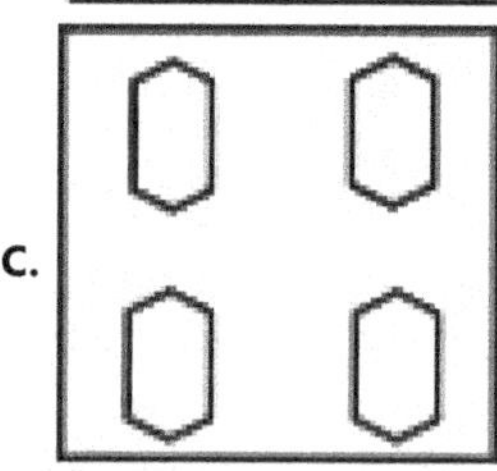   **D.** 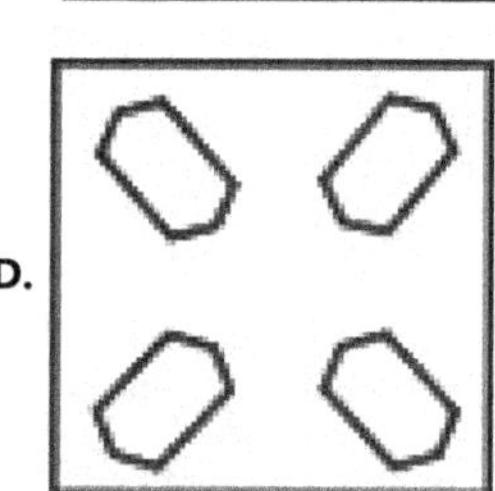

Q.11 Four usual dice are thrown on the ground. The total of numbers on the top faces of these four dice is 13 as the top faces showed 4, 3, 1 and 5 respectively. What is the total of faces touching the ground?

A. 12

B. 13

C. 15

D. Cannot be determined

Q.12 Directions: A series is given with one term missing. Select the correct alternative from the given ones that will complete the series.

K2S, Q4O, W8K, C16G, ?

A. I32B   **B.** I32C   **C.** J32B   **D.** J32C

Q.13 If ' — ' means addition, ' + ' means division, ' ÷ ' means multiplication, ' × ' means is subtraction, then,

$$34 - 25 + 5 \times 8 \div 4 + 2 - 7 = ?$$

A. 27   **B.** 30   **C.** 14   **D.** 12

Ques (14-15):Directions: In each of the following questions, select the related number from the given alternatives.

Q.14 224 : 817 :: 163 : ?

A. 497   **B.** 563   **C.** 572   **D.** 593

Q.15 6 : 42 :: 9 : ?

A. 81   **B.** 90   **C.** 72   **D.** 99

Q.16 From the given answer figures, select two in which the question figure is hidden/embedded.

Question figure:

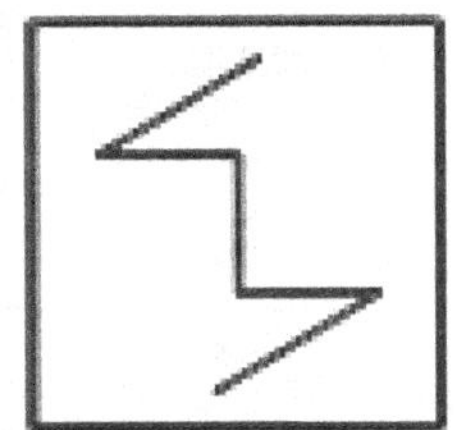

Answer figures:

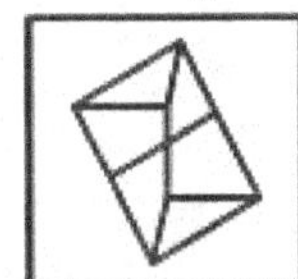 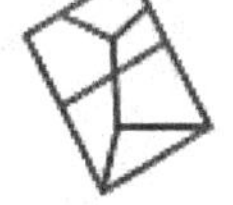 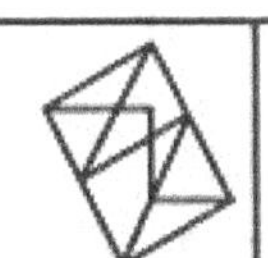 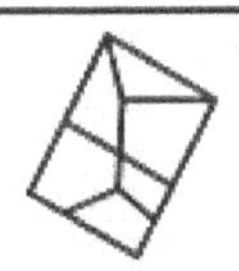

(A)   (B)   (C)   (D)

A. A & D   **B.** A & C   **C.** B & D   **D.** B & C

Q.17 In a certain code, **VISHWANATHAN** is written as **NAAWTHHSANIV**. How is **KARUNAKARANA** written in that code?

A. AKNUARRANKA

B. KAANRAURNAAK

C. NKKRANKRAUK

D. RURNKAAUNAK

Q.18 In the question given below, two statements are given followed by two Conclusion I, II. You have to consider the statements to be true even if they seem to be at variance from commonly known facts. You have to decide which of the given conclusion. if any follow the given statements

Statements:

All Teachers are experienced.

Some teachers are sprinters.

Conclusion:

I. Some experienced are spinsters

II. Some sprinters are experienced

A. Only conclusion I follows

B. Only conclusion II follows

C. Neither I conclusion II follows

D. Both I conclusions II follows

Q.19 Nurse Kemp has worked more night shifts in a row than Nurse Rogers, who has worked five. Nurse Miller has worked fifteen night shifts in a row, more than Nurses Kemp and Rogers combined. Nurse Calvin has worked eight-night shifts in a row, less than Nurse Kemp. How many night shifts in a row has Nurse Kemp worked?

A. Eight   **B.** Nine   **C.** Ten   **D.** Eleven

Q.20 In the following question, select the odd image from the given alternatives.

A. 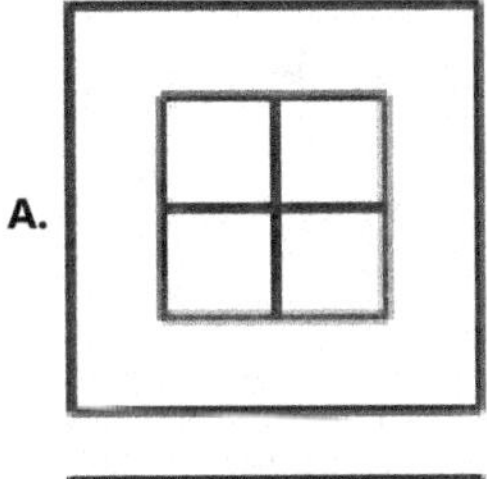   **B.** 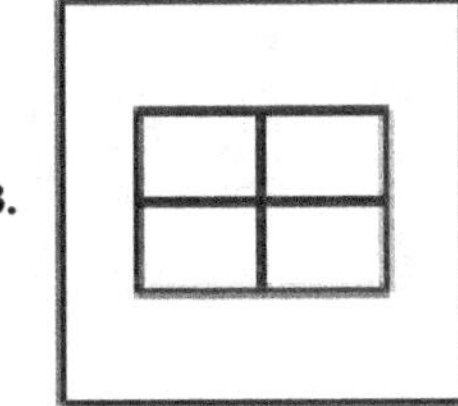

C. 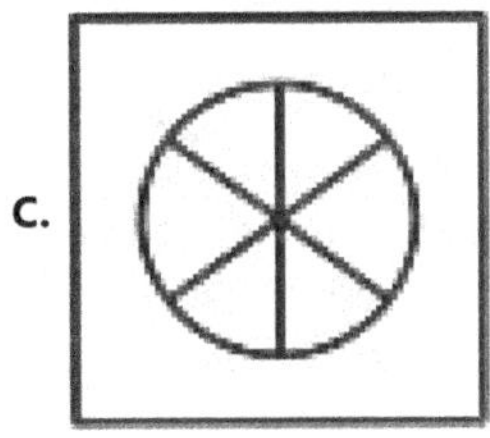   **D.** 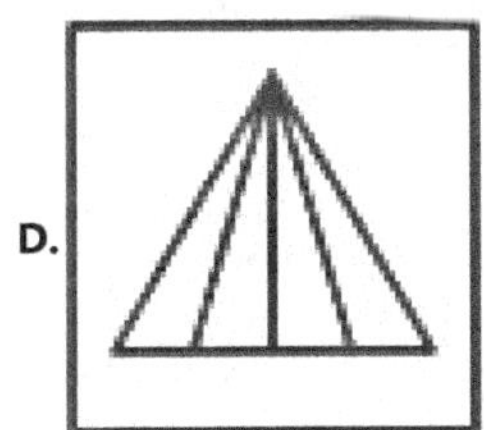

Q.21 Direction: Select the odd number from the given series.

331, 482, 551, 263, 383, 362, 284

A. 263   **B.** 383   **C.** 331   **D.** 551

Q.22 Select the odd letters from the given alternatives.

A. MPR   **B.** HKN   **C.** PSV   **D.** DGJ

Q.23 Identify the diagram that best represents the relationship among the given classes.

Red, Car, Bike

A. 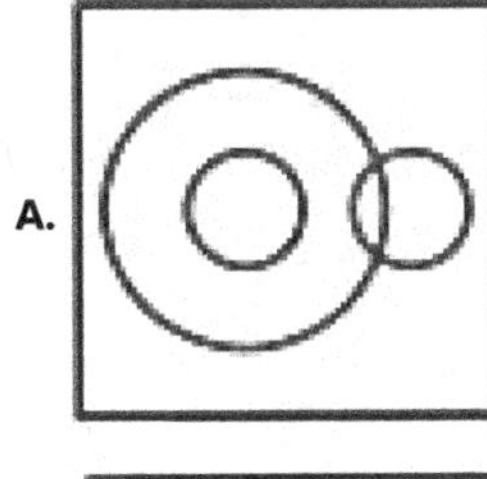   **B.** 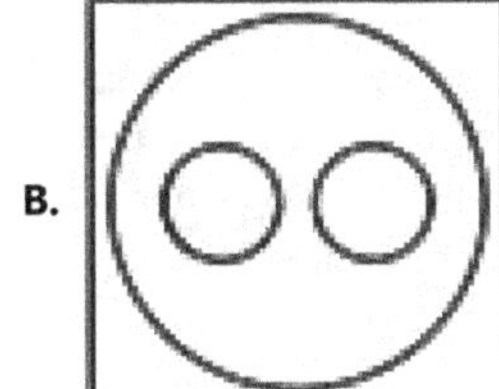

C. 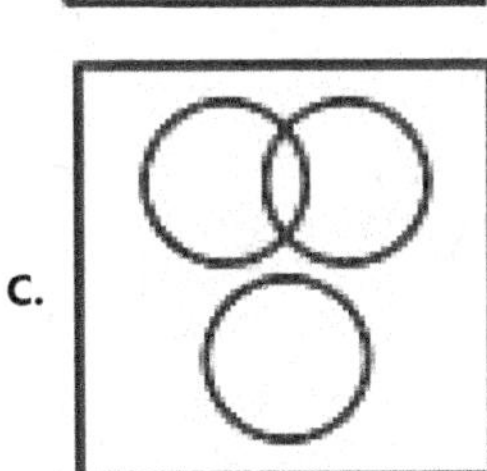   **D.** 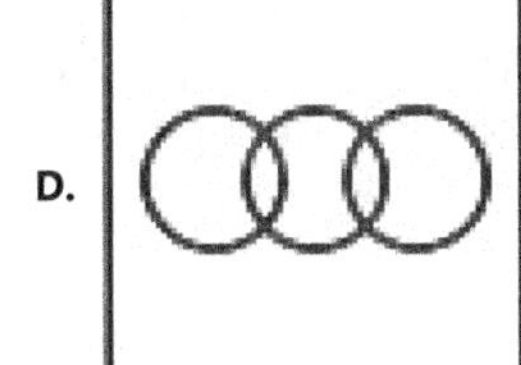

Q.24 In a certain code 'MDSC' is written as '69', how can 'KTAP' be written in that code?

A. 48 **B.** 55 **C.** 60 **D.** 64

Q.25 From the given alternatives find the word which can be formed from the letters used in the given word.

RATIONALIST

A. NATIONAL **B.** RATIONAL
C. FRACTIONAL **D.** VOCATIONAL

Numerical Aptitude/ Quantitative Ability

Q.26 The average of ten numbers is 7. If each number is multiplied by 12, then what will be the average of a new set of numbers?

A. 7 **B.** 19 **C.** 82 **D.** 84

Q.27 If $N = \sqrt{9} + \sqrt{6}$, then what is the value of $\dfrac{1}{N}$?

A. $\sqrt{9} - \sqrt{6}$ **B.** $3(\sqrt{9} - \sqrt{6})$
C. $\dfrac{\sqrt{9}-\sqrt{6}}{3}$ **D.** $\dfrac{\sqrt{9}-\sqrt{6}}{4}$

Q.28 If Q got 40% less marks than P, then the marks of P is how much percent more than that of Q?

A. 40 **B.** 33.33 **C.** 25 **D.** 66.66

Q.29 The population of a country increases at the rate of 8% per annum. If the present population of the country is 46656, then what was the population 2 years ago?

A. 15000 **B.** 40000 **C.** 50000 **D.** 80000

Q.30 In ΔABC, AD is drawn perpendicular from A on BC. If AD² = BD × CD; then ∠BAC is :

A. 30° **B.** 45° **C.** 60° **D.** 90°

Q.31 What is the simple interest (in Rs) on a principal of Rs 2000 at the rate of 5% per annum for 2 years?

A. 250 **B.** 200 **C.** 150 **D.** 225

Q.32 The angles of a triangle are in the ratio $2 : 3 : 7$. The measure of the smallest angle is:

A. 30° **B.** 60° **C.** 45° **D.** 90°

Q.33 A, B and C together can finish a job in 3 days. A and B together can finish the same job in 4 days. In how many days, C alone will finish the same job?

A. 12 **B.** 16 **C.** 20 **D.** 24

Q.34 A car travels at a speed of 50 m/s. for 5 hours. What is the distance (in km.) travelled by the car?

A. 1000 **B.** 900 **C.** 990 **D.** 500

Q.35 The area of the square is equal to six times the area of a rectangle of dimensions 216 cm × 100 cm. What is the perimeter of the square?

A. 1660 **B.** 1440 **C.** 1400 **D.** 1000

Q.36 An article is sold at a loss of 20%. If the selling price is doubled, then what will be the profit percentage?

A. 160 **B.** 100 **C.** 60 **D.** 37.5

Q.37 Points P and Q lie on side AB and AC of triangle ABC respectively such that segment PQ is parallel to side BC. If the ratio of AP : PB is 2 : 5, and area of ΔAPQ is 4 sq cm, what is the area of trapezium PQCB?

A. 49 sq cm **B.** 45 sq cm **C.** 25 sq cm **D.** 21 sq cm

Q.38 The ratio of the present income of A and B is 2 : 3 respectively. The total present income of A and B together is Rs. 21500, then find the income of B?

A. 6000 **B.** 7000 **C.** 12900 **D.** 13500

Q.39 The successive discount of 15%, 20% and 25% on an article is equivalent to the single discount of:

A. 60% **B.** 47% **C.** 49% **D.** 40%

Q.40 The average of 20 numbers is 15 and the average of the first 5 numbers is 12. The average of the rest is-

A. 16 **B.** 15 **C.** 14 **D.** 13

Ques (41-45): The bar graph given below shows the sales of books (in thousand number) from six branches of a publishing company during two consecutive years 2000 and 2001.

Sales of Books (in thousand numbers) from Six Branches - B1, B2, B3, B4, B5 and B6 of a publishing Company in 2000 and 2001.

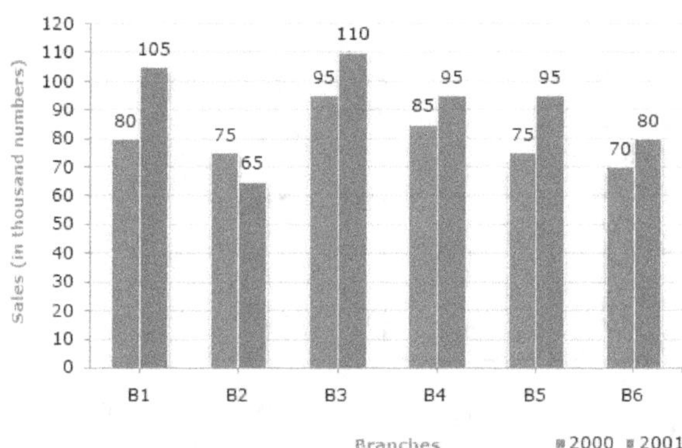

Q.41 What is the ratio of the total sales of branch B2 for both years to the total sales of branch B4 for both years?

A. 2:3 **B.** 3:5 **C.** 4:5 **D.** 7:9

Q.42 Total sales of branch B6 for both the years is what percent of the total sales of branches B3 for both the years?

A. 68.54% **B.** 71.11% **C.** 73.17% **D.** 75.55%

Q.43 What percent of the average sales of branches B1, B2 and B3 in 2001 is the average sales of branches B1, B3 and B6 in 2000?

A. 75% **B.** 77.5% **C.** 82.5% **D.** 87.5%

Q.44 What is the average sales of all the branches (in thousand numbers) for the year 2000?

A. 73 **B.** 80 **C.** 83 **D.** 88

Q.45 Total sales of branches B1, B3 and B5 together for both the years (in thousand numbers) is?

A. 250 **B.** 310 **C.** 435 **D.** 560

Q.46 If the cost price of 6 articles is equal to the selling price of 9 articles, then what is the loss percentage?

A. 25   **B.** 33.33   **C.** 50   **D.** 20

Q.47 Find the sum of all odd natural numbers less than 130.

A. 4286   **B.** 4275   **C.** 3456   **D.** 4225

Q.48 A seller offers 11% discount on a mini-refrigerator with a marked price of Rs. 8200. If he still earns a profit of Rs. 600, what is the cost price of the refrigerator?

A. Rs. 6698   **B.** Rs. 7600   **C.** Rs. 7350   **D.** Rs. 4960

Q.49 If sin 3A = cos (A − 26°), where 3A is an acute angle then the value of A is-

A. 33°   **B.** 29°   **C.** 45°   **D.** 52°

Q.50 If $\tan \theta = \tan 30°. \tan 60°$ and θ is an acute angle, then 2θ is equal to-

A. 30°   **B.** 45°   **C.** 90°   **D.** 0°

General English & Comprehension

Ques (51-52):Direction: Read each sentence to find out whether there is any grammatical error in it. The error, if any will be in one part of the sentence. If there is no error choose option (D) 'No error' as the answer.

Q.51 The expansion of the People's Liberation Army (1)/ and its assertive actions (2)/ have damaging the bilateral relation. (3)/ No error (4)

A. (1)   **B.** (2)   **C.** (3)   **D.** (4)

Q.52 They said they will (1)/ be focusing on developing healthy ties,(2)/ signaled towards a new start. (3)/ No error (4)

A. (1)   **B.** (2)   **C.** (3)   **D.** (4)

Ques (53-54):Direction: Out of the four alternatives, choose the one which can be substituted for the given words/sentences.

Q.53 One who abandons his religious faith.

A. Apostate   **B.** Prostate   **C.** Profane   **D.** Agnostic

Q.54 Hater of knowledge and learning.

A. Bibliophile   **B.** Philologist
C. Misogynist   **D.** Misologist

Q.55 Direction: Four alternatives are given for the idiom/phrase. Choose the correct alternative that best expresses the meaning of the idiom/phrase.

To catch a tartar.

A. To trap wanted criminal with great difficulty
B. To catch a dangerous person
C. To meet with disaster
D. To deal with a person who is more than one's match

Ques (56-57):Direction: Fill in the blank with the correct word.

Q.56 A pony can be arranged for the ride up, but only _____ the cafeteria.

A. Until   **B.** At   **C.** Till   **D.** Unless

Q.57 It is estimated to _____ at the rate of 42% over the next five years annually

A. Grows   **B.** Grow   **C.** Growing   **D.** Grown

Q.58 You are given a sentence with an underlined part. Four options are given which may improve the underlined part. Choose the best correction of the underlined part as your answer.

BJP govt. <u>has always in</u> favour of a "HINDU RASTRAH".

A. Has always been favoured
B. Has always favoured
C. Has always been in favour
D. Is always favorite

Q.59 Select the correctly spelt word.

A. lisence   **B.** Patner
C. Knowledge   **D.** Neice

Q.60 Direction: Select the most appropriate meaning of the given idiom.

Stand one's ground

A. To maintain one's position
B. To confess completely
C. To try to attain something
D. To be at a distance

Ques (61-62):Direction: A sentence has been given in Direct/Indirect speech. Out of the four alternatives choose the one which best expresses the same sentence in Direct/Indirect speech.

Q.61 Raman said to Harish, "Where were you sitting?"

A. Raman asked Harish where he has been sitting
B. Raman asked Harish where he was sitting
C. Raman asked Harish where he would be sitting
D. Raman asked Harish where he had been sitting

Q.62 Indira said to Biren, "This is a nice house!"

A. Indira told Biren that it was being a nice house
B. Indira told Biren that it is a nice house
C. Indira told Biren that it was a nice house
D. Indira exclaimed that it was a nice house

Ques (63-64):Direction: In the following questions, a sentence has been given in Active/Passive voice. Out of four alternatives suggested, select the one, which best expresses the same sentence in Passive/Active voice.

Q.63 They will visit the hospital tomorrow.

A. The hospital would be visited by them tomorrow
B. The hospital will be visited by them tomorrow
C. The hospital will be visited tomorrow
D. The hospital has been visited tomorrow

Q.64 Sell off this bicycle.

A. Should the bicycle be sold off
B. Let the bicycle be sold
C. You should sell off this bicycle
D. Let this bicycle be sold off

Q.65 Direction: Select the most appropriate synonym of the given word.

Bliss

A. Upset   **B.** Euphoria   **C.** Sadness   **D.** Mirage

Q.66 Direction: Identify the tense of the main verb.

The plane had left by the time I got to the airport.

A. Simple past
B. Past perfect
C. Past perfect continuous
D. Past continuous

Ques (67-68):Direction: Choose the word SIMILAR in meaning to the given word.

Q.67 Encumbrance

A. Torture   **B.** Trauma
C. Hindrance   **D.** Bulwark

Q.68 Eternal

A. Perpetual   **B.** Esteem
C. Quell   **D.** Instigated

Ques (69-70):Direction: Choose the word OPPOSITE in meaning to the given word.

Q.69 Petulant

A. Sycophant   **B.** Pragmatic
C. Affable   **D.** Frugal

Q.70 Opine

A. Taciturn   **B.** Usurp   **C.** Ornate   **D.** Perish

Ques (71-75):Direction: Read the passage and answer the following questions.

The organization is working to end the inhumane culling of stray dogs, which many countries do in a **misguided** effort to eliminate rabies. The organization points out that vaccination programs are the only effective way to eliminate rabies and work with governments on vaccination programs. In 2012, a mass vaccination program was started in the Shaanxi, Guizhou, and Anhui provinces of China, working with the Chinese Animal Disease Control Centre; as of June 2014, 750 veterinarians have been trained and over 90,000 dogs have been vaccinated. A second focus is on stray dog population management itself, through proven humane methods such as education, improved legislation, registration and identification of dogs, sterilisation, and contraception, holding facilities, and rehoming centres. The charity has two disaster operations teams located in Asia and Latin America. In the **aftermath** of disasters, they travel to the worst affected areas to administer, distribute food and reunite animals with their owners where possible. The work is of particular benefit in developing world countries, where communities rely on animals for food, transport, and income.

Q.71 What is the major function of the organization?

A. To educate people on animal health
B. Disaster management in China
C. To take proper care of animals
D. To improve living conditions after disasters

Q.72 What does the organization suggest as a way to end rabies?

A. Emergency veterinary care
B. Stop culling of stray dogs
C. Vaccination programs
D. Establishment of rehoming centres

Q.73 Which of the following is MOST SIMILAR in meaning to the word 'aftermath'?

A. Casualty   **B.** After effects
C. Illness   **D.** Recovery

Q.74 Why is work particularly significant in developing countries?

A. The reliance on animals is more in these places
B. The number of animals is more in this place
C. These are disaster-prone areas.
D. The animals are treated in the worst way here.

Q.75 Which of the following is MOST OPPOSITE in meaning to the word 'misguided'?

A. Effective   **B.** Fallacious
C. Obstruct   **D.** Well informed

General Awareness

Q.76 In which of the following sports, the words 'crawl', 'breaststroke', and 'butterfly' are used?

A. Swimming   **B.** Shooting
C. Tennis   **D.** Badminton

Q.77 When was the World Chess Federation founded?

A. 1935   **B.** 1924   **C.** 1905   **D.** 1896

Q.78 Who invented Polio Vaccine?

A. Ernest Rutherford   **B.** Jonas E. Salk
C. Richard Taylor   **D.** Karl Jansky

Q.79 In computers, which is the full form NIC?

A. Network Interface Card
B. Network Information Card
C. New Interface Card
D. New Information Card

Q.80 Which of the following is an ore of both Calcium and Magnesium?

A. Magnesite   **B.** Gypsum
C. Epsom Salt   **D.** Dolomite

Q.81 The atomic number of which of the following elements is greater than that of Bromine

A. Silver   **B.** Copper
C. Iron   **D.** Chromium

Q.82 Which among the following is the strongest force?

A. Gravitational Force
B. Nuclear Force
C. Electromagnetic Force
D. Frictional Force

Q.83 What is the SI unit of Heat?

A. Lux   B. Tesla   C. Joule   D. Farad

Q.84 Vitamin A is also known as _____.

A. Thiamine   B. Riboflavin
C. Retinol   D. Calciferol

Q.85 Which among the following is a factor of production?

1. Land
2. Labor
3. Physical capital

A. Only I   B. Both I & II
C. Both II & III   D. All I, II & III

Q.86 Which of the following is better known as the City of Prime Ministers?

A. Jaipur   B. Kolkata
C. Allahabad   D. Mumbai

Q.87 Which country recently (in Feb'21) launched the 'Arktika-M' satellite to monitor the climate change in Artic?

A. Japan   B. France   C. India   D. Russia

Q.88 The rise in the temperature in the stratosphere is caused by the absorption of _______.

A.   Visible Spectrum
B.   Ions present in the stratosphere
C.   Ultra Violet radiations
D.   Infrared radiations

Q.89 The Saddle Peak in Andaman and Nicobar is located in which of the following part of the territory?

A. Little Andaman   B. North Andaman
C. Great Nicobar   D. South Nicobar

Q.90 The concept of single citizenship in the Indian Constitution is inspired from which country?

A. Germany   B. France
C. Ireland   D. England

Q.91 Lord canning described which among the following groups as "breakwaters in the storm", who aided in the suppression of 1857 revolt?

A.   Zamindars
B.   Princely States
C.   Indian public servants
D.   Money lenders

Q.92 Satpura National Park is situated in-

[SBI PO, 2021]

A. Himachal Pradesh   B. Andhra Pradesh
C. Madhya Pradesh   D. Kerala

Q.93 What is the theme of 2021's National Science Day that was observed on 28th February?

A.   Make in India: S&T driven innovations
B.   Science and Technology for a sustainable future
C.   Future of STI: Impacts on Education, Skills, and Work
D.   Science for the People, and People for the Science

Q.94 Warli Painting is indigenous to which state?

A. Maharashtra   B. Rajasthan
C. Gujrat   D. Himachal Pradesh

Q.95 Which is the smallest continent?

A. Australia   B. Antarctica
C. Africa   D. South America

Q.96 With reference to Indian history, who among the following is a future Buddha, yet to come to save the world?

[UPSC Prelims, 2018]

A. Avalokiteshvara   B. Lokesvara
C. Maitreya   D. Padmapani

Q.97 What will be used to place headers and footers in handouts?

A. The Title Master   B. Notes and Handouts
C. The Slide Master   D. F-1

Q.98 The portion of profits that a company distributes among its shareholders in the form of cash is usually known as _____?

A. Yield   B. Dividend
C. Stock Split   D. Free Float

Q.99 A relatively dense layer of the band which is found in the thermosphere is known as?

A. Troposphere   B. Mesosphere
C. Stratosphere   D. Ionosphere

Q.100 Who amongst the following is the longest-serving Lok Sabha speaker?

A.   G V Mavalankar
B.   Somnath Chatterjee
C.   Balram Jakhar
D.   Neelam Sanjiva Reddy

// Smart Answer Sheet //

Correct Percentage of students who answered correctly. **Skipped** Percentage of students who skipped.

Q.	Ans.	Correct / Skipped	Q.	Ans.	Correct / Skipped	Q.	Ans.	Correct / Skipped	Q.	Ans.	Correct / Skipped	Q.	Ans.	Correct / Skipped	Q.	Ans.	Correct / Skipped
1	C	60.3 % / 1.44 %	18	D	45.98 % / 1.25 %	35	B	57.96 % / 1.52 %	52	C	69.79 % / 1.28 %	69	C	58.86 % / 1.09 %	86	C	87.95 % / 0.0 %
2	D	63.12 % / 1.73 %	19	B	68.2 % / 1.63 %	36	C	53.94 % / 1.09 %	53	A	63.09 % / 1.47 %	70	A	87.35 % / 0.0 %	87	D	67.26 % / 1.9 %
3	B	76.29 % / 0.0 %	20	C	78.58 % / 0.0 %	37	B	44.35 % / 1.48 %	54	D	58.24 % / 1.19 %	71	C	40.73 % / 1.73 %	88	C	65.77 % / 1.46 %
4	D	47.37 % / 1.28 %	21	B	42.92 % / 1.67 %	38	C	62.14 % / 1.68 %	55	B	56.21 % / 1.09 %	72	C	44.25 % / 1.53 %	89	B	46.25 % / 1.1 %
5	A	62.61 % / 1.95 %	22	A	50.17 % / 1.44 %	39	C	54.19 % / 1.41 %	56	C	76.25 % / 0.0 %	73	B	55.87 % / 1.1 %	90	D	44.7 % / 1.04 %
6	A	81.12 % / 0.0 %	23	D	58.48 % / 1.0 %	40	A	68.26 % / 1.04 %	57	B	80.08 % / 0.0 %	74	A	53.89 % / 1.14 %	91	B	50.34 % / 1.55 %
7	B	56.85 % / 1.77 %	24	C	62.98 % / 1.18 %	41	D	49.4 % / 1.84 %	58	C	15.06 % / 3.81 %	75	D	40.64 % / 1.08 %	92	C	84.12 % / 0.0 %
8	D	57.66 % / 1.17 %	25	B	80.39 % / 0.0 %	42	C	53.14 % / 1.43 %	59	C	83.9 % / 0.0 %	76	A	53.44 % / 1.21 %	93	C	41.93 % / 1.71 %
9	C	87.76 % / 0.0 %	26	D	54.4 % / 1.38 %	43	D	63.53 % / 1.76 %	60	A	64.67 % / 1.11 %	77	B	45.5 % / 1.29 %	94	A	59.6 % / 1.0 %
10	A	56.48 % / 1.76 %	27	C	46.69 % / 1.52 %	44	B	47.3 % / 1.57 %	61	D	49.34 % / 1.71 %	78	B	11.35 % / 4.17 %	95	A	56.33 % / 1.61 %
11	C	85.62 % / 0.0 %	28	D	52.56 % / 1.11 %	45	D	48.57 % / 1.96 %	62	D	52.23 % / 1.94 %	79	A	57.17 % / 1.46 %	96	C	60.0 % / 1.46 %
12	B	54.78 % / 1.23 %	29	B	67.99 % / 1.96 %	46	B	69.19 % / 1.34 %	63	B	18.43 % / 4.62 %	80	D	40.66 % / 1.19 %	97	B	41.71 % / 1.03 %
13	B	59.5 % / 1.93 %	30	D	67.75 % / 1.79 %	47	D	42.47 % / 1.55 %	64	D	53.12 % / 1.05 %	81	A	46.0 % / 1.37 %	98	B	58.17 % / 1.83 %
14	A	45.2 % / 1.53 %	31	B	59.57 % / 1.15 %	48	A	55.83 % / 1.55 %	65	B	42.54 % / 1.74 %	82	B	65.69 % / 1.25 %	99	D	60.42 % / 1.6 %
15	B	87.52 % / 0.0 %	32	A	55.91 % / 1.44 %	49	B	43.26 % / 1.92 %	66	B	54.12 % / 1.28 %	83	C	54.34 % / 1.74 %	100	C	62.17 % / 1.49 %
16	B	41.69 % / 1.89 %	33	A	43.24 % / 1.75 %	50	C	59.18 % / 1.39 %	67	C	81.58 % / 0.0 %	84	C	42.18 % / 1.09 %			
17	B	45.96 % / 1.76 %	34	B	77.48 % / 0.0 %	51	C	53.36 % / 1.02 %	68	A	66.95 % / 1.59 %	85	D	52.96 % / 1.1 %			

//Hints and Solutions//

1. $13^2 - 10 = 159$

$12^2 - 9 = 135$

$11^2 - 8 = 113$

$10^2 - 7 = 93$

So, the missing term is 113.

Hence, the correct option is (C).

2.

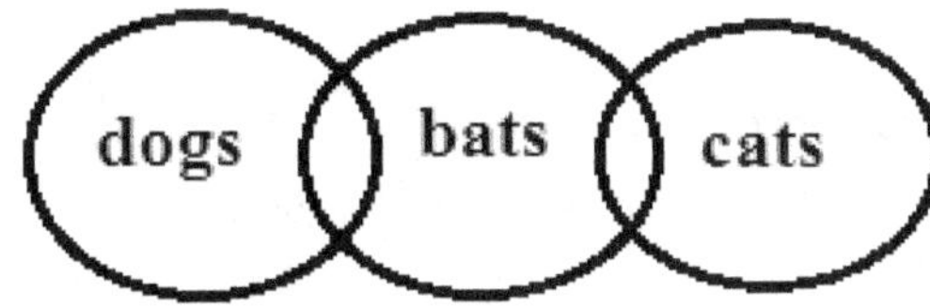

Both conclusions cannot be a definite case, therefore neither Conclusion I nor II follows

Hence, the correct option Is (D).

3. On arranging given word as per dictionary order,

1) **Tom**orrow

2) **Ton**ight

3) **Too**thless

4) **Top**per

5) **Tow**er

So, Topper comes fourth.

Hence, the correct option is (B).

4. Given equation is 36 × 2 + 3 - 10 ÷ 4 = 18

Let's check each of the options,

1. Interchanging × and ÷

Equation will become, 36 × 2 + 3 - 10 ÷ 4 =72.5 ≠ 18

2. Interchanging × and +

Equation will become, 36 + 2 × 3 - 10 ÷ 4 = 39.5 ≠ 18

3. Interchanging + and -

Equation will become, 36 × 2 - 3 + 10 ÷ 4 = 71.5 ≠ 18

4. Interchanging ÷ and +

Equation will become, 36 × 2 ÷ 3 - 10 + 4 = 18

Therefore, by interchanging ÷ and +, we get the correct answer.

Hence, the correct option is (D).

5.

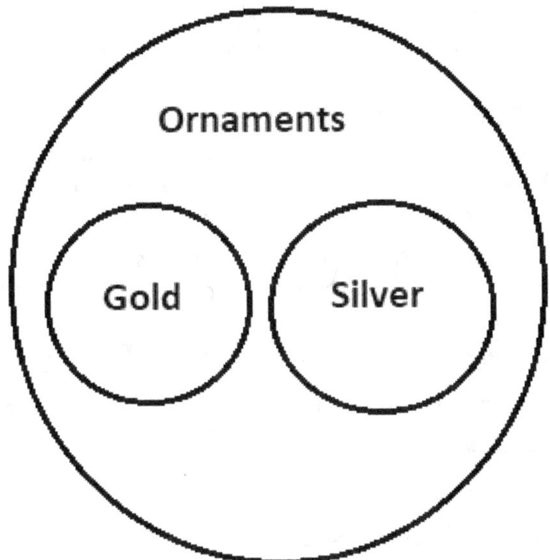

Hence, the correct option is (A).

6. The following pattern of series –

Y **Z** Y/ X Z X /**Y** Z **Y**/ X Z X/ Y Z **Y**/ X Z **X** /Y

= ZYXYX

Hence, the correct option is (A).

7. $\dfrac{18 \times 3}{9} = 6$

$\dfrac{36 \times 5}{30} = 6$

Similarly,

$\dfrac{19 \times 18}{A} = 6 \Rightarrow A = 57$

Hence, the correct option is (B).

8. Based on the given information we can summarise information in the below diagram,

$\boxed{2}\ \textcircled{5}\ 6 \longrightarrow \text{red}\ \widehat{\text{colour}}\ \boxed{\text{chalk}}$

$\textcircled{5}\ 8\ 9 \longrightarrow \text{green}\ \widehat{\text{colour}}\ \text{flower}$

$\boxed{2}\ 4\ \textcircled{5} \longrightarrow \text{white}\ \widehat{\text{colour}}\ \boxed{\text{chalk}}$

So, the Code for 'green' will be either '8' or '9'

Therefore, Can't be determined is the correct option.

Hence, the correct option is (D).

9. As we use gold to make jewellery, brick is used to make a wall.

So, 'Brick: Wall' is the correct alternative.

Hence, the correct option is (C).

10.

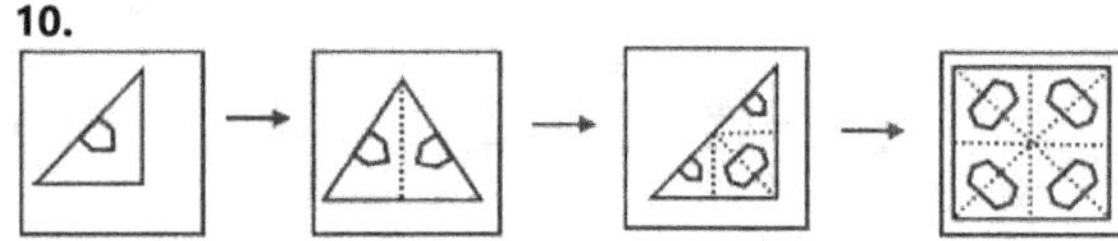

Hence, the correct option is (A).

11. In the usual dice, the sum of the numbers on any two opposite faces is always 7. Thus, 1 is opposite 6, 2 is opposite 5 and 3 is opposite 4.

Consequently, when 4, 3, 1 and 5 are the numbers on the top faces, then 3, 4, 6 and 2 respectively are the numbers on the face touching the ground.

The total of these numbers = 3 + 4 + 6 + 2 = 15.

Hence, the correct option is (C).

12. Given Series:

K2S, Q4O, W8K, C16G,?

The logic followed for the first letter:

The first letters are K, Q, W, C,

$$K \xrightarrow{+6} Q \xrightarrow{+6} W \xrightarrow{+6} C \xrightarrow{+6} I$$

The logic followed for numbers is:

Digits are: 2, 4, 8, 16,

$2 \times 2 = 4$

$4 \times 2 = 8$

$8 \times 2 = 16$

$16 \times 2 = \mathbf{32}$

The logic followed for the second letter is:

The second letters are S, O, K, G,

$$S \xrightarrow{-4} O \xrightarrow{-4} K \xrightarrow{-4} G \xrightarrow{-4} C$$

So, the next term will be I32C.

Hence, the correct option is (B).

13. Given,

$$34 - 25 + 5 \times 8 \div 4 + 2 - 7 = ?$$

After changing the signs-

$$34 + 25 \div 5 - 8 \times 4 \div 2 + 7$$

$$= 34 + 5 - 8 \times 2 + 7$$

$$= 39 - 16 + 7 = 30$$

Hence, the correct option is (B).

14. Given,

$2 + 2 + 4 = 8$

And $8 + 1 + 7 = 16$

Similarly,

$1 + 6 + 3 = 10$

And $4 + 9 + 7 = 20$

Here, the sum of the digits of the second group of numbers is twice the sum of the digits of the first group of numbers.

Hence, the correct option is (A).

15. First, the two terms are related in this way.

$6 + 6^2 = 42$

Similarly,

$9 + 9^2 = 90$

Hence, the correct option is (B).

16. Given question figure is hidden in answer figures (A) and (C) as shown below:

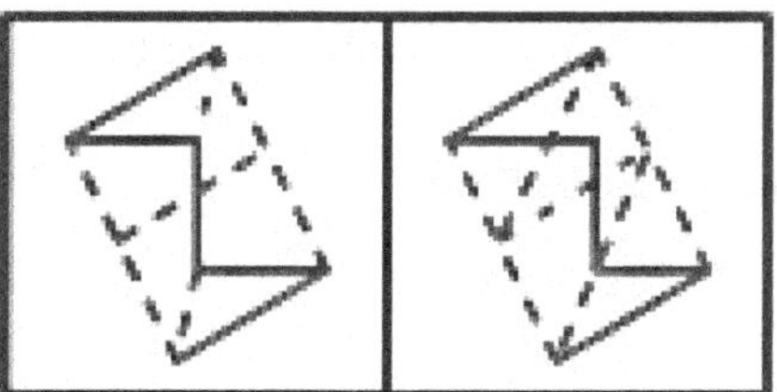

Hence, the correct option is (B).

17. Divide the word into six sets of two letters each and label these sets from 1 to 6.

Then, the code contains these sets in the order 4, 3, 5, 2, 6, 1 with the letters of sets 3, 2, 1 written in reverse order.

Thus, we have :

$$\frac{VI\ SH\ WA\ NA\ TH\ AN}{1\quad 2\quad 3\quad 4\quad 5\quad 6} \rightarrow \frac{NA\ AW\ TH\ HS\ AN\ IV}{4\quad 3\quad 5\quad 2\quad 6\quad 1}$$

Same as

$$\frac{KA\ RU\ NA\ KA\ RA\ NA}{1\quad 2\quad 3\quad 4\quad 5\quad 6} \rightarrow \frac{KA\ AN\ RA\ UR\ NA\ AK}{4\quad 3\quad 5\quad 2\quad 6\quad 1}$$

Hence, the correct option is (B).

18. According to the statements, the diagram is

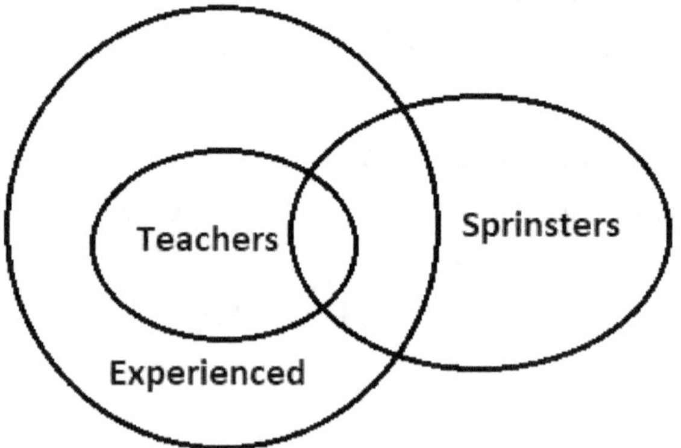

So, both conclusions I and II follow

Hence, the correct option is (D).

19. Nurse Kemp has worked more shifts in a row than Nurse Calvin; therefore, Kemp has worked more than eight shifts. The number of Kemp's shifts plus the number of Rogers's shifts (five) cannot equal fifteen or more, the number of Miller's shifts.

Therefore, Kemp has worked nine shifts in a row (5 + 9 = 14).

Hence, the correct option is (B).

20. Here all the given images are divided into 4 equal parts except the image in option (C) which is divided into 6 parts.

Thus image at option (C) is the odd one.

Hence, the correct option is (C).

21. In each number except 383, the product of the first and third digits is the middle one.

Hence, the correct option is (B).

22.

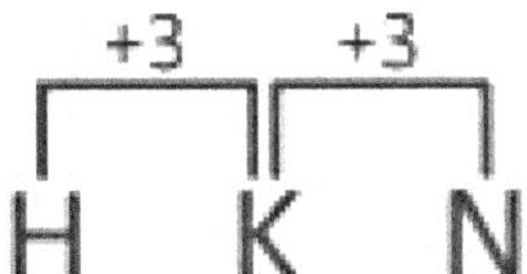

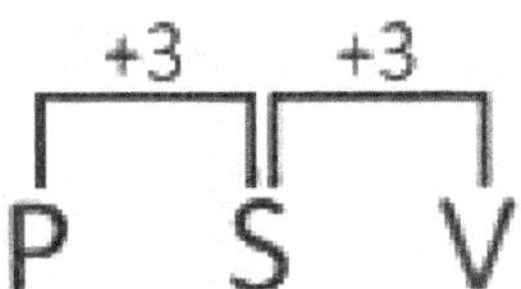

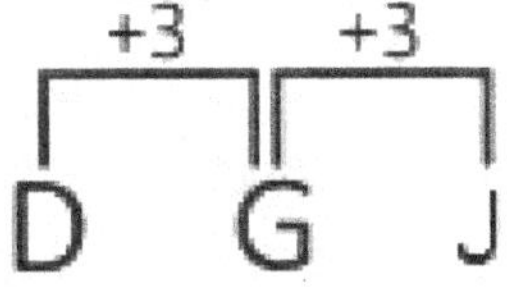

But,

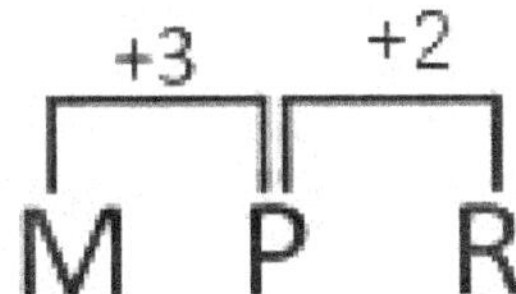

Hence, the correct option is (A).

23. Given:

Red, Car, Bike → Both 'Car' and 'Bike' can be 'Red' in colour.

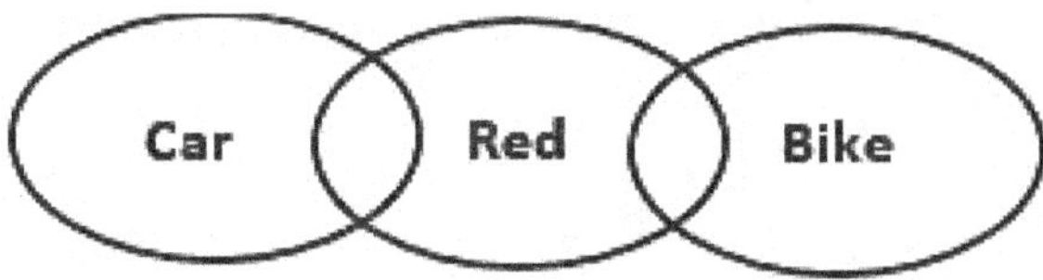

Thus the Venn diagram that represents the given relation correctly is shown in option (D).

Hence, the correct option is (D).

24. MDSC ↔ NWHX (opposite letters)

Now add the position number of the opposite letters i,e, 14 + 23 + 8 + 24 = 69

Similarly,

KTAP ↔ PGZK (16 + 7 + 26 + 11 = 60)

Hence, the correct option is (C).

25. 1) NATIONAL → only 1 N is present in RATIONALIST, so it can't be formed.

2) RATIONAL → it can be formed.

3) FRACTIONAL → the letter F and C is not present in RATIONALIST, it also can't be formed.

4) VOCATIONAL → the letter V and C is not present in RATIONALIST, then it can't be formed.

Thus, the word RATIONAL can be formed from the letters used in RATIONALIST.

Hence, the correct option is (B).

26. Average of ten numbers = 7

Each number is multiplied by 12

Then, the average will also get multiplied by 12

therefore, new average = 12 × 7 = 84

Hence, the correct option is (D).

27. $N = \sqrt{9} + \sqrt{6}$

$$\therefore \frac{1}{N} = \frac{1}{\sqrt{9}+\sqrt{6}}$$

$$\Rightarrow \frac{1}{N} = \frac{\sqrt{9}-\sqrt{6}}{(\sqrt{9}+\sqrt{6})(\sqrt{9}-\sqrt{6})}$$

$$\Rightarrow \frac{1}{N} = \frac{\sqrt{9}-\sqrt{6}}{(\sqrt{9})^2-(\sqrt{6})^2}$$

$$\Rightarrow \frac{1}{N} = \frac{\sqrt{9}-\sqrt{6}}{9-6}$$

$$\Rightarrow \frac{1}{N} = \frac{\sqrt{9}-\sqrt{6}}{3}$$

Hence, the correct option is (C).

28. Let P gets x marks.

Then, $Q = x - \left(\frac{40x}{100}\right) = \frac{3x}{5}$

Now we have, $P = x$ and $Q = \frac{3x}{5}$

$$\Rightarrow \frac{P-Q}{Q} \times 100$$

$$\Rightarrow \frac{x - \frac{3x}{5}}{\frac{3x}{5}} \times 100 = 66.66\%$$

Hence, the correct option is (D).

29. Given present population = 46656

Increase in population annually = 8%

Let, population 2 years ago = x

According to problem,

$$\Rightarrow x\left(1 + \frac{8}{100}\right)^2 = 46656$$

$$\Rightarrow x \times 1.08^2 = 46656$$

$$\Rightarrow x = \frac{46656}{1.1664}$$

$$\Rightarrow x = 40000$$

∴ Population 2 years ago = 40000

Hence, the correct option is (B).

30. Given,

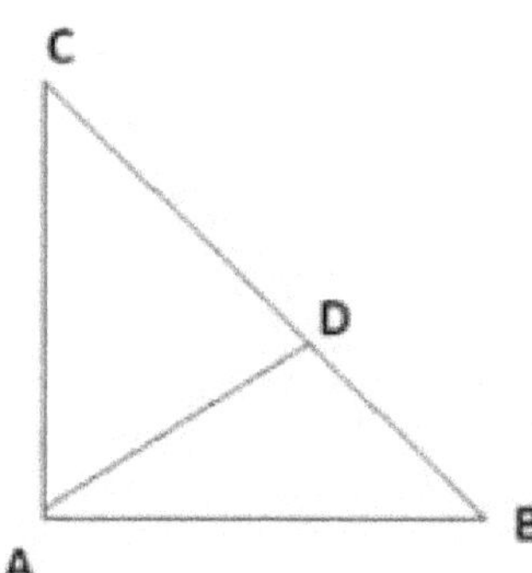

In right triangles ADB & ADC, we have:

$AB^2 = AD^2 + BD^2 \ldots \ldots \ldots 1$

$AC^2 = AD^2 + DC^2 \ldots \ldots \ldots 2$

From 1 & 2,

$AB^2 + AC^2 = 2AD^2 + BD^2 + DC^2$

$= 2BD \cdot CD + BD^2 + CD^2$ [Given: AD × 2 = BD . CD]

$= (BD + CD)^2 = BC^2$

Thus, in triangle ABC we have , $AB^2 + AC^2 = BC^2$

Triangle ABC is a right triangle right angled at A.

Hence, the correct option is (D).

31. We know the formula for simple interest-

$$SI = \frac{(P \times T \times R)}{100}$$

Where,

SI = Simple interest

P = Principal

R = Rate of interest

T = Time period

$$\Rightarrow SI = \frac{(2000 \times 2 \times 5)}{100} = \text{Rs. } 200$$

∴ Simple interest = Rs. 200

Hence, the correct option is (B).

32. Let angles of a triangle be $2x$, $3x$ and $7x$.

By angle sum property:-

$$2x + 3x + 7x = 180°$$

$$\Rightarrow 12x = 180°$$

$$\Rightarrow x = \frac{180°}{12} = 15°$$

$$2x = 2 \times 15 = 30°$$

$$3x = 3 \times 15 = 75°$$

$$7x = 7 \times 15 = 105°$$

Therefore, smallest angle $= 30°$

Hence, the correct option is (A).

33. (A + B + C) can do a job in = 3 days

∴ 1 day's work of (A + B + C) = $\frac{1}{3}$

(A + B) can do a job in = 4 days

∴ 1 day's work of (A + B) = $\frac{1}{4}$

∴ 1 day's work of C,

$$\Rightarrow \frac{1}{3} - \frac{1}{4}$$

$$\Rightarrow \frac{1}{12}$$

∴ C can complete the work in = 12 days

Hence, the correct option is (A).

34. Speed = 50 m/s $= \frac{(50 \times 18)}{5} = 180$ km/hr

Time = 5 hours

∴ Distance = Speed × Time = 180 × 5 = 900 km

Hence, the correct option is (B).

35. Area of square = side × side

$A^2 = 6 \times (216 \times 100)$

A = 360 cm

Perimeter = 4 × side

Perimeter = 1440 cm

Hence, the correct option is (B).

36. Let the cost price of the article be x.

Loss % = 20%

Then, SP = CP - Loss

Loss = 20% of x = 0.2x

$\Rightarrow$ SP = x - 0.2x = 0.8x

If the selling price is doubled,

SP = 2 × 0.8x = 1.6x

Profit = SP - CP = 1.6x - x = 0.6x

$$\text{Profit } \% = \frac{(Profit \times 100)}{CP}$$

$$\text{Profit } \% = \frac{(0.6x \times 100)}{x} = 60\%$$

Hence, the correct option is (C).

37.

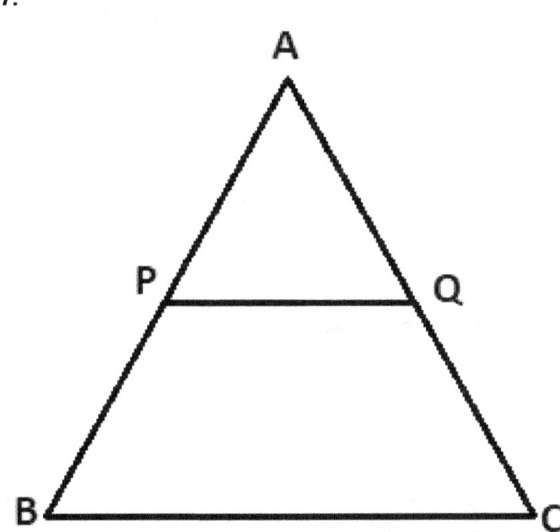

As per the given data,

∠ QPA = ∠ CBA

∠ PAQ = ∠ BAC

∴ ΔPAQ ~ ΔABC

Also given that ratio of AP : PB = 2 : 5

$$\frac{AP}{PB} = \frac{2}{5}$$

$$PB = \frac{5}{2} AP$$

Area ot ΔPAQ = 4 sq.cm

Area of ΔABC = (AP + PB)²

$$= \left(\frac{AP + 5}{2\,AP}\right)^2$$

$$= \left(\frac{7AP}{2}\right)^2$$

$$= \frac{49(AP)^2}{4}$$

$$= \frac{49(2)^2}{4}$$

= 49 sq.cm

We know that area of trapezium PQCB = area of ΔABC – area of ΔPAQ

= 49 sq.cm – 4 sq.cm

= 45 sq.cm

Hence, the correct option is (B).

38. The total present income of A and B together is Rs. 21500

The ratio of the present income of A and B are 2 : 3

Let the present income of A = 2x

Let the present income of B = 3x

According to the question,

3x + 2x = 21500

$$x = \frac{21500}{5} = 4300$$

So, the income of B,

$$\Rightarrow 3x = 3 \times 4300 = 12900$$

Hence, the correct option is (C).

39. Effective discount $\% = x + y - \frac{(xy)}{100}$

Where x and y are the success rates of discount

Therefore,

Effective discount on 15% and $20\% = 15 + 20 - \frac{(15 \times 20)}{100} = 32\%$

Now apply it on 25% and 32%

Effective discount on 25% and $32\% = 25 + 32 - \frac{(25 \times 32)}{100} = 49\%$

Hence, the correct option is (C).

40. The average of 20 numbers is 15.

∴ Sum of 20 numbers = 15 × 20

= 300

The average of the first five is 12.

∴ The sum of first five = 12 × 5

= 60

Sum of remaining 15 numbers = 300 – 60

= 240

Average of remaining 15 numbers $= \dfrac{240}{15}$

$= 16$

Hence, the correct option is (A).

41. Sales of Books from branch B2 in 2000 = 75

Sales of Books from branch B2 in 2001 = 65

Sales of Books from branch B4 in 2000 = 85

Sales of Books from branch B4 in 2001 = 95

Required ratio $= \dfrac{(75+65)}{(85+95)} = \dfrac{140}{180} = \dfrac{7}{9}$

Hence, the correct option is (D).

42. Required ratio $= \left[\dfrac{(70+80)}{(95+110)} \times 100\right]\%$

$= \left[\dfrac{150}{205} \times 100\right]\%$

$= 73.17\%$

Hence, the correct option is (C).

43. Average sales (in thousand number) of branches B1, B3 and B6 in 2000

$= \dfrac{1}{3} \times (80 + 95 + 70) = \left(\dfrac{245}{3}\right)$

Average sales (in thousand number) of branches B1, B2 and B3 in 2001

$= \dfrac{1}{3} \times (105 + 65 + 110) = \left(\dfrac{280}{3}\right)$

$\therefore$ Required percentage $= \left[\dfrac{\frac{245}{3}}{\frac{280}{3}} \times 100\right]\% =$

$\left(\dfrac{245}{280} \times 100\right)\% = 87.5\%.$

Hence, the correct option is (D).

44. Average sales of all the six branches (in thousand numbers) for the year 2000

$= \dfrac{1}{6} \times [80 + 75 + 95 + 85 + 75 + 70]$

$= 80$

Hence, the correct option is (B).

45. Total sales of branches B1, B3 and B5 for both the years (in thousand numbers)

$= (80 + 105) + (95 + 110) + (75 + 95)$

$= 560$

Hence, the correct option is (D).

46. Let the cost price of 1 article be Rs. 1

The cost price of 6 articles = Rs.6

Given,

The cost price of 6 articles = The selling price of 9 articles

$\therefore$ The selling price of 9 articles = Rs.6

And the cost price of 9 article = Rs.9

We know that,

Loss% $= \dfrac{C.P - S.P}{C.P} \times 100 = \dfrac{9-6}{9} \times 100 = \dfrac{100}{3} = 33.33\%$

Hence, the correct option is (B).

47. The sum of all odd natural numbers less than 130

$= 1 + 3 + 5 + 7 + \ldots\ldots + 129$

We can clearly observe that the above series is in $A.P.$

The no. of terms in the series, $n = \dfrac{130}{2} = 65$

Here, $a = 1$ and $l = 129$

According to the $A.P$, the sum of the following series,

$= \left(\dfrac{n}{2}\right) \times (a + l)$

$= \left(\dfrac{65}{2}\right) \times (1 + 129)$

$= \left(\dfrac{65}{2}\right) \times 130$

$= 4225$

Hence, the correct option is (D).

48. Let cost price of the mini-refrigerator = x

$\Rightarrow$ Marked price × (1 - discount%) = Selling price

$\Rightarrow 8200 \times \left(\dfrac{1 - 11}{100}\right) =$ Selling price

$\Rightarrow$ Selling price = Rs. 7298

Cost price = Selling price - profit

$\Rightarrow$ x = 7298 - 600 = Rs. 6698

Hence, the correct option is (A).

49. Given,

sin 3A = cos (A – 26°)

$\Rightarrow$ cos (90° – 3A) = cos (A – 26°) [$\because$ cos (90° – θ) = sin θ]

$\Rightarrow$ 90° – 3A = A – 26°

$\Rightarrow$ 4A = 116°

$\Rightarrow$ A = 29°

Hence, the correct option is (B).

50. Given,

$\tan \theta = \tan 30°. \tan 60°$

$$\tan \theta = \frac{1}{\sqrt{3}} \times \sqrt{3} = 1$$

$$\tan \theta = \tan 45°$$

$$\therefore \quad \theta = 45°$$

$$\Rightarrow 2\theta = 2 \times 45° = 90°$$

Hence, the correct option is (C).

51. The error lies in part 3 of the sentence as the word 'been' is missing after the verb 'have.' The correct tense here is a present perfect progressive tense form which is used to signify an activity that has started and is in continuity. Thus 'have been damaging' is correct. It should read as:'..have been damaging the bilateral relation.'

Hence, the correct option is (C).

52. The error lies in part 3 of the sentence as the verb 'signaled' in the past tense is incorrect. The sentence has the verbs in future continuous form thus the uniformity has to be maintained. It should read as:'.. signaling towards a new start.'

Hence, the correct option is (C).

53. The apostate is the right word which means a person who renounces or abandons a religious or political belief or principle.

The meaning of the rest of the words are:

Prostate: a gland surrounding the neck of the bladder in male mammals and releasing a fluid component of semen.

Profane: (of a person or their behaviour) not respectful of religious practice; irreverent.

Agnostic: a person who believes that nothing is known or can be known of the existence or nature of God.

Hence, the correct option is (A).

54. Misologist is the right word which means hater of knowledge and learning, debate, argument.

The meaning of the rest of the words are:

Bibliophile: a person who collects or has a great love for books.

Philologist: learner of the language, or linguist.

Misogynist: a person who hates women.

Hence, the correct option is (D).

55. The phrase "To catch a tartar" means to deal with someone or something that proves unexpectedly troublesome or powerful.

Ex: They thought that I would simply give up if my complaint had to go to court, but they'll soon realize that they've caught a Tartar.

Hence, the correct option is (B).

56. The only word which conveys the correct meaning is 'till' which means the ride can only be till the cafeteria. The other options do not fit here.

Hence, the correct option is (C).

57. The correct form of the verb is transitive as 'to' is mentioned before the blank thus 'grow' is the correct word.

Hence, the correct option is (B).

58. Option (A) is grammatically wrong as it shows a sentence in a passive voice with an object. Option (B) Would have been correct if "of " had not been given in sentence option (D) doesn't make any sense.

Hence, the correct option is (C).

59. Option (C) is the correctly spelt word as knowledge which means facts, information, and skills acquired through experience or education; the theoretical or practical understanding of a subject.

Other correct spellings and their meanings are:-

Partner = either of a pair of people engaged together in the same activity.

License = permit (someone) to do something.

Niece = a daughter of one's brother or sister, or of one's brother-in-law or sister-in-law.

Hence, the correct option is (C).

60. The idiom 'stand one's ground' means ' not retreat or lose one's advantage in the face of opposition.

For example, you will be able to hold your ground and resist the enemy's attack.

Hence, the correct option is (A).

61. Since this is an interrogative sentence the word 'asked' must be used here. The tense indirect speech is past continuous thus the correct tense in indirect speech is past perfect continuous.

Hence, the correct option is (D).

62. In indirect speech, the words of the speaker are not written in quotes. Usually, the word 'that' is used to convey the words of the speaker. The correct tense should be simple past as the tense in direct speech is simple present. The word 'this' needs to be written as 'that' but 'it' can be used as well and we can see in the options "that" is not given so we will use the word "it " as "it " also represents indirect speech. The sentence given is an exclamatory sentence so in place of "said to" we will use "exclaimed".

Hence, the correct option is (D).

63. The sentence is in active voice thus in the passive voice the object 'hospital' must be written before the subject 'they.'

In active voice :

Subject+verb+object

In a passive voice:

Object+verb+subject

The tense here is future So 'will be visited' is the correct verb to be used here.

The other options use incorrect tenses or change the meaning of the sentence.

Hence, the correct option is (B).

64. The sentence is in active voice thus in the passive voice the object 'bicycle' must be written before the subject 'you.'

In active voice :

Subject+verb+object

In a passive voice:

Object+verb+subject

Here 'you' is not mentioned thus 'let' is the correct word to be used here. The correct verb to be used here is 'sold' as the sentence is in the present tense.

Hence, the correct option is (D).

65. The meanings of the words are:

Bliss: Perfect happiness; great joy.

Euphoria: A feeling or state of intense excitement and happiness.

Upset: Make (someone) unhappy, disappointed, or worried.

Sadness: The condition or quality of being sad.

Mirage: An optical illusion caused by atmospheric conditions, especially the appearance of a sheet of water in a desert or on a hot road caused by the refraction of light from the sky by heated air.

Hence, the correct option is (B).

66. The PAST PERFECT TENSE indicates that an action was completed (finished or "perfected") at some point in the past before something else happened.

The form is: Subject + had + past participle = past perfect tense.

Hence, the correct option is (B).

67. The word 'Encumbrance' means 'Hindrance.'

Hindrance => Obstruction

Torture => Torment

Trauma => A deeply distressing or disturbing experience.

Bulwark => Support

Hence, the correct option is (C).

68. The word 'eternal' means 'perpetual; endless.'

Esteem => Respect and admiration

Quell => Reduce

Instigated => Bring about or initiate (an action or event)

Hence, the correct option is (A).

69. The word 'petulant' means '(of a person or their manner) childishly sulky or bad-tempered.' The meanings of the words are:

Affable => Good humoured

Sycophant => A person who acts obsequiously towards someone important in order to gain the advantage.

Pragmatic => Practical

Frugal => Thrifty

Hence, the correct option is (C).

70. The word 'opine' means 'express opinion;suggest.' The meanings of the words are:

Taciturn => Uncommunicative

Usurp => Take (a position of power or importance) illegally or by force.

Ornate => Decorate

Perish => Die

Hence, the correct option is (A).

71. The passage clearly states that the organization wants to improve the living conditions of the animals and stop all sorts of cruel treatment against them. The author talks about the effective measures taken by the organization as well.

Hence, the correct option is (C).

72. It is mentioned in the passage 'The organization points out that vaccination programs are the only effective way to eliminate rabies, and work with governments on vaccination programs.'

Hence, the correct option is (C).

73. The word 'aftermath' means 'the consequences or after-effects of a significant unpleasant event'.

Hence, the correct option is (B).

74. It is mentioned in the passage ' The work is of particular benefit in developing world countries, where communities rely on animals for food, transport, and income.'

Hence, the correct option is (A).

75. The word 'misguided' means 'having or showing faulty judgment or reasoning.' Thus the word 'well informed' conveys the opposite meaning.

Hence, the correct option is (D).

76. The words crawl, breaststroke, and butterfly are associated with the game of swimming.

In this game, the entire body of the person is moved through the water. In pools or open water, the sports take place. The events butterfly, breaststroke, freestyle, and individual medley are associated with swimming. A set of specific techniques is required by swimming. There are distinct regulations in competition.

Hence, the correct option is (A).

77. The Federation Internationale des Echecs (FIDE), or World Chess Federation, was formed on Sunday, July 20, 1924.

Hence, the correct option is (B).

78.

- **Jonas Edward Salk** invented the Polio vaccine.

- **Polio Vaccines** are used to prevent **poliomyelitis**. Two types are used that is inactivated poliovirus given by injection and weak end poliovirus given by mouth.

Scientist	Known For
Ernest Rutherford	Father Of Nuclear Physics
Richard Taylor	Nobel Prize In Physics (1990)
Karl Jansky	Founding Figures Of Radio Astronomy

Hence, the correct option is (B).

79.

- A Network Interface Card (NIC) is a computer hardware component that allows a computer to connect to a network. NICs may be used for both wired and wireless connections.

- A NIC is also known as a network interface controller (NIC), a network interface controller card.

Hence, the correct option is (A).

80. Dolomite is an ore of both Calcium (Ca) and Magnesium (Mg). The chemical formula of Dolomite is $CaCO_3.MgCO_3$.

Trick: MaCaDonalds> Ma- Magnesium, Ca- Calcium, Do- Dolomite.

Hence, the correct option is (D).

81.

- Silver is greater than Bromine.

- Silver has a higher atomic number when compared to Bromine.

- In the periodic table also Silver has an atomic number 47, whereas bromine has atomic number 35.

Hence, the correct option is (A).

82.

- The nuclear force is a force that acts between the protons and neutrons of atoms.

- The nuclear force plays an essential role in storing energy that is used in nuclear power and nuclear weapons.

- Gravitational force is the weakest force.

Hence, the correct option is (B).

83.

- Joule is the SI unit of Heat.

- 1 joule of work done is equal to the energy transferred to an object when a force of one newton acts on that object in the direction of its motion through a distance of one metre

Physical Quantities	Unit
Illuminance	Lux
Magnetic flux density	Tesla
Capacitance	Farad

Hence, the correct option is (C).

84.

- Vitamin A is also known as Retinol.

- It helps in maintaining the vision in humans and is also essential for the correct functioning of epithelial cells.

Hence, the correct option is (C).

85.

- The inputs that are used in the production of goods or services in order to make an economic profit, is known as a factor of production.

- The factors of production include land, labour, capital, entrepreneurship etc.

Hence, the correct option is (D).

86. Allahabad is known as the City of Prime Ministers as 7 Prime Ministers have connections to Allahabad city.

Hence, the correct option is (C).

87. Russia launched the 'Arktika-M' 1st satellite to monitor climate change in the Arctic Region. The satellite was launched from a Soyuz-2.1b carrier rocket from the Baikonur Cosmodrome, Kazakhstan. Arktika-M is 1st of the two satellites launched by Russia for creating a Hydrometeorological & climate monitoring system to monitor the climate & environment in the Arctic. The Arctic holds huge reserves of Oil & Gas which are being eyed by countries like the United States, Canada, Norway & Russia.

Hence, the correct option is (D).

88.

- The rise in the temperature in the stratosphere is caused by the absorption of Ultra Violet radiations.

- The ozone layer in the stratosphere is formed due to a reaction between UV rays and oxygen.

- The ozone is capable of absorbing radiations from the Sun and this causes an increase in temperature towards the upper part of the stratosphere while the lower part shows less temperature. This is called temperature inversion.

Hence, the correct option is (C).

89.

- Saddle Peak is located on the North Andaman.

- It is the highest peak on Andaman and Nicobar islands with an elevation of 731m.

- It is located near Diglipur, a town in North Andaman Island.

Hence, the correct option is (B).

90.

- Though the Indian Constitution is federal and envisages dual polity, it provides for only single citizenship unlike U.S.A that has dual citizenship.

- This feature has been adopted from the British Constitution.

Hence, the correct option is (D).

91. Lord canning described princely states as the breakwaters in the storms because it was the timely aid of princely state helped in the suppression of revolt of 1857

Hence, the correct option is (B).

92. Satpura National Park is located in the Hoshangabad district of Madhya Pradesh in India. Its name is derived from the Satpura range. Along with the adjoining Bori and Pachmarhi wildlife sanctuaries, it provides 1,427 km sq. of unique central Indian highland ecosystem. It was set up in 1981.

Hence, the correct option is (C).

93. National Science day is annually observed across India on 28th February to commemorate the discovery of 'Raman Effect' by Indian Physicist Sir CV Raman for which he was awarded the Nobel Prize in Physics in 1930. The theme of the National Science Day 2021 is "Future of Science and Technology and Innovation(STI): Impact on Education, Skills and Work". In the 2021 Union Budget, the Government of India has allocated Rs.50000 crores over 5 years for the National Research Foundation to support research in the field of Science.

Hence, the correct option is (C).

94. Warli painting is a style of tribal art mostly created by the tribal people from the North Sahyadri Range in India. This tribal art was originated in Maharashtra, where it is still practised today.

Hence, the correct option is (A).

95. Australia is a country and continent surrounded by Indian and Pacific ocean. Its landmass is of 7,617,930 square kilometers. It is world's smallest continent and sixth largest country of the total area.

Hence, the correct option is (A).

96. According to Buddhist tradition, Maitreya is a bodhisattva who will appear on Earth in the future, achieve complete enlightenment, and teach pure dharma. According to scriptures, Maitreya will be a successor to the present Buddha, Gautama Buddha (also known as Śākyamuni Buddha).

Hence, the correct option is (C).

97. Notes and Handouts will be used to place headers and footers in handouts. After clicking to "insert" button, go to "header & footer" and then "notes and handouts". One can insert the header and footer there.

Hence, the correct option is (B).

98. The dividend is the portion of profits that a company distributes among its shareholders in the form of cash. Usually, it is expressed per share. In some cases, it is expressed as a percentage of the share's face value. Dividend Yield is the ratio of dividend amount per share to the prevailing market price of the share is a yardstick to identify attractively-valued stocks. Other things remaining equal, the higher the dividend yield, the more attractive is the stock for investors

Hence, the correct option is (B).

99. The thermosphere extends 1000 km above the earth's crust. The ionosphere is a dense band of charged particles, specifically found in the thermosphere.

Hence, the correct option is (D).

100. Balram Jakhar has the distinction of beginning his career in Parliament by occupying the office of the Speaker immediately after his election to the seventh Lok Sabha for the first time. He has the distinction of being the longest serving Speaker in the Lok Sabha.

Hence, the correct option is (C).

General Intelligence and Reasoning

Q.1 A series is given with one word missing. Choose the correct alternative from the given ones that will complete the series.

Pen, Apron, Top, Teapot, Cheap,?

A. Prayer **B.** Output **C.** Occupy **D.** Backup

Q.2 In the following question, select the related letters from the given alternatives.

MEAT : LDZS :: PALE : ?

A. OKZD **B.** OBMF **C.** OZKD **D.** OZDK

Q.3 Direction: Select from Answer Figures, the appropriate figure to complete the series.

Problem Figures

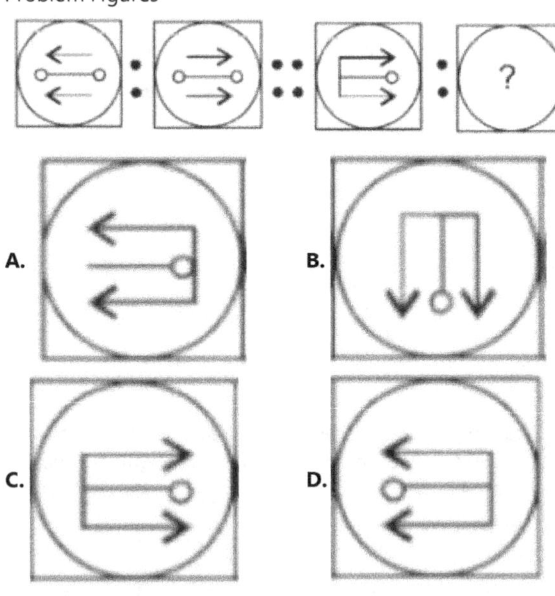

Q.4 Direction: Find the wrong number in the given series.

4131, 1377, 461, 153, 51

A. 461 **B.** 153 **C.** 1377 **D.** 51

Q.5 A walks 5 km toward the west. He turns right and walks 10 km. He again turns right and walks 15 km. how far (in km) is he from his starting point?

A. $10\sqrt{2}$ **B.** $10\sqrt{3}$ **C.** 20 **D.** 10

Q.6 In the following question, select the odd word from the given alternatives.

A. Black **B.** Yellow **C.** Rainbow **D.** Pink

Q.7 Direction: Arrange the given words in a meaningful order and select the option indicating the correct order:

1) Input
2) Output
3) Data
4) Information
5) Processing

A. 43251 **B.** 23541 **C.** 31524 **D.** 53421

Q.8 In a certain code language, "ODD" is written as "22" and "SAD" is written as "23". How is "CUP" written in that code language?

A. 38 **B.** 39 **C.** 40 **D.** 37

Q.9 Direction: Select the one which is different from the other three responses.

A. 32-42 **B.** 48-58 **C.** 96-106 **D.** 86-78

Q.10 In the following question, select the related numbers from the given alternatives.

APE : 23 : : BS : ?

A. 12 **B.** 21 **C.** 22 **D.** 18

Q.11 In the following question, select the word which cannot be formed using the letters of the given word.

FROLICSOME

A. Colors **B.** Crimes **C.** Looser **D.** Frame

Q.12 What does the area mark 1 in the figure given below represent?

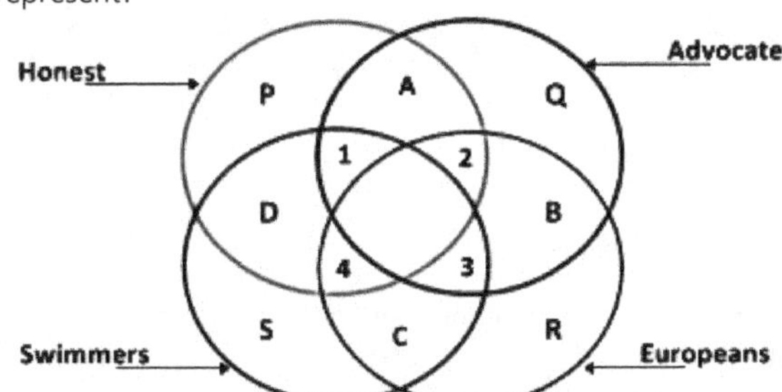

A. All honest European swimmers
B. All honest advocates who are swimmers
C. All no-European advocates who are honest swimmers
D. All non-Europeans who are honest swimmers

Q.13 If in a certain code language, URECKON is written as VSFDLPO then which word will be written as ECSTASI?

A. DSRBZRH **B.** DBZRSHR
C. DBRSZRH **D.** DZRBHZS

Q.14 Direction: In the following question, select the odd word from the given alternatives.

A. Tungsten **B.** Nickel
C. Diamond **D.** Gold

Q.15 In the following question, four groups of three numbers are given. In each group, the second and third numbers are related to the first number by a Logic/Rule/Relation. Three are similar on basis of the same Logic/Rule/Relation. Select the odd one out from the given alternatives.

| A. (17, 21, 25) | B. (12, 16, 20) |
| C. (19, 23, 27) | D. (22, 26, 32) |

Q.16 In the following question, by using which mathematical operators will the expression become correct?

(69_63) _6_36

A. -, +, =   B. -, -, =   C. -, ×, =   D. +, ÷,=

Q.17 If a mirror is placed on line AB, which of the option figures shows the correct image of the given question figure?

A

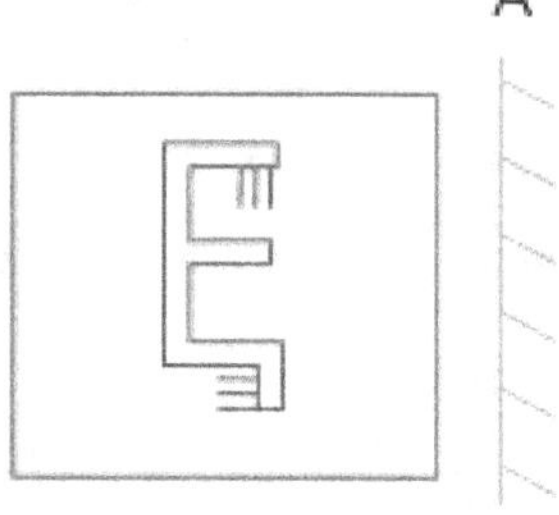

B

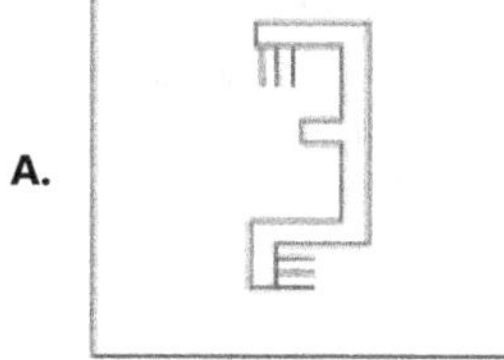  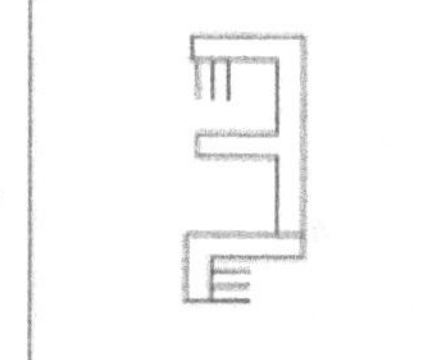

A.   B.

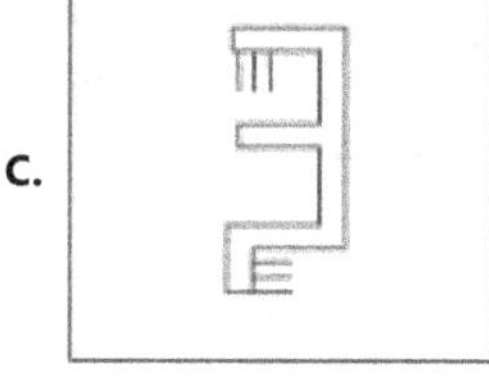 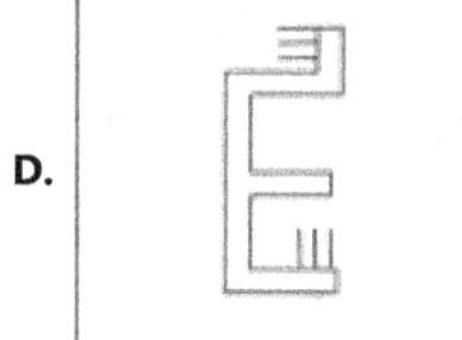

C.   D.

Q.18 A series is given with one term missing. Select the correct alternative from the given ones that will complete the series.

XQC, UNZ, RKW, OHT, ?

A. LFP   B. MED   C. LEQ   D. MFQ

Q.19 Among the four answer figures which can be formed from the cut-out pieces given below.

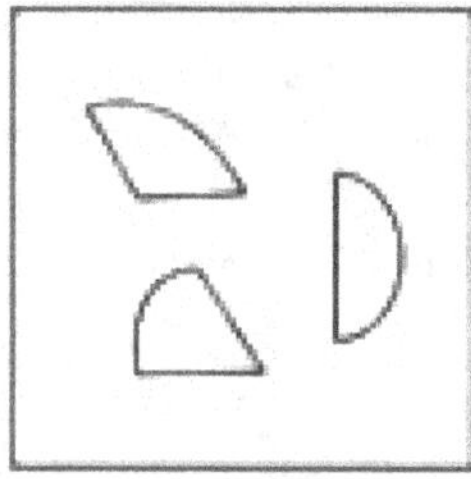

A.

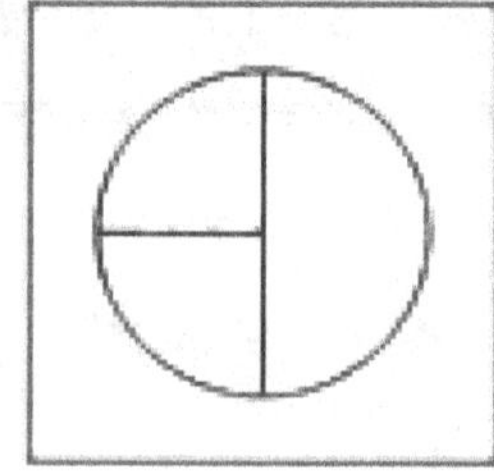

B.

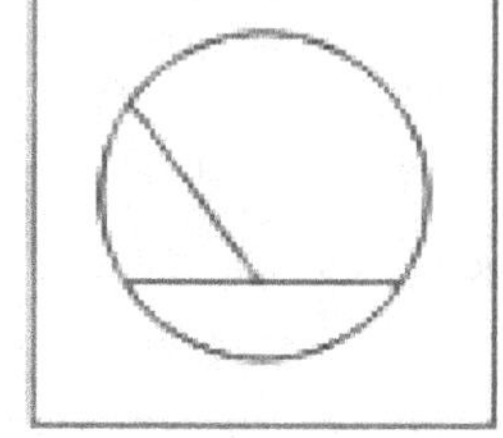

C.

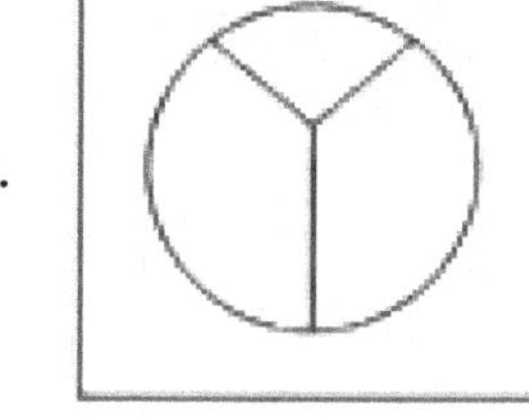

D.

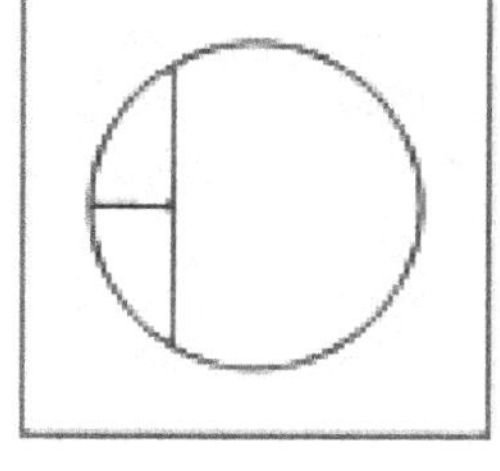

Q.20 A piece of paper is folded and punched as shown below in the question figures. From the given answer figures, indicate how it will appear when opened:

 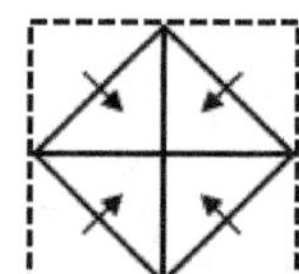  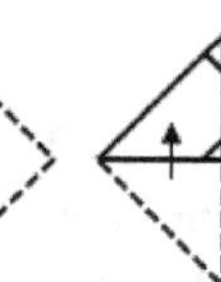

[SSC MTS, 2019], [UP Police Constable, 2019]

A. 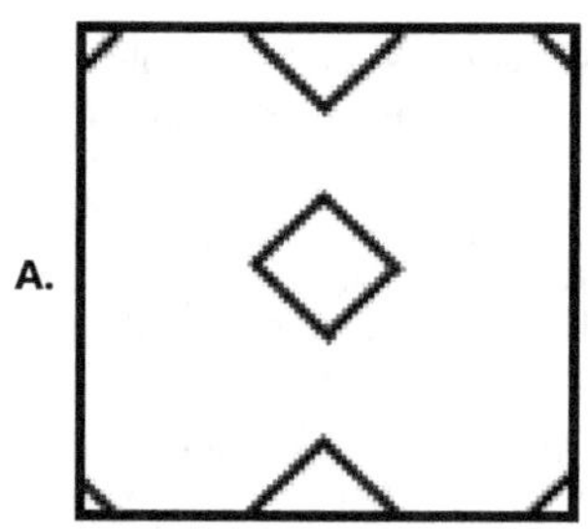   B. 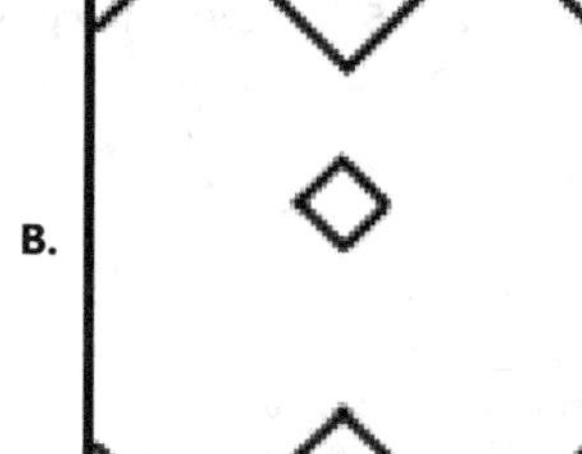

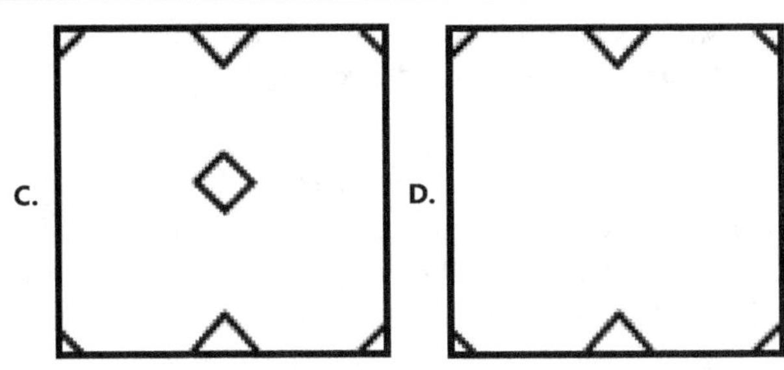

C.

D.

Q.21 In the following question four figures are given. One figure is different from other, find out that figure.

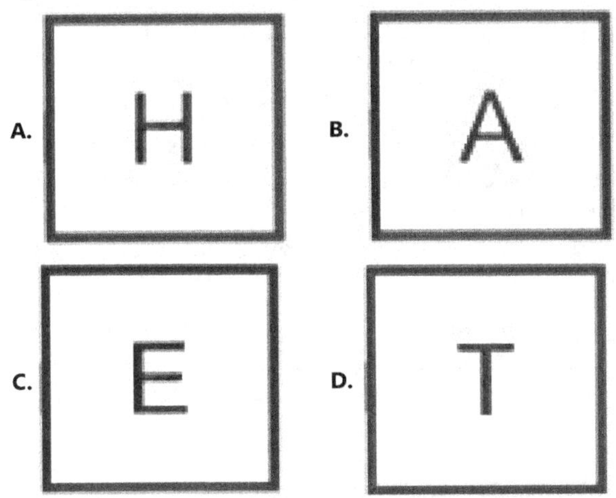

A. H

B. A

C. E

D. T

Q.22 In the following diagram, Positive, Negative, and Neutral people are represented by Circle, Triangle, and Heptagon respectively. How many people are Negative and Neutral but not positive?

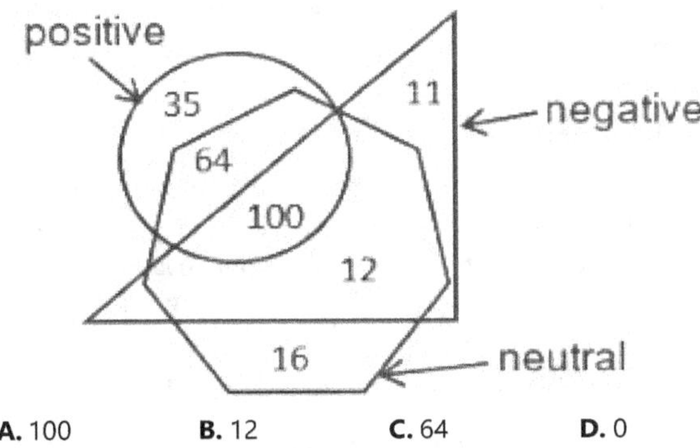

A. 100　　B. 12　　C. 64　　D. 0

Q.23 Direction: If + stands for division, × stands for addition, − stands for multiplication, ÷ stands for subtraction, which of the following is correct?

1. $15 \div 5 \times 2 - 6 + 3 = 28$
2. $15 \times 5 + 2 - 6 \div 3 = 56.5$
3. $15 + 5 - 2 \div 6 \times 3 = 3$
4. $15 - 5 + 2 \times 6 \div 3 = 41$

A. 3　　B. 1　　C. 2　　D. 4

Q.24 Direction: From the given answer figures select the one in which the question figure is hidden/embedded.

A. 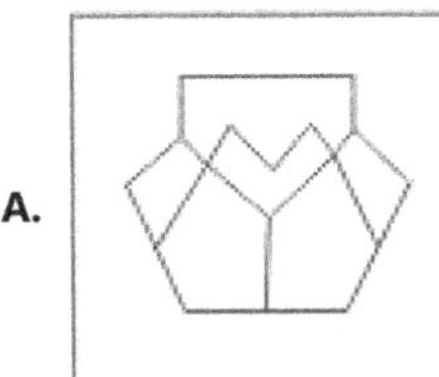

B. 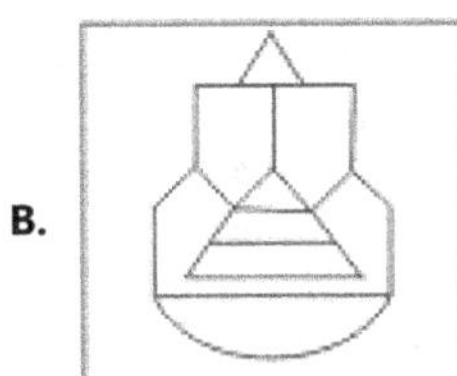

C. 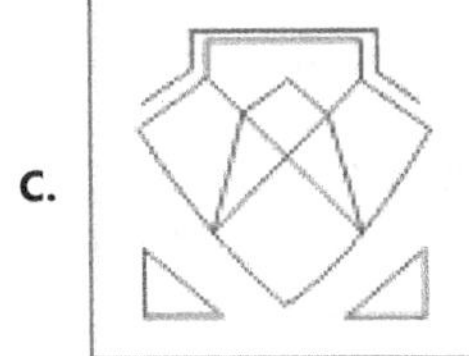

D. 

Q.25 Direction: In the question, a piece of paper is folded and cut as shown below in the question figures. The given option figure indicates how it will appear when opened.

A. 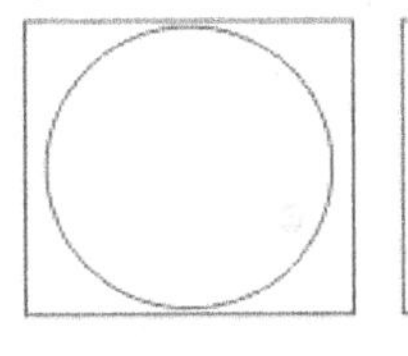

B. 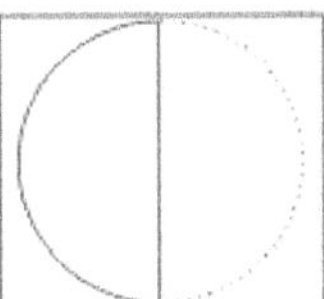

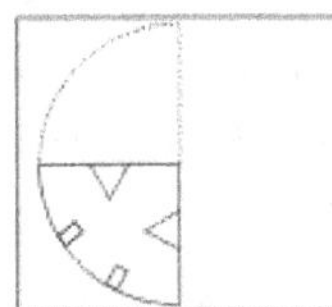

C. 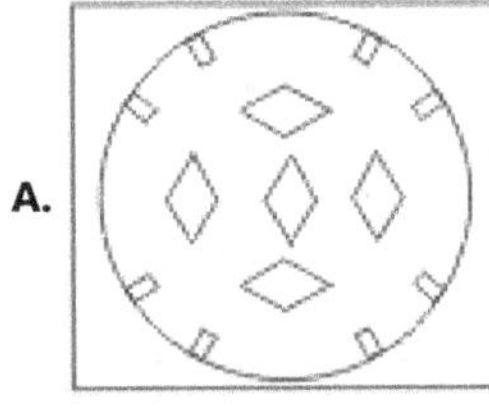

D. 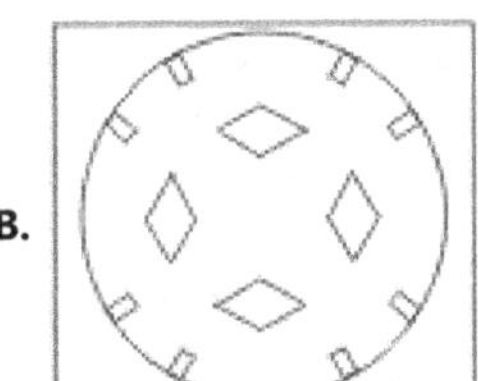

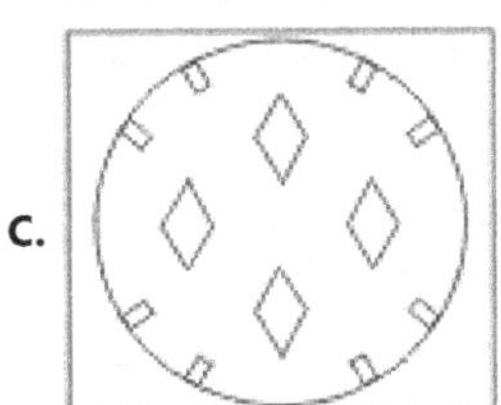

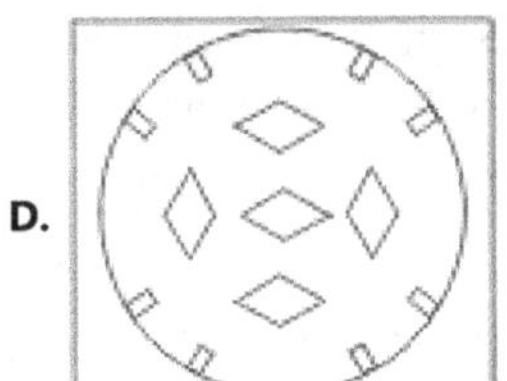

Numerical Aptitude/ Quantitative Ability

Q.26 What is the value of $[(1.4)^3 + (0.9)^3] \div [(1.4)^2 + (0.9)^2 - (1.4) \times (0.9)]$?

A. 0.5　　B. 2.3　　C. 1.6　　D. 2.2

Q.27 What is the value of x?

$x = 33.33\%$ of $81 + 77.78\%$ of $171 - 62.5\%$ of 144

A. 70 B. 120 C. 60 D. 82

Q.28 What is the average of first 31 multiples of 19?
A. 304
B. 418
C. 279
D. Cannot be determined

Q.29 If the price of almonds rises from Rs. 450 to Rs. 500 per kg, then Raj will have to reduce his consumption of almonds by (if the expenditure is constant):
A. 25% B. 10% C. 30% D. 90%

Q.30 The average of 17 numbers is 7. If one number is excluded, the average becomes 4. What is the excluded number?
A. 21 B. 55 C. 24 D. 20

Q.31 A cone of radius 15 cm and height 18 cm is completely filled with water. This water is emptied into an empty cylindrical vessel of the radius of 4.5 cm. What will be the height of water in this vessel?
A. $\frac{100}{3}$ cm B. $\frac{200}{3}$ cm C. 200 cm D. 320 cm

Q.32 A can do a particular work in 6 days. B can do the same work in 8 days. A and B signed to do it for Rs. 3200. They completed the work in 3 days with the help of C. How much is to be paid to C ?
A. 600 B. 420 C. 400 D. 380

Q.33 In a factory, there are three machines A, B and C. Efficiency of A is thrice of the efficiency of B and the efficiency of C is half of the combined efficiency of A and B. If all the three machines working together can manufacture 360 units in 15 hours then how much time machine A will take alone to manufacture these units?
A. 30 hours B. 20 hours C. 45 hours D. 90 hours

Q.34 Sudhir bought an almirah for Rs. 13600 and spent Rs. 400 on its transportation. He sold it for Rs. 16800. Find his gain percent.
A. 20% B. 30% C. 35% D. 15%

Q.35 How many balls each of radius 1 cm can be made by melting a bigger ball whose diameter is 8?
A. 65 B. 66 C. 68 D. 64

Q.36 If some articles are bought at Rs. 16 each and sold at Rs. 18 each, then what is the profit percentage?
A. 11.11 B. 12.5 C. 25 D. 9.09

Q.37 A, B and C enter into a partnership. A invests some money at the beginning, B invests double the amount after six months and C invests thrice the amount after eight months. If the annual profit be Rs. 27000; C's share (in Rs.) is ?
A. 10508 B. 9000 C. 11340 D. 15002

Q.38 Two successive discounts of 20% and 25% are given. What will be the net discount (in percentage)?
A. 43.5 B. 42.5 C. 45 D. 40

Q.39 Amit had an urgent requirement of Rs. 200000. He borrowed Rs. 120000 from Veer at a simple interest of 5% per annum, and Rs. 80000 from Ayush at a simple interest of 4% per annum. He cleared his debt from Veer in 6 months and that from Ayush in 9 months. How much total interest did he paid?
A. Rs. 5100 B. Rs. 5400 C. Rs. 5500 D. Rs. 5800

Q.40 Find the value of $\frac{\sin\theta-\cos\theta+1}{\sin\theta+\cos\theta-1}$
A. $\frac{1+\sin\theta}{\cos\theta}$ B. $\frac{1-\sin\theta}{\cos\theta}$ C. $\frac{1-\cos\theta}{\sin\theta}$ D. $\frac{1+\cos\theta}{\sin\theta}$

Q.41 What will be the compound interest on a sum of ₹ 9000 at compound interest compounded annually at 8% per annum in two years?
A. Rs. 1498.76 B. Rs. 1497.6
C. Rs. 1597.6 D. Rs. 1480.60

Q.42 If a 210 m long train crosses a 240 m long platform in 20 seconds, find the speed of the train.
A. 37.8 km/hr B. 43.2 km/hr
C. 54 km/hr D. 81 km/hr

Q.43 Two pipes P and Q can fill the tank alone in 200 and 300 hours respectively. If they are opened together, then in how many hours will the tank be filled?
A. 240 B. 120 C. 50 D. 250

Q.44 A room is 6 m long, 5 m broad and 4 m high. IF all the walls are to be covered with paper 50 cm wide, the length of the paper is:
A. 96 m B. 176 m C. 421 m D. 208 m

Q.45 The ratio of the number of boys to the number of girls in a school of 640 students, is $5:3$. If 30 more girls are admitted in the school, then how many more boys should be admitted so that the ratio of boys to that of the girl becomes $14:9$.
A. 20 B. 15 C. 25 D. 30

Q.46 In the adjoining figure A, B, C, D are the concyclic points. The value of 'x' is:

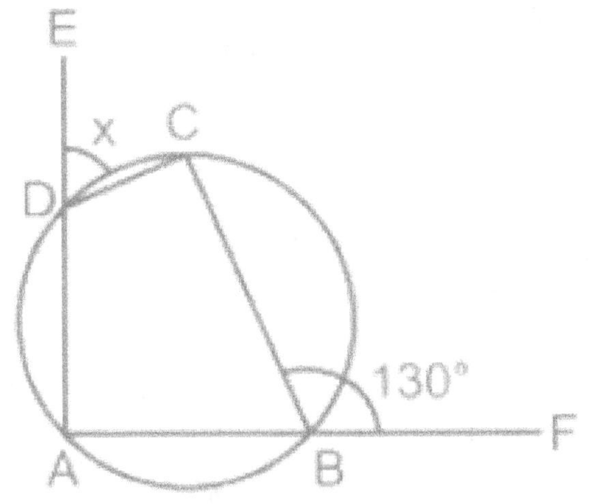

A. 50°   **B.** 60°   **C.** 70°   **D.** 90°

Q.47 At a point P on the ground the angle of elevation of the top of a 10 m tall building and of a helicopter hovering some distance over the top of the building are $30°$ and $60°$ respectively. Then, the height of the helicopter above the ground is

A. $\frac{10}{\sqrt{3}}$ m   **B.** $10\sqrt{3}$ m   **C.** $\frac{20}{\sqrt{3}}$ m   **D.** 30 m

Ques (48-50):Direction: The bar chart given below shows the sales (in lakh) by 2 companies X and Y from year 2011 to 2015.

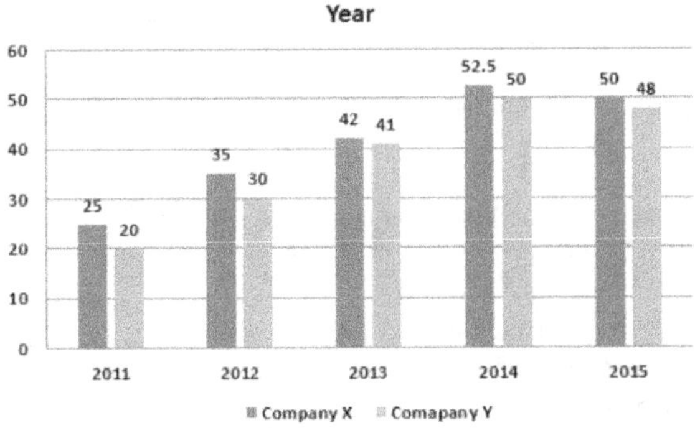

Q.48 Companies X and Y show the same difference in sales for which of the following years?

A. 2012 and 2013   **B.** 2011 and 2012
C. 2012 and 2014   **D.** None of these

Q.49

What is the average sale (in lacs) of company Y over the 5 given years?

A. 47   **B.** 37.8   **C.** 84   **D.** 42

Q.50

What is the percentage change in sales of company X from year 2011 to 2013?

A. 68   **B.** 84   **C.** 78   **D.** 34

General English & Comprehension

Ques (51-52):Direction: In the following question, one part of the sentence may have an error. Find out which part of the sentence has an error and click the option corresponding to it. If the sentence is free from error, click the 'No error' option.

Q.51 Nancy was (A) / accompanied with (B) / her mom on her first day at college (C) / No error. (D)
A. (A)   **B.** (B)   **C.** (C)   **D.** (D)

Q.52 Jay was under the illusion (A) / that the world (B) / revolved in him (C) / No error. (D)
A. (A)   **B.** (B)   **C.** (C)   **D.** (D)

Q.53 Direction: The sentence(s) given with blanks are to be filled with an appropriate word(s). Four alternatives are suggested for each question. For each question, choose the correct alternative and click the button corresponding to it.

A 9-year-old Indian chess genius ________ battle today to stay in the UK after the expiry of his father's work visa.
A. Had won a   **B.** Has won a
C. Is winning a   **D.** Was winning a

Q.54 Direction: The sentence(s) given with blanks are to be filled with an appropriate word(s). Four alternatives are suggested for each question. For each question, choose the correct alternative and click the button corresponding to it.

Shreyas, who was born in India, moved to the UK aged three with parents Jitendra and Anju Singh from Bangalore ________.
A. Six years ago   **B.** Six years ahead
C. Six years since   **D.** Six years hence

Q.55 Direction: In the following question, out of the four alternatives, select the word opposite in meaning to the given word.

Enlarge
A. Condense   **B.** Glorify
C. Amplify   **D.** Augment

Q.56 Direction: In the following question, out of the four alternatives, select the word opposite in meaning to the given word.

Tranquil
A. Unruffled   **B.** Perpetual
C. Temporal   **D.** Agitated

Q.57 Direction: In the following question, out of the four alternatives, select the alternative which best expresses the meaning of the Idiom/Phrase.

Hear it on the grapevine:
A. To hear rumors about something or someone though informal means
B. To present a counter-argument
C. People's intentions can be judged better by what they do than what they say
D. Believe someone's statement, without proof

Q.58 Direction: A sentence has been given in active/passive voice. Out of the four alternatives suggested selecting the one which best expresses the same sentence in active/passive voice.

Flowers were being plucked by the students.
- **A.** The flowers are being plucked by the students
- **B.** The students have been plucking flowers
- **C.** The students plucked flowers
- **D.** The students were plucking flowers

Q.59 Direction: A sentence has been given in active/passive voice. Out of the four alternatives suggested selecting the one which best expresses the same sentence in active/passive voice.

The work had already been completed by them.
- **A.** They are completing the work
- **B.** They had already completed the work
- **C.** They have already completed the work
- **D.** They already completed the work

Q.60 Direction: In the following question, out of the four alternatives, select the alternative which best expresses the meaning of the Idiom/Phrase.

Raining cats and dogs:
- **A.** To rain heavily
- **B.** To win a big lottery
- **C.** To get wealth beyond what one deserves
- **D.** To become filthy rich by honest means

Q.61 Direction: Improve the bracketed part of the sentence.

(As good as) an investor concerned, the high relating to indemnities is of no importance.
- **A.** As far as
- **B.** As soon as
- **C.** As much as
- **D.** No improvement

Ques (62-66):Direction: Choose the correct word by filling up the numbered blanks and complete the passage.

Opinions have been __(A)__ that the pace of development of the Indian Himalayan Region (IHR) has been slow. At the same time, its fragile nature and difficulty of taking up conventional development initiatives have not been __(B)__. In this report, arguments have been presented recommending __(C)__ of policies to bring in the "mountain perspective" for the IHR, in the national planning. __(D)__ has also been laid on developing norms for good governance and for __(E)__ social capital at the grassroots.

Q.62 Which of the following fits in the blank labeled (A)?
- **A.** Tormented
- **B.** Sanguine
- **C.** Expressed
- **D.** Demented

Q.63 Which of the following fits in the blank labeled (B)?
- **A.** Scurrilous
- **B.** Appreciated
- **C.** Mocked
- **D.** Underrated

Q.64
Which of the following fits in the blank labeled (C)?
- **A.** Signaling
- **B.** Vilifying
- **C.** Reshaping
- **D.** Depriving

Q.65

Which of the following fits in the blank labeled (D)?
- **A.** Travesty
- **B.** Emphasis
- **C.** Laws
- **D.** Censure

Q.66 Which of the following fits in the blank labeled (E)?
- **A.** Rescinding
- **B.** Commenting
- **C.** Procuring
- **D.** Harnessing

Q.67 Direction: Improve the bracketed part of the sentence.

I usually (make) a shower after I play tennis, but today I couldn't.
- **A.** Has
- **B.** Give
- **C.** Take
- **D.** No improvement

Q.68 Direction: In the following question, out of the four alternatives, choose the word which is opposite in meaning of the given word and click the button corresponding to it.

Torrid
- **A.** Slack
- **B.** Rushed
- **C.** Flashy
- **D.** Frigid

Q.69 Direction: In the following question, out of the four alternatives, choose the word which best expresses the meaning of the given word and click the button corresponding to it.

Conceal
- **A.** Receive
- **B.** Connive
- **C.** Hide
- **D.** Reveal

Q.70 Direction: In the following question, out of the four alternatives, choose the word which best expresses the meaning of the given word and click the button corresponding to it.

Dawdle
- **A.** Rumble
- **B.** Amble
- **C.** Fumble
- **D.** Tumble

Q.71 Direction: Improve the bracketed part of the sentence.

There (are demonstrations against) the government by Japanese university students in the 1960's.
- **A.** Is demonstrations against
- **B.** Were demonstrations against
- **C.** Are demonstrations from
- **D.** No improvement

Q.72 Direction: In the following question, a sentence has been given in Direct/Indirect Speech. Out of the four alternatives suggested, select the one which best expresses the same sentence in Indirect/Direct Speech.

Prakash will say, "I will always know where to find him".
- **A.** Prakash will say that he will always know where to find him
- **B.** Prakash will say that he would always know where to find him
- **C.** Prakash would say that he would always know where to find him
- **D.** Prakash says that he would always know where to find him

Q.73 Direction: In the following question, a sentence has been given in Direct/Indirect Speech. Out of the four alternatives suggested, select the one which best expresses the same sentence in Indirect/Direct Speech.

He said, " bathe regularly".

A. He said that he had taken bath regularly

B. He said that he bathed regularly

C. He said that he has taken a bath regularly

D. He said that he took a bath regularly

Q.74 Direction: Choose an option, which can be substituted for a given word/sentence/phrase out of given options.

To draw out; to cause to be emitted in vapour.

A. Conceal   **B.** Exhale   **C.** Repress   **D.** Quell

Q.75 Direction: In the following question, out of the four alternatives, select the word similar in meaning to the given word.

Superstitious

A. Pious

B. Traditional

C. Irrational

D. Sacred

General Awareness

Q.76 The Vishvamitra honour of Madhya Pradesh given for excellent performance in which Field?

A. Excellent performance in sports

B. Social work-related activities

C. Excellent performance in sports training

D. Out-standing award for literature

Q.77 What is the motto of Olympic Council of Asia?

A. Ever Onward

B. Ever Freedom

C. Ever Unity

D. All Together

Q.78 Who invented the Band-aid?

A. Earle Dickson

B. Alan Gant

C. Louis Pasteur

D. Frank Epperson

Q.79 Which of the following one founded the State of Hyderabad?

A. Murshid Quli Khan

B. Alivardi Khan

C. Nizam-ul-Mulk

D. None of these

Q.80 'Gypsum' is an ore of _______.

A. Copper

B. Magnesium

C. Silver

D. Calcium

Q.81 Which of the following elements has the highest atomic number?

A. Lead

B. Tin

C. Germanium

D. Silicon

Q.82 In which case greater force is required?

Case 1: accelerating a 6 kg mass at 3m/s^2

Case 2: accelerating a 9 kg mass at 2 m/s^2

A. Case 1 > Case 2

B. Case 1 < Case 2

C. Case 1 = Case 2

D. Can not be determined

Q.83 The SI unit of momentum is _______.

A. kilogram-meter per second

B. kilogram-meter per second squared

C. kilogram-meter-second

D. kilogram-meter-second squared

Q.84 Battle for Delhi during the Mughal period took place in which of the following area of Delhi?

A. Red Fort

B. Purana Qila

C. Tughlaqabad Fort

D. Badarpur

Q.85 Programs or instructions are in _______ system.

A. Hardware

B. Icon

C. Instructions

D. Software

Q.86 Messaging application named 'Secure Application for the Internet' (SAI) developed by which Indian armed force?

A. Indian Navy

B. Indian Coast Guard

C. Indian Air Force

D. Indian Army

Q.87 Which city is known as Manchester of India?

A. Ahmedabad

B. Allahabad

C. Agra

D. Asansol

Q.88 Varanasi is located on the banks of which river?

A. Ganga

B. Yamuna

C. Saraswati

D. Narmada

Q.89 The climate of India has broadly been described as of which type?

A. Dry

B. Monsoon

C. Arid

D. Humid

Q.90 The stage of connecting two or more computers with each other to share information is _______.

A. The network

B. Router

C. Server

D. Tunnel

Q.91 To which party does Kalvakuntala Chandrasekhar Rao, the Chief Minister of Telangana belong?

A. Telangana Rashtara Samithi

B. Congress Party

C. Telangana Parja Front

D. Jana Sena

Q.92 The Israeli Parliament is also known as _______.

A. Knesset

B. Senate

C. Congress

D. General Council

Q.93 In which conference of 1888, the constitution was created for Congress?

A. Bombay

B. Calcutta

C. Madras

D. Allahabad

Q.94 Bhadra Wildlife Sanctuary is in _______.

A. Chhattisgarh

B. Karnataka

C. Assam

D. Andhra Pradesh

Q.95 In which year Bombay Stock Exchange has established?

A. 1865   **B.** 1876   **C.** 1875   **D.** 1886

Q.96 When does Bangladesh celebrate its Independence Day?

A. March 26, 1971

B. March 26, 1972

C. June 22, 1976   **D.** June 22, 1977

Q.97 The Sangai Festival is organized in ________:
A. Assam   **B.** Manipur
C. Bihar   **D.** Nagaland

Q.98 Quantum theory was proposed by whom for the first time in the year 1900?
A. Albert Einstein   **B.** Max Planck
C. C V Raman   **D.** Louis de Broglie

Q.99 In which state prime minister Narendra Modi has launched the country's first seaplane service?
A. Gujrat   **B.** Kerala
C. Odisha   **D.** Maharashtra

Q.100 Prime Minister Narendra Modi is scheduled to flag off the country's first-ever fully-automated driverless train in which city?
A. Nagpur   **B.** New Delhi
C. Mumbai   **D.** Chennai

// Smart Answer Sheet //

Correct — Percentage of students who answered correctly. **Skipped** — Percentage of students who skipped.

Q.	Ans.	Correct	Skipped	Q.	Ans.	Correct	Skipped	Q.	Ans.	Correct	Skipped	Q.	Ans.	Correct	Skipped	Q.	Ans.	Correct	Skipped	Q.	Ans.	Correct	Skipped
1	D	60.44 %	1.47 %	18	C	55.3 %	1.34 %	35	D	18.86 %	4.97 %	52	C	42.13 %	1.76 %	69	C	12.54 %	3.71 %	86	D	52.19 %	1.56 %
2	C	16.27 %	4.2 %	19	B	46.11 %	1.46 %	36	B	79.18 %	0.0 %	53	B	20.04 %	3.5 %	70	B	22.24 %	3.36 %	87	A	85.06 %	0.0 %
3	D	10.15 %	3.89 %	20	B	40.96 %	1.57 %	37	B	83.86 %	0.0 %	54	A	27.23 %	3.73 %	71	B	43.89 %	1.84 %	88	A	88.02 %	0.0 %
4	A	26.11 %	3.99 %	21	C	88.1 %	0.0 %	38	D	51.27 %	1.84 %	55	A	86.98 %	0.0 %	72	A	45.23 %	1.78 %	89	B	11.43 %	3.41 %
5	A	19.65 %	3.65 %	22	B	17.59 %	4.13 %	39	B	12.16 %	4.59 %	56	D	29.84 %	3.73 %	73	B	44.52 %	1.44 %	90	A	29.45 %	4.78 %
6	C	60.78 %	1.44 %	23	A	47.87 %	1.75 %	40	A	29.24 %	3.44 %	57	A	82.19 %	0.0 %	74	B	43.73 %	1.42 %	91	A	68.21 %	1.31 %
7	C	79.7 %	0.0 %	24	D	86.68 %	0.0 %	41	B	45.93 %	1.42 %	58	D	55.64 %	1.31 %	75	C	78.05 %	0.0 %	92	A	21.97 %	4.54 %
8	B	14.58 %	3.43 %	25	B	24.12 %	4.23 %	42	D	89.16 %	0.0 %	59	B	49.23 %	1.52 %	76	C	54.01 %	1.73 %	93	D	89.64 %	0.0 %
9	D	47.25 %	1.84 %	26	B	62.88 %	1.34 %	43	B	65.0 %	1.61 %	60	A	20.54 %	3.48 %	77	A	51.9 %	1.85 %	94	B	52.74 %	1.31 %
10	C	17.08 %	4.5 %	27	A	13.83 %	3.55 %	44	B	83.29 %	0.0 %	61	A	49.53 %	1.14 %	78	A	58.66 %	1.35 %	95	C	57.11 %	1.48 %
11	D	80.05 %	0.0 %	28	A	11.37 %	3.94 %	45	A	55.86 %	1.47 %	62	C	41.19 %	1.32 %	79	C	17.53 %	3.57 %	96	A	64.1 %	1.41 %
12	C	22.06 %	3.87 %	29	B	16.08 %	3.42 %	46	A	54.34 %	1.68 %	63	B	42.56 %	1.88 %	80	D	76.04 %	0.0 %	97	B	19.55 %	4.88 %
13	C	64.69 %	1.82 %	30	B	87.44 %	0.0 %	47	D	32.79 %	4.63 %	64	C	54.77 %	1.46 %	81	A	16.26 %	3.47 %	98	B	31.04 %	3.67 %
14	C	67.17 %	1.48 %	31	B	62.79 %	1.12 %	48	B	55.22 %	1.94 %	65	B	66.78 %	1.73 %	82	C	65.28 %	1.79 %	99	A	57.45 %	1.12 %
15	D	53.53 %	1.98 %	32	C	49.59 %	1.58 %	49	B	45.65 %	1.85 %	66	D	45.32 %	1.9 %	83	A	43.35 %	1.41 %	100	B	59.31 %	1.95 %
16	C	30.28 %	3.8 %	33	A	29.73 %	3.53 %	50	A	48.92 %	1.34 %	67	C	86.01 %	0.0 %	84	C	17.25 %	3.21 %				
17	B	59.12 %	1.27 %	34	A	42.59 %	1.91 %	51	B	56.72 %	1.86 %	68	D	51.01 %	1.29 %	85	D	44.7 %	1.37 %				

//Hints and Solutions//

1. The pattern followed here is:

Pen, Apron, Top, Teapot, Cheap

Here, the letter 'p' is each term is shifted one place to the right.

Thus, the letter 'p' in the next term will be at the 6th position.

So, the next term will be 'Backup'.

Hence, the correct option is (D).

2. The pattern followed here is as follows,

M – 1 = L

E – 1 = D

A – 1 = Z

T – 1 = S

Similarly,

P – 1 = O

A – 1 = Z

L – 1 = K

E – 1 = D

Thus PALE is related to OZKD.

Hence, the correct option is (C).

3. In the first two problem figures, arrows change direction. Similarly, the direction of arrows in the third problem figure should be reversed to replace the question mark.

Hence, the correct option is (D).

4. The given series follows the following pattern:

$$\frac{4131}{3} = 1377$$

$$\frac{1377}{3} = 459$$

$$\frac{459}{3} = 153$$

$$\frac{153}{3} = 51$$

Thus, 461 is the wrong entry, it should be 459.

Hence, the correct option is (A).

5. A द्वारा चली गई दूरी को निम्न आरेख द्वारा दर्शाया गया है:

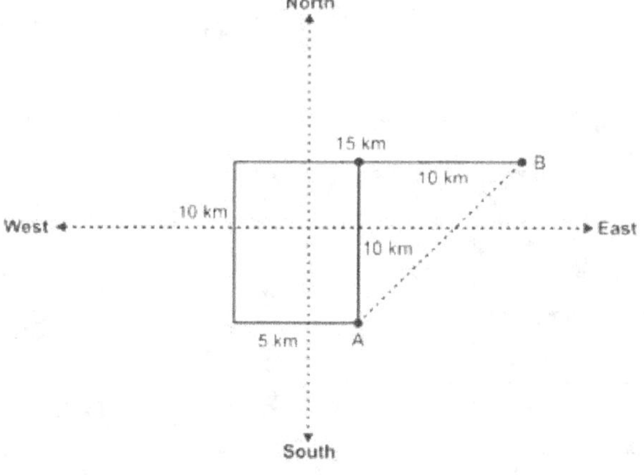

Using Pythagoras theorem:

$$10^2 + 10^2 = AB^2$$

$$AB = \sqrt{200}$$

$$= 10\sqrt{2}$$

Hence, the correct option is (A).

6. Black, Yellow and Pink are colour where is Rainbow is a combination of colours.

So, "Rainbow" is the odd word from the given alternatives.

Hence, the correct option is (C).

7.

- The sequence represents the process of conversion of data into information.
- Firstly there should be some "data".
- Then such data is entered into a computer which is called "Input".
- After that computer works on it which is called "Processing".
- After processing an "Output" is given by the computer.
- That output becomes the "Information" for the end-user.
- So, the correct sequence is 31524.

Hence, the correct option is (C).

8. The logic here is as follows,

ODD → (15 + 4 + 4) – 1 = 22

SAD → (19 + 1 + 4) – 1 = 23

Similarly,

CUP → (3 + 21 + 16) – 1 = 39

Hence, the correct option is (B).

9. The given series follows the following pattern:

42 - 32 = 10

58 - 48 = 10

106 - 96 = 10

But, 86 - 78 = 8

Hence, the correct option is (D).

10. With reference to English alphabets,

A = 1; P = 16; E = 5

(A + P + E) = (1 + 16 + 5) = 22; 22 + 1 = 23

Similarly,

B = 2; S = 19

(B + S) = (2 + 19) = 21; 21 + 1 = 22

Hence, the correct option is (C).

11. Let's check each option,

(A) Colors → can be formed from F**ROL**IC**SO**ME

(B) Crimes → can be formed from FROL**ICS**O**ME**

(C) Looser → can be formed from F**ROL**IC**SO**ME

(D) Frame → cannot be formed as there is no A in F**ROL**IC**SO**ME.

So, the word 'Frame' cannot be formed from the given word.

Hence, the correct option is (D).

12. Area marked 1 in the given figure represents "All non-European advocates who are honest swimmers."

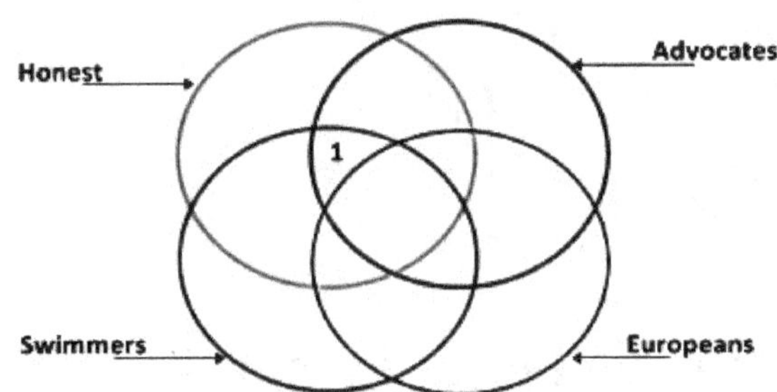

Hence, the correct option is (C).

13. The pattern for this code is as follows

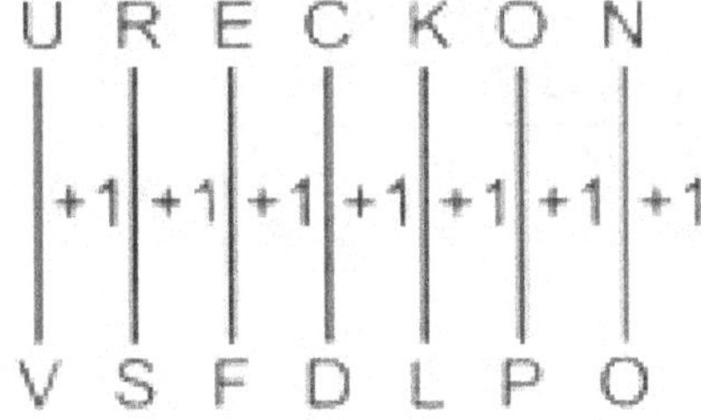

Similarly,

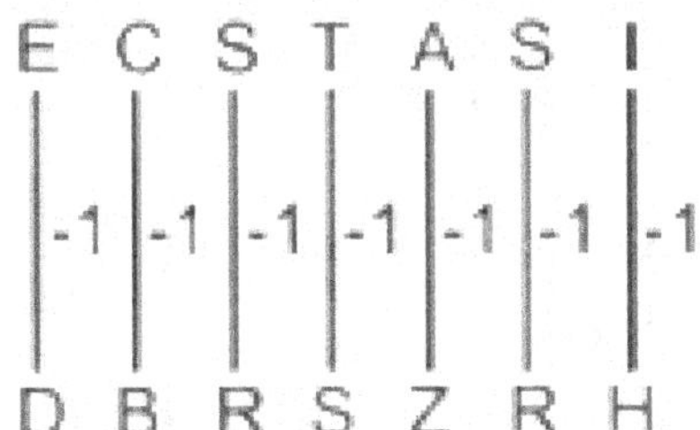

So, DBRSZRH is written as ECSTASI.

Hence, the correct option is (C).

14. Since diamond is an allotrope of carbon and the other four are metals.

Therefore, a diamond does not belong to that group.

So, diamond is different from others.

Hence, the correct option is (C).

15. The followed logic is:

(x, x + 4, x + 4)

On checking each option:

1) (17, 21, 25) → 17 + 4 = 21; 21 + 4 = 25

2) (12, 16, 20) → 12 + 4 = 16; 16 + 4 = 20

3) (19, 23, 27) → 19 + 4 = 23; 23 + 4 = 27

4) (22, 26, 32) → 22 + 4 = 26; 26 + 6 = 32

Hence, the correct option is (D).

16. Let us check for each option,

1) (69 - 63) + 6 = 36, False

2) (69 - 63) - 6 = 36, False

3) (69 - 63) × 6 = 36, True

4) (69 + 63) ÷ 6 = 36, False

So, "-, ×, =" is the correct set of signs.

Hence, the correct option is (C).

17. If a mirror is placed on the line AB then the following of the answer figures is the right image of the given figure:

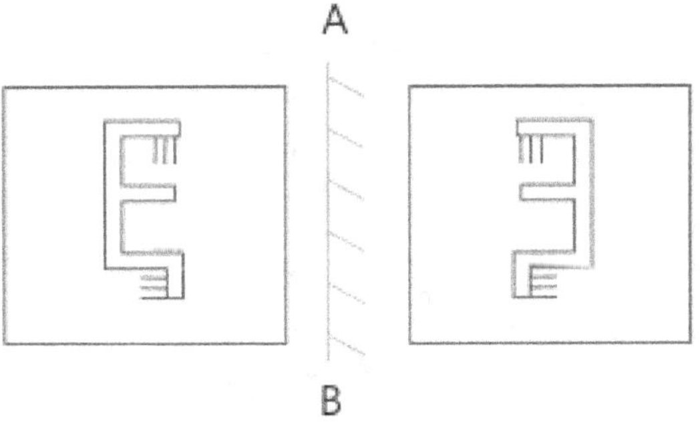

Hence, the correct option is (C).

18. The pattern/logic followed here is:

X – 3 = U; U – 3 = R; R – 3 = O; O – 3 = L

Q – 3 = N; N – 3 = K; K – 3 = H; H – 3 = E

C – 3 = Z; Z – 3 = W; W – 3 = T; T – 3 = Q

Hence, the correct option is (C).

19.

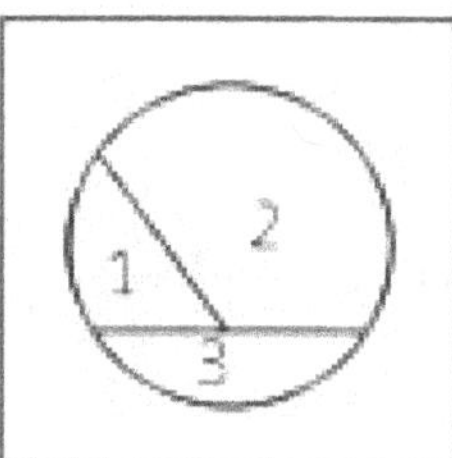

When we assemble the part given in question we will find that option (B) image will be formed.

Hence, the correct option is (B).

20. After folding a piece of paper, opening it after punching, it will look like the following figure:

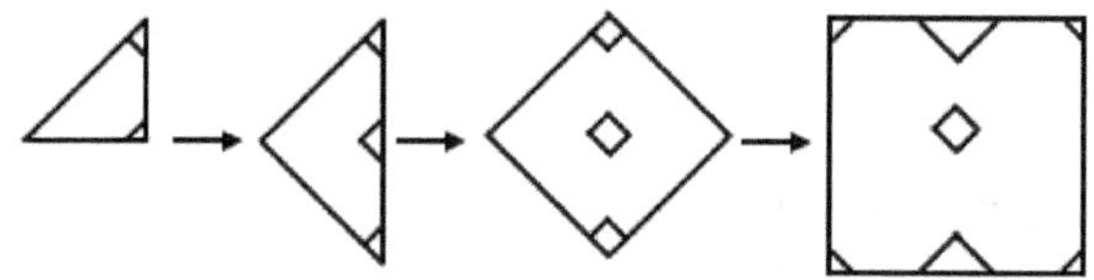

Hence, the correct option is (B).

21.

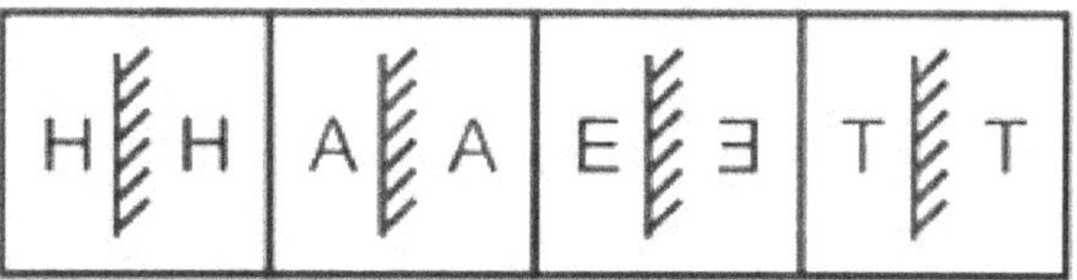

As we can H, A, and T's mirror image does not change, and is it similar to itself but E's mirror image changed.

Hence, the correct option is (C).

22. Positive, Negative, and Neutral are represented by Circle, Triangle, and Heptagon respectively. The area which represents Negative and Neutral but not positive is denoted by 12.

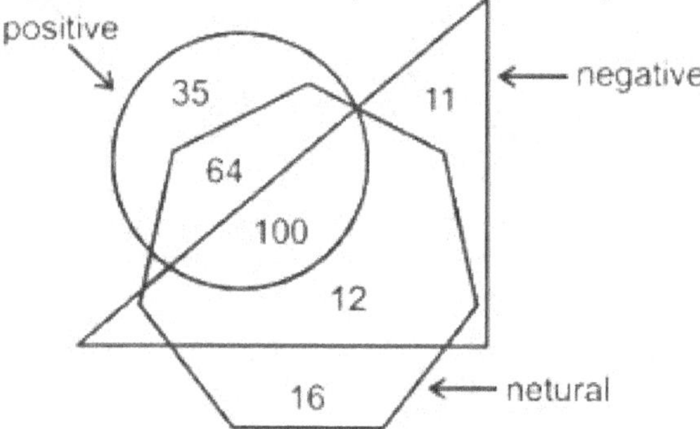

Hence, the correct option is (B).

23. From the third equation, we get

15 + 5 – 2 ÷ 6 × 3 = 3

After interchanging the symbol

⇒ 15 ÷ 5 × 2 – 6 + 3 = 3

⇒ 3 × 2 – 6 + 3 = 3

⇒ 6 – 6 + 3 = 3

⇒ 3 = 3

Hence, the correct option is (A).

24. On close observation, we find that the question figure is embedded in option (D) as shown below:

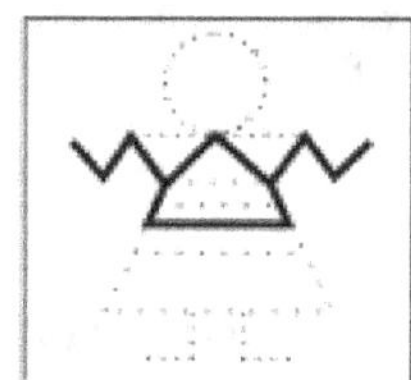

Hence, the correct option is (D).

25. After folding a piece of paper, opening it after cutting, it will look like the following figure:

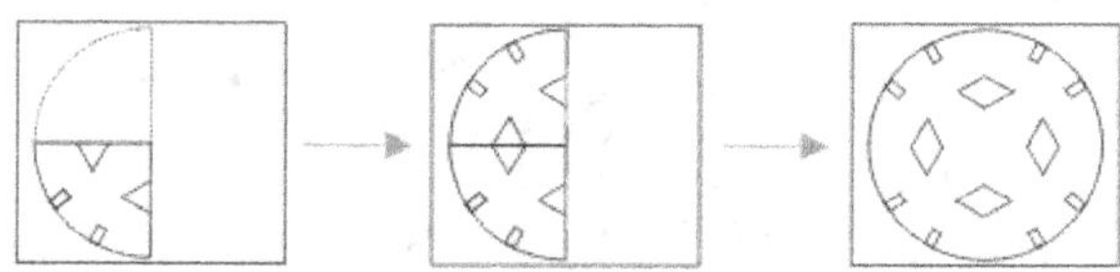

Hence, the correct option is (B).

26. Given:

$$[(1.4)^3 + (0.9)^3] \div [(1.4)^2 + (0.9)^2 - (1.4) \times (0.9)]$$

$$\Rightarrow \frac{[(1.4)^3 + (0.9)^3]}{(1.4)^2 + (0.9)^2 - (1.4) \times (0.9)}$$

We know that, $(a^3 + b^3) = (a + b)(a^2 + b^2 - ab)$

$$\Rightarrow \frac{[(1.4) + (0.9)][(1.4)^2 + (0.9)^2 - (1.4) \times (0.9)]}{[(1.4)^2 + (0.9)^2 - (1.4) \times (0.9)]}$$

$$\Rightarrow 1.4 + 0.9 = 2.3$$

Hence, the correct option is (B).

27. Given:

$$x = 33.33\% \text{ of } 81 + 77.78\% \text{ of } 171 - 62.5\% \text{ of } 144$$

$$\Rightarrow x = \frac{1}{3} \times 81 + \frac{7}{9} \times 171 - \frac{5}{8} \times 144$$

$$\Rightarrow x = 27 + 133 - 90$$

$$\Rightarrow x = 160 - 90$$

$$\Rightarrow x = 70$$

Hence, the correct option is (A).

28. First 31 multiples of 19 are $19, 38, 57 \ldots \ldots 589$

Sum of all multiples $= 19 + 38 + 57 + \cdots + 589$

$\Rightarrow 19(1 + 2 + 3 + \cdots + 31)$

$\Rightarrow 19 \times 496 = 9424$

$\therefore$ Average $= \dfrac{9424}{31} = 304$

Hence, the correct option is (A).

29. As we know,

Expenditure = price $\times$ consumption

Let original consumption of almonds $= 100$ kg

New consumption is $M\%$ of original consumption $= M$ kg

Original price of almonds $=$ Rs. 450

New price of almonds $=$ Rs. 500

Then,

$\Rightarrow 100 \times 450 = 500 \times M$

$\Rightarrow M = \dfrac{45000}{500}$

$\Rightarrow M = 90\%$

$\therefore$ There is a reduction in consumption of almonds by $100 - 90 = 10\%$

Hence, the correct option is (B).

30. Let the excluded number be x.

Average of 17 number $= 7$

$\therefore$ Sum of 17 number $= 17 \times 7 = 119$

According to the question,

$\Rightarrow 119 - x = (17 - 1) \times 4$

$\Rightarrow 119 - x = 64$

$\Rightarrow x = 55$

$\therefore$ The excluded number $= 55$

Hence, the correct option is (B).

31. Given:

Height of cylinder $= h$ cm and radius, $r = 4.5$ cm

Height of cone, $H = 18$ and Radius, $R = 7$ cm

According to question, Volume of cylinder $=$ Volume of a cone

$\Rightarrow \pi r^2 h = \dfrac{1}{3} \pi R^2 H$

$\Rightarrow (4.5)^2 h = \dfrac{1}{3} \times (15)^2 \times 18$

$\Rightarrow 20.25 \times h \times 3 = 225 \times 18$

$\Rightarrow h = 225 \times \dfrac{18}{20.25 \times 3}$

$\Rightarrow h = \dfrac{200}{3}$

Hence, the correct option is (B).

32. Amount of work A can do in 1 day $= \dfrac{1}{6}$

Amount of work B can do in 1 day $= \dfrac{1}{8}$

Amount of work $A + B$ can do in 1 day $= \dfrac{1}{6} + \dfrac{1}{8} = \dfrac{7}{24}$

Amount of work $A + B + C$ can do $= \dfrac{1}{3}$

Amount of work C can do in 1 day $\dfrac{1}{3} - \dfrac{7}{24} = \dfrac{1}{24}$

work A can do in 1 day: work B can do in 1 day:

work C can do in 1 day $= \dfrac{1}{6} : \dfrac{1}{8} : \dfrac{1}{24} = 4 : 3 : 1$

Amount to be paid to $C = 3200 \times \left(\dfrac{1}{8}\right) = 400$

Hence, the correct option is (C).

33. Let's assume a number of units produced by $B = N$

Therefore the number of units produced by $A = 3N$

So, the number of units produced by $C = \dfrac{(N + 3N)}{2} = 2N$

Total number of units produced by all the three machines in one-hour

$= (N + 3N + 2N)$ units $= 6N$ units

Thus; $6N = \dfrac{360}{15}$

$\Rightarrow N = 4$

Therefore time taken by A to manufacture 360 units $= \dfrac{360}{12}$ hours

$= 30$ hours

Hence, the correct option is (A).

34. Given:

Cost price of an almirah $=$ Rs. 13600

Transportation cost $=$ Rs. 400

Total cost price $=$ Rs. $(13600 + 400) =$ Rs. 14000

Selling price $=$ Rs. 16800

Now, $SP > CP$

Gain $= SP - CP = (16800 - 14000) =$ Rs. 2800

Gain $\% = \left(\dfrac{\text{Gain}}{CP} \times 100\right)\%$

$= \left(\dfrac{2800}{14000} \times 100\right)\%$

$= \dfrac{2800}{140}\%$

$= 20\%$

Hence, the correct option is (A).

35. Given:

The diameter of bigger ball $= 8$ cm

Therefore, the Radius of the bigger ball $= 4$ cm

$\therefore$ Volume $= \dfrac{4}{3}\pi r^3$

$= \dfrac{4}{3}\pi \times 4 \times 4 \times 4 = \dfrac{265\pi}{3}\ cm^3$

Radius of small ball $= 1$ cm

$\therefore$ Volume $= \dfrac{4}{3}\pi r^3$

$= \dfrac{4}{3}\pi \times 1 \times 1 \times 1 = \dfrac{4\pi}{3}$ cm ^{3}

Number of balls $= \dfrac{\frac{256x}{3}}{\frac{4\pi}{3}}$

$= \dfrac{256\pi}{3} \times \dfrac{3}{4\pi}$

$= 64$

Hence, the correct option is (D).

36. Given:

Cost price $=$ Rs. 16

Selling Price $=$ Rs. 18

Profit $= SP - CP = 18 - 16 =$ Rs. 2

$\therefore$ Profit $\% = \dfrac{Profit}{CP} \times 100 = \dfrac{2}{16} \times 100 = 12.5\%$

Hence, the correct option is (B).

37. Let the money invested by A, B and C be Rs. x, Rs. $2x$ and Rs. $3x$ respectively.

Then, $A : B : C = (x \times 12) : (2x \times 6) : (3x \times 4)$

$= 12x : 12x : 12x$

$= 1 : 1 : 1$

$\therefore$ C's share $=$ Rs. $\left(27000 \times \dfrac{1}{3}\right)$

$=$ Rs. 9000

Hence, the correct option is (B).

38. Let, cost price $=$ Rs. x

After first discount of 20%,

Price $= x - x \times \dfrac{20}{100}$

$\Rightarrow x - \dfrac{20x}{100} =$ Rs. $0.8x$

After second discount of 25%,

Price $= 0.8x - 0.8x \times \dfrac{25}{100}$

$=$ Rs. $0.6x$

$\therefore$ Net discount $= \dfrac{x - 0.6x}{x} \times 100\%$

$= 40\%$

Hence, the correct option is (D).

39. As we know, Simple interest $= \dfrac{Principal \times Rate \times Time}{100}$

He borrowed Rs. 120000 from Veer at 5% per annum for 6 months,

Simple interest paid $= \dfrac{120000 \times 5 \times 6}{100 \times 12} =$ Rs. 3000

He borrowed Rs. 80000 from Ayush at 4% per annum for 9 months,

Simple interest paid $= \dfrac{80000 \times 4 \times 9}{100 \times 12} =$ Rs. 2400

$\therefore$ Total interest paid $= 3000 + 2400 =$ Rs. 5400

Hence, the correct option is (B).

40. Given,

$\dfrac{\sin\theta - \cos\theta + 1}{\sin\theta + \cos\theta - 1}$

By rationalizing the denominator,

$= \dfrac{(\sin\theta - \cos\theta + 1)(\sin\theta + \cos\theta + 1)}{(\sin\theta + \cos\theta - 1)(\sin\theta + \cos\theta + 1)}$

$= \dfrac{(1 + \sin\theta)^2 - \cos^2\theta}{(\sin\theta + \cos\theta)^2 - 1^2}$

$= \dfrac{1 + \sin^2\theta - 2\sin\theta - \cos^2\theta}{1 + 2\sin\theta\cos\theta - 1}$

We know that $(1 - \cos^2\theta = \sin^2\theta)$

$= \dfrac{2\sin^2\theta + 2\sin\theta}{2\sin\theta \cdot \cos\theta} = \dfrac{1 + \sin\theta}{\cos\theta}$

Hence, the correct option is (A).

41. Given, $P =$ Rs. $9000; R = 8\%; n = 2$ years

We know that, $CI = A - P$

$$\Rightarrow CI = P\left(1 + \frac{R}{100}\right)^n - P$$

$$= 9000\left(1 + \frac{8}{100}\right)^2 - 9000$$

$$= 9000\left(\frac{27}{25}\right)^2 - 9000$$

$$= 9000\left(\frac{729}{625} - 1\right)$$

$$= 9000 \times 104 = \text{Rs. } 1497.6$$

Hence, the correct option is (B).

42. Time taken to cross the platform $=$

$$\frac{\text{(length of train + length of platform)}}{\text{speed of train}}$$

$\therefore$ Speed of train $= \dfrac{(210+240)}{20} = 22$ m/sec

$\Rightarrow 22.5 \times \dfrac{18}{5} = 81$ km/hr

Hence, the correct option is (D).

43. Given:

Pipe P can fill the tank $= 200$ hours

Pipe P's one-hour work $= \dfrac{1}{200}$

Pipe Q can fill the tank $= 300$ hours

Pipe Q's one-hour work $= \dfrac{1}{300}$

When both the pipes are opened together,

$$P + Q = \left(\frac{1}{200} + \frac{1}{300}\right)$$

$$= \frac{(3+2)}{600}$$

$$= \frac{5}{600}$$

$$= \frac{1}{120}$$

Therefore, $(P + Q)$ working together can complete the whole work in 120 hours.

Hence, the correct option is (B).

44. We know that, Total area of walls $= 2(l \times h) + 2(b \times h)$

$$= 2(6 \times 4) + 2(5 \times 4) = 88$$

Area of paper $= b \times l$

$\Rightarrow 88 = 0.5 \times$ length of paper

$\therefore$ Length of paper $= 176$ m

Hence, the correct option is (B).

45. Given:

Total students $= 640$

The ratio of boys to girls $= 5:3$

Number of boys $= \left[\dfrac{5}{8}\right]640 = 400$

Number of girls $= 640 - 400 = 240$

Let x boys admitted in the school.

So, number of boys $= 400 + x$

Ratio of boys to that of the girls $= 14:9$

According to the question,

$$\frac{(400+x)}{(240+30)} = \frac{14}{9}$$

$$\Rightarrow 400 + x = \left[\frac{14}{9}\right] \times 270$$

$$\Rightarrow x = 420 - 400$$

$$\Rightarrow x = 20$$

$\therefore 20$ students admitted in the school.

Hence, the correct option is (A).

46. Given:

$\angle CBF = 130°$

As known,

$\angle CBA + \angle CBF = 180°$

$\Rightarrow \angle CBA = 180° - 130°$

$\Rightarrow \angle CBA = 50°$

By exterior angle theorem,

$\angle EDC = \angle CBA$

$\therefore \angle EDC = x = \angle CBA = 50°$

Hence, the correct option is (A).

47. Let the distance between point and building be y.

Building $AB = 10$ m

And the height of the helicopter from the top of the building be r m.

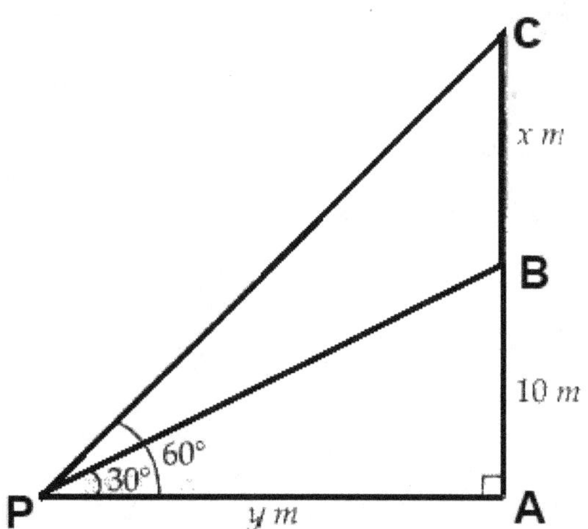

height of the helicopter from ground $= (10 + x)$ m

$\Rightarrow \dfrac{10}{y} = \dfrac{1}{\sqrt{3}}$

$\Rightarrow y = 10\sqrt{3}$ ...(i)

In $\triangle ACP$ $\dfrac{AC}{PA} = \tan 60°$

$\Rightarrow \dfrac{10+x}{y} = \sqrt{3}$

$\Rightarrow 10 + x = y\sqrt{3}$ ...(ii)

From (i) and (ii)

$10 + x = 10\sqrt{3} \times \sqrt{3}$

$\Rightarrow x = 30$

Thus, height of the helicopter $= 10 + 20 = 30$ m

Hence, the correct option is (D).

48. Difference in sales in $2011 = 25$ lacs -20 lacs $= 5$ lacs

Difference in sales in $2012 = 35$ lacs -30 lacs $= 5$ lacs

Difference in sales in $2013 = 42$ lacs -41 lacs $= 1$ lacs

Difference in sales in $2014 = 52.5$ lacs -50 lacs $= 2.5$ lacs

Difference in sales for 2011 and 2012 are same.

Hence, the correct option is (B).

49. The sum of sale of company Y for 5 years $= 20 + 30 + 41 + 50 + 48 = 189$ lacs

Average sale $= \dfrac{189}{5} = 37.8$ lacs

Hence, the correct option is (B).

50. From the table,

Sales of company X in $2011 = 25$ lacs

Sales of company X in $2013 = 42$ lacs

Percentage change $= \dfrac{42-25}{25} \times 100 = 68\%$

Hence, the correct option is (A).

51. The error lies in part (B) of the sentence. Here, the sentence refers to Nancy's mother accompanying her on her first day at college. Since we are referring to the act of accompanying, we cannot use the preposition 'with' because we are not referring to a place or position. The correct usage is 'accompanied by' which is why part (B) is incorrect.

Thus, the correct sentence is, 'Nancy was accompanied by her mom on her first day at college'.

Hence, the correct option is (B).

52. The error lies in part (C) of the sentence. The sentence speaks about Jay's illusion and the verb 'revolved' is used. The correct preposition to be used with 'revolved' (which is a circular motion) is 'around'. Here, the preposition used is 'in' which is used to denote 'inside' or 'within' and this is incorrect.

Thus, the correct sentence is, 'Jay was under the illusion that the world revolved around him'.

Hence, the correct option is (C).

53. There is no way we can use Past/Present continuous tense here. So options (C) and (D) are canceled. Since it says 'today' we must go for "has won a".

Hence, the correct option is (B).

54. This is a past event. The subject moved to the UK in the past. We use 'ago' for past events. Thus forth and anything 'forth' refers to the future.

Hence, the correct option is (A).

55. The condense is the opposite word of the enlarge.

Enlarge means to make something bigger; to become bigger.

Condense means reduce; to put something into fewer words.

Glorify means to make glorious by bestowing honor, praise, or admiration.

Amplify means to make larger or greater (as in amount or intensity).

Augment means make (something) greater by adding to it; increase.

Hence, the correct option is (A).

56. The agitated is the opposite word of the tranquil.

Tranquil (Adjective) means free from disturbance; calm.

Agitated means feeling or appearing troubled or nervous or disturbed.

Unruffled means not disordered or disarranged.

Perpetual means never ending or changing.

Temporal means relating to worldly as opposed to spiritual affairs; secular.

Hence, the correct option is (D).

57. To hear something through the grapevine is to learn of something informally and unofficially by means of gossip or rumor. The usual implication is that the information was passed person to person by word of mouth, perhaps in a confidential manner among friends or colleagues.

Hence, the correct option is (A).

58. The sentence is in the passive voice. The verb here expresses the action on the object. To Change it into active, we need to use the following formation.

Taking into consideration the fact that the sentence is in the past continuous tense.

Passive: Object+was/were+being+V3+Subject

Active voice: Subject+was/were+V1-ing+Object

Here "flowers" is the object "pluck" is the verb and 'The students" is the subject.

Active voice of given sentence: The students were plucking flowers.

Hence, the correct option is (D).

59. The sentence is in the passive voice. The verb here expresses the action on the object. To Change it into active, we need to use the following formation.

taking into consideration the fact that the sentence is in the past perfect tense.

Passive: Object+had+been+V3+Subject

Active: Subject+had+V3+Object

Here "the work" is the object "complete" is the verb and "They" is the subject.

Active voice of given sentence: They had already completed the work.

Hence, the correct option is (B).

60. It's raining cats and dogs is an idiom that means it's raining extremely heavily. The origin of the phrase raining cats and dogs is steeped in mystery. There are several theories, one being that the phrase raining cats and dogs references the mythologies of the Norse god Odin and English witches.

Hence, the correct option is (A).

61. 'As far as' also means 'with reference to' and the context to sentence demands this as it is in the reference of the investors.

Correct sentence: "As far as an investor concerned, the high relating to indemnities is of no importance".

Hence, the correct option is (A).

62. The word 'tormented' means 'disturbed' and 'sanguine' means 'hopeful'. Thus they cannot be fit in the blank. Opinions cannot be demented as the word means 'made mad'. The word

'expressed' which means 'conveyed' fits here correctly meaning that there have been opinions about the pace of development in the Himalayan region.

Hence, the correct option is (C).

63. The words at the same time give us the hint that this sentence should have the same tone as that of the previous one thus a negative meaning should be conveyed. The word 'scurrilous' means 'abusive' and does not convey any meaning. The word 'appreciated' means 'accepted and encouraged' and conveys a proper meaning that the fragility of the region and the difficulties existing in the region which are hindrances to any sort of development have not been considered. 'Mocked' means 'ridiculed' and 'underrated' means 'undervalued.'

Hence, the correct option is (B).

64. The sentence talks about recommending something thus the word 'reshaping' which means 'reframing' is the correct word. It means that policies should be framed. The other words do not convey any meaning here. 'vilifying' means 'speak or write about in an abusively disparaging manner.

Hence, the correct option is (C).

65. The word 'travesty' means a false, absurd, or distorted representation of something and does not fit here. 'Emphasis' means 'focus' and conveys the proper meaning that importance has been given to the development of norms.

Hence, the correct option is (B).

66. The sentence talks about social capital which means the network of relationships among people of a society. Thus 'harnessing' which means 'utilizing' frames a proper meaning here that norms should be such that can bring about good governance and use social capital at the basic level. The other words do not convey any meaning here.

Hence, the correct option is (D).

67. Here, the sentence needs a verb that goes with 'a shower'. Take is the only verb that goes with it.

Correct sentence: "I usually take a shower after I play tennis, but today I couldn't".

Hence, the correct option is (C).

68. The meaning of the word "torrid" is "very hot and dry" so the antonym must be "frigid" which means "very cold in temperature".

Slack: not taut or held tightly in position; loose

Rushed: done or completed too hurriedly; hasty

Flashy: ostentatiously attractive or impressive.

Hence, the correct option is (D).

69. The correct word here is "conceal" which means "not allow to be seen; hide" and therefore they are synonyms.

Receive: be given, presented with, or paid

Connive: secretly allow (something immoral, illegal, or harmful) to occur

Reveal: make (previously unknown or secret information) known to others

Hence, the correct option is (C).

70. The meaning of the word "dawdle" is "move slowly and idly in a particular direction" and therefore the synonym is "amble" which means "walk or move at a slow, relaxed pace'.

Rumble: make a continuous deep, resonant sound

Fumble: do or handle something clumsily

Tumble: fall suddenly, clumsily, or headlong

Hence, the correct option is (B).

71. "In the 1960's" shows that the sentence is in the past tense. So we use a past verb "were demonstrations against" in place of "are demonstrations against".

Correct sentence: "There were demonstrations against the government by Japanese university students in the 1960's".

Hence, the correct option is (B).

72. Whenever the main verb is in simple present/future tense, the tense of the verb in indirect speech remains as it is.

So, 'Prakash will say' remains unchanged.

The next simple future tense verb 'will know', will also remain unchanged.

Thus, the indirect sentence is: Prakash will say that he will always know where to find him.

Hence, the correct option is (A).

73. The original sentence is in 'direct speech' and this needs to be converted to 'indirect speech'.

In order to convert from direct speech to indirect speech, the inverted commas need to be removed.

The conjunction 'that' is added in order to join the 2 clauses in the sentence.

There will be a change in the tense of the reported speech as this is cannot be considered a habitual action.

Therefore, The correct indirect speech will be: "He said that he bathed regularly".

Hence, the correct option is (B).

74. Quell: put an end to (a rebellion or other disorder), typically by the use of force.

Repress: subdue (someone or something) by force.

Conceal: not allow to be seen; hide.

Exhale meaning: to breathe out.

And other words are the antonyms of Exhale.

Hence, the correct option is (B).

75. The irrational is a similar word to the superstitious.

Superstitious means having or showing a belief in superstitions, not logical.

Pious means strongly believing in religion.

Traditional means existing in or as part of a tradition; long-established.

Irrational means not logical or reasonable.

Sacred means connected with God or dedicated to a religious purpose and so deserving veneration.

Hence, the correct option is (C).

76. Vishvamitra honour of Madhya Pradesh has given for excellent performance in sports training.

- Vishwamitra honour was started in the year 1996.
- As of 2018, a total of 72 trainers have been awarded the Vishwamitra Award.
- Kabir Samman award was established by the Government of Madhya Pradesh in 1986.
- It is conferred annually for distinguished works in Literature (Poetry).

Hence, the correct option is (C).

77. "Ever Onward" is the motto of the Asian Games. The Asian Games, also known as Asiad, is a continental multi-sport event held every four years among athletes from all over Asia.

Hence, the correct option is (A).

78. The Band-Aid was invented in 1920 by Earle Dickson for his wife Josephine, who frequently cut and burned herself while cooking. He was an employee of American pharmaceutical and medical devices giant Johnson & Johnson Company.

Hence, the correct option is (A).

79. Hyderabad, the former princely state of south-central India that was centered on the city of Hyderabad. It was founded by Nizam-ul-Mulk, who was intermittently viceroy of the Deccan under the Mughal emperors from 1713 to 1721.

Hence, the correct option is (C).

80.

- Gypsum is an ore of Calcium (Ca). The chemical formula of Gypsum is $CaSO_4. 2H_2O$.
- Gypsum is mainly used as a fertilizer, as the main constituent in plaster, chalk, etc.

Hence, the correct option is (D).

81. The atomic number of the lads is the highest of all the given elements. Lead is extracted mainly from its ore galling (Pbs). Lead is the most stable element.

Element	Atomic number	Symbol
Lead	82	Pb
Tin	50	Sn
Germanium	32	Ge
Silicon	14	Si

Hence, the correct option is (A).

82. According to the question,

$m_1 = 6$ Kg, $m_2 = 9$ Kg and $a_1 = 3$m/s^2, $a_2 = 2$ m/s^2

We know that, $F = ma$,

Where F= Force, m = Mass, and a = acceleration

$F_1 = 6$kg $\times$ 3m/s^2 = 18N

$F_2 = 9$kg $\times$ 2m/s^2 = 18N

Thus $F_1 = F_2$, So both cases required equal Forces.

Hence, the correct option is (C).

83.

- Mathematically, momentum is defined as the product of mass and velocity.

- Momentum = Mass × Velocity

- Since the SI unit of mass is kilograms and that of velocity is meters per second, therefore, the SI unit of momentum is kilogram meters per second (kg-m/s).

Hence, the correct option is (A).

84. The Battle of Tughlaqabad (also known as the Battle of Delhi) was a notable battle fought on 7 October 1556 between Hem Chandra Vikramaditya, also known as Hemu, and the forces of the Mughal emperor Akbar led by Tardi Beg Khan at Tughlaqabad near Delhi.

Hence, the correct option is (C).

85. Computer programs or instructions are in the software of the system; These instructions collectively raise an algorithm that meets the software's functions for which the software is created. The program is written in programming languages such as Java, C +, C ++, Python, etc.

Hence, the correct option is (D).

86. The Indian Army has developed and launched an in-house messaging application called the 'Secure Application for the Internet (SAI)'.

This messaging application supports end-to-end secure voice, text, and video calling services for the android platform over the Internet.

SAI was first developed by Colonel Sai Shankar, the commanding officer of a signals unit in Rajasthan, and then upgraded to military-grade standards.

India's first Chief of Defence Staff: General Bipin Rawat.

Hence, the correct option is (D).

87. Ahmedabad city of Gujarat is known as Manchester or Boston of India. Ahmedabad is called Manchester as it derives its name from the famous Manchester city of Great Britain known for cotton textile industries. Ahmedabad has the largest textile center in India.

City	Sobriquet
Ahmedabad	Manchester or Boston of India.
Allahabad	Sangam city
Agra	City of Taj
Asansol	Land of Black Diamond

Hence, the correct option is (A).

88. Varanasi also called Banaras or Kashi. It is located on the left bank of the Ganges River and is one of the seven sacred cities of Hinduism.

River	Cities Located Nearby
Ganga	Haridwar, Banaras, Patna, Allahabad, Kolkata, etc
Yamuna	Delhi, Allahabad, Agra, Mathura, etc
Narmada	Jabalpur

Hence, the correct option is (A).

89.

- Indian Climate is described as the Monsoon type of climate due to seasonal reversal of winds.

- This happens due to the differential heating of land and water bodies and pressure situations.

- The monsoon type of climate is based on distinct season.

- India is home to an extraordinary variety of climatic regions, ranging from tropical in the south to temperate and alpine in the Himalayan north however, it is broadly believed to be monsoon type climate.

Hence, the correct option is (B).

90. A computer network is a group of computers connected together to share resources. Computers and devices that allocate resources to a network are called servers. Computer network supports a large number of applications and services such as access to the World Wide Web and digital video. The most famous computer network is the internet.

Hence, the correct option is (A).

91.

- Kalvakuntala Chandrasekhar Rao is the Chief Minister of Telangana belongs to Telangana Rashtra Samithi.

- He is the second Chief Minister of the newly formed state of Telangana in the year 2014 and again becoming Chief Minister since December 2018.

- The Party election symbol is CAR.

Hence, the correct option is (A).

92.

- The Israeli Parliament is also known as Knesset.

- Yuli-Yoel Edelstein is the Speaker of Knesset since 2013.

- Elections in Israel are based on nationwide proportional representation.

- Knesset is located in Givat Ram, Jerusalem.

Hence, the correct option is (A).

93.

- 1888 session of Indian National Congress was held in Allahabad

- The session was chaired by George.

- He was the first non-Indian president.

Hence, the correct option is (D).

94. Bhadra Wildlife Sanctuary is a protected area and a tiger reserve as part of Project Tiger, located 38 km northwest of Chikkamagaluru town in Karnataka state, India.
Hence, the correct option is (B).

95. The oldest stock exchange in Asia, the Bombay Stock Exchange(BSE), was established in 1875. It is in the name of Dalal street. BSE was corporatized and renamed BSE Limited in 2005. There are 23 stock exchanges in India. Among them, two are the national stock exchange, namely the Bombay Stock Exchange (BSE) and National Stock Exchange (NSE). The rest 21 are Regional stock exchange (RSE).

Hence, the correct option is (C).

96.

- The Independence Day of Bangladesh is celebrated on 26 March 1971.
- It commemorates the country's declaration of independence from Pakistan in the late hours of 25 March 1971.

Hence, the correct option is (A).

97. The Sangai festival is an annual cultural festival organized by the Manipur Tourism Department every year from November 21 to 30.

The festival as named the Sangai Festival to stage the uniqueness of the shy and gentle brow-antlered deer popularly known as the Sangai Deer, which is the state animal of Manipur.

Hence, the correct option is (B).

98. Max Planck was a German theoretical physicist who discovered the quantum of action, now known as Planck's constant, h, in 1900. This work laid the foundation for quantum theory, which won him the Nobel Prize for Physics in 1918.

Hence, the correct option is (B).

99. Prime Minister Narendra Modi launched the country's first seaplane service between the Statue of Unity near Kevadiya in Gujarat's Narmada district and Sabarmati Riverfront in Ahmedabad.

The 19-seater seaplane will be managed by private airline SpiceJet.

The chief minister of Gujrat: Vijay Rupani, Governor: Acharya Devvrat.

Hence, the correct option is (A).

100. Prime Minister Narendra Modi is scheduled to flag off the country's first-ever fully-automated driverless train service which will be on the Magenta Line of Delhi Metro on December 28.

The 37-km Magenta Line connects Janakpuri West and Botanical Garden metro stations.

He will also be launching the fully operational National Common Mobility Card for travel on the 23-km Airport Express Line.

Hence, the correct option is (B).

Q.1 Pick out the word opposite in meaning to the given word.
SENTIENT

A. Abnormal

B. Irregular

C. Unconscious

D. Irrelevant

Q.2 Pick out the word opposite in meaning to the given word.
SEQUESTER

A. Discover

B. Correlate

C. Integrate

D. Convict of

Q.3 Pick out the word opposite in meaning to the given word.
SERE

A. Humid   **B.** Livid   **C.** Parched   **D.** Drained

Q.4 In the following question, any part of the sentence may have errors. Find out which part of the sentence has an error and select the appropriate option. If a sentence is free from error, select 'No Error'.

I have watched many movies (1)/ of Rajnikanth's who Is called the (2)/ Amitabh Bachchan of Tollywood. (3)/ No error

A. 1   **B.** 2   **C.** 3   **D.** No error

Q.5 In the following question, any part of the sentence may have errors. Find out which part of the sentence has an error and select the appropriate option. If a sentence is free from error, select 'No Error'.

There are some people who believe (1)/ asking for government assistance is (2)/ akin with admitting one is a failure. (3)/ No error

A. 1   **B.** 2   **C.** 3   **D.** No error

Q.6 In the following question, out of the four alternatives, select the word similar in meaning to the given word.

Licentious

A. Immoral

B. Intellectual

C. Moral

D. Without license

Q.7 In the following question, out of the four alternatives, select the word similar in meaning to the given word.

Commemorate

A. Boast

B. Harmonize

C. Manipulate

D. Remember

Q.8 In the following question, out of the four alternatives, select the word similar in meaning to the given word.

Squander

A. Expensive

B. Waste

C. Litter

D. Economical

Q.9 In the following question, out of the four alternatives, select the alternative which best expresses the meaning of the Idiom/Phrase.

In black and white

A. Useless

B. In writing

C. In short

D. In full swing

Q.10 In the following question, out of the four alternatives, select the alternative which best expresses the meaning of the Idiom/Phrase.

Stick one's neck out

A. Interfere

B. Look outside

C. Move

D. Invite trouble

Ques (11-15):Direction: Read the passage carefully and select the best answer to each question out of the four alternatives.

The Great Leap Forward of the People's Republic of China (PRC) was an economic and social plan used from 1958 to 1960 which aimed to use China's vast population to rapidly transform mainland China from a primarily agrarian economy dominated by peasant farmers into a modern, industrialized communist society.

Mao Zedong based this program on the Theory of Productive Forces, a widely-used concept in communism and Marxism placing primary emphasis on achieving abundance in a nominally socialist economy before real communism, or even real socialism can have a hope of being achieved. It was allegedly necessitated by the fact that, despite the theoretical predictions of Marxism, China's revolution took place, not in modern, industrialized society, but a poor, agrarian one. It was epitomized by the absurdity of rural farmers having backyard furnaces to increase national steel production (yet what was produced was nearly unusable pig iron).

The concept has been used in all examples of state-supervised socialism to date. Joseph Stalin is one proponent of this view. The most influential philosophical defense of this idea has been promulgated by Gerald Cohen in his book Karl Marx's Theory of History: A Defence. According to this view, technical change can beget social change; in other words, changes in the means (and intensity) of production cause changes in the relations of production, i.e., in people's ideology and culture, their interactions with one another, and their social relationship to the wider world.

In this view, actual socialism or communism, based on the "redistribution of wealth" to the most oppressed sectors of society, cannot come to pass until that society's wealth is built up enough to satisfy whole populations. Using this theory as a basis for their practical programs meant that communist theoreticians and leaders, while paying lip service to the primacy of ideological change in individuals to sustain a communist society, actually put productive forces first, and ideological change second.

The Theory of Productive Forces was the basis of Stalin's Five Year Plans, Mao Zedong's Great Leap Forward, and most other examples of attempts to build and refine communism throughout the world in the 20th Century.

Q.11 According to the passage, in increasing which of the following did the rural farmers in China succeed?

A. Iron ore production **B.** Cotton
C. Steel production **D.** None of these

Q.12 Which of the following best describe 'The Great Leap Forward of the People's Republic of China'?

A. Economic and environmental
B. Social and economic
C. Social and ecological
D. Economic and theoretical

Q.13 On the basis of which of the following theories was communism honed across the globe?

A. Theory of Production Forces
B. Theory of Product Forces
C. Theory of Productive Forces
D. Theory of Produce Forces

Q.14 What does the word 'Beget' refers to in the passage?

A. Be the cause of **B.** Be the result of
C. Be the yield of **D.** Be the gape of

Q.15 What does the word 'Primacy' refer to in the passage?

A. Sub-ordinate **B.** Pre-eminence
C. Peripheral **D.** Ancillary

Q.16 In the following question, a sentence has been given in Direct/Indirect Speech. Out of the four alternatives suggested, select the one which best expresses the same sentence in Indirect/Direct Speech.

I told her, "It was raining last night when you left".

A. I told her that it had been raining the previous night when she had left.
B. I told her that it has been raining last night when she had left.
C. I told her that it had been raining the night before when she left.
D. I told her that it have been raining last night when she had left.

Q.17 In the following question, a sentence has been given in Direct/Indirect Speech. Out of the four alternatives suggested, select the one which best expresses the same sentence in Indirect/Direct Speech.

The beggar said, "Poverty is a great curse".

A. The beggar said poverty has a great curse.
B. The beggar said that poverty is a great curse.
C. The beggar said that poverty were a great curse.
D. The beggar said that poverty had been a great curse.

Q.18 A sentence is given below in jumbled order. Arrange the sentence in the right order to form a meaningful and coherent sentence.

Let us all be
P) until we realize
Q) we are all the same
R) unique together

A. QPR **B.** PRQ **C.** PQR **D.** RPQ

Q.19 A sentence is given below in jumbled order. Arrange the sentence in the right order to form a meaningful and coherent sentence.

The author has chosen
P) on this story
Q) responses
R) not to show

A. PQR **B.** QPR **C.** RQP **D.** PRQ

Q.20 In the following question, a sentence has been given in Active/Passive Voice. Out of the four alternatives suggested, select the one which best expresses the same sentence in Passive/Active Voice.

The washerman will return the clothes in the evening.

A. The clothes will have to be returned by the washerman in the evening.
B. The clothes will be returned by the washerman in the evening.
C. The clothes will return by the washerman in the evening.
D. In the evening the clothes will have been returned by the washerman.

Q.21 In the following question, a sentence has been given in Active/Passive Voice. Out of the four alternatives suggested, select the one which best expresses the same sentence in Passive/Active Voice.

Do the children play football?

A. Does football played by children?
B. Is football played by the children?
C. Football is played by the children?
D. The children do play football?

Q.22 In the following question, a sentence has been given in Active/Passive Voice. Out of the four alternatives suggested, select the one which best expresses the same sentence in Passive/Active Voice.

They have made a film based on this novel.

A. A film was based on this novel and made.
B. A film have been made based on this novel.
C. A film based on this novel has been made.
D. A film has been based and made on this novel.

Q.23 In the following question, the sentence is given with blank to be filled in with an appropriate word. Select the correct alternative out of the four and indicate it by selecting the appropriate option.

The servant _______ the picture on the wall.

A. Hang **B.** Hung **C.** Hanged **D.** Hunged

Q.24 In the following question, the sentence is given with blank to be filled in with an appropriate word. Select the correct alternative out of the four and indicate it by selecting the appropriate option.

She is one of the best _______ I know.

A. Teachers **B.** Student **C.** Doctor **D.** Lawyer

Q.25 Choose an option, which can be substituted for a given word/sentence/phrase out of given options.

A person who is skilled in horsemanship

A. Cavalier   B. Equestrian
C. Jockey   D. Cavalryman

// Smart Answer Sheet //

Correct		Percentage of students who answered correctly.	Skipped		Percentage of students who skipped.

Q.	Ans.	Correct / Skipped	Q.	Ans.	Correct / Skipped	Q.	Ans.	Correct / Skipped	Q.	Ans.	Correct / Skipped	Q.	Ans.	Correct / Skipped	Q.	Ans.	Correct / Skipped
1	C	33.03 % / 1.81 %	6	A	18.7 % / 10.11 %	11	C	29.56 % / 8.0 %	16	A	22.62 % / 11.01 %	21	B	24.43 % / 16.44 %			
2	C	29.86 % / 9.81 %	7	D	18.55 % / 13.73 %	12	B	42.08 % / 7.24 %	17	B	38.16 % / 2.87 %	22	C	25.49 % / 14.78 %			
3	A	25.94 % / 4.98 %	8	B	25.79 % / 11.01 %	13	C	30.17 % / 8.59 %	18	D	20.06 % / 11.46 %	23	B	23.68 % / 12.67 %			
4	B	32.28 % / 12.52 %	9	B	30.62 % / 14.18 %	14	A	29.41 % / 6.03 %	19	C	31.37 % / 9.2 %	24	A	34.99 % / 1.21 %			
5	C	24.43 % / 14.48 %	10	D	17.5 % / 10.55 %	15	B	25.49 % / 8.75 %	20	B	40.72 % / 5.43 %	25	B	23.08 % / 4.22 %			

//Hints and Solutions//

1. Sentient means conscious or alert. The opposite of conscious is unconscious.

Hence, the correct option is (C).

2. To sequester means; to separate, segregate, or isolate. The opposite of that is to integrate which means to blend, coordinate, or form.

Hence, the correct option is (C).

3. Sere means arid, droughty, dry, thirsty, waterless. The opposite of that is humid which means wet, damp, moist.

Hence, the correct option is (A).

4. "Rajnikanth" will come instead of "Rajnikanth's" because in the sentences which have the construction like "Many + Noun + of ", we don't use an apostrophe. So, the correct sentence is,

I have watched many movies of Rajinikanth who is called the Amitabh Bachchan of Tollywood.

Hence, the correct option is (B).

5. 'Akin' is always used with the preposition 'to' instead of 'with'. So, the correct sentence is,

There are some people who believe asking for government assistance is akin to admitting one is a failure.

Hence, the correct option is (C).

6. Licentious means behaving in a way that is considered sexually immoral. Hence, the word "immoral" is the correct synonym of the given word.

Hence, the correct option is (A).

7. Commemorate means to remember officially and give respect to a great person or event, especially by a public ceremony or by making a statue or special building. So, the word similar in the meaning is "Remember".

Hence, the correct option is (D).

8. Squander means to waste money, time etc in a stupid or careless way. So, the opposite meaning to 'squander' is 'waste'.

Hence, the correct option is (B).

9. The idiom "in black and white" means in writing or in print.

Hence, the correct option is (B).

10. The idiom "stick your neck out" means risk incurring criticism or anger by acting or speaking boldly, to take a risk or invite trouble by your actions.

Hence, the correct option is (D).

11. Refer to the following statement of the passage, 'It was epitomized by the absurdity of rural farmers having backyard furnaces to increase national steel production (yet what was produced was nearly unusable pig iron).'

Hence, the correct option is (C).

12. Refer to the first statement of the passage, 'The Great Leap Forward of the People's Republic of China (PRC) was an economic and social plan'.

Hence, the correct option is (B).

13. Communism was honed on the theory of productive forces.

Hence, the correct option is (C).

14. Beget means to be the cause of something.

Hence, the correct option is (A).

15. Primacy means the state of being the most important thing. Pre-eminence also means the state of being the most important thing.

Hence, the correct option is (B).

16. Rules for changing the direct speech into indirect speech are given below:

The inverted commas (" ") used in direct narration is removed in indirect narration and "that" conjunction is used. The direct narration is in past continuous tense, so it will be changed into past perfect continuous tense. Also, 'last night' will be changed into 'previous night'. So, the indirect speech of the given sentence will be:

I told her that it had been raining the previous night when she had left.

Hence, the correct option is (A).

17. The reported speech shows a universal truth. It means there will be no changes in its tense while converting the narration to indirect speech.

Hence, the correct option is (B).

18. The starting statement starts with 'let us', the continuing statement will be talking about the uniqueness of all i.e. R. P follows R as it describes up to when we all can be unique. Q will be the concluding statement as it talks about the realization that we all are the same. The correct option is RPQ as only that arrangement would make a coherent paragraph.

The correct formation would be, 'let us all be unique together until we realize, we all are the same'.

Hence, the correct option is (D).

19. Since the statement talks about the choice of an author, the continuing statement would be his choice of not showing responses on something. So, R follows Q and P will be the concluding statement as he chooses not to respond on his writings. Thus, the correct option is RQP as only that arrangement would make a coherent paragraph.

The correct formation would be, 'The author has chosen not to show responses on this story'.

Hence, the correct option is (C).

20. The given sentence is in the active voice. It is in future indefinite tense. Let us understand the structures for active/passive voices for such sentences.
Active: Subject + will/shall + verb (Ist form) + object.

Passive: Object+ will/shall + be + verb (IIIrd form) + by + subject.
So, with the help of the above structures, we can convert the sentence into passive voice:
The clothes will be returned by the washerman in the evening.

Hence, the correct option is (B).

21. The given sentence is in the active voice. It is in interrogative form of present indefinite tense. The structures for active/passive voices are:

Active: Do/does + subject + verb (Ist form) + object?

Passive: Is/are/am + object + verb (IIIrd form) + by + subject?

So, based on the above structures, we can convert the given sentence into passive voice:

Is football played by the children?

Hence, the correct option is (B).

22. The given sentence is of present perfect tense and it is the active form. The structures for active/passive voices are:

Active: Subject + has/have + verb (IIIrd form) + object.

Passive: Object + has/have + been + verb (IIIrd form) + by + subject.

So, the passive voice of the given sentence would be:

A film based on this novel has been made.

Hence, the correct option is (C).

23. Hang means kill (someone) by tying a rope attached from above around their neck and removing the support from beneath them (often used as a form of capital punishment).

Forms- Hang, Hanged, Hanged.

He was hanged for murder.

Hang- to have been suspended in the air or placed on a wall

Forms- Hang, Hung, Hung.

He hung up his coat.

Hence, the correct option is (B).

24. After the phrase 'one of the', a plural noun is used. Hence, 'teachers' is the only suitable choice for this blank.

Hence, the correct option is (A).

25. An equestrian is a person who is skilled in horsemanship.

A cavalier is an arrogant person or someone indifferent or casual about important matters.

A jockey is a person who rides horses in races, especially as a profession.

A cavalryman is a soldier who is in the cavalry, especially one who rides a horse.

Hence, the correct option is (B).

Q.1 In the following question, out of the four alternatives, select the word opposite in meaning to the given word.

Desecration

A. Hopelessness   **B.** Disbelief

C. Veneration   **D.** Manifestation

Q.2 In the following question, out of the four alternatives, select the word opposite in meaning to the given word.

Impoverished

A. Pure   **B.** Affluent

C. Important   **D.** Efficient

Q.3 In the following question, out of the four alternatives, select the word opposite in meaning to the given word.

Pensive

A. Careless   **B.** Thoughtful

C. Penitent   **D.** Unattached

Q.4 In the following question, some part of the sentence may have errors. Find out which part of the sentence has an error and select the appropriate option. If a sentence is free from error, select 'No Error'.

He has decided to visit Mumbai (1)/ with a view to explore the new (3)/ opportunities lying in front of him. (3)/ No error

A. 1   **B.** 2   **C.** 3   **D.** No Error

Q.5 In the following question, some part of the sentence may have errors. Find out which part of the sentence has an error and select the appropriate option. If a sentence is free from error, select 'No Error'.

I expected that you would (1)/ score much better (2)/ marks but unfortunately you didn't. (3)/ No error

A. 1   **B.** 2   **C.** 3   **D.** No Error

Q.6 In the following question, some part of the sentence may have errors. Find out which part of the sentence has an error and select the appropriate option. If a sentence is free from error, select 'No Error'.

My husband told me that he (1)/ will be coming to Singapore (2)/ next year for the new project. (3)/ No error

A. 1   **B.** 2   **C.** 3   **D.** No Error

Q.7 In the following question, out of the four alternatives, select the word similar in meaning to the given word.

Dogma

A. Possibility   **B.** Feeling

C. Tenet   **D.** Doubt

Q.8 In the following question, out of the four alternatives, select the word similar in meaning to the given word.

Smear

A. Mark   **B.** Laud   **C.** Blank   **D.** Hymn

Q.9 In the following question, a sentence has been given in Active/Passive Voice. Out of the four alternatives suggested, select the one which best expresses the same sentence in Passive/Active Voice.

They should shoot the traitor dead.

A. The traitor should be shot at by them.

B. The traitor should be shot them.

C. The traitor should be shot dead by them.

D. The traitor is shot dead by them.

Q.10 In the following question, a sentence has been given in Active/Passive Voice. Out of the four alternatives suggested, select the one which best expresses the same sentence in Passive/Active Voice.

Is a letter being written by you?

A. Are you writing a letter?

B. Were you writing a letter?

C. Had you been writing a letter?

D. Did you write a letter?

Ques (11-15):Direction: Read the passage carefully and select the best answer to the question out of the given four alternatives.

The saddest part of life lies not in the act of dying, but in failing to truly live while we are alive. Too many of us play small with our lives, never letting the fullness of our humanity see the light of day. I've learned that what really counts in life, in the end, is not how many toys we have collected or how much money we've accumulated, but how many of our talents we have liberated and used for a purpose that adds value to this world. What truly matters most are the lives we have touched and the legacy that we have left. Tolstoy put it so well when he wrote: "We live for ourselves only when we live for others." It took me forty years to discover this simple point of wisdom.

Forty long years to discover that success cannot really be pursued. Success ensues and flows into your life as the unintended yet inevitable by-product of a life spent enriching the lives of other people. When you shift your daily focus from a compulsion to survive towards a lifelong commitment to serving, your existence cannot help but explode into success. I still can't believe that I had to wait until the "half-time" of my life to figure out that true fulfillment as a human being comes not from achieving those grand gestures that put us on the front pages of the newspapers and business magazines, but instead from those basic and incremental acts of decency that each one of us has the privilege to practice each and every day if we simply make the choice to do so.

Mother Teresa, a great leader of human hearts if ever there was one, said it best: "There are no great acts, only small acts done with great love." I learned this the hard way in my life. Until recently, I had been so busy striving, I had missed out on living. I was so busy chasing life's big pleasures that I had missed out on the little ones, those micro joys that weave themselves in

and out of our lives on a daily basis but often go unnoticed. My days were overscheduled, my mind was overworked and my spirit was underfed.

Q.11 According to the passage, what does "failing to truly live while we are alive" answer?

A. End up thinking of death all our lives

B. Never letting the fullness of our humanity see the light of day

C. Focus on basic and incremental acts of decency

D. Over scheduling our days and overpaying ourselves

Q.12 Suggest a suitable title for the passage?

A. True happiness as experienced by Mother Teresa

B. Forty years of discovery Tolstoy

C. Living truly

D. Learning it the hard way

Q.13 According to the passage, what took Tolstoy forty years to discover?

A. Simple point of happiness

B. That we live for ourselves only when we live for others

C. That his spirit was undeterred

D. That he was a great leader of human hearts

Q.14 What according to the passage is success?

A. Success cannot be pursued

B. Success is an unintended yet inevitable byproduct of a life spent enriching the lives of others

C. Success is true fulfillment

D. Success is an incremental act of decency

Q.15 According to the passage, what did Mother Teresa learn in a hard way in her life?

A. That there are no great acts, only small acts are done with great love

B. That she had been so busy striving that she had missed out on living

C. That her days were overscheduled and her mind was overworked

D. That she was so busy chasing life's big pleasures that she had missed out on the little ones

Q.16 In the following question, a sentence has been given in Direct/Indirect Speech. Out of the four alternatives suggested, select the one which best expresses the same sentence in Indirect/Direct Speech.

The teacher asked me why I had been absent the day before.

A. The teacher asked me, "Why were you absent yesterday?".

B. The teacher asked me, "Why are you absent yesterday?".

C. The teacher asked me, "Why are you absent the day before?".

D. The teacher asked me, "Were you absent the day before?".

Q.17 In the following question, a sentence has been given in Direct/Indirect Speech. Out of the four alternatives suggested, select the one which best expresses the same sentence in Indirect/Direct Speech.

He said, "Thanks for reminding me".

A. He thanked me reminding him.

B. He thanked me for reminding him.

C. He said to me thanks for reminding him.

D. He said that he is thankful to me for reminding him.

Q.18 In the following question, a sentence has been given in Direct/Indirect Speech. Out of the four alternatives suggested, select the one which best expresses the same sentence in Indirect/Direct Speech.

He said, "Where shall I be this time next year!"

A. He asked that where should he be that time next year.

B. He wondered where he should be that time the next year.

C. He contemplated where shall he be that time the following year.

D. He wondered where he would be that time the following year.

Q.19 In the following question, out of the four alternatives, select the alternative which best expresses the meaning of the Idiom/Phrase.

To carry weight

A. To carry burden

B. Carry the day

C. Be important

D. Carry through

Q.20 In the following question, out of the four alternatives, select the alternative which best expresses the meaning of the Idiom/Phrase.

To be fair and square

A. Worthy

B. Honest

C. Successful

D. Obedient

Q.21 A sentence is given below in jumbled order. Arrange the sentence in the right order to form a meaningful and coherent sentence.

Seeking help
P) always easy
Q) is not
R) for everyone

A. PQR

B. QPR

C. RPQ

D. QRP

Q.22 A sentence is given below in jumbled order. Arrange the sentence in the right order to form a meaningful and coherent sentence.

I will sign
P) the cheque
Q) the work
R) when you finish

A. PQR

B. PRQ

C. RPQ

D. QPR

Q.23 In the following question, the sentence is given with blank to be filled in with an appropriate word. Select the correct alternative out of the four and indicate it by selecting the appropriate option.

Soldiers are not prepared __________ that kind of attack.

A. At

B. By

C. For

D. About

Q.24 Choose an option, which can be substituted for a given word/sentence/phrase out of given options.

One who loves mankind is called

A. Optimist

B. Philanthropist

C. Optometrist

D. Truant

Q.25 Choose an option, which can be substituted for a given word/sentence/phrase out of given options.

A remedy for all diseases is

A. Medicine
B. Medical
C. Panacea
D. None of these

// Smart Answer Sheet //

Correct — Percentage of students who answered correctly. **Skipped** — Percentage of students who skipped.

Q.	Ans.	Correct / Skipped	Q.	Ans.	Correct / Skipped	Q.	Ans.	Correct / Skipped	Q.	Ans.	Correct / Skipped	Q.	Ans.	Correct / Skipped
1	C	68.99 % / 1.22 %	6	B	79.08 % / 0.0 %	11	B	56.86 % / 1.7 %	16	A	67.87 % / 1.11 %	21	B	81.59 % / 0.0 %
2	B	41.43 % / 1.99 %	7	C	66.29 % / 1.61 %	12	C	52.34 % / 1.85 %	17	B	60.15 % / 1.68 %	22	B	86.79 % / 0.0 %
3	A	55.94 % / 1.2 %	8	A	65.87 % / 1.19 %	13	B	58.97 % / 1.48 %	18	D	58.34 % / 1.05 %	23	C	83.91 % / 0.0 %
4	B	77.09 % / 0.0 %	9	C	43.36 % / 1.96 %	14	B	61.22 % / 1.1 %	19	C	62.69 % / 1.08 %	24	B	67.85 % / 1.82 %
5	A	69.73 % / 1.3 %	10	A	48.09 % / 1.94 %	15	A	60.74 % / 1.51 %	20	B	79.62 % / 0.0 %	25	C	63.09 % / 1.42 %

//Hints and Solutions//

1. Desecration means making lose face or showing disrespect.

Veneration means having and showing a lot of respect for something.

Manifestation means the action or fact of showing something.

Hopelessness means the absence of hope.

Disbelief means inability or refusal to accept that something is true or real.

Hence, the correct option is (C).

2. Impoverished means very poor.

Affluent means having a lot of money or owning a lot of things; a rich person.

Efficient means working or operating quickly and effectively in an organized way.

Hence, the correct option is (B).

3. Pensive means thinking deeply or seriously.

Careless means not giving sufficient attention or thought to avoid harm or errors.

Thoughtful means absorbed in or involving thought.

Penitent means feeling or showing sorrow and regret for having done wrong; repentant.

Unattached means not working for or belonging to a particular body or organization.

Hence, the correct option is (A).

4. We always use gerund (V+ing) form with the structure like "with the view to". Therefore, it should be "exploring" instead of "explore" in part (2) of the sentence. The correct sentence is-

He has decided to visit Mumbai with a view to exploring the new opportunities lying in front of him.

Hence, the correct option is (B).

5. The Past Perfect tense is used with words like hope, expect, intend etc to indicate hope, expectation, intension etc. The correct sentence is-

I had expected that you would score much better marks but unfortunately you didn't.

Hence, the correct option is (A).

6. Since the reporting verb is in the past tense, therefore reporting speech will also be in the past tense. Hence 'would be coming' will come instead of 'will be coming'. So, the correct sentence is-

My husband told me that he would be coming to Singapore next year for the new project.

Hence, the correct option is (B).

7. Dogma = a belief or set of beliefs held by a group or organization, which others are expected to accept without argument.

Tenet = a principle or belief, especially one of the main principles of a religion or philosophy.

So, 'Tenet' is the word similar in meaning to the word 'Dogma'.

Hence, the correct option is (C).

8. Smear refers to a mark or streak of a greasy or sticky substance. So, 'Mark' is the word similar in meaning to "Smear".

Hence, the correct option is (A).

9. The given sentence is of active voice and it uses a modal verb. The structures for active/passive voices for modal verbs are:

Active: Subject + modal verb + verb (Ist form) + object.

Passive: Object + modal verb + be + verb (IIIrd form) + by + subject.

So, with the help of the above structures, we can convert the given sentence into passive voice:

The traitor should be shot dead by them.

Hence, the correct option is (C).

10. The given sentence is in the passive voice. Here, the tense is present continuous interrogative. The structures for passive/active voices are:

Passive: Is/are/am + object + being + verb (IIIrd from) + by + subject?
Active: Is/are/am + subject + verb (ing) + object?

So, with the help of the above structures, we can convert the given sentence into active voice:
Are you writing a letter?

Hence, the correct option is (A).

11. The passage reflects on the importance of humanity. The line here reflects that as human beings we live our whole life believing that our life is only about achieving goals that will give us monetary benefits. What we fail to see is that we never let our humanity see that living fully means living for others.

Hence, the correct option is (B).

12. The passage reflects on the importance of humanity and states that we forget to live or help others and become selfish to achieve things, which won't satisfy our soul. What should matter here is that the loves we will touch or bring a change in other's life for good. The passage is all about reflecting the living purpose of humans.

Hence, the correct option is (C).

13. The last lines of the first paragraph state that Tolstoy learned that we live for ourselves only when we live for others and it took him forty years to discover this simple point of wisdom.

Hence, the correct option is (B).

14. The second line of the second paragraph clearly states that success ensues and flows into our life as the unintended yet inevitable byproduct of a life spent enriching the lives of other people. This is not understood by most people and they live their life without enriching the lives of others.

Hence, the correct option is (B).

15. The last paragraph states that "Mother Teresa, a great leader of human hearts if ever there was one, said it best: "There are no great acts, only small acts done with great love."

Hence, the correct option is (A).

16. The given sentence is in indirect speech. While converting it to direct speech, following changes are made:
1. "asked" will change to "said to".
2. The reported verb will be of simple past and the question word "why" will start the sentence in reported verb.
3. Word "the day before" will change to "yesterday". The question mark will be placed at the end of reported verb.
We can see that only option A follows the above rules correctly, so, it is the correct answer.

Hence, the correct option is (A).

17. This is a sentence of optative direct speech. Rules for changing such sentences into indirect narrations are given below:

Said changes to prayed/wished/bade/cursed/thanked etc as per the sense of the sentence. Inverted commas (" ") are removed and "that" is used instead. However, in some sentences, "that" is not used. Reported speech (which has the verb and subject) is now written in the form of (subject + verb); reported speech is made assertive. So, the answer will be:

He thanked me for reminding him.

Hence, the correct option is (B).

18. The given sentence is in interrogative form. To convert such sentences into the direct narration, the below rules are followed:

'Said/say' is changed to ask/asked/wonder/wondered/enquire of/enquired of. If the reported speech is in the form of WH-Question (who/what/why/how/where/when/which etc), no conjunction is used before the question word. The question word itself works as conjunction. The reported verb is made assertive; i.e. it is kept in the order of subject + verb.

So, the answer will be:

He wondered where he would be that time the following year.

Hence, the correct option is (D).

19. The idiom "to carry weight" means be important; effective or strong.

Hence, the correct option is (C).

20. The idiom "fair and square" means being very accurate or honest.

Hence, the correct option is (B).

21. As the starting statement talks about the seeking help, the next statement would be carrying a verb, so, Q follows. P follows Q as it describes that taking help is not that easy. R will be the concluding statement as it states that it is not easy for everyone.

Thus, the correct option is QPR as only that arrangement would make a coherent paragraph.

The correct formation would be, 'Seeking help is not always easy for everyone'.

Hence, the correct option is (B).

22. As the work can't be signed, so P follows the opening statement as it talks about the signing of the cheque. The next statement will be the condition on which the cheque will get signed. So, R follows P. The concluding statement would be Q as it talked about the work that is yet to be finished. Thus, the correct option is PRQ as only that arrangement would make a coherent paragraph.

The correct formation would be, 'I will sign the check when you finish the work'.

Hence, the correct option is (B).

23. 'For' is the most appropriate choice of preposition here as 'prepare for' means to make plans for a future event. So, the sentence is-

Soldiers are not prepared for that kind of attack.

Hence, the correct option is (C).

24. One who loves mankind is called a philanthropist.

A person who is inclined to be hopeful and to expect good outcomes is called an optimist.

A healthcare professional who provides primary vision care ranging from sight testing and correction to the diagnosis, treatment and management of vision changes is called an optometrist.

A child who stays away from school without permission is called a truant.

Hence, the correct option is (B).

25. A remedy for all diseases is called a panacea.

The art, science, and practice of caring for a patient and managing the diagnosis are called medicine.

An examination of the body by a doctor to check your state of health is called medical.

Hence, the correct option is (C).

Q.1 In the following question, out of the four alternatives, select the word opposite in meaning to the given word.

Calumny

A. Revoke

B. Slander

C. Cantankerous

D. Accolade

Q.2 In the following question, out of the four alternatives, select the word opposite in meaning to the given word.

Eternity

A. Perpetuity

B. Yonder

C. Aeon

D. Ephemeral

Q.3 In the following question, out of the four alternatives, select the word opposite in meaning to the given word.

Dawdle

A. Loiter **B.** Mosey **C.** Hasten **D.** Saunter

Q.4 In the following question, some part of the sentence may have errors. Find out which part of the sentence has an error and select the appropriate option. If the sentence is free from error, select 'No error'.

I purchased (A)/ this ball yesterday (B)/ and have given it to my friend. (C)/ No error (D)

A. A **B.** B **C.** C **D.** No Error

Q.5 In the following question, some part of the sentence may have errors. Find out which part of the sentence has an error and select the appropriate option. If the sentence is free from error, select 'No error'.

The actress (A)/ with all her fans (B)/ are sent to the theatre. (C)/ No error (D)

A. A **B.** B **C.** C **D.** No Error

Q.6 In the following question, some part of the sentence may have errors. Find out which part of the sentence has an error and select the appropriate option. If the sentence is free from error, select 'No error'.

Aradhaya learnt (A)/ the alphabets (B)/ at her playschool. (C)/ No error (D)

A. A **B.** B **C.** C **D.** No Error

Q.7 Choose an option, which can be substituted for a given word/sentence/phrase out of given options.

A doctor who specializes in diseases of the nose

A. Rhinologist

B. Otologist

C. Pathologist

D. Podiatrist

Q.8 In the following question, out of the four alternatives, select the word similar in meaning to the given word.

Jeer

A. Compliment

B. Hoot

C. Flatter

D. Praise

Q.9 In the following question, out of the four alternatives, select the word similar in meaning to the given word.

Bombastic

A. Eloquent

B. Ornate

C. Glorious

D. Grandiloquent

Q.10 In the following question, out of the four alternatives, select the word similar in meaning to the given word.

Engross

A. Dismiss

B. Oppress

C. Absorb

D. Endanger

Ques (11-15):Direction: Read the passage carefully and select the best answer to each question out of the four alternatives.

The Ebola virus causes an acute, serious illness that is often fatal if untreated. Ebola virus disease (EVD) first appeared in 1976 in two simultaneous outbreaks, one in what is now, Nzara, South Sudan, and the other in Yambuku, Democratic Republic of Congo. The latter occurred in a village near the Ebola River, from which the disease takes its name. The 2014 - 2016 outbreak in West Africa was the largest and most complex Ebola outbreak since the virus was first discovered in 1976. There were more cases and deaths in this outbreak than all others combined. It also spread between countries, starting in Guinea then moving across land borders to Sierra Leone and Liberia.

The virus family Filoviridae includes three genera: Cuevavirus, Marburgvirus, and Ebolavirus. Within the genus Ebolavirus, five species have been identified: Zaire, Bundibugyo, Sudan, Reston and Taï Forest. The first three, Bundibugyo ebolavirus, Zaire ebolavirus, and Sudan ebolavirus have been associated with large outbreaks in Africa. The virus causing the 2014 - 2016 West African outbreak belongs to the Zaire ebolavirus species.

It is thought that fruit bats of the Pteropodidae family are natural Ebola, virus hosts. Ebola is introduced into the human population through close contact with the blood, secretions, organs or other bodily fluids of infected animals such as chimpanzees, gorillas, fruit bats, monkeys, forest antelope and porcupines found ill or dead or in the rainforest.

Q.11 How did the Ebola Virus get its name?

A. It is not known how the virus was named Ebola

B. The name was kept on the name of the person who was first diagnosed with it

C. It was kept on the name of a river near the village where the virus was first reported

D. Ebola is the name of the Vaccine used to cure it

Q.12 Which of the following is not the genus of the virus family Filoviridae?

A. Cuevavirus

B. Ebolavirus

C. Hyphomycetes

D. Marburgvirus

Q.13 The virus causing the 2014–2016 West African outbreak belonged to which ebolavirus species?

A. Bundibugyo   **B.** Sudan

C. Reston   **D.** Zaire

Q.14 Which of the following is not the way the Ebola virus is introduced into human body?

A. Through contaminated water

B. Through fruit bats

C. Through infected animals

D. Through antelope and porcupines

Q.15 Which of the following is the opposite in meaning to the word "outbreak"?

A. Berserk   **B.** Epidemic

C. Doldrums   **D.** Insurgence

Q.16 In the following question, a sentence has been given in Active/Passive Voice. Out of the four alternatives suggested, select the one which best expresses the same sentence in Passive/Active Voice.

He was not given the information he needed.

A. Somebody was not given the information he needed.

B. The information he needed wasn't given to him.

C. He needed the information he wasn't given.

D. They didn't give him the information he needed.

Q.17 In the following question, a sentence has been given in Active/Passive Voice. Out of the four alternatives suggested, select the one which best expresses the same sentence in Passive/Active Voice.

Bipin was not told about the meeting.

A. Somebody did not tell Bipin about the meeting.

B. There was nobody who could tell Bipin about the meeting.

C. Nobody told Bipin about the meeting.

D. The meeting was not told about Bipin.

Q.18 In the following question, a sentence has been given in Active/Passive Voice. Out of the four alternatives suggested, select the one which best expresses the same sentence in Passive/Active Voice.

End the war now.

A. Now must the war be ended.

B. Let the war be ended now.

C. You must end the war now.

D. Must the war be ended now.

Q.19 In the following question, out of the four alternatives, select the alternative which best expresses the meaning of the Idiom/Phrase.

No room to swing a cat.

A. An open public area

B. To catch a cat in a closed room

C. To have a bad luck

D. To be in a very small and crowded place

Q.20 In the following question, out of the four alternatives, select the alternative which best expresses the meaning of the Idiom/Phrase.

Crocodile tears

A. To feel sad for another person's misfortunes

B. To laugh so much that your eyes start to water

C. A person whose sadness is never noticed

D. Expressions of sorrow that are insincere

Q.21 In the following question, a sentence has been given in Direct/Indirect Speech. Out of the four alternatives suggested, select the one which best expresses the same sentence in Indirect/Direct Speech.

Tom said to me, "I shall meet you at the station".

A. Tom told me that he would meet me at the station.

B. Tom told me that he will meet me at the station.

C. Tom told me that I would meet me at the station.

D. Tom told me that he would have met me at the station.

Q.22 In the following question, a sentence has been given in Direct/Indirect Speech. Out of the four alternatives suggested, select the one which best expresses the same sentence in Indirect/Direct Speech.

The boss said to her secretary, "Did you discuss this matter with the manager?"

A. The boss asked her secretary whether she discussed that matter with the manager.

B. The boss asked her secretary if you have discussed that matter with the manager.

C. The boss asked her secretary if she had discussed that matter with the manager.

D. The boss asked her secretary whether she has discussed that matter with the manager.

Q.23 In the following question, a sentence has been given in Direct/Indirect Speech. Out of the four alternatives suggested, select the one which best expresses the same sentence in Indirect/Direct Speech.

The robber said to Alexander, "I am your captive".

A. The robber told Alexander that he is his captive.

B. The robber told Alexander that he was your captive.

C. The robber told to Alexander that he was his captive.

D. The robber told Alexander that he was his captive.

Q.24 Choose the correct option from the given alternatives and improve the bracketed part of the sentence.

400 million people speak English as (there first language).

A. There native language

B. Their first language

C. His first language

D. No improvement

Q.25 Choose the correct option from the given alternatives and improve the bracketed part of the sentence.

She could have left then, and might have if curiosity hadn't gotten (best of her).

A. The best of her

B. The most best of her

C. A best of her

D. No improvement

// Smart Answer Sheet //

Correct Percentage of students who answered correctly.   **Skipped** Percentage of students who skipped.

Q.	Ans.	Correct / Skipped	Q.	Ans.	Correct / Skipped	Q.	Ans.	Correct / Skipped	Q.	Ans.	Correct / Skipped	Q.	Ans.	Correct / Skipped	Q.	Ans.	Correct / Skipped
1	D	56.34 % / 1.53 %	6	B	86.9 % / 0.0 %	11	C	76.1 % / 0.0 %	16	D	32.21 % / 3.01 %	21	A	56.91 % / 1.36 %			
2	D	87.02 % / 0.0 %	7	A	58.51 % / 1.01 %	12	C	86.39 % / 0.0 %	17	C	10.29 % / 3.36 %	22	C	42.92 % / 1.2 %			
3	C	63.41 % / 1.02 %	8	B	69.48 % / 1.56 %	13	D	80.83 % / 0.0 %	18	B	52.86 % / 1.63 %	23	D	48.07 % / 1.15 %			
4	C	79.94 % / 0.0 %	9	D	45.56 % / 1.18 %	14	A	67.38 % / 1.01 %	19	D	55.89 % / 1.05 %	24	B	76.14 % / 0.0 %			
5	C	79.75 % / 0.0 %	10	C	48.38 % / 1.53 %	15	C	61.55 % / 1.45 %	20	D	82.35 % / 0.0 %	25	A	81.8 % / 0.0 %			

//Hints and Solutions//

1. Calumny = a statement about someone that is not true and is intended to damage the reputation

Accolade = a formal expression of praise

Revoke = official cancel a decree, decision or promise

Cantankerous = quarrelsome, arguing and complaining a lot

Slander = a false spoken statement about someone that damages their reputation

So, 'Accolade' is the opposite word for 'Calumny'.

Hence, the correct option is (D).

2. Eternity means forever; infinite or unending time.

Ephemeral means short-lived; lasting for a very short time.

Perpetuity means continuance; the state or quality of lasting forever.

Yonder means farther; at some distance in the direction indicated.

Aeon means lifetime; an indefinite and very long period of time.

So, 'Ephemeral' is the opposite word for 'Eternity'.

Hence, the correct option is (D).

3. Dawdle = waste time; be slow

Hasten = be quick to do something

Loiter = walk slowly and with no apparent purpose; dawdle

Mosey = walk or move in a leisurely manner

Saunter = walk in a slow, relaxed manner; a leisurely stroll

So, 'Hasten' is the opposite word for 'Dwadle'.

Hence, the correct option is (C).

4. The error is in part (C) of the sentence. The use of verb "purchased" and the word "yesterday" makes it clear that the given sentence is in past tense. Therefore, it is grammatically incorrect to use present verb "have given" in part (C) of the sentence. Thus, The correct sentence is-

I purchased this ball yesterday and gave it to my friend.

Hence, the correct option is (C).

5. If the subject is joined by 'as well as', 'with', 'along with', 'together with' etc. the verb will agree with the first subject. Here, the first subject is "the actress" which is singular; hence, the verb used should also be singular. Hence, replace 'are' with 'is'. So, the correct sentence is-

The actress with all her fans is sent to the theatre.

Hence, the correct option is (C).

6. The error is in part (B) of the sentence. The noun 'alphabet' is not used in plural form. It is because it is a collective noun which is used for the letters referring to a to z in English language. So, the correct sentence is-

Aradhaya learnt the alphabet at her playschool.

Hence, the correct option is (B).

7. A doctor who specializes in diseases of the nose is called a Rhinologist.

A doctor who specializes in diseases of the ears is called an Otologist.

A medical healthcare provider who examines bodies and body tissues is called a Pathologist.

A physician and surgeon who treats the foot, ankle and related structures of the leg is called Podiatrist.

Hence, the correct option is (A).

8. Jeer = a rude and mocking remark

Hoot = a shout expressing scorn or disapproval

Compliment = a polite expression of praise or admiration

Flatter = lavish praise and compliments on (someone), often insincerely and with the aim of furthering one's own interests

Praise = express warm approval or admiration

So, the word 'Hoot' has a similar meaning as 'Jeer'.

Hence, the correct option is (B).

9. Bombastic = sounding important but in actual meaningless; pompous, grandiloquent

Grandiloquent = pompous or extravagant in language, style, or manner, especially in a way that is intended to impress; bombastic

Eloquent = fluent or persuasive in speaking or writing

Ornate = highly decorated

Glorious = having great beauty and splendor

So, the word 'Grandiloquent' has a similar meaning as 'Bombastic'.

Hence, the correct option is (D).

10. Engross = absorb all the attention or interest of; to occupy completely, as the mind or attention

Absorb = take up the attention of (someone); interest greatly

Dismiss = order or allow to leave; send away; treat as unworthy of serious consideration

Oppress = to govern people in an unfair and cruel way and prevent them from having opportunities and freedom

Endanger = put (someone or something) at risk or in danger

So, the word 'Absorb' has a similar meaning as 'Engross'.

Hence, the correct option is (C).

11. It is given in the first paragraph that the virus first appeared at two places in 1976. Out of these two places, one was found in a village near the river "Ebola" in Yambuku, Democratic Republic of Congo.

Hence, the correct option is (C).

12. There are only three genera of virus family Filoviridae has been given in the passage which are Cuevavirus, Marburgvirus, and Ebolavirus.

Hence, the correct option is (C).

13. It is clearly mentioned in the following line of the passage, "The virus causing the 2014–2016 West African outbreak belongs to the Zaire ebolavirus species".

Hence, the correct option is (D).

14. As mentioned in the passage, the Ebola virus can infect the human body through the blood, secretions, organs or other bodily fluids of infected animals such as chimpanzees, gorillas, fruit bats, monkeys, forest antelope and porcupines found ill or dead or in the rainforest. The aspects of its affecting the human body through contaminated water is nowhere mentioned in the passage.

Hence, the correct option is (A).

15. Outbreak = a sudden and unusual occurrence of something, such as a war or a disease

Doldrums = unsuccessful or showing no activity or development

Berserk = out of control with anger or excitement; wild or frenzied.

Epidemic = a widespread occurrence of an infectious disease in a community at a particular time.

Insurgence = an act of rebellion

So, the correct opposite meaning of the given word "outbreak" is "doldrums".

Hence, the correct option is (C).

16. The given sentence is in passive form and its structure is:

Passive: Object + was/were (not) + verb (IIIrd form) + (by + subject).

Its active structure would be:

Active: Subject + did not + verb (Ist form) + object.

It is optional to include the part (By + subject) in the passive voice. In sentences where the subject is hidden or not given, we need to create a subject accordingly.

The active form of the given sentence would be:

They didn't give him the information he needed.

Hence, the correct option is (D).

17. The sentence is in passive form and needs to be changed into active voice. The structure for passive/active voice has been shown below:

Passive: Object + was/were + verb (IIIrd form) + (by + subject).

Active: Subject + verb (IInd form) + object.

So, according to the above structure, the active voice of the given sentence would be:

Nobody told Bipin about the meeting.

Hence, the correct option is (C).

18. The given sentence is an imperative sentence. It is given in the form:

Active: Verb + object

So, the passive form of the sentence will be:

Passive: Let + object + be + past participle

So, the passive voice of the given sentence would be:

Let the war be ended now.

Hence, the correct option is (B).

19. The idiom "no room to swing a cat" means a place is very small and crowded.

Hence, the correct option is (D).

20. The idiom "crocodile tears" means to show sadness which is not sincere or actual; fake cry. The same meaning is depicted by option (D).

Hence, the correct option is (D).

21. The given sentence is of direct speech. "Said to" will change to "told". Since the reporting verb is in the past tense, changes will be made to the reported verb. "Shall" will change to "would" as the pronoun "I" will change to "he". Option (A) follows the rules correctly, so, it is the correct answer. So, the answer is-

Tom told me that he would meet me at the station.

Hence, the correct option is (A).

22. The given sentence is in interrogative form. To convert such sentences into the indirect narration, the below rules are followed:

Say/Said is changed to ask/asked/wonder/wondered/enquire of/enquired of etc as per the sense of the sentence.

If the reported speech is in the form of WH-Question (who/what/why/how/where/when/which etc), no conjunction is used before the question word. The question word itself works as conjunction.

So, the correct answer is:

The boss asked her secretary if she had discussed that matter with the manager.

Hence, the correct option is (C).

23. The given sentence is indirect speech. To convert it into indirect speech, we'll convert "said to" into "told". The tense of the reported speech is simple present which will change to simple past. The pronoun "I" is the first-person pronoun. First-person pronoun changes according to the subject of the reporting speech which is "robber" in the sentence. So, "I" will change to "he" in indirect speech. "Your" is a second-person pronoun. Second-person pronoun changes according to the object of the reporting verb which is Alexander in the sentence. So, "your" will change to "his". So, the correct answer is-

The robber told Alexander that he was his captive.

Hence, the correct option is (D).

24. The word "there" refers to a place, "their" means belonging to, or associated with, a group of people. Here, "their" should be used in place of there. So, the correct sentence is-

400 million people speak English as their first language.

Hence, the correct option is (B).

25. Before the superlative degree "best", article 'the' should come. Hence option A is correct. For option B, "most" can't be used before "best". So, the correct sentence is-

She could have left then, and might have if curiosity hadn't gotten the best of her.

Hence, the correct option is (A).

Q.1 Which of the following awards has NOT been won by Australian cricket all-rounder Ellyse Perry?

A. ICC Women's ODI Player of the Year 2019

B. Rachael Heyhoe-Flint Award 2017

C. ICC Women's Emerging player of the Year 2019

D. Rachael Heyhoe-Flint Award 2019

Q.2 What is the capital of Bhutan?

A. Paro | **B.** Punakha
C. Thimphu | **D.** None of these

Q.3 The metallic constituents of hard water are:

A. Magnesium, Calcium and Tin

B. Iron, Tin and Calcium

C. Calcium, Magnesium and Iron

D. Magnesium, Tin and Iron

Q.4 Which is the largest peninsular river in India?

A. Krishna | **B.** Godavari
C. Kaveri | **D.** Mahanadi

Q.5 'Ampere' is the unit of _______.

A. Electric current | **B.** Speed
C. Temperature | **D.** Pressure

Q.6 What is the brain of a computer?

A. ALU | **B.** CPU
C. Keyboard | **D.** Monitor

Q.7 Under which article of the Constitution of India, the fundamental rights of members of armed forces can be specifically restricted?

A. Article 21 | **B.** Article 25
C. Article 33 | **D.** Article 33

Q.8 If you want to create an animated presentation, which application program would be best for it?

A. MS PowerPoint | **B.** MS Word
C. MS Access | **D.** MS Excel

Q.9 Who discovered the electromagnetic nature of light?

A. Snell | **B.** Newton | **C.** Maxwell | **D.** Young

Q.10 Akbar given the title 'Mian' to whom?

A. King Todar Mal | **B.** Man Singh I
C. Birbal | **D.** Tansen

Q.11 Which of the following is an extension to save a video?

A. JEPG | **B.** PNG | **C.** DOX | **D.** MPEG

Q.12 British Government appointed an Indian Statutory Commission to review the Government of India Act 1919, this commission is also known as?

A. Simon Commission | **B.** Hunter Commission
C. Elbert Commission | **D.** Cripps Mission

Q.13 Who is the current Union Steel Minister?

A. Rajkumar Saini

B. Ramesh Chandra

C. Dharmendra Pradhan

D. Ashwini Kumar

Q.14 Which of the following fundamental rights cannot be canceled during the Emergency?

A. Organization liberty

B. Freedom of speech and expression

C. Life and Personal Liberty

D. Freedom to organize without arms

Q.15 Who was the first Chief Election Commissioner of India?

[DSSSB TGT Social Science, 2014]

A. K. V. K. Sundaram | **B.** S. P. Sen Verma
C. Sukumar Sen | **D.** Rajmannar

Q.16 Which of the following laws does not relate to gases?

A. Charle's law | **B.** Dalton's law
C. Lenz's law | **D.** Boyle's law

Q.17 The working principle of a washing machine is:

A. Reverse osmosis | **B.** Diffusion
C. Centrifugation | **D.** Dialysis

Q.18 Which of the following household substances is not basic in nature?

A. Toothpaste

B. Vinegar

C. Solution of washing soda

D. Detergent solution

Q.19 Which of the following types of farming is more suitable for the production of crops like sugarcane, wheat and rice?

A. Irrigated farming | **B.** Subsistence farming
C. Shifting farming | **D.** Terrace farming

Q.20 Which is a salt water lake located in Rajasthan?

A. Sambhar Lake | **B.** Chilka Lake
C. Barapani | **D.** Dal lake

Q.21 Who among the following occupies the second highest office in India?

A. President of India

B. Chief Justice of India

C. Prime Minister of India

D. Vice President of India

Q.22 Luciferin is found in which of the following insects?

A. Firefly | **B.** Sandfly | **C.** Housefly | **D.** Fruitfly

Q.23 Which country has successfully launched its first-ever Arctic-monitoring satellite that will monitor the Arctic's climate and environment?

A. Japan   **B.** Russia   **C.** China   **D.** India

Q.24 Which one of the following layer of the atmosphere is responsible for the deflection of the radio waves?

A. Troposphere   **B.** Ionosphere
C. Stratosphere   **D.** Mesosphere

Q.25 Who among the following had founded The Congress - Khilafat Swaraj Party?

A.   Mahatma Gandhi
B.   Subhash Chandra Bose
C.   Jawaharlal Nehru
D.   Motilal Nehru

// Smart Answer Sheet //

| Correct | Percentage of students who answered correctly. | Skipped | Percentage of students who skipped. |

Q.	Ans.	Correct / Skipped	Q.	Ans.	Correct / Skipped	Q.	Ans.	Correct / Skipped	Q.	Ans.	Correct / Skipped	Q.	Ans.	Correct / Skipped	Q.	Ans.	Correct / Skipped
1	C	43.28 % / 1.76 %	6	B	87.76 % / 0.0 %	11	D	40.63 % / 1.37 %	16	C	56.43 % / 1.7 %	21	D	83.52 % / 0.0 %			
2	C	55.63 % / 1.77 %	7	C	68.49 % / 1.87 %	12	A	63.15 % / 1.85 %	17	C	54.83 % / 1.08 %	22	A	66.17 % / 1.35 %			
3	C	53.09 % / 1.39 %	8	A	86.86 % / 0.0 %	13	C	46.76 % / 1.94 %	18	B	79.66 % / 0.0 %	23	B	29.99 % / 3.13 %			
4	B	49.13 % / 1.47 %	9	C	42.18 % / 1.24 %	14	C	44.47 % / 1.02 %	19	A	77.26 % / 0.0 %	24	B	40.93 % / 1.49 %			
5	A	79.96 % / 0.0 %	10	D	82.96 % / 0.0 %	15	C	55.92 % / 1.12 %	20	A	57.22 % / 1.47 %	25	D	55.4 % / 1.28 %			

//Hints and Solutions//

1.

- ICC Women's Emerging Player of the Year 2019 has not been won by Australian cricket all-rounder Ellyse Perry.
- Ellyse Perry is an Australian sportswoman who has represented her country in cricket and association football.
- She holds the distinction of having represented Australia in both cricket and soccer World Cups.
- Chanida Sutthiruang won the Women's Emerging Cricketer of the Year.

Hence, the correct option is (C).

2. Thimphu is the capital and largest city of Bhutan. It is situated in the western central part of Bhutan.

Hence, the correct option is (C).

3. The metallic constituents of hard water are calcium, magnesium and iron.

Though iron, aluminum, and manganese may also be found in certain metals. These metals are water-soluble, meaning they will dissolve in water.

Hence, the correct option is (C).

4. The Godavari is the largest peninsular river in India.

In terms of length, catchment area and discharge, the Godavari is the largest in peninsular India.

Hence, the correct option is (B).

5. 'Ampere' is the unit of electric current.

The ampere unit is named after 'Andre-Marie Ampere', from France. One ampere is equivalent to a charge of one coulomb per second flowing in a circuit.

Hence, the correct option is (A).

6. CPU is the brain of a computer.

This includes the control system of the computer system and the Arithmetic Logic Unit. All major calculations and compilers in the computer system are executed by the CPU. It controls all the internal and external devices.

Hence, the correct option is (B).

7. Under article 33 of the Constitution of India, the fundamental rights of members of armed forces can be specifically restricted.

Article 33 empowers the Parliament to restrict, modify or abrogate the fundamental rights to the members of armed forces, para-military forces, police forces, members of intelligence agencies or similar services. This is required to make the proper discharge of their duties which are sensitive and urgent in nature.

Hence, the correct option is (C).

8. MS PowerPoint would be best to create an animated presentation.

In the field of 'Built-In Transitions and Animations', PowerPoint has received approximately 95% of the presentation software by 2012, making the inning presentation really simple. This allows users to create advanced and custom animations.

Hence, the correct option is (A).

9. Maxwell discovered the electromagnetic nature of light.

An electrical theory called classical electromagnetism was developed by various physicists during the 19th century, which coincided with the conclusion of the work of James Clerk Maxwell, who integrated the earlier development in the same theory.

Hence, the correct option is (C).

10. Akbar gave the title 'Mian' to Tansen.

Tansen was a court musician in the darbar of Raja Ramachandra of Bandavagarh (Rewa). When Akbar heard of his prodigious talent, he sent a decree to the king asking for Tansen and made him one of the Navaratnas in his court.

Hence, the correct option is (D).

11. MPEG is an extension to save a video.

MPEG stands for 'Moving Picture Experts Group'. MPEG is an organization that develops standards for encoding digital audio and video. It works with the International Organization for Standardization (ISO) and the International Electrotechnical Commission (IEC) to ensure media compression standards are widely adopted and universally available.

Hence, the correct option is (D).

12. British Government appointed an Indian Statutory Commission to review the Government of India Act 1919, this commission is also known as Simon Commission.

The Indian Statutory Commission, also known as the Simon Commission, was a group of seven Members of Parliament under the chairmanship of Sir John Simon. The commission arrived in British India in 1928 to study constitutional reform in Britain's largest and most important possession.

Hence, the correct option is (A).

13. Dharmendra Pradhan is the current Union Steel Minister.

Dharmendra Pradhan is the Cabinet Minister for Petroleum & Natural Gas and Steel in the Government of India. On 31 May 2019, Shri Pradhan began his second consecutive tenure at the Ministry of Petroleum & Natural Gas becoming the first such incumbent in the history of independent India.

Hence, the correct option is (C).

14. During the Emergency, the right to life and personal liberty cannot be canceled.

During the National Emergency, many fundamental rights of Indian citizens can be suspended. Under the right to freedom, six independents are automatically suspended. In contrast, the right to life and personal freedom can not be suspended as per the original constitution.

Hence, the correct option is (C).

15. Sukumar Sen was the first Chief Election Commissioner of India.

Sukumar Sen (1898–1963) was an officer of the Indian Civil Services (ICS). He was the first Chief Election Commissioner (CEC) of India, serving from 21 March 1950 to 19 December 1958. Two general elections (1951–52 and in 1957) were administered under his watch.

Hence, the correct option is (C).

16. Lenz's law does not relate to gases.

Lenz's law states that the induced electromotive force with different polarities induces a current whose magnetic field opposes the change in magnetic flux through the loop in order to ensure that original flux is maintained through the loop when current flows in it.

Hence, the correct option is (C).

17. The working principle of a washing machine is centrifugation.

Centrifugation is a separation process that uses the action of centrifugal force to promote accelerated settling of particles in a solid-liquid mixture. The washing machine consists of a centrifuge for this purpose. A centrifuge is a piece of equipment that puts an object in rotation around a fixed axis, applying a force perpendicular to the axis of spin that can be very strong.

Hence, the correct option is (C).

18. Vinegar is not basic in nature.

Toothpaste, solution of washing soda, detergent solution and slaked lime are the household substances having basic nature.

Substances like bathroom acid, vitamin C tablets, lemon juice, orange juice, vinegar, fizzy drinks etc are acidic in nature.

Hence, the correct option is (B).

19. Irrigated farming is more suitable for the production of crops like sugarcane, wheat and rice.

Irrigated farming is practiced in the areas where average rainfall is between 80 and 200cms which is sufficient for the crops like sugarcane, wheat and rice.

Such system of farming is practiced only in those regions of the country where the source of water is from underground or surface water bodies like rivers, tanks and lakes is sufficient throughout the year.

Hence, the correct option is (A).

20. Sambhar Lake is a salt water lake located in Rajasthan.

The Sambhar Salt Lake is India's largest inland salt lake. It is the bowl-shaped lake that encircles historical Sambhar Lake Town located 96 km south west of the city of Jaipur and 64 km northeast of Ajmer along National Highway 8 in Rajasthan.

Hence, the correct option is (A).

21. Vice-President of India occupies the second highest office in India.

He is accorded a rank next to the President of India in the official warrant of precedence. This office is modelled on the lines of the American Vice-President.

Hence, the correct option is (D).

22. Luciferin is an organic substance found in insects called Luciferin firefly or present in insects.

That produces light when oxidized by the action of the enzyme luciferase. Firefly luciferin is used in a luciferin-luciferase system that requires ATP as a co-factor. It can also be used as a bio-indicator of the presence of energy or life.

Hence, the correct option is (A).

23. Russia has successfully launched its first-ever Arctic-monitoring satellite that will monitor the Arctic's climate and environment. The name of Russia's space agency is Roscosmos.

Hence, the correct option is (B).

24. The Ionosphere layer of the atmosphere is responsible for the deflection of the radio waves.

In the lower part of the thermosphere region, between 100 and 400 kms, the ionisation of the atmospheric gases takes place and the layer is called ionosphere. The ionosphere is ionized by solar radiation. There is a peak concentration of ionized particles at 250 kms which is responsible for the deflection of radio waves.

Hence, the correct option is (B).

25. The Congress - Khilafat Swaraj Party was founded by Chittaranjan Das and Motilal Nehru in December 1922.

Chittaranjan Das was the party president while Motilal Nehru was one of the secretaries.

The new party was to function as a group within the Congress.

Hence, the correct option is (D).

Q.1 Who founded the International Tennis Hall of Fame, the largest tennis museum in the world?
A. Walter Clopton Wingfield
B. Jimmy Van Alen
C. Arthur Ashe
D. Harry Hopman

Q.2 Which countries participated in the final match of the first FIFA Football World Cup held in 1930?
A. Yugoslavia Vs United States of America
B. Uruguay Vs Argentina
C. France Vs Mexico
D. Uruguay Vs United States of America

Q.3 The alloy 'solder' used for soldering, is a composition of which of the following two elements?
A. Copper and Zinc
B. Copper and Nickel
C. Lead and Silver
D. Lead and Tin

Q.4 What is the SI Unit of luminous intensity?
A. Mole
B. Kelvin
C. Candela
D. Ampere

Q.5 Which of the following fields of an e-mail hides the identity of the recipients?
A. To
B. From
C. Cc
D. Bcc

Q.6 What is the national currency of Myanmar?
A. Ngultrum
B. Euro
C. Rial
D. Kyat

Q.7 Which of the following physical quantities is vector quantity?
A. Mass
B. Speed
C. Time
D. Velocity

Q.8 Which of the following acid found in red ants?
A. Hydrochloric acid
B. Oxalic acid
C. Formic acid
D. Boric acid

Q.9 'Anemophily' is a form of pollination in which the pollen is distributed by ______.
A. Butterflies
B. Ants
C. Wind
D. Bees

Q.10 Which of the following is not a necessary micronutrient required for plants?
A. Zinc
B. Chromium
C. Manganese
D. Molybdenum

Q.11 Who among the following administers oath to the Protem speaker?
A. President
B. Leader of the Lok Sabha
C. Outgoing speaker
D. Chief Justice of India

Q.12 Who among the following had moved the crucial "Objectives Resolution"?
A. Jawaharlal Nehru
B. Motilal Nehru
C. Dr. Bhimrao Ambedkar
D. Mahatma Gandhi

Q.13 What is the type of Indian Economy?
A. Independent Economy
B. Mixed Economy
C. Capitalist Economy
D. Communist Economy

Q.14 Which is the oldest language of South India?

[NCERT National Talent Search Exam, 2020]

A. Malayalam
B. Tamil
C. Telugu
D. Kannada

Q.15 "Hyperinflation" in the economy will lead to ________ .
A. Easy loans
B. Fall in value of money
C. Increased production of goods
D. Increased deposits in banks

Q.16 Which of the following country is not a member of SAARC?
A. Nepal
B. Maldives
C. China
D. Afghanistan

Q.17 LISP is a programming language built by whom?
A. John McCar
B. Dennis Ritchie
C. Larry Wall
D. Rasmus Lerdorf

Q.18 Goods whose demand is proportional to price are called:
A. Inferior goods
B. Veblen goods
C. Normal goods
D. Exclusive goods

Q.19 A computer cannot "boot" if it does not have a/an __________.
A. Compiler
B. Loader
C. Operating system
D. Assembler

Q.20 Where has the first of its kind "Organ Donor Memorial" been inaugurated virtually in the country on the occasion of the 11th National Organ Donation Day celebration?
A. Gujarat
B. Maharashtra
C. Rajasthan
D. Punjab

Q.21 Which of the following folk dance forms is associated with Gujarat?
A. Nautanki
B. Garba
C. Kathakali
D. Bhangra

Q.22 Which Petroleum Company launched India's first 100 Octane Petrol also known as XP 100?

A. Indian Oil Corporation
B. Bharat Petroleum
C. Gas Authority of India Ltd
D. Oil and Natural gas Corporation

Q.23 Where has India's first Moss Garden been inaugurated?
A. Kevadia, Gujrat
B. Nainital, Uttarakhand
C. Mandi, Himachal Pradesh
D. Kochi, Kerela

Q.24 Who was the inventor of the telephone?
A. Alexander Graham Bell
B. Thomas Edison
C. Archimedes
D. Nikola Tesla

Q.25 Who has authored the book titled "Advantage India: The Story of Indian Tennis"?
A. Sania Mirza
B. Anindya Dutta
C. Vijay Amritraj
D. Mahesh Bhupati

// Smart Answer Sheet //

Correct — Percentage of students who answered correctly.   **Skipped** — Percentage of students who skipped.

Q.	Ans.	Correct / Skipped	Q.	Ans.	Correct / Skipped	Q.	Ans.	Correct / Skipped	Q.	Ans.	Correct / Skipped	Q.	Ans.	Correct / Skipped	Q.	Ans.	Correct / Skipped
1	B	11.51 % / 4.26 %	6	D	66.34 % / 1.05 %	11	A	77.22 % / 0.0 %	16	C	79.17 % / 0.0 %	21	B	79.01 % / 0.0 %			
2	B	13.7 % / 3.87 %	7	D	78.19 % / 0.0 %	12	A	61.75 % / 1.45 %	17	A	12.97 % / 4.47 %	22	A	16.06 % / 4.7 %			
3	D	63.33 % / 1.86 %	8	C	81.2 % / 0.0 %	13	B	89.71 % / 0.0 %	18	B	84.45 % / 0.0 %	23	B	47.0 % / 1.5 %			
4	C	54.0 % / 1.88 %	9	C	45.66 % / 1.87 %	14	B	65.7 % / 1.37 %	19	C	87.03 % / 0.0 %	24	A	59.31 % / 1.59 %			
5	D	66.28 % / 1.42 %	10	B	82.87 % / 0.0 %	15	B	68.5 % / 1.27 %	20	C	66.81 % / 1.76 %	25	B	21.67 % / 3.41 %			

//Hints and Solutions//

1. Jimmy Van Alen founded the International Tennis Hall of Fame, the largest tennis museum in the world. James Van Alen was an American tennis official. In 1954, the late tennis innovator Jimmy Van Alen founded the Hall of Fame in Newport, Rhode Island as a "shrine to the ideals of the game."

Hence, the correct option is (B).

2. In the final, hosts and pre-tournament favourites Uruguay defeated Argentina 4–2 in front of a crowd of 68,346 people to become the first nation to win the World Cup. The final was played at the Estadio Centenario in Montevideo, Uruguay, on 30 July, a Wednesday.

Hence, the correct option is (B).

3. The alloy 'solder' used for soldering is the composition of two elements, lead and tin.

An alloy is a mixture of two or more different elements and at least one of which is metal. Solder is used for soldering electronic appliances and to create firm joints between metals. Solder is the composition of lead and tin.

Hence, the correct option is (D).

4. The SI Unit of luminous intensity is candela.

Mole is the SI unit of amount of substance. Kelvin is the SI unit of temperature. Ampere is the SI unit of electric current.

Hence, the correct option is (C).

5. Bcc (blind carbon copy) e-mail hides the identity of the recipients is a copy of an email message sent to a recipient whose email address does not appear (as a recipient) in the message.

By being hidden, 'Bcc recipients' differ from 'To and Cc recipients', whose addresses do appear in the respective header lines.

Every recipient of the message can see all the 'To and Cc recipients', but only the sender knows about 'Bcc recipients'.

Hence, the correct option is (D).

6. The national currency of Myanmar is Kyat. Ngultrum is the currency of Bhutan. There are many countries that use the euro as their national currency. Some of them are Austria, Belgium, Cyprus, Estonia, Finland, France, Germany etc. Rial is the currency of Iran, Oman, and Yemen.

Hence, the correct option is (D).

7. Velocity is vector quantity.

The physical quantity which has magnitude only but no direction called scalar quantity. For example – physical quantities like speed, mass, volume, time, work energy, power etc are called scalar quantities.

The physical quantity which has magnitude, as well as direction, called vector quantity. For example – physical quantities like force, acceleration, velocity, displacement, torque etc are called vector quantities.

Hence, the correct option is (D).

8. Formic acid is found in red ants.

Formic acid, systematically called methanoic acid, is the simplest carboxylic acid, and its chemical formula is $HCOOH$. It is an important intermediate in chemical synthesis and occurs naturally, most notably in some ants.

Hence, the correct option is (C).

9. 'Anemophily' is a form of pollination in which the pollen is distributed by wind.

It is also called as a wind pollination which is predominant in grasses, most conifers and many deciduous trees.

Other common anemophilous plants are oaks, sweet chestnuts, alders etc.

Hence, the correct option is (C).

10. Chromium is not a necessary micronutrient required for plants.

For a plant to grow, chemical elements like carbon, hydrogen and oxygen are the necessary nutrients that can be available from air and water.

The elements like Nitrogen, Phosphorus, Potassium, Manganese and Molybdenum are the necessary elements needed to grow a plant. Plants can receive these nutrients from the soil and fertilizers. Chromium is considered a serious environmental pollutant.

Hence, the correct option is (B).

11. President appoints and administers oath to the 'Protem' speaker.

The 'Protem' speaker is appointed when speaker of the lower house vacates his/her office before the first meeting of the newly elected members of the lower house of the parliament.

The major duty of 'Protem' speaker is to administer oath to the new members of the Lok Sabha.

Hence, the correct option is (A).

12. Jawaharlal Nehru had moved the crucial "Objectives Resolution".

The Constituent Assembly had 300 members, of these, six members played particularly important roles.

Three were representatives of the Congress, namely, Jawaharlal Nehru, Vallabh Bhai Patel and Rajendra Prasad.

Hence, the correct option is (A).

13. Indian Economy is a mixed economy.

The feature of a mixed economy which exist in India is private ownership of means of production. This is observed in most of the agricultural, industrial and service sectors.

Hence, the correct option is (B).

14. The oldest language of South India is Tamil (200 BC). It is also one of the 7 ancient languages in the world that is still spoken.

Malayalam is a dialect of tamil which dates back to 9th century, Kannada to 400 AD and Telugu to 571 AD.

Hence, the correct option is (B).

15. "Hyperinflation" in the economy will lead to fall in value of money.

In Hyperinflation, the prices of goods and services increases at a rapid rate (usually more than 50% increase in the prices of goods and services). This regularly erodes the value of domestic currency. The value of money falls leading to a weaker purchasing power.

Hence, the correct option is (B).

16. China is not a member of SAARC.

SAARC is South Asian Association for Regional Cooperation, which is a regional intergovernmental organisation.

It's members are these nations- India, Afghanistan, Pakistan, Bhutan, Nepal, Maldives, Sri Lanka and Bangladesh.

Hence, the correct option is (C).

17. LISP, a computer programming language developed in 1960 by John McCarthy at the Massachusetts Institute of Technology (MIT). LISP was founded on the mathematical theory of recursive functions (in which a function appears in its own definition).

Hence, the correct option is (B).

18. Veblen goods are those, for which demand increases as the price increases because of their exclusive nature and status symbol. Veblen goods are named after American economist Thorstein Veblen, who first identified conspicuous consumption as a mode of status-seeking in The Theory of the Leisure Class (1899).

Hence, the correct option is (B).

19. A computer cannot "boot" if it does not have an operating system.

An operating system is the system software that handles the software and hardware resources and provides services for the computer programs.

Hence, the correct option is (C).

20. On 27 November 2020 on the occasion of the 11th National Organ Donation Day celebration at Jaipur, Rajasthan CM Ashok Gehlot inaugurated virtually the first of its kind "Organ Donor Memorial" in the country.

Hence, the correct option is (C).

21. Garba is a form of dance that originates from the state of Gujarat in India. The name is derived from the Sanskrit term Garbha ("womb") and Deep ("a small earthenware lamp"). Many traditional garbas are performed around centrally lit lamp or a picture or statue of the Goddess Shakti.

Hence, the correct option is (B).

22. Ministry of Petroleum and Natural gas(MOP&NG) Minister Dharmendra Pradhan launched India's first 100 Octane Petrol also known as XP 100 manufactured by Indian Oil

Corporation(IOC). XP 100, the premium grade petrol is manufactured at IOC's Mathura refinery in Uttar Pradesh, and will be rolled out in two Phases at selected Petrol stations.

Hence, the correct option is (A).

23. India's First Moss Garden was inaugurated at Khurpatal, Nainital District of Uttarakhand by renowned Water Conservation Activist of India, Rajendra Singh (also known as Water Man of India). The Garden has been set up for the purpose of conservation of different species of moss.

Hence, the correct option is (B).

24. Alexander Graham Bell was an inventor, scientist, and engineer who is credited with inventing and patenting the first practical telephone. He also co-founded the American Telephone and Telegraph Company.

Hence, the correct option is (A).

25. Anindya Dutta has authored the book titled "Advantage India: The Story of Indian Tennis". The book is published by Westland publications. The book provides the extensive history of Indian tennis on both men's and women's sides.

Hence, the correct option is (B).

Q.1 Who is the only female track and field athlete to win 6 Olympic gold medals?

A. Allyson Felix
B. Jenny Thompson
C. Natalie Coughlin
D. Allison Schmitt

Q.2 Who among the following is NOT an Indian weightlifter?

A. Karnam Malleswari
B. Dipika Pallikal
C. Dipika Pallikal
D. Rakhi Haldar

Q.3 How does the sun get its energy?

A. From gravitational pressure
B. From nuclear fission
C. From nuclear fusion
D. None of these

Q.4 The gas, which usually causes explosions in coal mines is:

A. Hydrogen
B. Carbon monoxide
C. Air
D. Methane

Q.5 Where did Iltutmish establish a center of learning?

A. Multan
B. Kolkata
C. Alwar
D. Patna

Q.6 The largest freshwater lake located in the Sahara desert is __________.

A. Lake Chad
B. Lake Michigan
C. Lake Superior
D. None of these

Q.7 Which were the two dynasties, which ruled immediately before and after the Khiljis?

A. Mamluk and Lodhi
B. Saiyyad and Lodhi
C. Mamluk and Tughlaq
D. Tughlaq and Lodhi

Q.8 Which Article deals with Freedom of Press?

A. Article 19(1) A
B. Article 20
C. Article 22
D. Article 21

Q.9 What are the basic laws of physics?

A. Classical physics
B. Atomic physics
C. Both (A) and (B)
D. None of above

Q.10 Bilateral monopoly situation is:

A. When there are only two sellers of a product
B. When there are only two buyers of a product
C. When there is only one buyer and one seller of a product
D. When there are two buyers and two sellers of a product

Q.11 The Residuary powers of legislation under Indian Constitution rests with:

A. President
B. Prime Minister
C. Parliament
D. States

Q.12 What is the correct formula for finding acceleration?

A. $a = \frac{v-u}{t}$
B. $a = \frac{v+u}{t}$
C. $a = u + at$
D. $a = u - vt$

Q.13 Franchising is:

A. Not having to pay any fee
B. A form of licensing
C. Operating a business without a license
D. Operating a business without a license

Q.14 Under which amendment special provision was adopted to give the status of a state to Nagaland?

A. 10th Amendment
B. 12th Amendment
C. 13th Amendment
D. 14th Amendment

Q.15 Which device is used to determine longitude at sea?

A. Fathometer
B. Chronometer
C. Hygrometer
D. Anemometer

Q.16 Which Organization appointed Sandeep Kataria as the CEO (1st Indian to be appointed as the global CEO) of the organization?

A. Red Chief
B. Bata
C. Patanjali
D. Liberty

Q.17 Eastern ghats and Western ghats meet at the ______.

A. Annamalai hills
B. Palani hills
C. Nilgiri hills
D. None of these

Q.18 Bhangra is a folk dance of ________.

A. Arunachal Pradesh
B. Punjab
C. Assam
D. Nagaland

Q.19 Tadoba national park known for sheltering tiger, panther and bear is located in:

A. Assam
B. Maharashtra
C. Karnataka
D. Tamil Nadu

Q.20 The Rath Yatra at Puri is celebrated in honor of which Hindu deity?

A. Ram
B. Jagannath
C. Shiva
D. Vishnu

Q.21 Who invented the air conditioner?

A. John Gorrie
B. Geraud Darnis
C. David Gitlin
D. Willis Haviland Carrier

Q.22 Which state will host the Indian Women's League (IWL)?

A. Madhya Pradesh
B. Haryana
C. Odisha
D. Gujarat

Q.23 Who won the silver medal at the 72nd Strandja Memorial Boxing Tournament in Sofia, Bulgaria?

A. Deepak Kumar
B. Manish Kaushik
C. Amit Panghal
D. Satish Kumar

Q.24 What is the capital of Afghanistan?

A. Herat
B. Jalalabad
C. Kabul
D. Balkh

Q.25 Who is the current Prime Minister of Nepal?

A. Sher Bahadur Deuba
B. Madhav Kumar Nepal
C. K. P. Sharma Oli
D. Baburam Bhattarai

// Smart Answer Sheet //

Correct — Percentage of students who answered correctly. **Skipped** — Percentage of students who skipped.

Q.	Ans.	Correct / Skipped	Q.	Ans.	Correct / Skipped	Q.	Ans.	Correct / Skipped	Q.	Ans.	Correct / Skipped	Q.	Ans.	Correct / Skipped	Q.	Ans.	Correct / Skipped
1	A	48.17 % / 1.44 %	6	A	69.41 % / 1.11 %	11	C	47.67 % / 1.94 %	16	B	60.45 % / 1.9 %	21	D	12.51 % / 3.51 %			
2	B	59.93 % / 1.05 %	7	C	63.47 % / 1.83 %	12	A	76.63 % / 0.0 %	17	C	85.97 % / 0.0 %	22	C	53.96 % / 1.97 %			
3	C	83.45 % / 0.0 %	8	A	57.18 % / 1.11 %	13	B	44.28 % / 1.22 %	18	B	88.75 % / 0.0 %	23	A	18.46 % / 4.52 %			
4	D	62.28 % / 1.05 %	9	C	83.42 % / 0.0 %	14	C	45.43 % / 1.22 %	19	B	45.3 % / 1.38 %	24	C	84.0 % / 0.0 %			
5	D	64.01 % / 1.54 %	10	C	58.62 % / 1.86 %	15	B	49.48 % / 1.44 %	20	B	76.61 % / 0.0 %	25	C	48.7 % / 1.43 %			

//Hints and Solutions//

1. Allyson Felix is the only female track and field athlete to ever win six Olympic gold medals and is tied with Merlene Ottey as the most decorated female Olympian in track and field history.

- She made her Olympic debut in Athens in 2004, winning silver in the 200-meter.
- She won another silver in the same event in 2008 and gold in 2012.
- She also has a silver in the 400-meter, won in 2016, and five relay golds won from 2008-2016.

Hence, the correct option is (A).

2. Dipika Pallikal is an Indian professional squash player.

- She is the first Indian to break into the top 10 in the PSA Women's rankings.

Karnam Malleswari is a retired Indian weightlifter.

- She is the first Indian woman to win a medal at the Olympics.

Saikhom Mirabai Chanu is an Indian weightlifter.

- She was awarded the Padma Shri by the Government of India for her contributions to the sport.

Rakhi Haldar is also a weight lifter.

- In 2019, She won a bronze medal at the Qatar International Cup.

Hence, the correct option is (B).

3. The Sun gets its energy from nuclear fusion.

- Nuclear fusion is a reaction in which two or more atomic nuclei come closer enough to form one or more different atomic nuclei and subatomic particles (neutrons or protons).
    - $1H2 + 1H2 \rightarrow 2He4$
- A hydrogen bomb is an immensely powerful bomb whose destructive power comes from the rapid release of energy during the nuclear fusion of isotopes of hydrogen (deuterium and tritium), using an atom bomb as a trigger.
- Sun is the best example of nuclear fusion in which smaller nuclei of atoms fused at very high temperatures and pressure into a larger nucleus.
- This fusion happens inside the core of the sun and the energy later escapes to the surface of the sun.
- It is responsible for the generation of solar radiation.

Hence, the correct option is (C).

4. Methane explosions occur in mines when a buildup of methane gas, a byproduct of coal, comes into contact with a heat source, and there is not enough air to dilute the gas to levels below its explosion point.

Hence, the correct option is (D).

5. Iltutmish was the third ruler of the Delhi Sultanate, belonging to the Mamluk dynasty. He established a center of learning at Azimabad in Patna. He re-organized the monetary system, the nobility and also the distribution of grounds and fiefs, and erected many buildings.

Hence, the correct option is (D).

6. Lake Chad is the largest freshwater lake situated in the South Central part of the Sahara Desert. Rivers Nile and Niger are the two important rivers that flow in the Eastern and Western parts of the Sahara Desert respectively.

Hence, the correct option is (A).

7. The Khilji dynasty was a Muslim dynasty of Turkic origin, which ruled large parts of South Asia between 1290-1320.

The Mamluk dynasty was just before the Khilji dynasty from 1193-1290 and the Tughlaq dynasty was just after it from 1320-1395.

Hence, the correct option is (C).

8. There is no specific provision in our constitution to guaranteeing the freedom of the press because freedom of press is included in the wider freedom expression which is guaranteed by the Article 19(1) A.

Freedom of expression means the freedom of express not only one's own views but also the views of others and by means including printing.

Hence, the correct option is (A).

9. The basic laws of physics fall into two categories: classical physics that deals with the observable world (classical mechanics) and atomic physics that deals with the interactions between elementary and subatomic particles (quantum mechanics).

Hence, the correct option is (C).

10. A bilateral monopoly is a market structure consisting of both a monopoly (a single seller) and a monopsony (a single buyer). It was a common phenomenon in the colonial period whereby the imperial powers were the sellers of the goods and the colonized country were the sole buyers.

Hence, the correct option is (C).

11. The subjects that are not mentioned in any of the three lists are known as residuary subjects. However, there are many provisions made in the constitution out side these lists permitting parliament or state legislative assembly to legislate.

The power to legislate on residuary subjects (not mentioned anywhere in the constitution), rests with the parliament exclusively per Article 248.

Article 248 (2) of the Constitution of India says that the Parliament has exclusive power to make any law with respect to any matter not enumerated in list II and III. Such power shall include the power of making any law imposing a tax not mentioned in either of those lists.

Hence, the correct option is (C).

12. The rate of change of velocity of an object with respect to time is called acceleration. The SI unit for acceleration is metre per second squared (ms^{-2}).

The formula of acceleration,

$$a = \frac{v-u}{t}$$

Where u is the initial velocity of the object, v is the final velocity and t is the time interval.

Hence, the correct option is (A).

13. Franchising is the practice of the right to use a firm's business model and brand for a prescribed period of time. To get franchise of any company one has to take license for it than he can open an office/ outlet of that company.

Hence, the correct option is (B).

14. 13th Amendment Act 1962, this amendment was passed to implement the agreement between the leaders of the Government of India and Nagaland People's Convention. This agreement was made to treat Nagaland as a state. This added a new Article 371A to the Constitution, which has some special provisions for the administration of Nagaland.

Hence, the correct option is (C).

15. Chronometer is a time piece or timing device with a special mechanism for ensuring and adjusting its accuracy, for use in determining longitude at sea or for any purpose where very exact measurement of time is required.

Hence, the correct option is (B).

16. Sandeep Kataria, the Chief Executive Officer (CEO) of Bata India has been elevated as the CEO of Bata Organization. He becomes the 1st Indian to be appointed as the global CEO of Bata. He succeeds Alexis Nasard.

Hence, the correct option is (B).

17. The Eastern Ghats and the Western Ghats meet at Nilgiri Hills. The Eastern Ghats are a discontinuous range of mountains along India's eastern coast whereas the Western Ghats are also known as Sahyadri is a mountain range that runs parallel to the western coast of the Indian peninsula.

Hence, the correct option is (C).

18. Bhangra is a type of traditional dance of the Indian subcontinent, originating in Sialkot in the Majha area of Punjab. The dance was associated primarily with the spring harvest festival Baisakhi.

Hence, the correct option is (B).

19. In the Chandrapur district of Maharashtra lies the Tadoba National Park which shelters around 43 tigers to date. The tiger reserve is one of the fifty tiger reserves in India which also happens to be the largest and oldest national park in the state.

Hence, the correct option is (B).

20. The Rath Yatra at Puri is celebrated in honor of the Hindu deity Jagannath. Lord Jagannath is considered an avatar (incarnation) of Lord Vishnu. In fact, he has the attributes of all the avatars of Lord Vishnu.

Hence, the correct option is (B).

21. The first modern air conditioner was invented in 1902 by Willis Haviland Carrier. He was an American engineer. In 1915, he founded Carrier Corporation, a company specializing in the manufacture and distribution of heating, ventilation, and air conditioning (HVAC) systems.

Hence, the correct option is (D).

22. According to the All India Football Federation (AIFF), Odisha will host the Indian Women's League (IWL). This is the fifth edition of IWL, the top division women's league in India.

Hence, the correct option is (C).

23. Deepak Kumar (52kg) won the silver medal at the 72nd Strandja Memorial Boxing Tournament in Sofia, Bulgaria.

Hence, the correct option is (A).

24. Kabul is the capital and largest city of Afghanistan, located in the eastern section of the country. It is also a municipality, forming part of the greater Kabul Province, and divided into 22 districts.

Hence, the correct option is (C).

25. K. P. Sharma Oli (Khadga Prasad Sharma Oli) is a Nepalese politician and the current Prime Minister of Nepal.

Hence, the correct option is (C).

Q.1 A librarian purchased 60 storybooks for his library but he found that he could get 4 extra books by spending Rs 336 more and then the overall average price per book reduces by Rs 1 . The previous average price of each book was:

A. Rs 84 **B.** Rs 83 **C.** Rs 68 **D.** Rs 100

Q.2 The average of 11 results is 50. The average of the 6 results is 49 and that of the last 6 results is 52. What is the 6th result?

A. 48 **B.** 51 **C.** 56 **D.** 49

Q.3 In the following figure, O is the centre of the circle and AB is a tangent to it at point B. $\angle BDC = 65°$. Find $\angle BAO$.

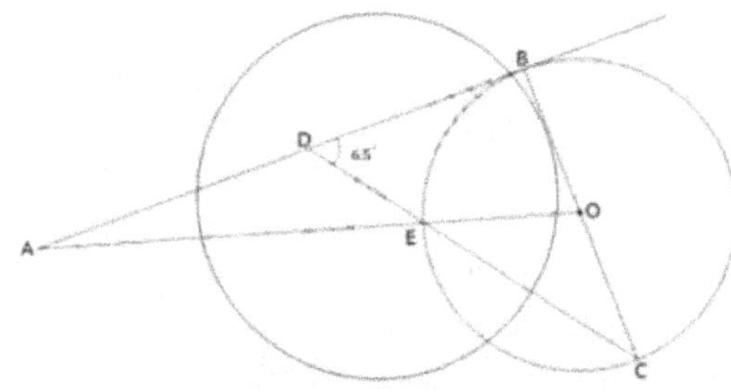

A. 40° **B.** 50° **C.** 80° **D.** 60°

Q.4 MRP of an electric iron is Rs. 75. A customer is given 2 successive discounts and it costed him Rs. 63.45 . If the first discount is 10% , what will be the second discount?

A. 5% **B.** 6.5% **C.** 4% **D.** 6%

Q.5 The LCM and HCF of two numbers are 168 and 6 respectively. If one of the numbers is 24, find the other.

A. 36 **B.** 38 **C.** 40 **D.** 42

Q.6 A dealer sold a bicycle at a profit of 10%. Had he bought the bicycle at 10% less price and sold it at a price Rs 60 more, he would have gained 25%. The cost price of the bicycle was:

A. 2,400 **B.** 2,200 **C.** 2,000 **D.** 2,600

Q.7 The area of a rectangle is 42sq.cm and its length is 7cm. Find its perimeter.

A. 14 cm **B.** 21 cm **C.** 26 cm **D.** 24 cm

Q.8 A truck travels at 90 km/hr for the first $1\frac{1}{2}$ hours. After that, it travels at 70km/hr. Find the time taken by the truck to travel 310 km.

A. 2.5 hrs **B.** 3 hrs **C.** 3.5 hrs **D.** 4 hrs

Q.9 A contractor undertook to make a road in 40 days and employed 25 men. After 24 days, he finds that only one-third of the road has been made. How many extra men should he employ so that he could able to complete the work 4 days earlier?

A. 100 **B.** 125 **C.** 110 **D.** 75

Q.10 The marked price of a watch is 800 . A shopkeeper gives two successive discounts and sells the watch at 612 . If the first discount is 10%, the second discount is:

A. 14% **B.** 13% **C.** 15% **D.** 12%

Q.11 What is the total surface area of a right circular cone of height 14 cm and base radius 7 cm?

A. $498.35\ cm^2$ **B.** $128.35\ cm^2$
C. $328.35\ cm^2$ **D.** $454.25\ cm^2$

Q.12 If $A:B:C = 2:3:4,$ then the ratio $\frac{A}{B}:\frac{B}{C}:\frac{C}{A}$ is equal to-

A. 8: 9: 16 **B.** 8: 9: 12 **C.** 4: 9: 16 **D.** 8: 9: 24

Q.13 If each side of a square is increased by 25%. What is the increase % in its area?

A. 15% **B.** 20% **C.** 44% **D.** 40%

Q.14 Sonu invented 10% more than the investment of Mona and Mona invested 10% less than the investment of Raghu. If the total investment of all the three persons is 5780 , find the investment of Raghu.

A. Rs 2010 **B.** Rs 2000 **C.** Rs 2100 **D.** Rs 2210

Q.15 Value of $\sin34° + \cos64° - \cos4°$ is?

A. 2 **B.** 0 **C.** 1 **D.** 3

Q.16 20 men working 10 hours per day can finish $\frac{2^{rd}}{3}$ of the work in 12 days, whille 15 women working 9 hours per day can finish $\frac{2^{th}}{5}$ of the work in X days. If one woman is twice as efficient as one man, then what is the value of X ?

A. $2\frac{2}{3}$ **B.** $3\frac{3}{5}$ **C.** $5\frac{1}{3}$ **D.** $6\frac{2}{5}$

Q.17 Manu sold a dozen watches for Rs.1454.64 per watch and made a profit of 16%. Find the cost price of a watch?

A. 1294 **B.** 1354 **C.** 1254 **D.** 1634

Q.18 If by selling 20 cycles Vinay incurs a loss equal to the selling price of 2 cycles, find his loss percentage.

A. 10% **B.** 11% **C.** $13\frac{1}{3}\%$ **D.** $9\frac{1}{11}\%$

Q.19 What will Rs. 40,000 amount to in 2 years at the rate of 20% p.a., if interest is compounded yearly?

A. Rs. 48,620 **B.** Rs. 58,564
C. Rs. 57,600 **D.** Rs. 60,000

Q.20 How long will it take for a sum of money to double itself if it is invested at a 9.09% rate of simple interest?

A. 12 year **B.** 14 year **C.** 11 year **D.** 13 year

Q.21 A train having a length of 500 m passes through a tunnel of 1000 m in 1 minute. What is the speed of the train in Km/hr?

A. 75 Km/hr

B. 90 Km/hr

C. 87 Km/hr

D. 96 Km/h

Ques (22-25):Directions: Answer the following question based on the information given below.

The table below shows the number of cases of various crimes reported at police stations in different states in 2015-16.

State	Domestic Violance	Dowry	Rape	Molestation	Trafficking
UP	354	496	263	132	342
MP	376	225	216	125	117
HP	87	125	53	56	57
Kerala	535	352	226	364	126
Gujarat	455	225	252	175	144
Bihar	475	576	675	764	852
Punjab	245	256	259	261	263
Assam	278	274	276	252	363

Q.22 How many cases have been reported from Gujarat in all?

A. 1751   **B.** 1331   **C.** 1251   **D.** 1221

Q.23 The Domestic violance and Dowry cases reported in Bihar are what percent more/less than the Rape and Trafficking cases reported in Punjab?

A. 98.7% less

B. 101.3% more

C. 101.3% less

D. 98.7% more

Q.24 Based on the average number of Rape and Molestation cases reported per state, Molestation is approximately how many times as prevalent as Rape?

A. 1.04   **B.** 0.96   **C.** 0.92   **D.** 0.86

Q.25 The total number of Dowry and Molestation cases reported in UP is approximate what percent of the total cases reported in that state, across all crimes?

A. 40   **B.** 45   **C.** 37   **D.** 47

// Smart Answer Sheet //

Correct — Percentage of students who answered correctly.   **Skipped** — Percentage of students who skipped.

Q.	Ans.	Correct / Skipped	Q.	Ans.	Correct / Skipped	Q.	Ans.	Correct / Skipped	Q.	Ans.	Correct / Skipped	Q.	Ans.	Correct / Skipped	Q.	Ans.	Correct / Skipped
1	D	87.12 % / 0.0 %	6	A	18.64 % / 4.94 %	11	A	81.54 % / 0.0 %	16	C	68.5 % / 1.46 %	21	B	80.0 % / 0.0 %			
2	C	63.91 % / 1.57 %	7	C	77.17 % / 0.0 %	12	D	44.69 % / 1.58 %	17	C	44.49 % / 1.39 %	22	C	63.56 % / 1.36 %			
3	A	32.48 % / 3.04 %	8	D	43.15 % / 1.5 %	13	C	85.77 % / 0.0 %	18	D	54.17 % / 1.21 %	23	B	45.21 % / 1.02 %			
4	D	45.53 % / 1.5 %	9	D	47.65 % / 1.27 %	14	B	11.43 % / 3.82 %	19	C	59.85 % / 1.37 %	24	B	66.21 % / 1.33 %			
5	D	77.56 % / 0.0 %	10	C	85.46 % / 0.0 %	15	B	48.37 % / 1.62 %	20	C	65.72 % / 1.08 %	25	A	51.82 % / 1.46 %			

//Hints and Solutions//

1. Let the previous average price be P.

According to the question,

$\Rightarrow 60P + 336 = (P - 1)64$

$\Rightarrow 60P + 336 = 64P - 64$

$\Rightarrow 64P - 60P = 336 + 64$

$\Rightarrow 4P = 400$

$\Rightarrow P = \dfrac{400}{4} = $ Rs 100

Hence, the correct option is (D).

2. According to the question,

The average of 11 numbers is = 50

The total of 11 results = 11 $\times$ 50 = 550

The sum of the first 6 results = 6 $\times$ 49 = 294

And the sum of the last 6 results = 6 $\times$ 51 - 312

So the 6th result = (294 + 312) - 550 = 56

Hence, the correct option is (C).

3. Form the given figure OB is the radius and therefore in triangle BDC.

$\angle DBC + \angle BDC + \angle BCD = 180°$

$\Rightarrow 90° + 65° + \angle BCD = 180°$

$\Rightarrow \angle BCD = 25$

Now, $OE = OC = $ radius, $\angle OEC = \angle OCE = 25°(\angle OCE = \angle BCD)$

$\Rightarrow \angle AED = \angle OEC = 25°$ (Vertically opposite angles)

Also, $\angle ADE = 180° - 65° = 115°$

Therefore in triangle AED $\angle BAO = 180° - 115° - 25° = 40°$

Hence, the correct option is (A).

4. Given:

MRP of an electric iron = Rs. 75

Price after 10% discounts $= 75 \times \dfrac{90}{100} = 67.5$

Diffrence $= 67.5 - 63.45 = 4.05$

Second discount $= \dfrac{4.05}{67.5} \times 100 = 6\%$

Hence, the correct option is (D).

5. We know that,

product of two numbers = L.C.M. × H.C.F. of those numbers

Let the second number be x.

$24 \times x = 168 \times 6$

$\Rightarrow x = 6 \times 7$

$\Rightarrow x = 42$

Hence, the correct option is (D).

6. Let the CP of bicycle = Rs x

Old SP of bicycle $= x \times 110\%$ ....(i)

Now, new $CP = x \times 90\%$

and new $SP = x \times 90\% \times 125\%$ ...(ii)

Difference between new SP and old SP

$x \times 90\% \times 125\% - x \times 110\% = 60$

$\Rightarrow \dfrac{x \times 11250}{10000} - \dfrac{x \times 110}{100} = 60$

$\Rightarrow x \left[\dfrac{1125 - 1100}{1000} \right] = 60$

$\Rightarrow x \left[\dfrac{60000}{25} \right]$

$\Rightarrow x = 2400$ Rs

Hence, the correct option is (A).

7. Given:

Area of rectangle = 42 sq.cm

Length of the rectangle (l) = 7 cm

Let the breadth be "b" cm.

We know that, Area of rectangle = Length × breadth

7 × b = 42

$\Rightarrow$ b = 6 cm

Perimeter = 2(l + b) = 2(7 + 6) = 26 cm

Hence, the correct option is (C).

8. We know that, Distance = Speed $\times$ Time

Distance covered by truck in $1\dfrac{1}{2}$ or $\dfrac{3}{2}$ hours

$= 90 \times 32 = 135$ km

Remaining distance $= 310 - 135 = 175$ km

Time taken at 70 kmph $= \dfrac{175}{70} = 2.5$ hours

Total time $= 1.5 + 2.5 = 4$ hours

Hence, the correct option is (D).

9. Given:

Scheduled time to complete the work $= 40$ days

25 men in 24 days do $\frac{1}{3}$ work.

$\therefore$ 1 man in 1 day does $= \dfrac{1}{3 \times 25 \times 24} = \dfrac{1}{1800}$ work.

Work remaining $= 1 - \dfrac{1}{3} = \dfrac{2}{3}$

The work is to be completed 4 days before schedule i.e., in

$(40 - 4) = 36$ days

Number of days left for $\frac{2}{3}$ rd work $= 36 - 24 = 12$ days

work is done in 1 day by 1 man.

$\therefore \frac{2}{3}$ work will be done in 12 days by

$= 1800 \times \dfrac{2}{3} \times \dfrac{1}{12} = 100$ men

25 men are already working

$\therefore$ Extra men to be employed $= 100 - 25 = 75$

Hence, the correct option is (D).

10. Given:

Marked price Rs 800 , First discount $= 10\%$

$\therefore$ Net price after the first discount $= 90\%$ of Rs 800

$= 0.9 \times$ Rs 800 = Rs 720

Final price after the second discount = Rs 612

$\therefore$ Second discount= Rs 720 - Rs 612 = Rs 108

$\Rightarrow$ Second discount rate $\dfrac{108}{720} \times 100\% = 15\%$

Hence, the correct option is (C).

11. Given:

Height $(h) = 14\ cm$ and radius $(r) = 7\ cm$

Using formula: length ^{2} = height ^{2} + radius ^{2} $l^2 = h^2 + r^2$

So, $l^2 = (14)^2 + (7)^2 = 245$

$l = 7\sqrt{5}\ cm$

Therefore, total surface area $= \pi r l + \pi r^2 = \dfrac{22}{7} \times 7 \times 7\sqrt{5} + \dfrac{22}{7} \times 7 \times 7$

$= 154(\sqrt{5} + 1)$

$= (154 \times 3.236) cm^2$

$= 498.35\ cm^2$

Hence, the correct option is (A).

12. Given:

$A : B : C = 2 : 3 : 4$

Let, $A = 2x,\ B = 3x, C = 4x$

$\therefore \dfrac{A}{B} : \dfrac{B}{C} : \dfrac{C}{A} = \dfrac{2x}{3x} : \dfrac{3x}{4x} : \dfrac{4x}{2x}$

$\Rightarrow \dfrac{2}{3} : \dfrac{3}{4} : \dfrac{2}{1}$

Multiply by the L.C.M of denominator to remove fraction

So, L.C.M of $(3,4,1) = 12$

$\therefore \dfrac{A}{B} : \dfrac{B}{C} : \dfrac{C}{A}$

$\Rightarrow \dfrac{2}{3} \times 12 : \dfrac{3}{4} \times 12 : \dfrac{2}{1} \times 12$

$\Rightarrow 8 : 9 : 24$

Hence, the correct option is (D).

13. Let each side of the square be a, then area $= a^2$

As given that the side is increased by 25%, then

New side $= \dfrac{125a}{100} = \dfrac{5a}{4}$

New area $= \left(\dfrac{5a}{4}\right)^2 = \dfrac{25a^2}{16}$

Increased area $= \dfrac{25a^2}{16} - a^2$

Increase $\% = \dfrac{\left[\dfrac{9a^2}{16}\right]}{a^2} \times 100\% = 56.25\%$

Hence, the correct option is (C).

14. Let Mona's investment $=$ Rs 100

Sonu's investment = Rs 110 and Raghu's investment $= \dfrac{100}{90} \times 100 =$ Rs $\dfrac{1000}{9}$

Ratio of Mona's, Sonu's and Raghu's investments $= 100 : 110 : \dfrac{1000}{9}$

$= 90 : 99 : 100$

Sum of ratios $= 90 + 99 + 100 = 289$

Raghu's investment = Rs $\left(\dfrac{100}{289} \times 5870\right)$

= Rs 2000

Hence, the correct option is (B).

15. Given:

$\sin 34° + \cos 64° - \cos 4°$

$= \sin 34° + [\cos 64° - \cos 4°]$

According to the formula,

$$\cos C - \cos D = 2\sin\left[\frac{(C+D)}{2}\right]\sin\left[\frac{(D-C)}{2}\right]$$

$$= \sin 34° + \left[-2\sin\left(\frac{64+4}{2}\right)\sin\left(\frac{4-64}{2}\right)\right]$$

$$= \sin 34° + 2\sin 34°\sin(-30)°$$

$$= \sin 34° - 2\sin 34°\sin 30°$$

$$= \sin 34° - 2\sin 34°\left(\frac{1}{2}\right)$$

$$= \sin 34° - \sin 34°$$

$$= 0$$

$$\therefore \sin 34° + \cos 64° - \cos 4° = 0$$

Hence, the correct option is (B).

16. Given:
$M_1 = 20, D_1 = 12, H_1 = 10, W_1 = \frac{2}{3}, M_2 = 15, D_2 = X, H_2 = 9, W_2 = \frac{2}{5}$

According to the question, one woman is twice as efficient as one man

So, the ratio of efficiency of woman and man is 2: 1 $\Rightarrow \dfrac{E_2}{E_1} = \dfrac{2}{1}$

Now, using MDH formula we get

$$\frac{M_1 D_1 H_1 E_1}{W_1} = \frac{M_2 D_2 H_2 E_2}{W_2}$$

$$\Rightarrow \frac{20\times12\times10}{\frac{2}{3}} = \frac{15\times X\times9}{\frac{2}{5}} \times \frac{E_2}{E_1}$$

$$\Rightarrow \frac{2400\times3}{2} = \frac{135\times5\times X}{2} \times 2$$

$$\Rightarrow X = 5\frac{1}{3} \text{ days}$$

Hence, the correct option is (C).

17. Let, the cost price of all the watches is x.

The selling price of one dozen watches = 12 × 1454.64
=Rs. 17455.68

But the selling price at 16% profit is = x+ $\dfrac{16x}{100}$ =1.16x

So, 1.16x = 17455.68

$\therefore$ x = 15048 Rs.

Cost Price of dozen watches = Rs.15048

Cost Price of each watch = Rs. $\dfrac{15048}{12}$ = Rs.1254

Hence, the correct option is (C).

18. Let the selling price of each cycle = x

Then loss = 2x

Selling price = 20x

Cost price = selling price + loss

= 20x + 2x = 22x

$$\text{Loss\%} = \left(\frac{Loss}{Cost\ price}\right) \times 100$$

$$= \frac{2x}{22x} \times 100 = \frac{100}{11} = 9\frac{1}{11}\%$$

Hence, the correct option is (D).

19. Given:

$$P = 40000 \text{ Rs.}, \quad r = 20\% \text{ and } \quad n = 2 \text{ years}$$

If P amount compounded yearly at $r\%$ rate of interest for n years, then amount become

$$A = P\left(1 + \frac{r}{100}\right)^n$$

$$= 40000\left(1 + \frac{20}{100}\right)^2$$

$$= 40000(1.2)^2$$

$$= 40000 \times 1.44$$

$$= 57600$$

Hence, the correct option is (C).

20. Given:

$$R = 9.09\%$$

We know that, $SI = \dfrac{P \times R \times T}{100}$, and $A = P + SI$

Here, Sl = Simple interset, P = Principle, A = Amount, R = Rate, and T = Time

According to the question, $A = 2P$

$$\Rightarrow 2P = P + \left(\frac{P \times 9.09 \times T}{100}\right)$$

$$\Rightarrow P = \frac{9.09PT}{100}$$

$$\Rightarrow T = \frac{100}{9.09} \approx 11 \text{ year}$$

Hence, the correct option is (C).

21. Let the speed of the train be x m/s.

Given the length of the train $= 500$ m

Length of the tunnel $= 1000$ m

Time taken to pass the tunnel $= 1$ minute $= 60$ seconds

$$\therefore x = \frac{(500+1000)}{60}$$

$$\Rightarrow x = 25 \text{ m/s}$$

Speed of the train in km/hr $= \left(25 \times \dfrac{18}{5}\dfrac{km}{hr}\right)$ = 90 km/hr

Hence, the correct option is (B).

22. Total cases reported from Gujarat = 455 + 225 + 252 + 175 + 144 = 1251

Hence, the correct option is (C).

23. Domestic Violance and Dowry in Bihar = 475 + 576 = 1051

Rape and Trafficking in Punjab = 259 + 263 = 522

Difference = 1051 − 522 = 529

$$\therefore \quad \text{Required } \% = \frac{529}{522} \times 100 = 101.3\% \text{ more}$$

Hence, the correct option is (B).

24. Total cases reported on Molestation = 132 + 125 + 56 + 364 + 175 + 764 + 261 + 252 = 2129

Total cases reported on Rape = 263 + 216 + 53 + 226 + 252 + 675 + 259 + 276 = 2220

$\therefore$ Required ratio = 2129 : 2220 = 0.96

Hence, the correct option is (B).

25. Total number of Dowry and Molestation cases reported in UP = 496 + 132 = 628

Total cases reported in UP = 496 + 132 + 354 + 263 + 342 = 1587

$$\therefore \text{Required } \% = \frac{628}{1587} \times 100 = 39.57\%$$

The closest value in the options is 40%.

Hence, the correct option is (A).

Q.1 10 men working 6 hours a day, can complete a work in 18 days. How many hours a day must 15 men work, to complete the same work in 12 days?

A. 4   **B.** 5   **C.** 6   **D.** 7

Q.2 In a Company, the average income of all the employees is Rs.20,000 per month. Recently the company announced increment of Rs. 2000 per month for all the employees. The new average income of all the employees is

A. Rs. 22,000   **B.** Rs. 24,000

C. Rs. 28,000   **D.** Rs. 26,000

Q.3 Suresh started his journey form P to Q by his bike at the speed of 40 km/h and then, the same distance he travelled on his foot at the speed of 10 km/h from Q to R. Then he returned from R to P via Q at the speed of 24 km/h. The average speed of the whole trip is:

A. 18.5 km/h   **B.** 19.8 km/h

C. 18.2 km/h   **D.** 19.2 km/h

Q.4 The true discount on a bill of Rs. 540 is Rs. 90. The banker's discount is-

A. Rs. 60   **B.** Rs. 108   **C.** Rs. 72   **D.** Rs. 75

Q.5 The H.C.F. of two numbers is 4 and the two other factors of L.C.M. are 5 and 7. Find the smaller of the two numbers.

A. 10   **B.** 4   **C.** 20   **D.** 28

Q.6 Find the simple interest on the Rs. 2000 at the rate of $\frac{25}{4}\%$ per annum for the period from 4 th Feb 2005 to 18 th April 2005.

A. 25   **B.** 30   **C.** 35   **D.** 40

Q.7 Bala travels the first one-third of the total distance at the speed of 10 km/h and the next one-third distance at the speed of 20 km/h and the last one-third distance at the speed of 60 km/h. What is the average speed of Bala?

A. 18 km/h   **B.** 19 km/h   **C.** 16 km/h   **D.** 12 km/h

Q.8 Tell the measurement of an angle that is equal to the measurement of its complementary angle?

A. 90°   **B.** 45°   **C.** 80°   **D.** 100°

Q.9 A truck moves at the speed of 84 after repairing and moves at the speed of 74 before repairing. It covers x distance in 6 hours after repair. How much time (in hours) will if take to cover $3x$ distance before repairing?

A. 48.12   **B.** 40.31   **C.** 20.43   **D.** 28.32

Q.10 A single discount equivalent to successive discounts of $20\%, 10\%$ and 5% is

A. 36.1%   **B.** 35%   **C.** 35.6%   **D.** 31.6%

Q.11 A candidate who gets 20% marks in an examination fails by 30 marks but another candidate who gets 32% gets 42 marks more than the pass marks. Then the percentage of pass marks is:

A. 52%   **B.** 50%   **C.** 33%   **D.** 25%

Q.12 The average expenditure of Mr. Sharma for January to June is Rs. 4200 and he spent Rs. 1200 in January and Rs. 1500 in July. The average expenditure for the months of February to July is?

[Intelligence Bureau Security Assistant, 2017]

A. Rs. 2750   **B.** Rs. 3250   **C.** Rs. 4250   **D.** Rs. 4500

Q.13 The ratio of incomes of A, B and C is 7: 9: 12 and that of their expenditures is 8: 9: 15 . If A saves $\frac{1}{4}$ th of his income then find the ratio of their savings?

A. 56: 99: 69   **B.** 69: 56: 99

C. 99: 56: 69   **D.** 99: 69: 56

Q.14 If 64 identical small spheres are made out of a big sphere of diameter 8 cm what is the surface area of each small sphere?

A. $\pi\ cm^2$ **B.** $2\pi\ cm^2$ **C.** $4\pi\ cm^2$ **D.** $8\pi\ cm^2$

Q.15 The average of 17 numbers is 7. If one number is excluded, the average becomes $4.$ What is the excluded number?

A. 21   **B.** 55   **C.** 24   **D.** 20

Q.16 Rs. 1500 were invested for 5 years in Scheme A which offers simple interest the rate of 14% p.a. The amount received after 5 years and some additional money, is then invested in Scheme B, for 2 years, which offers compound interest (compounded annually) at the rate of 20% p.a. If the compound interest received from Scheme B after 2 years is Rs. 1408 . What was the additional amount invested in Scheme B apart from the amount from Scheme A?

A. 450   **B.** 550   **C.** 500   **D.** 650

Q.17 If there are $0 \le \theta \le 90°$, and $\sin(8\theta + 12°) = \cos(4\theta + 6°)$, what is the value of θ (in degrees)?

A. 4°   **B.** 16°   **C.** 6°   **D.** 12°

Q.18 Aparna changes the marked price of an item to 50% above its C.P. What % of discount allowed in approximately to gain10%?

A. 27%   **B.** 25%   **C.** 35%   **D.** 37%

Q.19 $ABCD$ is a concyclic quadrilateral. The tangents at A and C intersect each other at P. If $\angle ABC = 100°$ then what is $\angle APC$ equal to?

A. 10°   **B.** 20°   **C.** 30°   **D.** 40°

Q.20 Two secants AB and CD of a circle intersect at point P externally, If AB =6 cm, CD = 3 cm and PD =4cm, then find the length of PB.

A. 5 cm **B.** 7.35 cm **C.** 6 cm **D.** 4 cm

Q.21 $\triangle ABC$ is right angled triangle with $AB = 6\ cm, BC = 8\ cm. O$ is the in-centre of the triangle. The radius of the in-circle is:

A. 2 cm **B.** 5 cm **C.** 4 cm **D.** 3 cm

Ques (22-25):Directions Study the following bar chart carefully and answer the question given beside.

In the bar chart, the total numbers of students enrolled in different years from 2015 to 2019 in Sunshine and Aryan Summer camps are given.

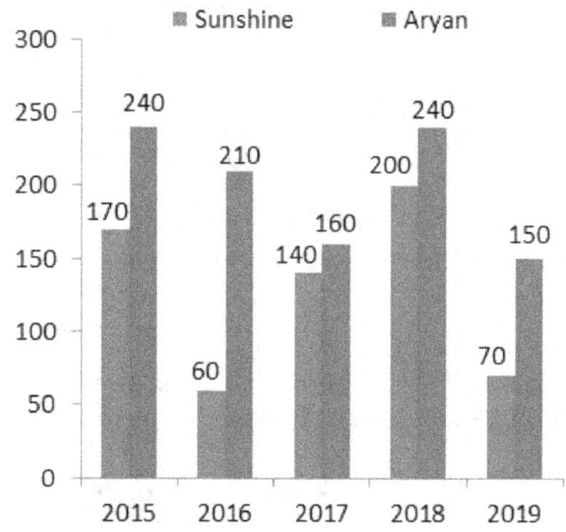

Q.22 If in the year 2020 there is 30% increase in total number of students enrolled as compared to 2019, find the total number of students enrolled in 2020?

A. 286 **B.** 245 **C.** 292 **D.** 234

Q.23 What is the ratio between total students in 2016 to the total students in 2019 of both summer camps?

A. 25 : 21 **B.** 27 : 22 **C.** 29 : 12 **D.** 31 : 11

Q.24 The number of students of Sunshine in 2015 is what percentage of the number of students of Aryan in 2017?

A. 101.25% **B.** 111.25% **C.** 106.25% **D.** 124.25%

Q.25 The total number of students enrolled in Sunshine from 2016 to 2019 is what percentage more than the total number of students enrolled in Aryan in 2018 and 2019?

A. 10.51% **B.** 15.51% **C.** 11.51% **D.** 20.51%

// Smart Answer Sheet //

Correct — Percentage of students who answered correctly. **Skipped** — Percentage of students who skipped.

Q.	Ans.	Correct / Skipped	Q.	Ans.	Correct / Skipped	Q.	Ans.	Correct / Skipped	Q.	Ans.	Correct / Skipped	Q.	Ans.	Correct / Skipped	Q.	Ans.	Correct / Skipped
1	C	89.98 % / 0.0 %	6	A	88.05 % / 0.0 %	11	D	58.69 % / 1.72 %	16	D	24.69 % / 3.73 %	21	A	29.73 % / 3.9 %			
2	A	57.7 % / 1.8 %	7	A	64.69 % / 1.69 %	12	C	40.67 % / 1.29 %	17	C	49.96 % / 1.27 %	22	A	41.64 % / 1.01 %			
3	D	62.63 % / 1.86 %	8	B	43.9 % / 1.91 %	13	A	65.54 % / 1.4 %	18	A	65.78 % / 1.19 %	23	B	59.62 % / 1.75 %			
4	B	80.42 % / 0.0 %	9	C	32.76 % / 4.18 %	14	C	68.98 % / 1.74 %	19	B	48.34 % / 1.88 %	24	C	43.78 % / 1.8 %			
5	C	82.66 % / 0.0 %	10	D	29.47 % / 3.67 %	15	B	79.42 % / 0.0 %	20	A	16.51 % / 4.65 %	25	D	56.98 % / 1.2 %			

//Hints and Solutions//

1. Given that,

$M_1 = 10, M_2 = 15$

$D_1 = 18, D_2 = 12$

$H_1 = 6$ and $H_2 = ?$

We know that, $M_1 D_1 H_1 = M_2 D_2 H_2$

$\Rightarrow 10 \times 18 \times 6 = 15 \times 12 \times H_2$

$\Rightarrow 180 \times 6 = 180 \times H_2$

$\Rightarrow H_2 = 6$

Hence, the correct option is (C).

2. The average income of all the employees is 20,000 per month.

The company announced an increment is 2000 per month for all employees.

$$\text{Average income} = \frac{\text{Total salary paid to all employees}}{\text{Number of employees}}$$

∵ Income is increased of each employee by the same value.

⇒ New average = Actual average salary + Increment per employee

∴ New average income = 20,000 + 2,000 = Rs. 22,000.00

Hence, the correct option is (A).

3. Given:

Suresh started his journey from P to Q by his bike at the speed of = 40 km/h

The same distance he travelled on his foot from Q to R at the speed = 10 km/hr

Then he returned from R to P via Q at the speed of = 24 km/hr

According to the question,

PQ = QR

RP = 2PQ

$$\text{Formula: Average speed} = \frac{\text{Total distance}}{\text{Total time}}$$

Let the distance between P and Q be 120 km.

⇒ PQ = QR = 120 km

⇒ RP = 2 × 120 = 240 km

$$\text{Time taken by Suresh from point P to Q} = \frac{\text{Distance}}{\text{Speed}} = \frac{120}{40} =$$

3 hours

$$\text{Time taken by Suresh from point Q to R} = \frac{\text{Distance}}{\text{Speed}} = \frac{120}{10} =$$

12 hours

$$\text{Time taken by Suresh from point R to P} = \frac{\text{Distance}}{\text{Speed}} = \frac{240}{24} =$$

10 hours

$$\text{Average Speed} = \frac{(120+120+240)}{(3+12+10)} = \frac{480}{25} = 19.2 \text{ km/hr}$$

Hence, the correct option is (D).

4. Present worth of bill = Rs. (540 - 90) = Rs. 450

∴ Simple interest on Rs. 450 = Rs. 90

$$\text{Simple interest on Rs. 540 = Rs. } \frac{90}{450} \times 540 = \text{Rs. 108}$$

banker's discount = Rs. 108

Hence, the correct option is (B).

5. Let the two numbers be 4x and 4y.

L.C.M. = 4 × 5 × 7

Since x and y are coprime numbers.

x = 5 and y = 7

Smaller number = 4 × 5 = 20

Hence, the correct option is (C).

6. Always remember that the day on which money is deposited is not counted while the day on which money is withdrawn is counted.

So, let's calculate the number of days now,

$$\text{Time} = (24 + 31 + 18) \text{ days} = \frac{73}{365} \text{ years} = \frac{1}{5} \text{ years}$$

$P = 2000$ and $R = \frac{25}{4}\%$

We know that,

$$S.I. = \frac{P \times R \times T}{100}$$

$$\Rightarrow S.I. = \frac{2000 \times 25 \times 1}{4 \times 5 \times 100} = 25$$

Hence, the correct option is (A).

7. Given:

Bala travels first one-third of the total distance at the speed of = 10 km/h

The next one-third distance at the speed of = 20 km/h

The last one – third distance at the speed of = 60 km/h

$$\text{Formula: Average speed} = \frac{\text{Total distance}}{\text{Total time}}$$

Let the total distance be 180 km.

$$\Rightarrow \frac{1^{rd}}{3} \text{ of total distance} = 180 \times \left(\frac{1}{3}\right) = 60 \text{ km}$$

Time taken by Bala to cover first one-third of the total distance $= \frac{60}{10} = 6$ hrs

Time taken by Bala to cover next one-third of the total distance

$$= \frac{60}{20} = 3 \text{ hrs}$$

Time taken by Bala to cover last one-third of the total distance

$$= \frac{60}{60} = 1 \text{ hrs}$$

Average speed $= \dfrac{\text{Total time}}{\text{total distance}} = \dfrac{180}{(6+3+1)} = \dfrac{180}{10} = 18$ km/hr

Hence, the correct option is (A).

8. Let one of the two equal complementary angles is x.

$$x + x = 90°$$

$$\Rightarrow 2x = 90°$$

$$\Rightarrow 2x = 45°$$

$\therefore 45°$ is equal to its complement.

Hence, the right option is (B).

9. Given: After repairing,

Speed $=84$ km/hr

Time taken $= 6$ hours

Distance covered $=$ speed $\times$ time $= 84 \times 6 = 504$ km

Let, Distance covered $x = 504$ km

Before repairing:

$$\Rightarrow \text{Distance} = 3x = 3 \times 504 = 1512 \text{ km}$$

$$\Rightarrow \text{Speed} = 74 \text{ km/hr}$$

$$\therefore \text{Time taken} = \frac{Distance}{speed} = \frac{1512}{74} = 20.43 \text{ hr}$$

Hence, the correct option is (C).

10. Successive discount $= 20\%, 10\%$ and 5%

Let M.P. Rs. $= 100$

$\therefore$ S.P. after three discounts,

$$\therefore \text{S.P.} = \frac{\text{M.P.} (100 - \text{Discount})}{100}$$

$$= \frac{100(100-20)(100-10)(100-5)}{100 \times 100 \times 100}$$

$$= \frac{100 \times 80 \times 90 \times 95}{100 \times 100 \times 100}$$

$$= \frac{342}{5}$$

$$\therefore \text{Total discount} = 100 - \frac{342}{5}$$

$$= \frac{500-342}{5} = \frac{158}{5}$$

$$\therefore \text{Single discount} = \frac{158}{5}\% = 31.6\%$$

Hence, the correct option is (D).

11. Let the maximum marks $= x$

According to the question,

Case (i) Pass marks $= \dfrac{20x}{100} + 30$

Case (ii) Pass marks $= \dfrac{32x}{100} - 42$

Pass marks would be the same in both cases.

$$\frac{20x}{100} + 30 = \frac{32x}{100} - 42$$

$$\Rightarrow \frac{12x}{100} = 72$$

$$\Rightarrow x = 600$$

Thus total marks $x = 600$

Required percentage $= \dfrac{\text{Pass marks}}{\text{Total marks}} \times 100$

$$= \frac{150}{600} \times 100 = 25\%$$

Hence, the correct option is (D).

12. Given:

The average expenditure of Mr. Sharma for the months January to June is Rs 4200.

Mr. Sharma spent Rs 1200 in January,

Mr. Sharma spent Rs 1500 in the month of July,

Formula: Average $= \dfrac{\text{Sum of all observation}}{\text{Total number of all observation}}$

Total expenditure of Mr. Sharma for January to June = 6 × 4200 = Rs 25200

$\Rightarrow$ Total expenditure of Mr. Sharma for the month February to June = 25200 – 1200

= Rs 24000

Total expenditure of Mr. Sharma for the months February to July = 24000 + 1500 = Rs 25500

$\therefore$ Average expenditure for the months February to July $= \dfrac{25500}{6} = $ Rs 4250

Hence, the correct option is (C).

13. Let the incomes of A, B and C be $7x, 9x$ and $12x$ respectively and spendings be $8y, 9y$ and $15y$ respectively.

According to the question,

$$\Rightarrow 7x - 8y = \frac{1}{4} \times 7x$$

$$\Rightarrow 7x - \frac{7x}{4} = 8y$$

$$\Rightarrow 28x - 7x = 32y$$

$$\Rightarrow 21x = 32y$$

$$\Rightarrow y = \frac{21}{22}x$$

As a saves $\dfrac{1}{4}$ of his income.

$\therefore$ A's savings $= \dfrac{7x}{4}$

B 's saving $= 9x - 9y = 9(x - y)$

$= 9\left(x - \dfrac{21x}{32}\right)$

$= \dfrac{9 \times 11x}{32} = \dfrac{99x}{32}$

C 's saving $= 12x - 15y = 12x - 15 \times \dfrac{21}{32}x = \dfrac{69x}{32}$

$\therefore$ Required ratio $= \dfrac{7x}{4} : \dfrac{99x}{32} : \dfrac{69x}{32}$

$= 56 : 99 : 69$

Hence, the correct option is (A).

14. Given that, the diameter of the big sphere = 8 cm

$\therefore$ Radius of the big sphere (R) =4 cm

Let the radius of each small sphere $= r$

We know that,

The Volume of each small sphere $= \dfrac{\text{Volume of big sphere}}{\text{Number of a small sphere}}$

$\Rightarrow \dfrac{4}{3}\pi r^3 = \dfrac{\frac{4}{3}\pi R^3}{64}$

$\Rightarrow r^3 = \dfrac{(4)^3}{64} = 1$

$\Rightarrow r = 1$ cm

Now, the surface area of each small sphere $= 4\pi r^2 = 4\pi(1)^2 = 4\pi \ cm^2$

Hence, the correct option is (C).

15. Let the excluded number be x.

Average of 17 numbers $= 7$

$\therefore$ Sum of 17 numbers $= 17 \times 7 = 119$

According to the question,

$119 - x = (17 - 1) \times 4$

$119 - x = 64$

$x = 55$

$\therefore$ the excluded number $= 55$

Hence, the correct option is (B).

16. We know that, S.I. $= \dfrac{\text{Principle} \times \text{Time} \times \text{Rate}}{100}$

$= \dfrac{1500 \times 5 \times 14}{100} = $ Rs 1050

Amount $=$ Rs. $(1500 + 1050)$ =Rs. 2550

If additional amount be Rs. x, then

$CI = P\left[\left(\dfrac{1+R}{100}\right)^T - 1\right]$

$\Rightarrow 1408 = (2550 + x)\left(\dfrac{36}{25} - 1\right)$

$\Rightarrow 1408 = (2550 + x)\left(\dfrac{36-25}{25}\right)$

$\Rightarrow (2550 + x) = \dfrac{1408 \times 25}{11} = 3200$

$\Rightarrow x = 3200 - 2550 = $ Rs. 650

Hence, the correct option is (D)

17. Given:

$\sin(8\theta + 12°) = \cos(4\theta + 6°)$

$\sin(8\theta + 12°) = \sin[90° - (4\theta + 6°)]$
$[\because \cos\theta = \sin(90° - \theta)]$

$8\theta + 12° = 90° - 4\theta - 6°$

$= 8\theta + 4\theta = 84° - 12°$

$\Rightarrow 12\theta = 72°$

$\Rightarrow \theta = \dfrac{72°}{12} = 6°$

$\Rightarrow \theta = 6°$

Hence, the correct option is (C).

18. As per the given data,

Let the cost price be Rs. 100, then marked price = Rs.150

Given required gain = 10%

$\therefore$ Selling price = Rs. 110

We know that discount = Marked price - selling price

So, discount = 150 - 110 = 40

Discount percentage $= \dfrac{40}{150} \times 100 = 26.66\% \approx 27\%$

Hence, the correct option is (A).

19.

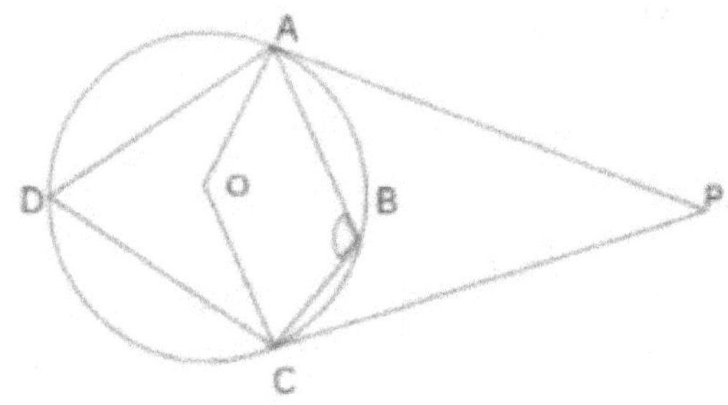

From the graph, ACD is a cyclic quadrilateral so,

$$\angle ABC + \angle ADC = 180°$$

$$\angle ADC = 180 - 100 = 80°$$

$$\angle AOC = 2 \times \angle ADC = 2 \times 80 = 160°$$

In quadrilateral $AOCP$ -

$$\angle OAP + \angle APC + \angle PCO + \angle COA = 360°$$

$$\angle OAP = \angle PCO = 90° \qquad .$$

($\because$ tangent angle)

$$\angle APC = 360 - 90 - 90 - 160 = 20°$$

Hence, the correct option is (B).

20.

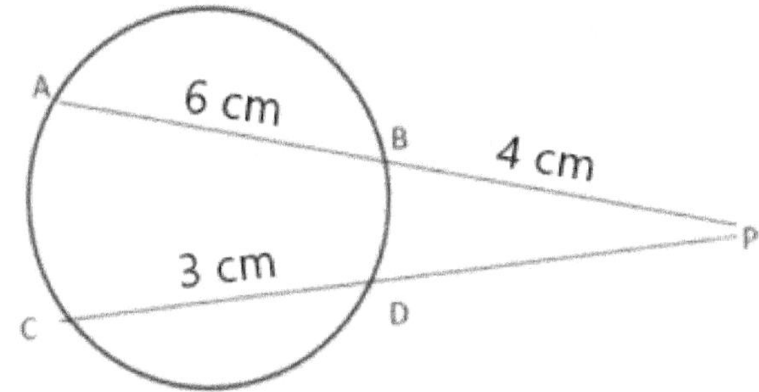

AB = 6 cm, CD = 3 cm and PB = 4 cm

We know by Secant Rule :

PB × PA = PD × PC

$$\Rightarrow 4 \times 10 = (x) \times (3 + x)$$

$$\Rightarrow 40 = 3x + x^2$$

$$\Rightarrow x^2 + 3x - 40 = 0$$

$$\Rightarrow x = 5 \text{ cm}$$

Length of PD is 5 cm.

Hence, the correct option is (A).

21. Let ABC be the right angled triangle such that ∠B = 90° , BC = 6 cm, AB = 8 cm. Let O be the centre and r be the radius of the in circle.

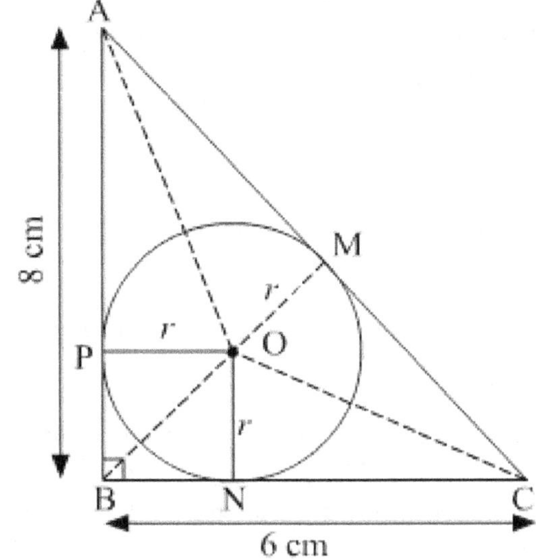

AB, BC and CA are tangents to the circle at P, N and M.

$\therefore$ OP = ON = OM = r (radius of the circle)

Area of $\triangle ABC = \frac{1}{2} \times 6 \times 8 = 24 \ cm^2$

By Pythagoras theorem,

$$CA^2 = AB^2 + BC^2$$

$$\Rightarrow CA^2 = 8^2 + 6^2$$

$$\Rightarrow CA^2 = 100$$

$$\Rightarrow CA = 10 \text{ cm}$$

Area of $\triangle ABC$ = Area $\triangle OAB$ + Area $\triangle OBC$ + Area $\triangle OCA$

$$24 = \frac{1}{2}r \times AB + \frac{1}{2}r \times BC + \frac{1}{2}r \times CA$$

$$24 = \frac{1}{2}r(AB + BC + CA)$$

$$\Rightarrow r = \frac{2 \times 24}{(AB + BC + CA)}$$

$$\Rightarrow r = \frac{48}{8 + 6 + 10}$$

$$\Rightarrow r = \frac{48}{24}$$

$$\Rightarrow r = 2 \text{ cm}$$

Hence, the correct option is (A).

22. Number of students enrolled in 2019 in both camps = 70 + 150 = 220

Total number of students enrolled in 2020 in both camps $= \frac{130 \times 220}{100} = 286$

Hence, the correct option is (A).

23. In 2016, total students in both camps = 60 + 210 = 270

In 2019, total students in both camps = 70 + 150 = 220

Required ratio = 270 : 220

= 27 : 22

Hence, the correct option is (B).

24. In 2015, the number of students in Sunshine = 170

In 2017, the number of students in Aryan = 160

Required $\% = \frac{170}{160} \times 100 = 106.25\%$

Hence, the correct option is (C).

25. Total number of students enrolled in Sunshine from 2016 to 2019 = 60 + 140 + 200 + 70 = 470

Total number of students enrolled in Aryan in 2018 and 2019 = 240 + 150 = 390

Difference = 470 - 390 = 80

Required $\% = \frac{80}{390} \times 100 = 20.51$

Hence, the correct option is (D).

Q.1 An isosceles right triangle has area 8 cm². The length of its hypotenuse is:

A. $\sqrt{32}$ cm **B.** $\sqrt{16}$ cm **C.** $\sqrt{48}$ cm **D.** $\sqrt{24}$ cm

Q.2 What is the value of 19% of 23% of 560?

A. 24.472 **B.** 23.572 **C.** 25.762 **D.** 27.342

Q.3 In $a \triangle ABC, AB = 4\ cm$ and $AC = 8\ cm$. If M is the midpoint of BC and $AM = 3\ cm$, then the length of BC in cm is:

A. $2\sqrt{26}$ **B.** $2\sqrt{31}$ **C.** $\sqrt{31}$ **D.** $\sqrt{26}$

Q.4 The average marks of 23 people is 78 and the average of top 12 marks is 90 and that of bottom 12 is 65 then what are the marks of 13th top scorer?

A. 62 **B.** 64 **C.** 66 **D.** 68

Q.5 If a man were to sell his chair for Rs. 720, he would lose 25 %. To gain 25% he should sell it for:

A. Rs. 1200 **B.** Rs. 1000 **C.** Rs. 960 **D.** Rs. 900

Q.6 An amount of money is to be divided between P, Q and R in the ratio of $3:7:12$. If the difference between the shares of P and Q is Rs. x and the difference between Q and R 's share is Rs. 3000. Find the total amount of money?

A. Rs. 11000 **B.** Rs. 12400
C. Rs. 13200 **D.** Rs. 14300

Q.7 A person travels from A to B at the speed of 120 km/hour and returns from B to A at the speed of 80 km/hour. What is his average speed?

A. 100 km/hr **B.** 96 km/hr
C. 90 km/hr **D.** 60 km/hr

Q.8 Sohan bought a second-hand refrigerator for Rs. 2500, then spent Rs. 500 on its repair and sold it for Rs. 3300. Find his loss or gain $\%$.

A. 10% **B.** 20% **C.** 30% **D.** 14%

Q.9 A can do a work in 15 days and B in 20 days. If they work on it together for 4 days, then the fraction of the work that is left is:

A. $\frac{1}{4}$ **B.** $\frac{1}{10}$ **C.** $\frac{7}{15}$ **D.** $\frac{8}{15}$

Ques (10-13):Direction: Read the following information carefully and answer the question.

The following line chart show the annual number of fire incidents between 2013 - 2016 in the USA, INDIA and AUSTRALIA.

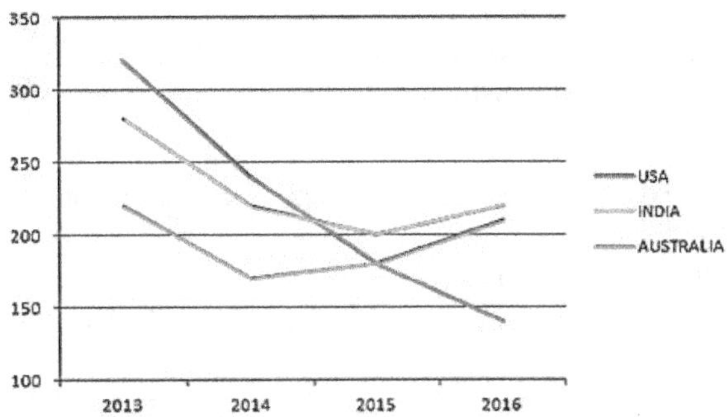

Q.10 What is the average number of fire accidents in the year 2014 in the given countries?

A. 190 **B.** 220 **C.** 210 **D.** 200

Q.11 If the average number of fire accidents in a country in the given time period is less than 250, the country is considered safe. How many of the given countries are safe?

A. 2 **B.** 3 **C.** 1 **D.** 0

Q.12 In how many countries there is an increase in the number of accidents for two consecutive years?

A. 0 **B.** 1 **C.** 2 **D.** 3

Q.13 What is the percentage change in number of accidents in INDIA in 2015 from 2014?

A. 11.11% **B.** -11.11% **C.** 9.09% **D.** -9.09%

Q.14 Raghav completes a certain journey by a car. If he covers 25% of the distance at the speed of 30 km/h, 50% of the distance at 45 km/h and the remaining of the distance at 15 km/h, his average speed is:

A. 23 **B.** 28 **C.** 43 **D.** 53

Q.15 The circumference of the base of a 12 m high conical tent is 66 m. Find the volume of the air contained in it.

A. 1432 **B.** 1386 **C.** 1614 **D.** 1321

Q.16 $1\frac{5}{6} + 2\frac{3}{5} + 4\frac{2}{3} = ?$

A. $2\frac{1}{10}$ **B.** $7\frac{1}{10}$ **C.** $6\frac{1}{10}$ **D.** $9\frac{1}{10}$

Q.17 A sum of Rs. 9000 is to be distributed among A, B and C in the ratic $4:5:6$. What will be the difference between A's and C's shares?

A. Rs. 1200 **B.** Rs. 1400 **C.** Rs. 1300 **D.** Rs. 1600

Q.18 The selling price of 12 articles is equal to the cost price of 15 articles. Find the gain percent?

A. 13% **B.** 16% **C.** 25% **D.** 19%

Q.19 Ravi marked the price of an article at 50% above the cost price. He allows a 20% discount to Kamal. Kamal sell it 50 more than cost price. This selling price is 30% more than cost price then, find profit % of Kamal.

A. 9% **B.** 10% **C.** 6.66% **D.** 8.33%

Q.20 Simple interest of Rs 1495 was obtained on a sum of money, invested for 4 years, at a rate of 12.5% per annum. Find the principal amount.

A. Rs. 4567 **B.** Rs. 2990 **C.** Rs. 6500 **D.** Rs. 1300

Q.21 A metal cube of side 11 cm is completely submerged in the water contained in a cylindrical vessel with a diameter 28 cm. Find the rise in the level of water.

A. 1.33 **B.** 2.16 **C.** 11.2 **D.** 3.21

Q.22 A can do a work in 15 days and B in 20 days. If they work on it together for 4 days, then the fraction of the work that is left is:

A. $\frac{1}{4}$ **B.** $\frac{1}{10}$ **C.** $\frac{7}{15}$ **D.** $\frac{8}{15}$

Q.23 $(3^{25} + 3^{26} + 3^{27} + 3^{28})$ is divisible by

A. 11 **B.** 16 **C.** 25 **D.** 30

Q.24 The radius of a circular wheel is $1\frac{3}{4}$m. How many revolutions will it make in traveling 11 $\left(\pi = \frac{22}{7}\right)$.

A. 1000 **B.** 1100 **C.** 900 **D.** 1200

Q.25 The arithmetic mean of the scores of a group of students in a test was 57. The brightest 20% of them secured a mean score of 80 and the dullest 25% had a mean score of 32. The mean score of the remaining 55% is:

A. 45 **B.** 50 **C.** 55 **D.** 60

// Smart Answer Sheet //

Correct   Percentage of students who answered correctly.   **Skipped**   Percentage of students who skipped.

Q.	Ans.	Correct / Skipped	Q.	Ans.	Correct / Skipped	Q.	Ans.	Correct / Skipped	Q.	Ans.	Correct / Skipped	Q.	Ans.	Correct / Skipped	Q.	Ans.	Correct / Skipped
1	A	69.05 % / 1.23 %	6	C	30.15 % / 3.57 %	11	B	77.27 % / 0.0 %	16	D	54.58 % / 1.99 %	21	B	83.42 % / 0.0 %			
2	A	46.66 % / 1.87 %	7	B	54.96 % / 1.41 %	12	D	80.38 % / 0.0 %	17	A	41.11 % / 1.35 %	22	D	65.57 % / 1.5 %			
3	B	21.77 % / 3.45 %	8	A	65.3 % / 1.88 %	13	D	56.14 % / 1.78 %	18	C	43.86 % / 1.75 %	23	D	60.09 % / 1.05 %			
4	C	17.4 % / 4.31 %	9	D	52.95 % / 1.24 %	14	B	47.2 % / 1.41 %	19	D	58.71 % / 1.17 %	24	A	76.09 % / 0.0 %			
5	A	65.31 % / 1.46 %	10	C	88.57 % / 0.0 %	15	B	87.91 % / 0.0 %	20	B	82.3 % / 0.0 %	25	D	42.48 % / 1.63 %			

//Hints and Solutions//

1. We know that, $A = \frac{(B \times H)}{2}$,

where A is area of triangle, B is base and H is height.

We know that for a right angled isosceles triangle, $B = H$

So, $A = \frac{(B)^2}{2}$

$8 \times 2 = B^2$

$\therefore B = H = 4$ cm

Now, hypotenuse $= \sqrt{(B^2 + H^2)}$

$= \sqrt{2B^2}$

$= \sqrt{2 \times 8 \times 2}$

$= \sqrt{32}$ cm

Hence, the correct option is (A).

2. By simplification we get,

$\Rightarrow 19\%$ of 23% of 560

$\Rightarrow \left(\frac{19}{100}\right) \times \left(\frac{23}{100}\right) \times 560$

$\Rightarrow 24.472$

Hence, the correct option is (A)

3. It is given that in $\triangle ABC$, $AB = 4\ cm$ and $AC = 8\ cm$

M is the midpoint of BC and $AM = 3\ cm$

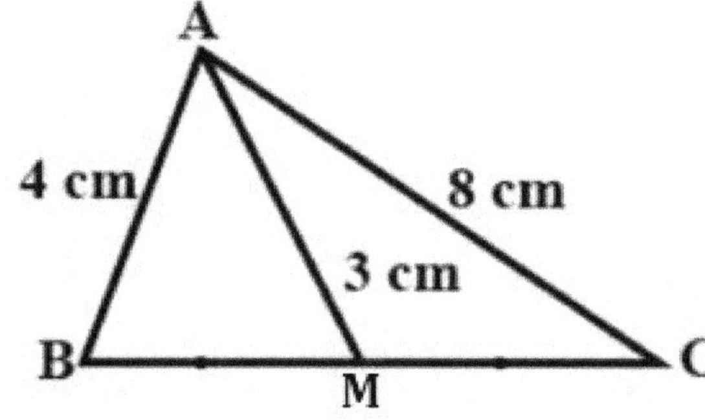

Using Apollonius theorem,

$AB^2 + AC^2 = 2(AM^2 + BM^2)$

$\Rightarrow 4^2 + 8^2 = 2(3^2 + BM^2)$

$\Rightarrow 16 + 64 = 2(9 + BM^2)$

$\Rightarrow BM^2 = 31$

$\Rightarrow BM = \sqrt{31}$

$\because BC = 2BM$

$\therefore BC = 2\sqrt{31}$

Hence, the correct option is (B).

4. Sum of marks of 23 people = 78 × 23 = 1794

Sum of marks of top 12 scorers = 12 × 90 =1080

Sum of marks of bottom 12 scorers = 12 × 65 = 780

Sum of marks of 23 people and 13th top scorer = 1080 + 780 = 1860

Marks of 13th top scorer = 1860 - 1794 = 66

Hence, the correct option is (C).

5. Let the cost price of the chair is x.

$SP = x - 25\%$ of x

$\Rightarrow 720 = 0.75x$

$\Rightarrow x = 960$

$\Rightarrow CP =$ Rs 960

So, To gain 25%, SP would be $= 960 + 25\%$ of $960 =$ Rs 1200

Hence, the correct option is (A).

6. Let the amount P, Q and R got is $3a, 7a$ and $12a$. So, according to the question,

$12a - 7a = 3000$

$\Rightarrow 5a = 3000$

$\Rightarrow a = 600$

Now it is given that the difference between P and Q's share is x.

$7a - 4a = x$

$\Rightarrow 3a = x$

$\Rightarrow x = 1800$

So, the total amount of money $= 22 \times 600 = 13200$

Hence, the correct option is (C).

7. Let the distance be x.

So, time taken to travel $= \frac{x}{120}$

Time taken to return $= \frac{x}{80}$

Average speed $= \dfrac{\text{Total distance}}{\text{Time taken}}$

$= \dfrac{2x}{\frac{x}{130} + \frac{1}{80}} = \dfrac{2x \times 240}{5x} = 96$ km/hr

Hence, the correct option is (B).

8. As per the question, the Cost price of refrigerator $=$ $2500 + 500 =$ Rs. 3000

Selling price $=$ Rs. 3300

Clearly, he is gaining here.

So, Gain $= SP - CP = 3300 - 3000 = 300$

Therefore, Gain percent $= \dfrac{gain \times 100}{CP} = \dfrac{300 \times 100}{3000} = 10\%$

Hence, the correct option is (A).

9. Let the total work is 1 unit.

A's 1 day's work $= \dfrac{1}{15}$;

B 's 1 day's work $= \dfrac{1}{20}$;

$(A + B)'s\,1$ day's work $= \left(\dfrac{1}{15} + \dfrac{1}{20}\right) = \dfrac{7}{60}$

$(A + B)$'s 4 day's work $= \left(\dfrac{7}{60} \times 4\right) = \dfrac{7}{15}$

Therefore, remaining work $= \left(1 - \dfrac{7}{15}\right) = \dfrac{8}{15}$

Hence, the correct option is (D).

10. The data in the line chart can be tabulated as below:

	2013	2014	2015	2016
USA	320	240	180	210
INDIA	280	220	200	220
AUSTRALIA	220	170	180	140

According to the table, the average number of fire accidents in $2014 = \dfrac{(240+220+170)}{3}$
$= \dfrac{630}{3} = 210$

Hence, the correct option is (C).

11. The data in the line chart can be tabulated as below:

	2013	2014	2015	2016
USA	320	240	180	210
INDIA	280	220	200	220
AUSTRALIA	220	170	180	140

So, according to the table, the average number of accidents in

$USA = \dfrac{(320+240+180+210)}{4} = 237.5$

The average number of accidents in INDIA $=$
$\dfrac{(280+220+200+220)}{4} = 230$

The average number of accidents in AUSTRALIA $=$
$\dfrac{(220+170+180+140)}{4} = 177.5$

Hence, the correct option is (B).

12. The data in the line chart can be tabulated as below:

	2013	2014	2015	2016
USA	320	240	180	210
INDIA	280	220	200	220
AUSTRALIA	220	170	180	140

From the table, we can conclude that there is no increase in the number of accidents for two consecutive years for any of the three countries.

Hence, the correct option is (D).

13. The data in the line chart can be tabulated as below:

	2013	2014	2015	2016
USA	320	240	180	210
INDIA	280	220	200	220
AUSTRALIA	220	170	180	140

According to the table, the percentage change in 2015 from 2014 in INDIA is $= \left(\dfrac{200-220}{220}\right) \times 100 = -9.09\%$

Hence, the correct option is (D).

14. Let the total distance be 100 km.

$$Time = \dfrac{Distance}{Speed}$$

$$Average\ speed = \dfrac{Total\ Distance\ Covered}{Time\ Taken}$$

$\Rightarrow$ Average speed $= \dfrac{100}{\left[\left(\frac{25}{30}\right)+\left(\frac{50}{45}\right)+\left(\frac{25}{15}\right)\right]}$

$\Rightarrow$ Speed $= \dfrac{100}{\left[\left(\frac{5}{6}\right)+\left(\frac{10}{9}\right)+\left(\frac{5}{3}\right)\right]}$

$\Rightarrow$ Speed $= \dfrac{20}{\left[\left(\frac{1}{6}\right)+\left(\frac{2}{9}\right)+\left(\frac{1}{3}\right)\right]}$

$\Rightarrow$ Speed $= \dfrac{(20 \times 6 \times 3)}{13}$

$\therefore$ Speed $= 27.69$ km/h $= 28$ km/h

Hence, the correct option is (B).

15. Circumference of the conical tent $= 66$ m

And height $(h) = 12$ m

$\therefore$ Radius $= \dfrac{c}{2\pi} = \dfrac{66 \times 7}{2 \times 22} = 10.5$ m

Therefore, volume of air contained in it $= \dfrac{1}{3}\pi r^2 h$

$= \dfrac{1}{3} \times \dfrac{22}{7} \times \dfrac{21}{2} \times \dfrac{21}{2} \times 12\ m^3$

$= 1386\ m^3$

Hence, the correct option is (B).

16. Given: $1\dfrac{5}{6} + 2\dfrac{3}{5} + 4\dfrac{2}{3}$

$$= (1 + 2 + 4) + \left(\frac{5}{6} + \frac{3}{5} + \frac{2}{3}\right)$$

$$= \left(7 + \frac{25+18+20}{30}\right)$$

$$= 7 + \frac{63}{30}$$

$$= 7 + \frac{21}{10}$$

$$= \frac{91}{10} = 9\frac{1}{10}$$

Hence, the correct option is (D).

17. Given:

Total amount Rs. $= 9000$

A's share $= 4x$

$\Rightarrow B$'s share $= 5x$ and C 's share $= 6x$

Then $4x + 5x + 6x = 9000$

$\Rightarrow 15x = 9000 \Rightarrow x = 600$

Now, A's share $= 4 \times 600 =$ Rs. 3600

Difference between A's and C's share $= (3600 - 2400) =$ Rs. 1200

Hence, the correct option is (A).

18. Let the CP of 1 article Rs. $= x$

Cost Price of 15 article $=$ Rs. $15x$

Selling Price of 12 article $=$ Rs. $15x$

SP of 1 article Rs. $= \frac{15}{12}x$

Gain $= \frac{15x}{12} - x$

$= \frac{3x}{12} = \frac{x}{4}$

Gain $\% = \frac{Gain \times 100}{CP}$

$= \frac{\frac{x}{4} \times 100}{x} = 25\%$

Hence, the correct option is (C).

19. Original value of the considered item $= 100\%$

Ravi marked the price $= 150\%$

Cost price of kamal $= \frac{80}{100} \times 150 = 120\%$

Selling price of kamal $= 120\% + 50 = 130\%$

$10\% =$ Rs. 50

Cost price of kamal $= 120 \times 5 = 600$

Profit percentage of kamal $= \frac{50}{600} \times 100 = 8.33\%$

Hence, the correct option is (D).

20. Given,

Simple interest = Rs 1495

Rate $(R) = 12.5\%$

Time $(T) = 4$ years

Simple Interest $= \frac{(P \times R \times T)}{100}$

$\Rightarrow 1495 = \frac{(P \times 12.5 \times 4)}{100}$

$\Rightarrow P =$ Rs 2990

Hence, the correct option is (B).

21. As per the question,

Volume of cube of side $11\ cm =$ Volume of water displaced in the cylinder

$\Rightarrow (11)^3 = \pi r^2 h$

$\Rightarrow 11 \times 11 \times 11 = \frac{22}{7} \times \frac{28}{2} \times \frac{28}{2} \times h$

$\Rightarrow h = \frac{11 \times 11 \times 11 \times 7 \times 2 \times 2}{22 \times 28 \times 28}$

$= \frac{121}{56} = 2.16\ cm$

Hence, the correct option is (B).

22. Given:

A's day's work $= \frac{1}{15}$

B 's day's work $= \frac{1}{20}$

$(A + B)$'s 1 day's work $= \left[\frac{1}{15} + \frac{1}{20}\right] = \frac{7}{60}$

$(A + B)$'s 4 day's work $= \left[\frac{7}{60} \times 4\right] = \frac{7}{15}$

Therefore, Remaining work $= \left[1 - \frac{7}{15}\right] = \frac{8}{15}$

Hence, the correct option is (D).

23. Given: $3^{25} + 3^{26} + 3^{27} + 3^{28}$

$= 3^{25}(1 + 3 + 3^2 + 3^3)$

$= 3^{25}(1 + 3 + 9 + 27)$

$= 3^{25} \times 40,$

$= 3^{24} \times 3^1 \times 4 \times 10$

$= 30 \times 4 \times 3^{24}$

Which is clearly divisible by 30.

So, the given expression is divisible by 30.

Hence, the correct option is (D).

24. Given: Traveling $= 11$ km $= 1100$ m

The radius of the circular wheel $r = 1\frac{3}{4} = \frac{7}{4} = 1.75$ m

Circumference of a circular wheel $= 2\pi r = 2 \times \frac{22}{7} \times 1.75$ m

$$\text{Number of revolutions} = \frac{\text{Distance to be covered}}{\text{Circumference of circle}}$$

$$= \frac{1100\ m}{2 \times \frac{22}{7} \times 1.75\ m} = \frac{1100}{11} = 1000$$

Hence, the correct option is (A).

25. Let the total number of students be x.

Total score of all students $= 57x$

Score of top 20% students $= \left(\frac{20}{100}\right) x \times 80 = 16x$

Score of last 25% students $= \left(\frac{25}{10}\right) x \times 32 = 8x$

Let y be the mean of 55% students.

Total score of these students $= \left(\frac{55}{100}\right) x \times y$

Total score $= 16x + 8x + \left(\frac{55}{100}\right) x \times y$

$$\Rightarrow 16x + 8x + \left(\frac{55}{100}\right) x \times y = 57x$$

$$\Rightarrow \left(\frac{55}{100}\right) y = 33$$

$$\Rightarrow y = 60$$

Hence, the correct option is (D).

Ques (1-3):Direction: A series is given with one term missing. Select the correct alternative from the given ones that will complete the series.

Q.1 7, 6, 10, 27, 104, ____
A. 520   **B.** 420   **C.** 525   **D.** 515

Q.2 ZWR, XUO, VSL,?
A. TQI   **B.** TQL   **C.** SQK   **D.** UQK

Q.3 120, 99, 80, 63,48,?
A. 35   **B.** 38   **C.** 39   **D.** 40

Ques (4-5):Direction: In the following question, select the related number from the given alternatives.

Q.4 381 : 160 : : 478 : ?
A. 347   **B.** 357   **C.** 247   **D.** 257

Q.5 4 : 48 : : 12 : ?
A. 96   **B.** 246   **C.** 432   **D.** 58

Q.6 Direction: In the following question, select the related word from the given alternatives.
Fan : Electricity :: Generator : ?
A. Kerosene   **B.** Diesel
C. Petrol   **D.** Hydraulic Liquid

Q.7 Which answer figure will complete the pattern in the question figure?

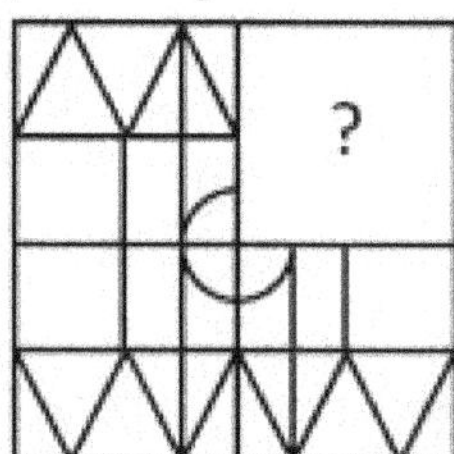

[UP Police Constable, 2019]

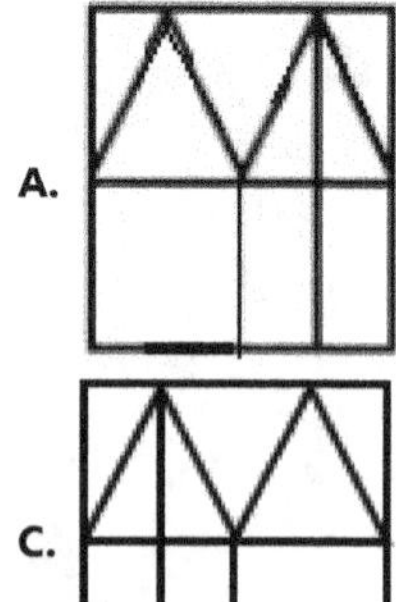

A.   **B.**

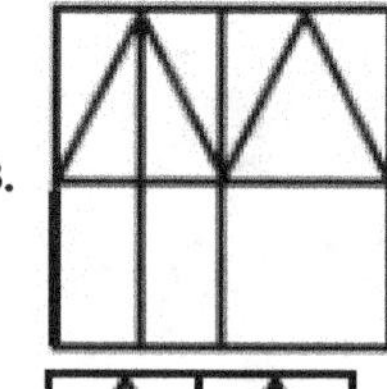
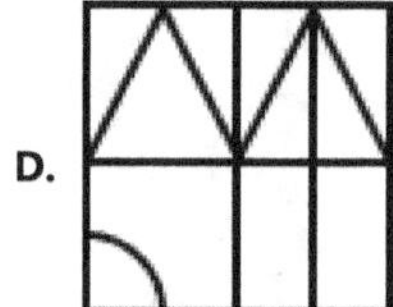

C.   **D.**

Q.8 Find the answer figure in which the question figure is embedded?

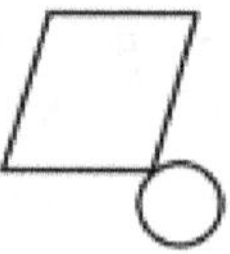

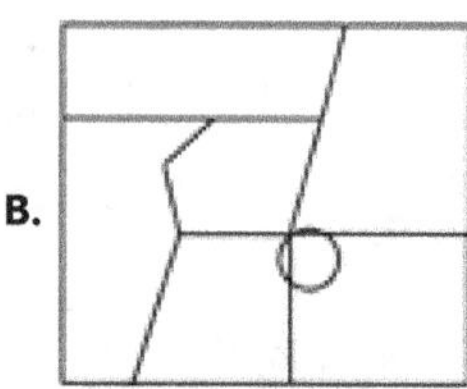

A.   **B.**

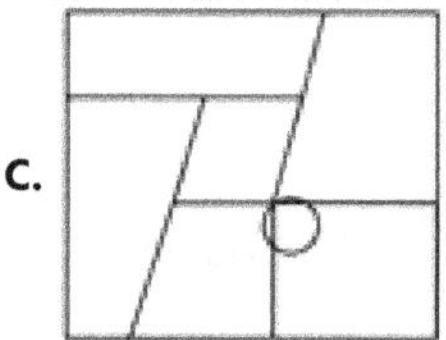
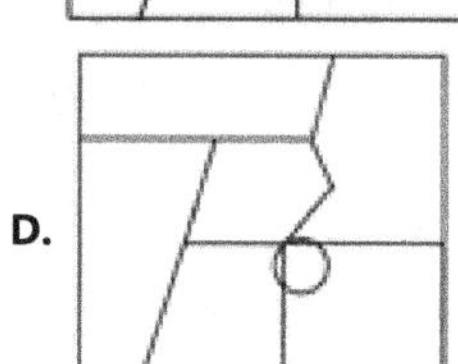

C.   **D.**

Q.9 Which of the following figure can be created by folding the following figure?

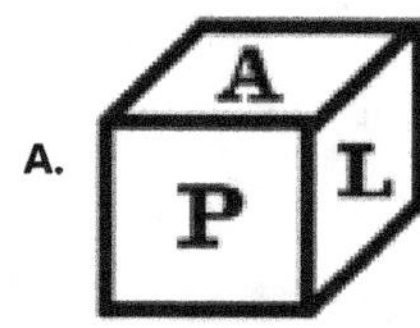

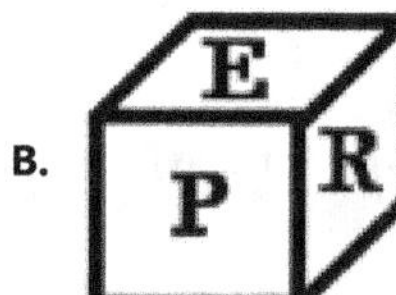

A.   **B.**

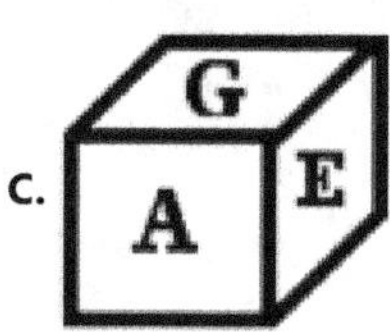

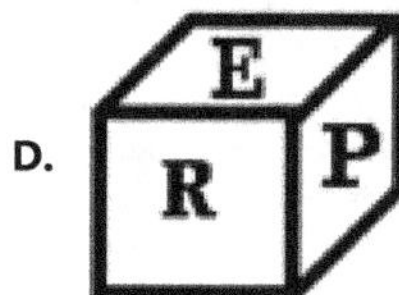

C.   **D.**

Q.10 In a certain code language,
'134' means nice and tasty
'478' means 'look nice pictures' and
'729' means 'pictures are colourful'.
Which of the following digits stands for 'look'?
A. 1   **B.** 2   **C.** 8   **D.** 9

Q.11 In a certain code language, "FRAK" is written as "35" and "MALT" is written as "45". How is "TRIM" written in that code language?

A. 59   B. 60   C. 30   D. 58

Q.12 In a certain code, FLOWERS is written as EKNVDQR. How is SUPREME written in that code?

A. TQDROLD   B. RTODQLD
C. TQDDROL   D. RTOQDLD

Q.13 Direction: Identify the diagram that best represents the relationship among the given classes.

Girl, Singer, Politician

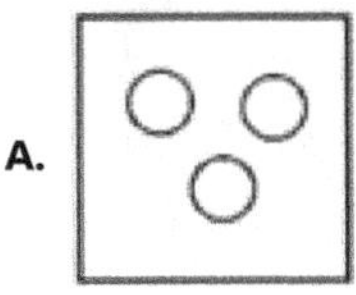
A.

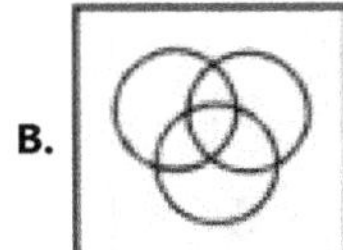
B.

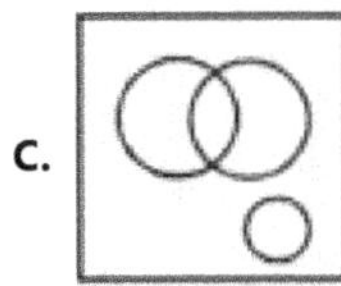
C.

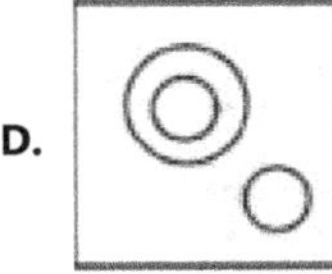
D.

Q.14 In the given diagram, Circle A represents Football players, Circle B represents Cricket players and Circle C represents Hockey players. Which portion represents the Cricket players who are also Football players?

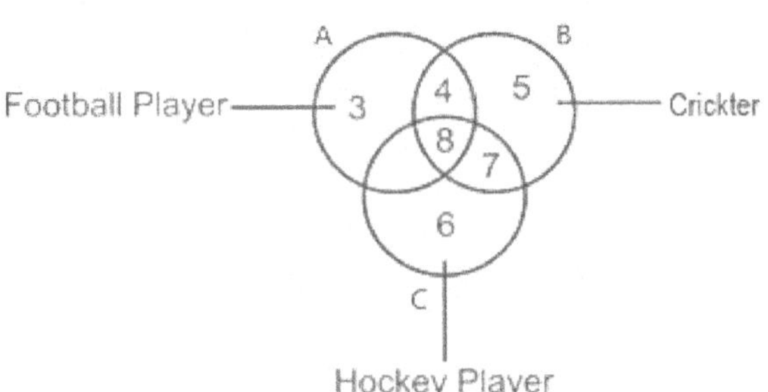

A. 8   B. 4   C. 7   D. 6

Q.15 Direction: Identify the diagram that best represents the relationship among the given classes.

Professionals, Chartered Accountant, Female

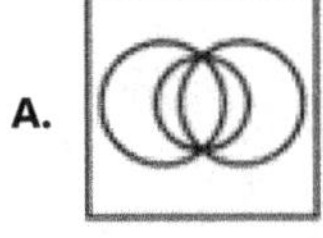
A.

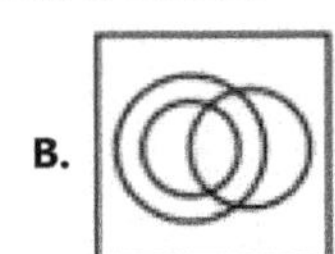
B.

C.

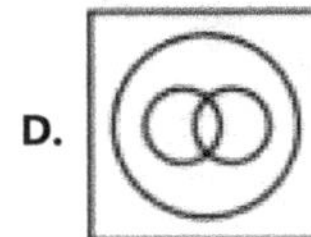
D.

Q.16 Find the odd one out.

A. 7251   B. 8231   C. 9211   D. 6321

Q.17 Find the odd one out.

A. MLN   B. ONP   C. PRQ   D. UTV

Q.18 Find the odd one out:

A. ZM   B. RH   C. XL   D. NG

Ques (19-20):Direction: Find the word that cannot be formed from the letters in the given word.

Q.19 WIDESPREAD

A. IDEA   B. DESIRE   C. SPEED   D. REPAIR

Q.20 REHABILITATION

A. HOBBY   B. HAPPY
C. BRIGHT   D. BRITTLE

Q.21 Direction: In the following question, from the given alternatives words, select the word which cannot be formed using the letters of the given word.

HANDSOME

A. HATS   B. HOME   C. NAME   D. SAND

Ques (22-23):Direction: In the following question, some statements are followed by some conclusions. Assuming the given statements to be true, find which of the following conclusions follow the given statements and choose the appropriate answer choice.

Q.22 Statements:

Some cars are windows.

Some windows are trees.

Some trees are hills.

Conclusions:

I. Some hills are cars.

II. Some trees are cars.

III. Some hills are windows.

IV. No car is a hill.

A. Only either I or II follows
B. Only either I or III follows
C. Only either I or IV follows
D. Only either II or IV follows

Q.23 Statements:

Some pens are keys.

Some keys are locks.

All locks are cards.

No card is paper.

Conclusions:

I. No lock is paper.

II. Some cards are keys.

III. Some keys are not paper.

A. I and II follow   B. Only I follows
C. Only II follows   D. All follow

Q.24 If '+' means '-', '÷' means '+', '-' means '+' and '+' means '÷', then which of the following equation is correct?

A. 40-10+10×5 = 92   B. 265+11-2×14 = 22
C. 66×3-11+12 = 230   D. 2-14×4÷11 = 16

Q.25 In a certain code language, '+' represents '×', '-' represents '÷', '' represents '÷' and '' represents '-'. What is the answer to the following question?

11 + 50 - 150 ÷ 200 = ?

A. 200   B. 500   C. 250   D. 50

// Smart Answer Sheet //

Correct — Percentage of students who answered correctly. **Skipped** — Percentage of students who skipped.

Q.	Ans.	Correct / Skipped	Q.	Ans.	Correct / Skipped	Q.	Ans.	Correct / Skipped	Q.	Ans.	Correct / Skipped	Q.	Ans.	Correct / Skipped	Q.	Ans.	Correct / Skipped
1	D	64.5 % / 1.87 %	6	B	44.66 % / 1.33 %	11	A	86.01 % / 0.0 %	16	D	55.61 % / 1.62 %	21	A	89.07 % / 0.0 %			
2	A	47.42 % / 1.13 %	7	C	53.15 % / 1.19 %	12	D	86.35 % / 0.0 %	17	C	88.31 % / 0.0 %	22	C	68.25 % / 1.7 %			
3	A	68.13 % / 1.15 %	8	C	54.68 % / 1.29 %	13	B	59.04 % / 1.55 %	18	B	47.25 % / 1.76 %	23	D	53.27 % / 1.69 %			
4	D	65.86 % / 1.84 %	9	A	78.74 % / 0.0 %	14	B	85.19 % / 0.0 %	19	D	82.25 % / 0.0 %	24	C	64.98 % / 1.16 %			
5	C	51.57 % / 1.72 %	10	C	40.79 % / 1.61 %	15	B	84.74 % / 0.0 %	20	D	53.13 % / 1.88 %	25	B	46.33 % / 1.73 %			

//Hints and Solutions//

1. According to the given series,

$7 \times 1 - 1 = 6$

$6 \times 2 - 2 = 10$

$10 \times 3 - 3 = 27$

$27 \times 4 - 4 = 104$

So, $104 \times 5 - 5 = 515$

Hence, the correct option is (D).

2. The pattern is 1st letter in each letter is decreased by 2 as Z and X and V are decrementing in order by 2 so next letter will be T now 2nd letter which is also decreased by 2 so next letter will be Q and now 3rd letter is in a difference of 3 as R-3 gives O and O-3 gives L now L-3 gives I so next word will be TQI.

Hence, the correct option is (A).

3. The pattern is - 21, -19, -17, -15, ...

So, missing term = 48 - 13 = 35.

Hence, the correct option is (A).

4. As given,

381 - 221 = 160

Similarly,

478 - 221 = 257

257 is the answer.

Hence, the correct option is (D).

5. As,

$4^2 = 16$; $16 \times 3 = 48$

Similarly,

$12^2 = 144$; $144 \times 3 = 432$

Thus 12 is related to 432.

Hence, the correct option is (C).

6. A fan is an electrical device that runs on electricity. Similarly, the generator runs with diesel.

Thus Generator is related to Diesel.

Hence, the correct option is (B).

7.

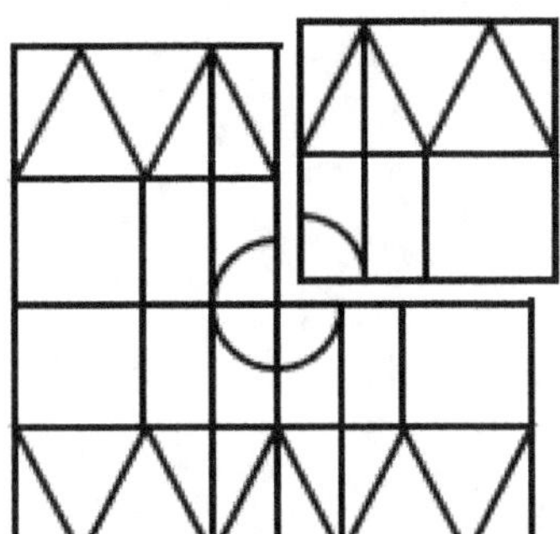

Thus option (C), completes the shape pattern.

Hence, the correct option is (C).

8. From the above figures, we get

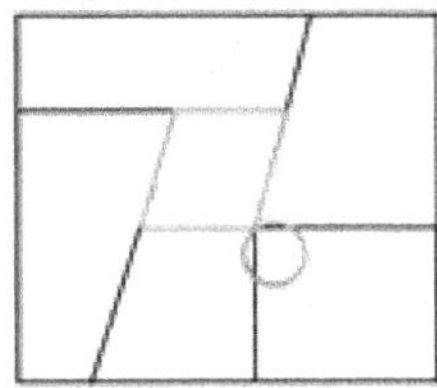

Hence, the correct option is (C).

9. learn from question figure that in Option (B) and (D) letter P and R are adjacent, in option (C) letters A and E are adjacent which is not possible so option (A) is correct where A, P & L can be adjacent.

Hence, the correct option is (A).

10. In the first and second statements, the common code digit is 4 and the common word is nice. Thus, 4 stands for nice. In the second and third statements, the common code digit is '7' and the common word is 'pictures'. Thus, '7' means 'pictures'. Thus, in the second statement, '8' means 'look'.

Hence, the correct option is (C).

11. The letters are coded by subtracting one from the sum of the positional value of the letters in the English alphabetical series.

FRAK = (6+18+1+11)-1 = 35

MALT = (13+1+12+20)-1 = 45

Thus, TRIM = (20+18+9+13)-1 = 59

Hence, the correct option is (A).

12. The letters are coded with the previous letter in the English alphabetical series.

FLOWER ⇒ EKNVDQR

Similarly,

SUPREME ⇒ RTOQDLD

Hence, the correct option is (D).

13. Some girls can be singer or politician or both.

Therefore, the best figure which describes this relationship is:

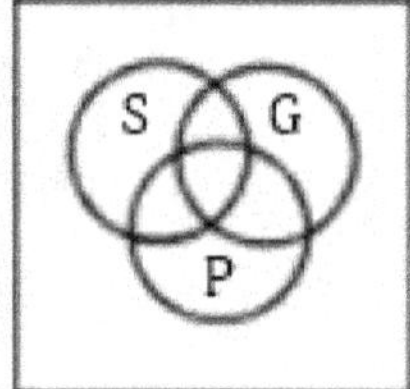

Hence, the correct option is (B).

14. As in the diagram labeled, the Cricket players who are also Football players is the number containing 4.

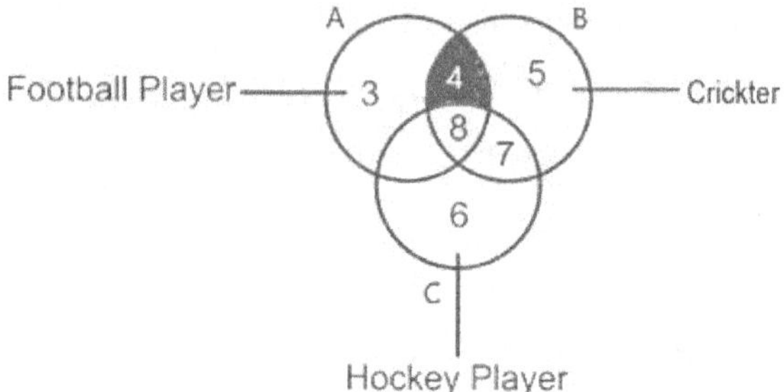

Hence, the correct option is (B).

15. A chartered accountant is a type of profession and a female may be a chartered accountant or maybe not.

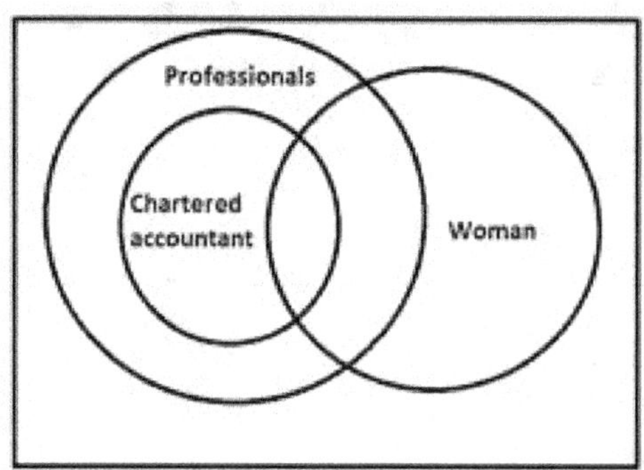

Hence, the correct option is (B).

16. The given numbers follow the following pattern:

$7 \times 2 + 5 \times 1 = 19$

$8 \times 2 + 3 \times 1 = 19$

$9 \times 2 + 1 \times 1 = 19$

$6 \times 3 + 2 \times 1 = 20 \neq 19$

Hence, the correct option is (D).

17. The pattern followed here is:

$$M(13) \overset{-1}{\to} L(12) \overset{+2}{\to} N(14)$$

$$O(15) \overset{-1}{\to} N(14) \overset{+2}{\to} P(16)$$

$$P(16) \overset{+2}{\to} R(18) \overset{-1}{\to} Q(17)$$

$$U(21) \overset{-1}{\to} T(20) \overset{+2}{\to} V(22)$$

Hence, the correct option is (C).

18. The positional value of the 1st alphabet is twice that of the positional value of the 2nd alphabet.

Z(26) M(13),

R(18) H(8),

X(24) L(12),

N(14) G(7),

As $8 \times 2 = 16$ and not 18, RH is the odd one out

Hence, the correct option is (B).

19. IDEA, DESIRE, SPEED all these words can be formed from the given word WIDESPREAD.

But REPAIR word can't be formed, as only a single R is available in the given word WIDESPREAD.

Hence, the correct option is (D).

20. BRITTLE: It can be formed, as it has all the needed letters.

A) HOBBY: The letter Y is not present in REHABILITATION, so it can't be formed.

B) HAPPY: The letter P and Y are not present in REHABILITATION, so it can't be formed

C) BRIGHT: The letter G is not present in REHABILITATION, so it can't be formed.

Thus, BRITTLE can be formed from the letters used in REHABILITATION.

Hence, the correct option is (D).

21.

H A N D S O M E ⇒ H O M E

H A N D S O M E ⇒ N A M E

H A N D S O M E ⇒ S A N D

Since there is no 'T' involved in 'HANDSOME', so 'HATS' can't be formed.

Hence, the correct option is (A).

22.

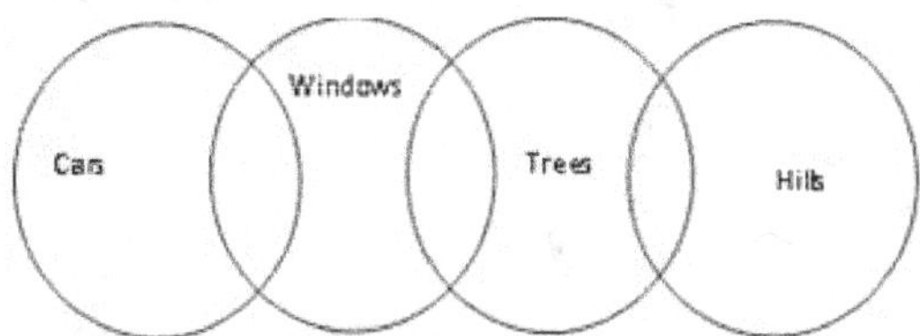

It is clear from the given diagram that only conclusion I and IV follow. As there is no direct relation given between conclusion I and conclusion IV, either of them can follow.

Hence, the correct option is (C).

23.

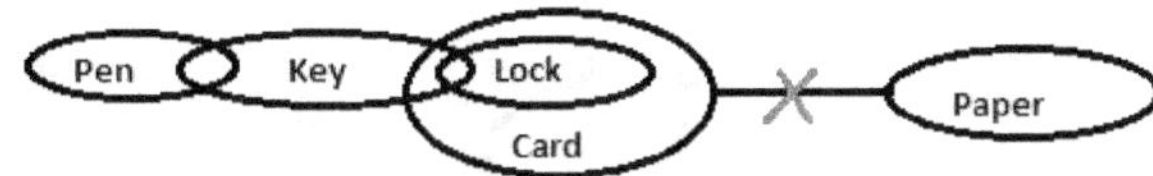

From conclusion 1: As it is given that no card is paper, then lock also cannot be a part of the paper.

From conclusion 2: It is clear from the above figure that some part of the key is a part of the card.

From conclusion 3: The part of the key which is also a part of the card, cannot be a part of the paper.

Thus, all the conclusions follow.

Hence, the correct option is (D).

24. Option (C) equation is correct

Given that, $66 \times 3 - 11 + 12 = 230$

After changing the signs according to the question,

$\Rightarrow 66 \div 3 \times 11 - 12 = 230$

$\Rightarrow 22 \times 11 - 12 = 230$

$\Rightarrow 242 - 12 = 230$

$\Rightarrow 230 = 230$

Thus, LHS = RHS

Hence, the correct option is (C).

25. Using the proper symbols, we get

$11 \times 50 + 150 - 200 = ?$

Now applying the BODMAS rule,

$11 \times 50 + 150 - 200$

$= 550 + 150 - 200$

$= 700 - 200 = 500$

Hence, the correct option is (B).

Q.1 If '÷' is coded as 'L', '+' is coded as 'M', '-' is coded as 'N', '×' is coded as 'P', then what is the value of 38 L 2 M 7 P 4 N 22?

A. 33 **B.** 25 **C.** 28 **D.** 21

Q.2 Find the odd word from the given alternatives.

A. Bajra **B.** Mustard **C.** Rice **D.** Wheat

Q.3 Direction: In the following question, select the related letters from the given alternatives.

SD : YJ :: HK : ?

A. LN **B.** MO **C.** OR **D.** NQ

Q.4 What is the next term in the given sequence?

2, 5, 11, 23, ?

A. 47 **B.** 53 **C.** 42 **D.** 34

Q.5 Identify the diagram which best represents the relationship among the classes given below.

Alphabets, Numbers, Vowels, Consonants

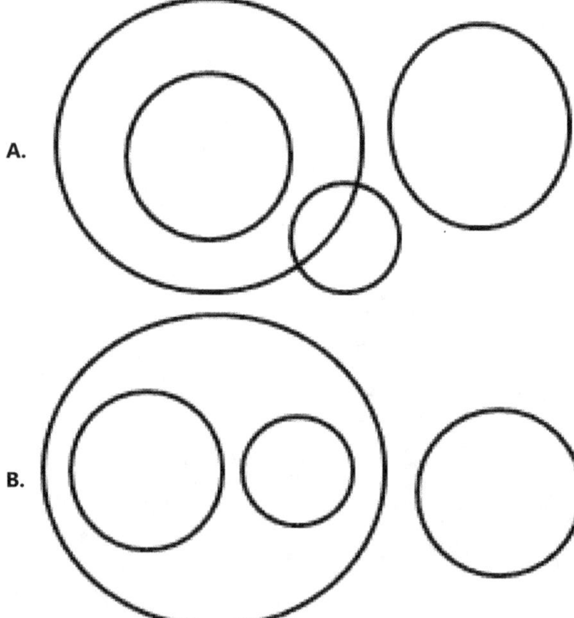

A.

B.

C.

D.

Q.6 If '$' means '÷', '@' means '×', '#' means '-', then find the value of 10 # 5 @ 1 $ 5.

A. 11 **B.** 9 **C.** 13 **D.** 7

Q.7 Direction: In the following question, some statements are given each followed by two conclusions I and II. You have to consider the statements to be true even if they seem to be at variance from commonly known facts. You have to decide which of the given conclusions, if any, follows from the given statements.

Statements:

I. Some Yellow are Red

II. No Red is Black

Conclusions:

I. No Yellow is Black

II. Some Yellow are Black

A. Only Conclusion I follows

B. Only Conclusion II follows

C. Either Conclusion I or Conclusion II follows

D. Both Conclusions I and II follow

Q.8 Direction: In the following question, select the related letters from the given alternatives.

Roof : Floor :: Sad : ?

A. Annoy **B.** Bitter **C.** Sweet **D.** Happy

Q.9 In a certain code language "QKAIT" is coded as " SMCKV" and "VGHRS" is coded as "XIJTU" then what is the code for "BHASR"?

A. DLDVT **B.** DKCVT **C.** DJCVT **D.** DJCUT

Q.10 Which of the following comes in the place of '?'

34 : 25 :: 47 : ?

A. 55   **B.** 65   **C.** 121   **D.** 39

Q.11 Direction: In the following question, select the related letters from the given alternatives.

Float : Sink :: Boat : ?

A. Ship   **B.** War

C. Submarine   **D.** Missile

Q.12 Direction: Identify the diagram which best represents the relationship among the classes given below -

student, teacher, school

A.

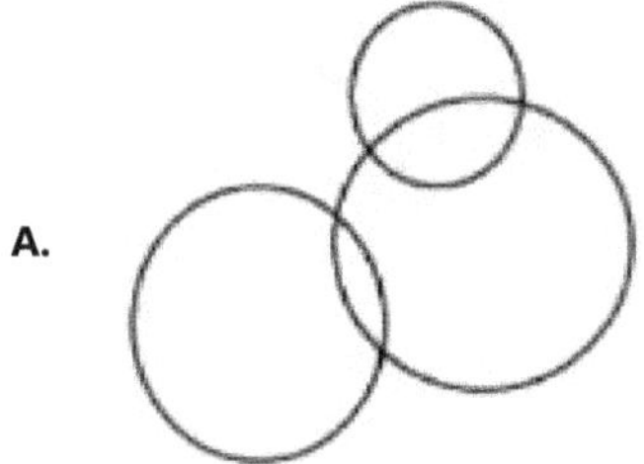

B.

C.

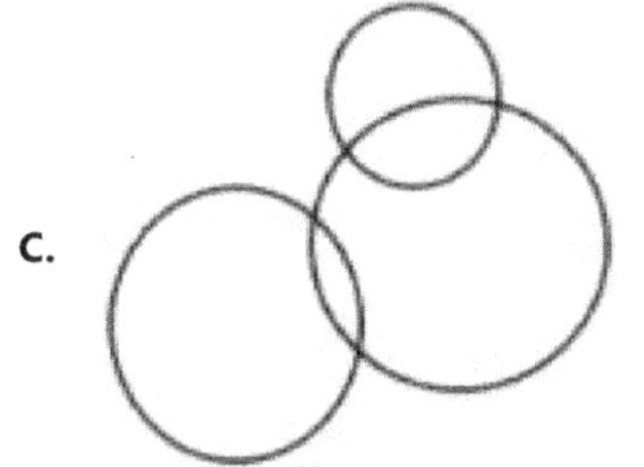

D.

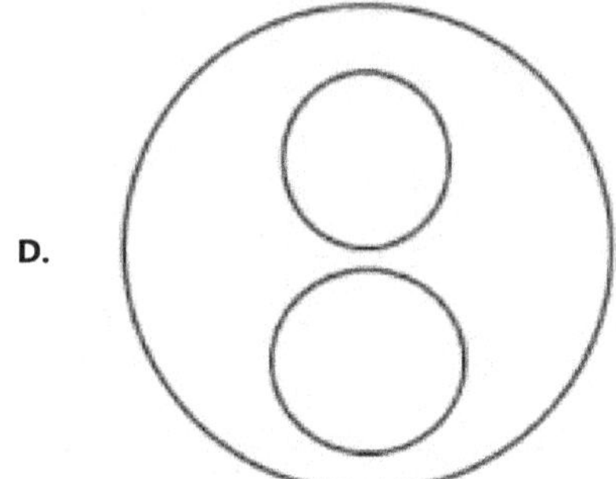

Q.13 Direction: Which of the following comes in the place of?

4224 : 6 :: ? : 8

A. 4960   **B.** 5600   **C.** 4880   **D.** 8632

Q.14 Direction: Find the missing term in the given series.

11, 13, 16, 21, 28, 39, ?, 69

A. 49   **B.** 55   **C.** 52   **D.** 57

Q.15 Direction: In the following questions, some statements are given each followed by two conclusions I and II. You have to consider the statements to be true even if they seem to be at variance from commonly known facts. You have to decide which of the given conclusions, if any, follows from the given statements.

Statements:

Statement I: All Circles are Squares

Statement II: No Square is a Rectangle

Conclusions:

Conclusion I: No Circle is a Rectangle

Conclusion II: All Squares are Circles

A. Only Conclusion I follows

B. Only Conclusion II follows

C. Either Conclusion I or Conclusion II follows

D. Both Conclusions I and II follow

Q.16 In a certain code language "LISTEN" is coded as "KGPPZH" and "MOTHER" is coded as "LMQDZL" then what is the code for "KITTEN" ?

A. JGQRZH   **B.** JHQRZH

C. JGQPZH   **D.** JFQPZH

Q.17 Direction: In the following words, select the word which cannot be formed by using the letters in the given word.

VISIONARINESS

A. Session   **B.** Season   **C.** Restore   **D.** Revision

Q.18 Direction: In the following question, select the related letters from the given alternatives.

Asia : Japan :: Europe :?

A. South Africa   **B.** England

C. USA   **D.** Canada

Q.19 Direction: In the following words, select the word which cannot be formed by using the letters in the given word.

CARBONISATION

A. Narcos   **B.** Satire   **C.** Carbon   **D.** Sanction

Q.20 Direction: On the basis of the given figure, answer the question given below:

Which letter represents the set of persons who play all three games?

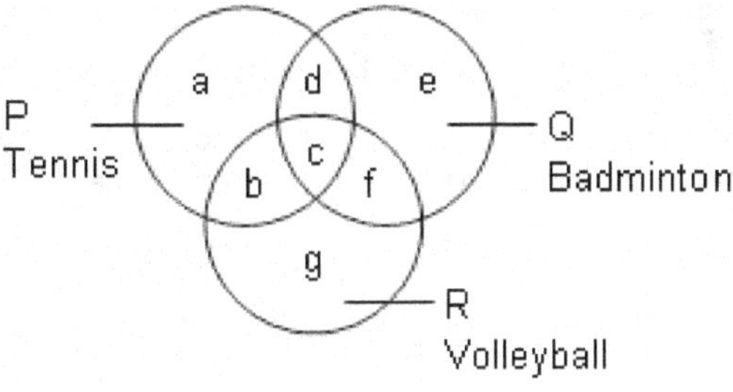

A. b   **B.** c   **C.** f   **D.** g

Q.21 Direction: Study the following question carefully and choose the right answer:

Statement: Warning: Cigarette smoking is injurious to health.

Assumption: I. Non-smoking promotes health.

II Really, this warning is not necessary.

A. If only assumption I is implicit

B. If only assumption II is implicit

C. If either I or II is implicit

D. If neither I nor II is implicit

Q.22 Direction: Study the following question carefully and choose the right answer:

If a mirror is placed on the line AB, which of the options figure shows the correct image of the given question figure?

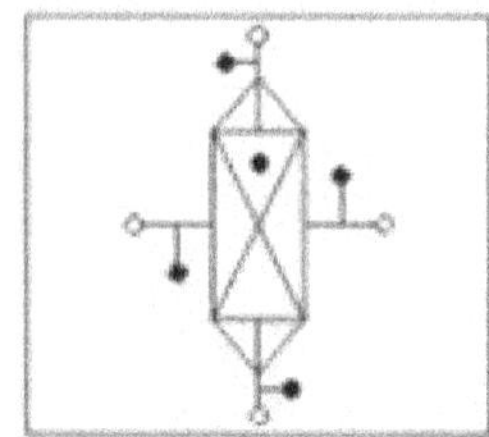

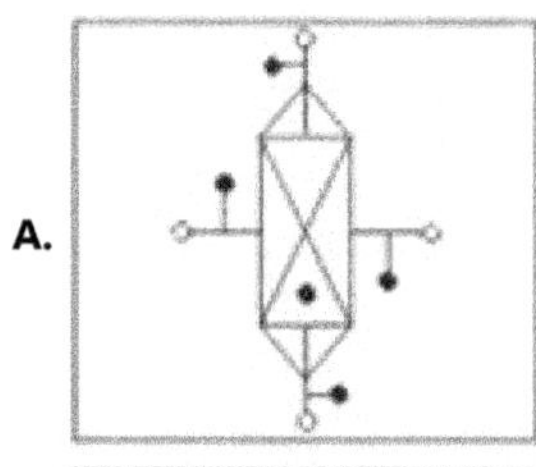

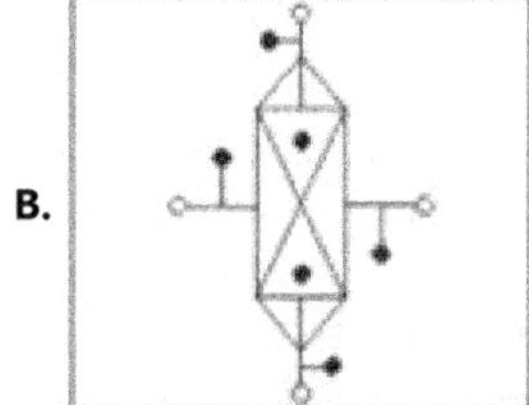

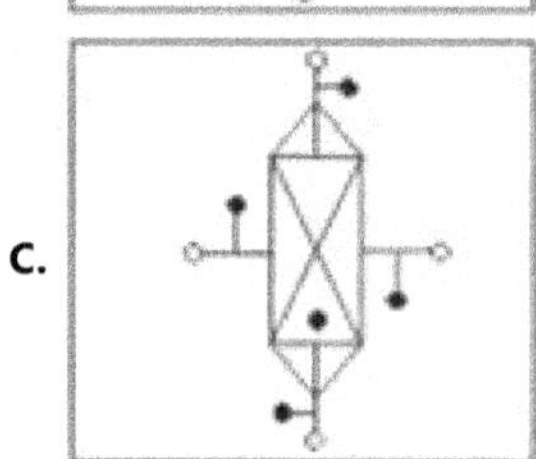

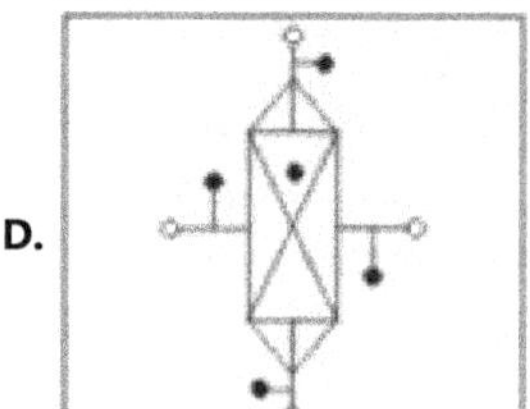

Q.23 From the following questions find the number from the given alternatives.

A. 93   **B.** 79   **C.** 97   **D.** 89

Q.24 In a certain code language, @ represents +, ⊕ represents '-', α represents '÷' and 'θ' represents '×'. Find out the answer to the following question.

107 θ 3 ⊕ 64 α 8 ⊕ 2 θ 9 = ?

A. 295   **B.** 290   **C.** 209   **D.** 105

Q.25 In a certain code language "OPERA" is coded as "LKVIZ" and "PAROL" is coded as "KZILO" then what is the code for "RAMBO"?

A. IZNYL   **B.** IZOZL   **C.** IZNYO   **D.** IZOYO

// Smart Answer Sheet //

Correct Percentage of students who answered correctly. **Skipped** Percentage of students who skipped.

Q.	Ans.	Correct / Skipped	Q.	Ans.	Correct / Skipped	Q.	Ans.	Correct / Skipped	Q.	Ans.	Correct / Skipped	Q.	Ans.	Correct / Skipped	Q.	Ans.	Correct / Skipped
1	B	89.31 % / 0.0 %	6	B	85.58 % / 0.0 %	11	C	50.53 % / 1.04 %	16	C	61.48 % / 1.94 %	21	D	22.49 % / 4.99 %			
2	B	80.09 % / 0.0 %	7	C	47.69 % / 1.91 %	12	D	49.99 % / 1.71 %	17	C	54.45 % / 1.41 %	22	C	55.05 % / 1.32 %			
3	D	84.86 % / 0.0 %	8	D	81.54 % / 0.0 %	13	D	53.36 % / 1.23 %	18	B	46.17 % / 1.89 %	23	A	46.51 % / 1.64 %			
4	A	43.64 % / 1.32 %	9	D	54.26 % / 1.03 %	14	C	66.44 % / 1.46 %	19	B	79.93 % / 0.0 %	24	A	45.77 % / 1.48 %			
5	B	83.41 % / 0.0 %	10	B	43.55 % / 1.9 %	15	A	40.09 % / 1.29 %	20	B	51.46 % / 1.43 %	25	A	51.01 % / 1.25 %			

//Hints and Solutions//

1. Given:

38 L 2 M 7 P 4 N 22

Changing the signs according to the question,

38 ÷ 2 + 7 × 4 - 22

Solving by using BODMAS,

= 19 + 28 - 22

= 25

Hence, the correct option is (B).

2. All except Mustard are foodgrains, while mustard is an oilseed,

Hence, the correct option is (B).

3. The given letters follow the following pattern,

S+6 = Y

D+6 = J

Similarly,

H+6 = N

K+6 = Q

Hence, the correct option is (D).

4. The pattern followed here is:

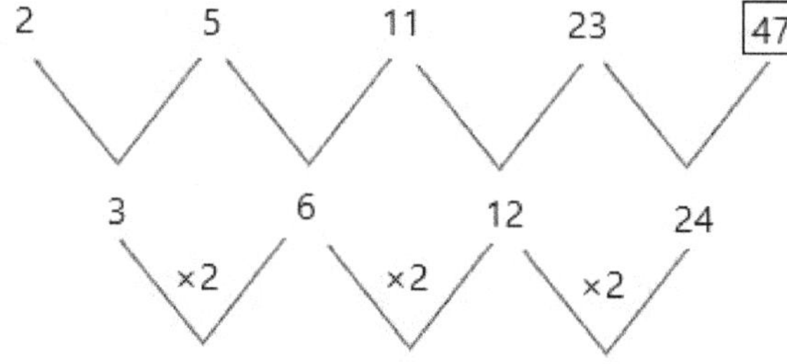

Hence, the correct option is (A).

5. Vowels and consonants are parts of alphabets while numbers are not alphabets.

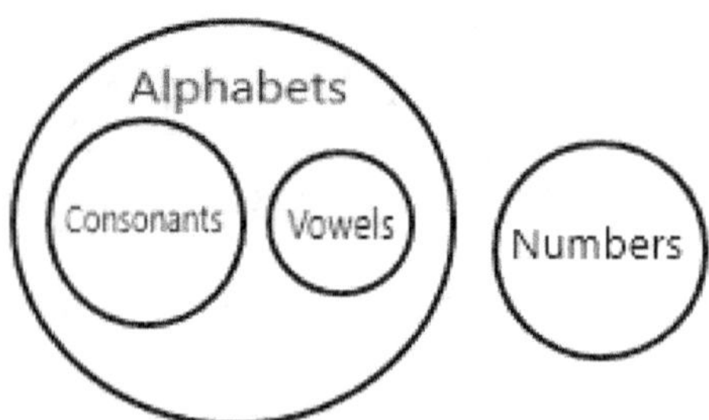

Hence, the correct option is (B).

6. Given:

10#5@1$5

Changing the signs according to the question,

10 - 5 × 1 ÷ 5

Solving by using BODMAS,

= 10 -1

= 9

Hence, the correct option is (B).

7. The below diagram can be drawn using the given statements,

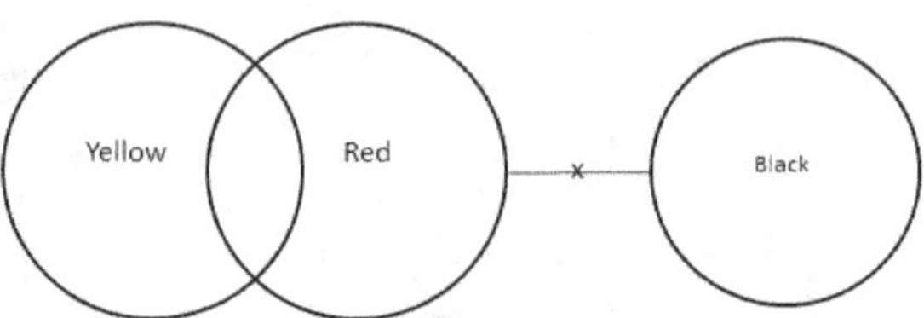

Conclusion I and Conclusion II cannot be true at the same time.

Therefore, Either I or II follows.

Hence, the correct option is (C).

8. The roof is the opposite of the Floor and similarly Happy is the opposite of Sad.

Hence, the correct option is (D).

9. The pattern followed here is,

Q+2 = S

K+2 = M

A+2 = C

I+2 = K

T+2 = V

Similarly for VGHRS,

So required code for BHASR is

B+2 = D

H+2 = J

A+2 = C

S+2 = U

R+2 = T

i.e, DJCUT

Hence, the correct option is (D).

10. The pattern followed here is,

Sum the squares of individual digits of 34.

= $3^2 + 4^2$

= 9+16 = 25

Similarly, for 47

= $4^2 + 7^2$

= 16+49 = 65

Hence, the correct option is (B).

11. Float means above water and sinks mean underwater. In the same way, the Boat floats on water, and the submarine moves underwater.

Hence, the correct option is (C).

12. Both teachers and students are part of the school. Also, no student can be a teacher.

Hence, the correct option is (D).

13. We have $6 \times x = 4224$

$x = 704$

Similarly,

$8 \times 704 = 5632$

Hence, the correct option is (D).

14. Consecutive prime numbers are being added in subsequent terms.

$$11 + 2 = 13$$
$$13 + 3 = 16$$
$$16 + 5 = 21$$
$$21 + 7 = 28$$
$$28 + 11 = 39$$
$$39 + 13 = 52$$
$$52 + 17 = 69$$

So, the missing term is 52

Hence, the correct option is (C).

15. The below diagram can be drawn using given statements.

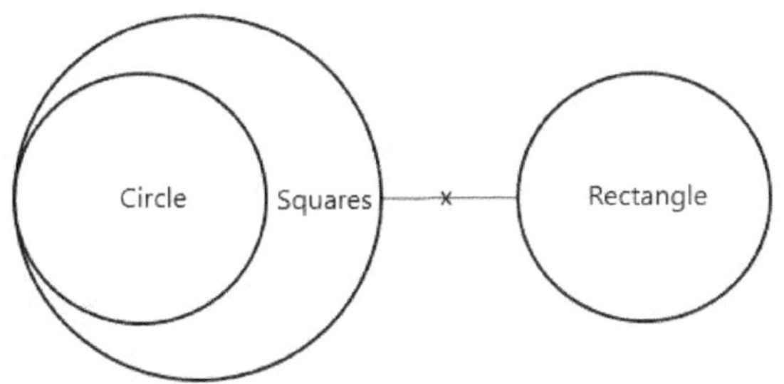

From the above diagram, All Circles are Squares that cannot be Rectangles. So, the conclusion (I) is true.

All Squares are Circles can only be a possibility and can't be a conclusion. So, conclusion (II) is not true.

Hence, the correct option is (A).

16. In this code

L - 1 = K

I - 2 = G

S - 3 = P

T - 4 = P

E - 5 = Z

N - 6 = H

Similarly for MOTHER and so required code for KITTEN is

K - 1 = J

I - 2 = G

T - 3 = Q

T - 4 = P

E - 5 = Z

N - 6 = H

I.e JGQPZH

Hence, the correct option is (C).

17. In the given option, Restore cannot be formed by using the letters in the given word, because there is no "T" letter present in it.

Hence, the correct option is (C).

18. Japan is present in Asia and similarly, England is present in Europe.

Hence, the correct option is (B).

19. Only "Satire" cannot be formed from the keyword.

It requires an extra 'E' from the keyword "CARBONISATION".

Option (A): Narcos can be formed by "CARBONISATION".

Option (C): Carbon can be formed by "CARBONISATION".

Option (D): Sanction can be formed by "CARBONISATION".

Hence, the correct option is (B).

20. It is clear from the diagram that the letter 'c' represents the set of persons who play all three games.

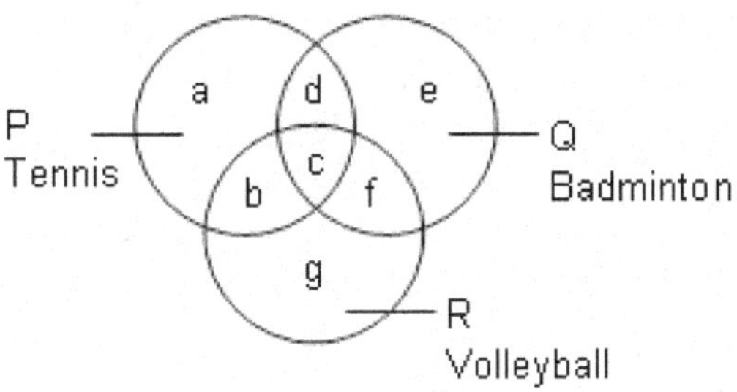

Hence, the correct option is (B).

21. None is implicit. The assumption I is a mere twisted form of the given statement. Smoking is injurious. It means that non-smoking is not injurious. And that's it. It doesn't mean that non-smoking promotes health.

II obviously is just the opposite of what is true. Public warnings are given only when they are assumed to be necessary.

Hence, the correct option is (D).

22. If a mirror is placed on the line AB then the following of the answer figures is the right image of the given figure:

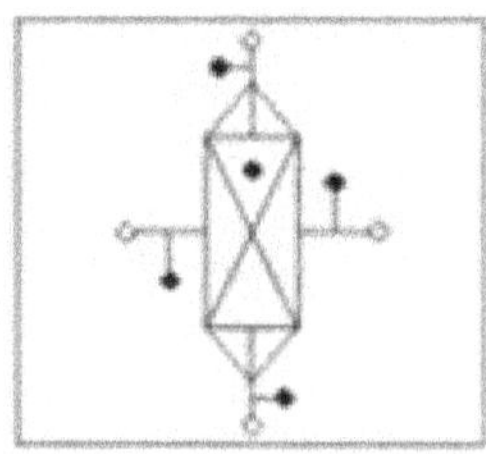

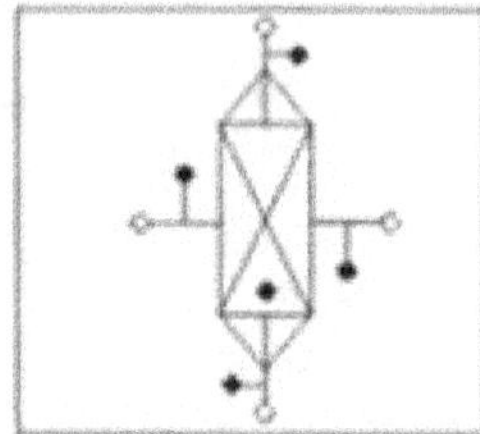

Hence, the correct option is (C).

23. 79, 97, 89 all are prime numbers. Expect 93 which is a composite number.

Hence, the correct option is (A).

24. According to the given equation,

10703 $\oplus$ 209=?

Using the proper symbols, we get

107 × 3 - 64 ÷ 8 - 2 × 9 (by BODMAS rule)

= 107 × 3 - 8 -2 × 9

= 321 - 8 - 18

= 321 - 26

= 295

Hence, the correct option is (A).

25. In this question, each letter of the first word is replaced by its opposite letter in its code i.e if B is the 2nd letter from the beginning it is replaced by the 2nd letter from the end i.e Y.

So, if "OPERA" is coded as "LKVIZ" and "PAROL" is coded as "KZILO" then "RAMBO" will be coded as "IZNYL".

Hence, the correct option is (A).

Q.1 Direction: In the following question, select the related word from the given alternatives.

Ornithology : Birds:: Oology:?

A. Plants   **B.** Viruses   **C.** Eggs   **D.** Shells

Q.2 Direction: In the following question, three of the four alternatives are exactly alike so form a group. Find a group that does not belong to that group.

A. G 9   **B.** M 15   **C.** S 21   **D.** W 26

Q.3 Direction: In the following question, three of the four alternatives are exactly alike so form a group. Find a group that does not belong to that group.

A. Vienna   **B.** Osaka
C. Colombo   **D.** Ottawa

Q.4 Direction: Read the following information carefully and answer the question given below-

In a certain language 'he is smart' is coded as 'mo ta pa', 'he knows nothing' is coded as 'pa la ha' and 'smart people knows' is coded as ' mo ki la'.

What is the code for 'is'?

A. Ta   **B.** La   **C.** Mo   **D.** Pa

Q.5 Direction: In the following question, select the related word/number from the given alternatives.

NEWS: 1452319:: TAPE:?

A. 201165   **B.** 231854   **C.** 115426   **D.** 201056

Q.6 Direction: From the following alternatives, select the word which cannot be formed using the letters of the given word.

REQUIREMENT

A. REQUIRE   **B.** RENTAL
C. QUIET   **D.** TREE

Q.7 Direction: In the following diagram, the square represents the male, the triangle represents the manager, and the circle represents the engineer. Which numbered section represents men who are managers but not engineers?

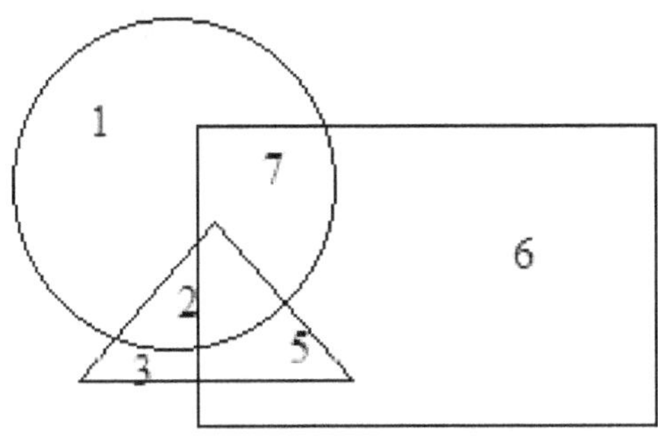

A. 5   **B.** 6   **C.** 2   **D.** 1

Q.8 Direction: Study the statements given in the question and two conclusions carefully and answer that (A) if only I follow. (B) If only II follows. (C) If neither I nor II follows. (D) If both I and II follow.

Statement:

All towers are doors.

All doors are temples.

conclusion:

I. Some temples are towers.

II. Some towers are doors.

A. (A)   **B.** (B)   **C.** (C)   **D.** (D)

Q.9 If 5 × 7 = 24 and 6 × 5 = 22, then 3 × 4 = ?

A. 18   **B.** 16   **C.** 10   **D.** 14

Q.10 Direction: Find the odd numbers from the given options.

A. 48 – 54   **B.** 38 – 44   **C.** 34 – 40   **D.** 32 – 39

Q.11 In a certain code language, **COMPUTER** is written as **RFUVQNPC**. How is **MEDICINE** written in the same code?

A. EOJDEJFM   **B.** EOJDJEFM
C. MFEDJJOE   **D.** MFEJDJOE

Q.12 In a certain code language, 'always tells truth' is written as 'vo, to, ko', 'truth of life difficult' is written as 'mo, ko, ri, si' and 'life tells everything' is written as 'ri, to, mi'. How is 'everything' written in that code language?

A. si   **B.** ri   **C.** mo   **D.** mi

Q.13 Direction: Select the word that cannot be formed from the word given below-

PHOTOSYNTHETIC

A. THOSE   **B.** SCENT
C. PRONE   **D.** COTTON

Q.14 In the given figure, the circle represents Indian, the square represents Dancer and the triangle represents Musicians. Find the region of Indian Musicians.

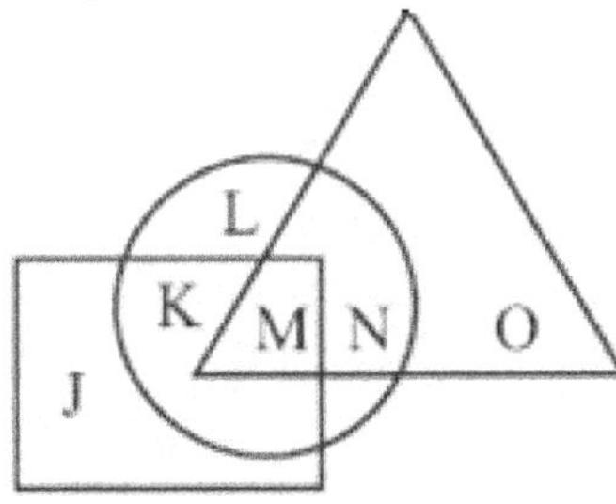

A. M   **B.** L   **C.** K   **D.** N

Q.15 If a mirror is placed on the line MN then which of the answer figures is the right image of the given figure?

Question Figure:

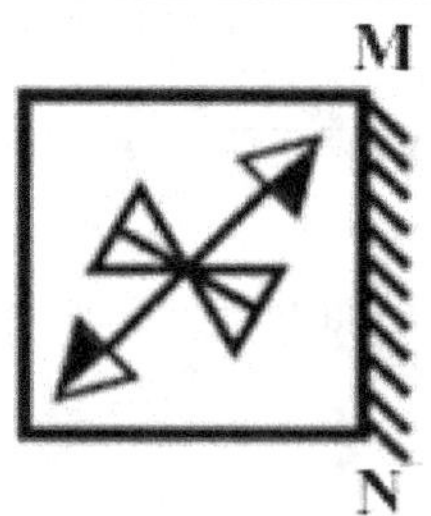

Answer Figure:

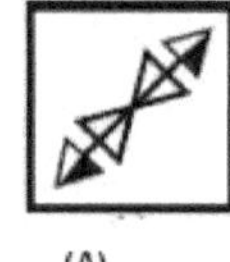 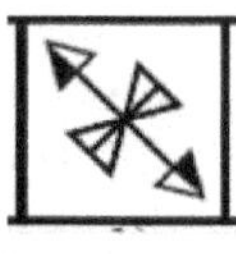  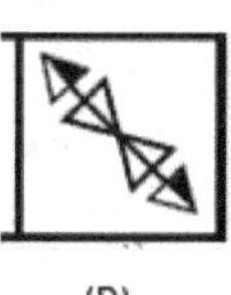

| (A) | (B) | (C) | (D) |

A. (A)   **B.** (B)   **C.** (C)   **D.** (D)

Q.16 If 56 × 11 = 9, 37 × 13 = 6, 42 × 12 = 3, then find the value of 87 × 34.

A. 8   **B.** 2   **C.** 3   **D.** 4

Q.17 Direction: In the following question, which of the two mathematical signs are to be interchanged to correct the following equation.

12 ÷ 6 × 5 + 5 − 7 = 20

A. × and −   **B.** ÷ and ×   **C.** × and +   **D.** ÷ and −

Q.18 If + means ÷, - means ×, × means +, ÷ means -, give the value for 45 + 9 - 3 × 15 ÷ 2 = ?

A. 40   **B.** 36   **C.** 55   **D.** 28

Q.19 Direction: In the following question, two statements are given each followed by two conclusions I and II. You have to consider the statements to be true even if they seem to be at variance from commonly known facts. You have to decide which of the given conclusions, if any, follows from the given statements.

Statements:

(I) Some bags are hot.

(II) All hot things are cakes.

Conclusion:

(I) All cakes are bags.

(II) All bags are cakes.

A. Conclusion I follows

B. Conclusion II follows

C. Neither I nor II follows

D. Both I and II follows

Q.20 Direction: In the following question below are given some statements followed by some conclusions. Taking the given statements to be true even if they seem to be at variance from commonly known facts, read all the conclusions and then decide which of the given conclusion logically follows the given statements.

Statements:

I. All flowers are toys.

II. Some toys are idiots.

III. Some angels are idiots.

Conclusions:

I. Some angels are toys.

II. Some idiots are flowers.

III. Some flowers are angels.

A. Only conclusion I and conclusion II follow

B. Only conclusion III follows

C. All conclusions follow

D. No conclusion follows

Q.21 From the following alternatives select the word which can be formed by using the letters of the word.

PRAGMATIC

A. GUITAR   **B.** AGMARK

C. GAME   **D.** MAGIC

Q.22 From the following alternatives select the word which cannot be formed by using the letters of the word.

INTERNATIONAL

A. LATTER   **B.** RELATION

C. TREATMENT   **D.** TRAIN

Q.23 Three positions of a cube are shown below. What will come opposite to face containing 'B'?

A. C   **B.** D   **C.** F   **D.** G

Ques (24-25):Direction: A series is given with one term missing. Select the correct alternative from the given ones that will complete the series.

Q.24 2, 5, 12, 27,?

A. 56   **B.** 57   **C.** 58   **D.** 59

Q.25 ?, 5, 30, 186, 1309, 10480

A. 0.25   **B.** 0.75   **C.** 1.00   **D.** 0

// Smart Answer Sheet //

Correct — Percentage of students who answered correctly. **Skipped** — Percentage of students who skipped.

Q.	Ans.	Correct / Skipped	Q.	Ans.	Correct / Skipped	Q.	Ans.	Correct / Skipped	Q.	Ans.	Correct / Skipped	Q.	Ans.	Correct / Skipped	Q.	Ans.	Correct / Skipped
1	C	66.97 % / 1.03 %	6	B	50.42 % / 1.23 %	11	B	26.58 % / 4.25 %	16	A	49.54 % / 1.08 %	21	D	52.41 % / 1.46 %			
2	D	43.65 % / 1.54 %	7	A	40.34 % / 1.02 %	12	D	57.94 % / 1.92 %	17	C	68.55 % / 1.24 %	22	C	62.55 % / 1.45 %			
3	B	77.46 % / 0.0 %	8	D	49.2 % / 1.12 %	13	C	47.32 % / 1.05 %	18	D	52.44 % / 1.98 %	23	D	47.78 % / 1.2 %			
4	A	57.79 % / 1.13 %	9	D	66.26 % / 1.82 %	14	D	63.46 % / 1.11 %	19	C	59.57 % / 1.24 %	24	C	60.0 % / 1.87 %			
5	A	89.52 % / 0.0 %	10	D	80.07 % / 0.0 %	15	B	64.45 % / 1.56 %	20	D	49.61 % / 1.77 %	25	A	58.92 % / 1.84 %			

//Hints and Solutions//

1. Ornithology is the study of birds. Similarly, Oology is the study or collecting of bird's eggs.

Hence, the correct option is (C).

2. G (Positional value = 7) $\Rightarrow$ 7 + 2 = 9

M (Positional value = 13) $\Rightarrow$ 13 + 2 = 15

S (Positional value = 19) $\Rightarrow$ 19 + 2 = 21

W (Positional value = 23) $\Rightarrow$ 23 + 2 = 25

Therefore, W 26 does not belong to that group.

Hence, the correct option is (D).

3. Osaka is a city in Japan except for the capital of all countries.

Hence, the correct option is (B).

4. He is <u>smart</u> → <u>mo</u> ta **pa**

He <u>knows</u> nothing → **pa** <u>la</u> ha

<u>Smart</u> people <u>knows</u> →<u>mo</u> ki <u>la</u>

is → ta, He → pa, Smart → mo, knows → la, People → ki

Thus, the code for 'is' is 'ta'.

Hence, the correct option is (A).

5. After writing the place value,

N	E	W	S
↓	↓	↓	↓
14	5	23	19

Similarly,

T	A	P	E
↓	↓	↓	↓
20	1	16	5

Therefore, ?= 201165

Hence, the correct option is (A).

6. 'RENTAL' cannot be formed using the letters of 'REQUIREMENT'.

Because letter A and L are not Present in **REQUIREMENT**

Hence, the correct option is (B).

7. The common area for the square and triangle represents male managers who are not engineers. The required field number is 5.

Hence, the correct option is (A).

8.

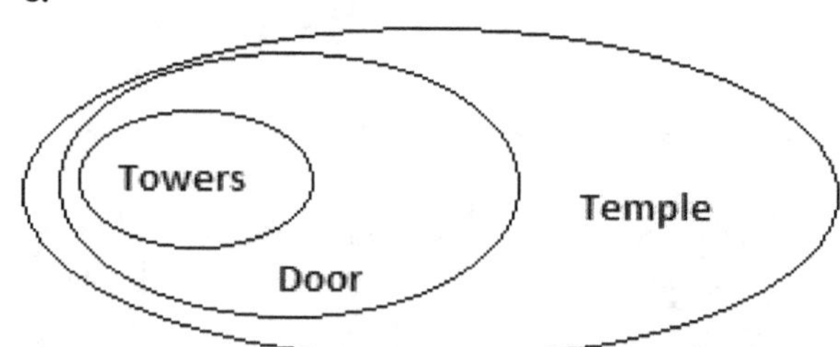

Both I and II follow.

Hence, the correct option is (D).

9. As, 5 × 7 = 24 $\Rightarrow$ (5 + 7) × 2

= 12 × 2 = 24

and

6 × 5 = 22 $\Rightarrow$ (6 + 5) × 2

= 11 × 2 = 22

Similarly,

3 × 4 $\Rightarrow$ (3 + 4) × 2

= 7 × 2 = 14

Hence, the correct option is (D).

10. Except option (D) the difference between the numbers in all others is 6.

Hence, the correct option is (D).

11. Coding is as follows:

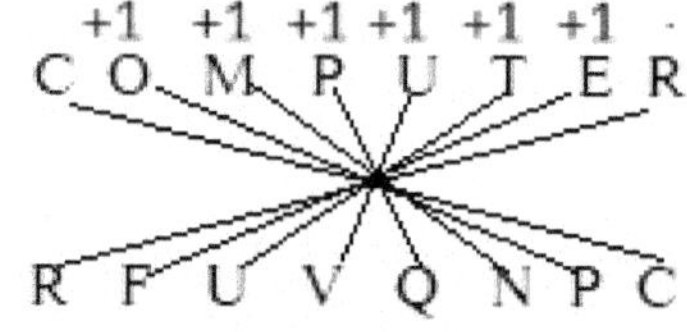

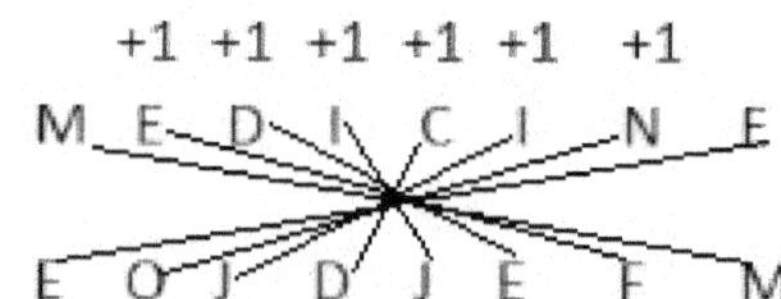

Hence, the correct option is (B).

12. (A) 'Always tells truth' is written as 'vo, to, ko'.

(B) 'Truth of life difficult' is written as 'mo, ko, ri, si'.

(C) 'Life tells everything' is written as 'ri, to, mi'.

From (A) and (B), 'truth' can be coded as 'ko'.

From (B) and (C), 'life' can be coded as 'ri'.

From (A), (B) and (C), 'everything' can be coded as 'mi'.

Hence, the correct option is (D).

13. R is not in the word PHOTOSYNTHETIC. Therefore, PRONE cannot be formed using letters of PHOTOSYNTHETIC.

Hence, the correct option is (C).

14. As circle represents Indian and triangle represents Musicians so the only N is common in both.

Hence, the correct option is (D).

15.

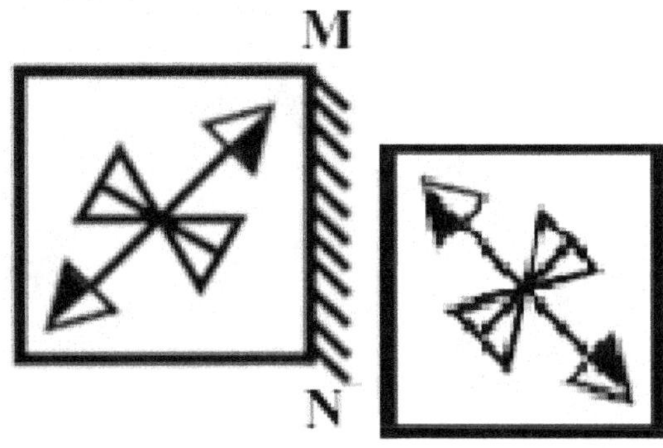

Hence, the correct option is (B).

16. Given:

56 × 11 = 9, 37 × 13 = 6, 42 × 12 = 3

The pattern is as follows:

(5 + 6) - (1 + 1) = 9

(3 + 7) - (1 + 3) = 6

(4 + 2) - (1 + 2) = 3

Similarly, for 87 × 34:

(8 + 7) - (3 + 4) = 8

Hence, the correct option is (A).

17. For option (C)

On interchanging signs × and +, we get new equation as:

12 ÷ 6 + 5 × 5 − 7 = 20

2 + 5 × 5 − 7 = 20

2 + 25 − 7 = 20

20 = 20

Hence, the correct option is (C).

18. Given:

45 + 9 - 3 × 15 ÷ 2 = ?

After interchanging the symbol,

45 ÷ 9 × 3 + 15 - 2

⇒ ? = 5 × 3 + 15 - 2

⇒ ? = 15 + 15 - 2

⇒ ? = 30 - 2

⇒ ? = 28

Hence, the correct option is (D).

19. Both the statements can be represented by the following figure:

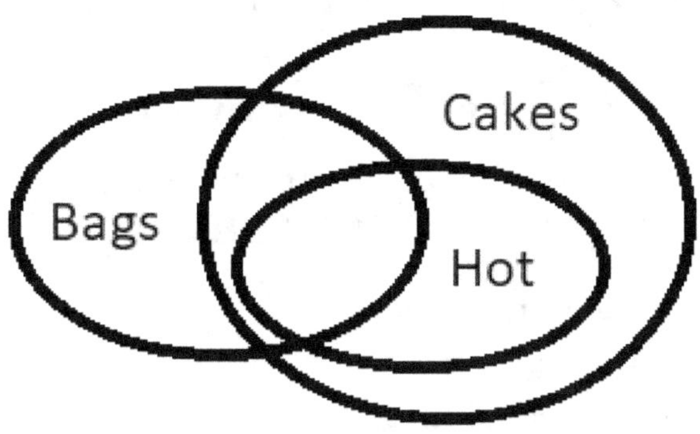

According to the above statements, neither conclusion I nor II follows.

Hence, the correct option is (C).

20. The possible diagram of the given statements is:

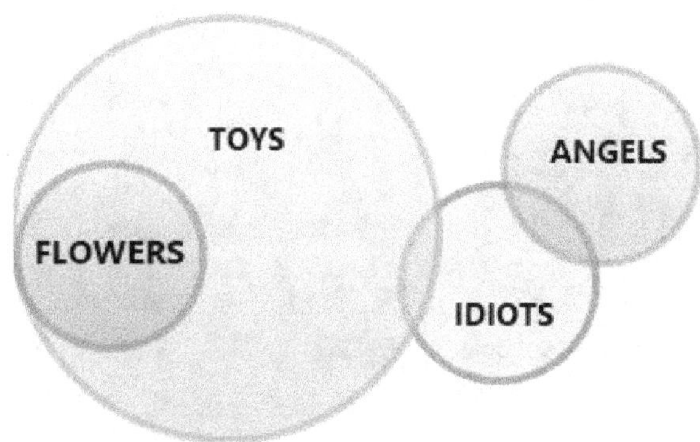

It's clear that no conclusion follows.

Hence, the correct option is (D).

21. The word 'MAGIC' can be formed from the given word as shown in the figure:

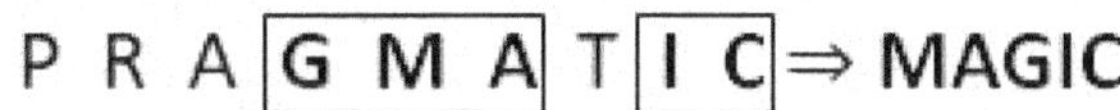

In option (A) - Here, the letter 'U' is missing. So, the word 'GUITAR' cannot be formed.

In option (B) - The letter 'K' is missing. So, the word 'AGMARK' cannot be formed.

In option (C) - The letter 'E' is missing. So, the word 'GAME' cannot be formed.

Hence, the correct option is (D).

22. The words which can be formed from the word 'INTERNATIONAL' are:

I N T̲E R̲ N A T̲ I O N A̲L̲ ⇒ LATTER

I N T̲E R̲ N A T̲ I O N̲A̲L̲ ⇒ RELATION

I N T̲E R̲ N A̲T̲I̲O N̲ A L ⇒ TRAIN

There are only two 'T's in the word 'INTERNATIONAL' and no 'M'. So, the word 'TREATMENT' can't be formed from the word 'INTERNATIONAL'.

Hence, the correct option is (C).

23. Considering cube 1 and cube 2,

In the clockwise direction from B,

B   D   C

B   F   E

Thus, G is the letter opposite to B

Hence, the correct option is (D).

24. According to the given series,

$$2 \times 2 + 1 = 5$$

$$5 \times 2 + 2 = 12$$

$$12 \times 2 + 3 = 27$$

$$27 \times 2 + 4 = 58$$

Hence, the correct option is (C).

25. According to the given series,

$0.25 \times 4 + 4 = 5$

$5 \times 5 + 5 = 30$

$30 \times 6 + 6 = 186$

$186 \times 7 + 7 = 1309$

$1309 \times 8 + 8 = 10480$

Hence, the correct option is (A).

// Notes //

// Notes //